Panentheism
The Other God of the Philosophers

Panentheism
The Other God of the Philosophers

From Plato to the present

John W. Cooper

APOLLOS (an imprint of Inter-Varsity Press)
Norton Street, Nottingham NG7 3HR, England
Email: ivp@ivpbooks.com
Website: www.ivpbooks.com

First published 2007

British Library Cataloguing in Publication Data
A catalogue record for this book is available from the British Library.

ISBN–10: 1–84474–174–5
ISBN–13: 978–1–84474–174–8

Typeset in the United States of America
Printed and bound in Great Britain by Ashford Colour Press Ltd,
Gosport, Hampshire

Inter-Varsity Press publishes Christian books that are true to the Bible
and that communicate the gospel, develop discipleship and strengthen
the church for its mission in the world.

Inter-Varsity Press is closely linked with the Universities and Colleges
Christian Fellowship, a student movement connecting Christian Unions
in universities and colleges throughout Great Britain, and a member
movement of the International Fellowship of Evangelical Students.
Website: www.uccf.org.uk

To the students of Calvin Theological Seminary
and all who seek to shape their ministries
according to sound doctrine

Contents

Acknowledgments

I wish to thank Calvin Theological Seminary for supporting this book in several ways. I was granted two sabbaticals and one publication leave during the years I worked on it and was provided comfortable work space and excellent technical support. Calvin Seminary also awarded me two Heritage Fund Grants to pay assistants during the final two summers of writing. Several Ph.D. student assistants helped with initial research and provided thoughtful feedback on early drafts. The excellent theology and philosophy collections of the Hekman Library of Calvin College and Seminary include all but half a dozen of the works cited.

I am thankful to my editor, Brian Bolger of Baker Academic, whose sound advice on early drafts helped greatly to improve the readability of the final product.

I am especially grateful to my son, John, and my daughter, Catherine, who helped with research, critical reading, and thorough editing.

Finally, I express my abiding gratitude to Sylvia, my wife, for her faithful support, interest, patience, and willingness to let me spend time and personal energy that rightfully belonged to her on this book. I cannot repay her, but I am trying.

Abbreviations

General

B.C.E.	before the Common Era
bk(s).	book(s)
C.E.	the Common Era
chap(s).	chapter(s)
d.	died
diss.	dissertation
e.g.	*exempli gratia,* for example
ed(s).	edited by; editor(s)
i.e.	*id est,* that is
intro.	introduced by
par.	paragraph(s)
p(p).	page(s)
q.	question
rev.	revised
sec.	section
trans.	translated by; translator
vol(s).	volume(s)

Primary Sources

Johannes Eckhart
    Serm.   *Sermones* (*Sermons*)
John Scotus Eriugena
    Div. nat.   *De divisione naturae* (*On the Division of Nature*)

Nicholas of Cusa
 Doc. ign. *De docta ignorantia* (*On Learned Ignorance*)
Plato
 Rep.   *Republic*
 Tim.   *Timaeus*
Plotinus
 Enn.   *Enneads*
Proclus
 Theol. plat. *Theologia platonica* (*The Platonic Theology*)
Pseudo-Dionysius
 Div. nom. *De divinis nominibus* (*The Divine Names*)
Thomas Aquinas
 ST   *Summa theologica*

Secondary Sources

Hist. Phil. Frederick Copleston, *History of Philosophy*. Westminster,
      MD: Newman Press, 1946–75. Repr., Garden City, NY:
      Doubleday, 1962–77
EncPhil   *Encyclopedia of Philosophy*. Edited by Paul Edwards. 8 vols.
      New York: Macmillan, 1967
EncRel   *The Encyclopedia of Religion*. Edited by Mircea Eliade.
      16 vols. New York: Macmillan, 1987
JAAR   *Journal of the American Academy of Religion*
JR   *Journal of Religion*
Schaff-Herzog *The New Schaff-Herzog Encyclopedia of Religious
      Knowledge*. New York: Funk and Wagnalls, 1910. Repr.,
      Grand Rapids: Baker, 1953
TSP   *Tulane Studies in Philosophy*

I

Panentheism

The Other God of the Philosophers

Classical Theism, Relational Theology, and "the God of the Philosophers"

When Pascal penned his famous warning against substituting the God of the philosophers for the God of Abraham, Isaac, and Jacob,[1] he was addressing the Enlightened intellectuals of his time who rejected biblical revelation and the supernatural God of the Judeo-Christian tradition. The Deists and Baruch Spinoza are prime examples. They constructed theologies based on reason alone, not on supernatural revelation. They either ignored Holy Scripture or reinterpreted it so that it makes no claims about God and salvation that an intelligent human could not discover merely by thinking clearly.[2] The gods of these philosophers are at odds with the God of Abraham, Isaac, Jacob, and Jesus Christ. They conflict with core Judeo-Christian beliefs about the particularity and supernatural character of God's redemptive dealings with humanity through Israel and Jesus Christ. Pascal was not criticizing traditional Christian theology so long as it is an expression of genuine devotion to God.

---

1. Blaise Pascal, "The Memorial," in *Pensées and Other Writings*, trans. Honor Levi (New York: Oxford University Press, 1995), 178.
2. James Livingston, "The Religion of Reason," chap. 2 in *Modern Christian Thought: From the Enlightenment to Vatican II* (New York: Macmillan, 1971).

13

When theologians of the last two centuries warn against the God of the philosophers, however, they are targeting something else. For them, the God of the philosophers is the God of *classical theism*, the standard mainstream doctrine of God in the Christian tradition from earliest times until the twentieth century. In brief, classical theism asserts that God is transcendent, self-sufficient, eternal, and immutable in relation to the world; thus he does not change through time and is not affected by his relation to his creatures.[3] A large majority of recent theologians—non-Christians, modernist Christians, and even traditional Christians—agree that the classical doctrine of God is neither biblical nor philosophically coherent. So they warn theology students and thoughtful believers away from "the God of the philosophers." It is important for us to consider classical theism and these criticisms more fully.

Classical theism is a complex doctrine of God that has been worked out over centuries in the Western church by such preeminent Christian teachers as Augustine, Anselm, Aquinas, and Scotus and carried on after the Reformation by Roman Catholic and Protestant theologians alike. Eastern Christianity embraces a slightly different version shaped by John Chrysostom, Basil and Gregory of Nyssa, and Gregory of Nazianzus. Classical theism intends to represent God as supernaturally revealed, not merely as known by reason. But it has borrowed philosophical and theological ideas from Greek philosophers, especially Plato and the Neoplatonists, to state clearly what it understands Scripture to teach about God. Many modern theologians believe that this use of Greek philosophy has distorted the biblical presentation of God. This is why they label classical theism negatively as "the God of the philosophers."

Western classical theism asserts that God in himself is maximal Being—absolutely self-sufficient, eternal, immutable, omnipotent, omniscient, completely active, and most excellent in every way.[4] Although he does not need the world, God eternally and freely chooses to create it from nothing and sustain it through time. He is immanent in the sense that he is supernaturally present to all beings and events at all times and places throughout the history of the world, empowering creatures and effectuating his eternal knowledge and will through their natural existence and free actions. But God in himself is utterly transcendent, all-determining, and changeless. The world is not

---

3. Thomas Morris, "The God of Abraham, Isaac, and Anselm," in *Anselmian Explorations: Essays in Philosophical Theology* (Notre Dame, IN: University of Notre Dame Press, 1987), 10–25, defines classical theism and its modifications in response to contemporary criticisms.

4. Eastern theology, following Neoplatonism, affirms that God in himself is eternal, immutable, and wholly transcendent of creation because he is *beyond* Being. We will note the differences between Eastern and Western classical theism and panentheism when relevant.

part of his nature or existence. He does not exist in time or as part of the cause-and-effect networks in terms of which creatures exist and relate within the world order. Nothing temporal affects his existence, knowledge, or will. In other words, classical theism affirms that God is eternal and immutable even in relationship with his creation.

Classical theism is not the exclusive property of traditional Christianity. Traditional Jewish and Islamic theologians endorsed it as well.[5] Most Deists at the time of Pascal still professed it even though they did not accept the distinctive doctrines of Christianity. Spinoza in fact used it to argue for his kind of pantheism: because God is eternal, immutable, perfect, and all-determining, he necessarily produces the world precisely as it is. Schleiermacher still held a fairly classical view of God in the first third of the nineteenth century.

Since then, however, an increasing number of thinkers have challenged the God of the philosophers—classical theism's eternal, immutable God— and presented dynamic alternatives.[6] The philosophers Hegel, Schelling, James, Bergson, and Whitehead developed theologies of divine develop-ment in nature and history. So did the Roman Catholic priest Teilhard de Chardin and the Jewish rabbi Martin Buber in the first half of the twentieth century. During the second half, it became commonplace for Christians and non-Christians alike to affirm a "relational God," a God who is involved in time, interacts with creatures, and is affected by them. Traditional Christians such as Richard Swinburne, Nicholas Wolterstorff, and William Craig affirm that God is involved in time.[7] The recent debate among evangelicals about "open" or "free-will theism" is whether God knows what people will choose to do in the future, not whether he interacts with creatures in time.[8] In the twenty-first century, relational views of God are

5. Philo, a contemporary of Jesus, used Platonic philosophy to articulate Jewish theology. The Jewish rabbi Moses Maimonides and the Islamic theologians Avicenna and Averroës were medieval classical theists addressed in the writings of Thomas Aquinas.

6. The atheist Ludwig Feuerbach in *The Essence of Christianity* (1841) drives the wedge between the God of the philosophers and the God of popular religion in order to reject both. Adolf von Harnack's seminal *History of Dogma* (3 vols., 1886–1889) is a prolonged attack on classical Christian theism as Greek philosophy disguised in biblical language.

7. Richard Swinburne, *The Coherence of Theism* (Oxford: Oxford University Press, 1993) and *The Christian God* (Oxford: Oxford University Press, 1994), affirms the temporal involvement of God; see also Gregory Ganssle, ed., *God and Time: Four Views* (Downers Grove, IL: InterVarsity, 2001), in which Alan Padgett, William Lane Craig, and Nicholas Wolterstorff affirm God's involvement in time, and Paul Helm defends the classical view of eternity.

8. See, e.g., Richard Rice, *The Openness of God: The Relationship between Divine Foreknowledge and Human Free Will* (Washington, DC: Review and Herald, 1980; rev. ed., Minneapolis: Bethany House, 1985); William Hasker, *God, Time, and Knowledge* (Ithaca, NY: Cornell University Press, 1989); Clark Pinnock et al., *The Openness of God: A Biblical Challenge to the Traditional Understanding of God* (Downers Grove, IL: InterVarsity, 1994); David Basinger, *The Case for Freewill Theism* (Downers Grove, IL:

endorsed by a large majority of theologians along a broad spectrum from religious pluralism, on one end, to evangelical Christianity, on the other.

These challenges to classical theism have been made for biblical, theological, and philosophical reasons. Let us note the key criticisms in each category.

Critics of classical theism point out that the Bible portrays God as a Great Person (or persons) who acts, interacts, and responds to the creatures he has made. The God of the Bible is dynamic and involved. Scripture does not present what classical theism seems to infer—a mysterious parallelism between God's eternal actuality and the temporal sequence of events that count as his acts in the world. Contemporary theologians claim to preserve the personal-relational character of the biblical God. If God is relational as Scripture presents him, they argue, then he is to some extent involved in time and change. A final point is that biblical Christianity emphasizes God's saving activity in this world as well as his future kingdom. Many contemporary theologians charge that traditional theology, following Greek philosophy, is too supernaturalistic, spiritualized, and otherworldly in its view of salvation and the Christian life.

One important theological issue is the relation of God, freedom, and evil. If God knows and wills everything in the world from all eternity, critics argue, then creatures do not have genuine freedom. Whatever they choose is known and determined from all eternity, including all the evil they do. Thus God is the cause of evil. Most contemporary theologians assign humans more freedom and God less determination, thereby shifting responsibility for evil away from God. This is a major motivation of theologians as diverse as Whitehead and free-will theists.

A second theological issue for Christians is the incarnation. In traditional orthodoxy, Jesus Christ is truly God and truly human, which implies that the eternal God has entered time. This is a conundrum for classical theism. Many defenders of historical orthodoxy believe that a relational view of God does a better job of accounting for the temporality of the incarnation.

Philosophical coherence is a third reason for criticizing classical theism. One issue, already raised, is the logic of eternity and time. If God is wholly eternal, critics charge, it is incoherent to claim that he performs individual acts that begin, end, and are in sequence, which are characteristics of temporality. Another alleged incoherence is the claim that although God eternally knows human actions, humans are free to choose among alternative possible actions. If God eternally knows that I choose eggs for breakfast tomorrow,

InterVarsity, 1996); John Sanders, *The God Who Risks* (Downers Grove, IL: InterVarsity, 1998); and Gregory Boyd, *God of the Possible* (Grand Rapids: Baker, 2000).

then inevitably I do choose eggs, however freely I make the choice. Freedom and inevitability do not seem to be compatible.

In sum, contemporary theologians of many religious and philosophical perspectives are critical of the God of the philosophers, that is, the God of classical theism, for biblical, theological, and philosophical reasons. They offer a variety of relational alternatives, from minor modifications of classical theism to major revisions of classical theism, to varieties of panentheism, to new versions of naturalistic pantheism.[9]

The Other God of the Philosophers: The Panentheistic Tradition

Many of these theologians take rhetorical advantage of identifying classical theism with "the God of the philosophers." Dismissing classical theism in this way allows them to claim the high ground with "the God of Abraham, Isaac, and Jacob." Now that the God of the philosophers has been exposed and dismissed, they suggest, we can get on with theology that is fresh, biblical, and intellectually adequate. The force of this rhetoric depends on an unstated premise, an exclusive disjunction: Theology is either philosophical-classical or biblical-relational. To reject the former is to endorse the latter.

But any suggestion that the modern alternatives to classical theism are free of philosophy is entirely false and misleading. Every contemporary theology has parallels and philosophical sources deep in history. Consider free-will theism, for example, which argues that God does not know the future actions of free creatures because his knowledge of them is temporal and those actions are not yet determined. This position was articulated in detail already by Faustus Socinus (1539–1604) just a generation after Luther and Calvin, and it adopts Aristotle's debatable view about future propositions.[10] Contemporary relational

9. Richard Swinburne, Nicholas Wolterstorff, William Craig, and many other conservative Christians are modified classical theists. Open or free-will theism is a major revision of classical theism. This book surveys the variety of contemporary panentheists. Einstein's quip "God does not roll dice" and Carl Sagan's quasi-religious view of the life-giving cosmos are popular examples of naturalistic pantheism. We discuss the variety of theologies and their objections to classical theism again in the final chapter.

10. See Charles Hartshorne and William Reese, "Temporalistic Theism," chap. 6 in *Philosophers Speak of God* (Chicago: University of Chicago Press, 1953), which presents Socinus as a forerunner of process theology.

Free-will theism asserts that propositions about contingent future events have no present truth value. "John goes home at 6 p.m." is neither true nor false until 6 p.m. Whether right or wrong, this position was argued by Aristotle. But Aristotle's God knows only himself, not temporal things. Socinus and free-will theists think that God knows temporal things only as they happen. But if God is eternal or everlastingly omniscient, then he knows the truth of all tensed propositions. In any case, the point is that all contemporary theology has philosophical roots.

theologies all have deep historical roots, roots that go back to the Greeks. In this sense they all represent "Gods of the philosophers."

These roots are not numerous, diverse, or hard to locate. Most contemporary alternatives to classical theism are branches of a single family tree with roots in Plato and Neoplatonism. Broadly speaking, this is the ancient tradition of *panentheism*, the topic of this book. Those theologies, such as neoorthodoxy and naturalistic pantheism, that are not in this family have been its neighbors and conversation partners. In brief, panentheism affirms that although God and the world are ontologically distinct and God transcends the world, the world is "in" God ontologically. In contrast, classical theism posits an unqualified distinction between God and the world: although intimately related, God and creatures are always and entirely other than one another. Ironically, panentheism shares important roots with classical theism, which also borrowed from Plato and Neoplatonism. This is why they make some common affirmations about God.

The crucial difference is how God relates to the world, and this reflects different aspects of Plato's theology. In his dialogue *Timaeus*, Plato presents a complex, somewhat ambiguous view of the Divine. God is the eternal transcendent Father, Mind, and Craftsman who makes the universe from matter. More precisely, God makes the universe as a World-Soul, which Plato calls "a god," with the material world as its body. For Plato, the world is "in" the World-Soul just as the human body is "in" the soul. This is the seed of the world's being "in" the Divine.

Broadly speaking, the difference between classical theism and panentheism is what each appropriated from Plato and Neoplatonism. To articulate the biblical doctrine of creation, the Christian church fathers adapted Plato's eternal transcendent God, the Father, Mind, and Craftsman, who is wholly other than the world he makes. They modified it to fit the doctrine of the Trinity: the Father, the Son as the Word including the Ideas, and the Holy Spirit as Creator but not as World-Soul.

The panentheist tradition found two options in Plato. Most panentheists followed Plotinus, the Neoplatonist who reframed Plato's theological cosmology as a divine hierarchy, a "Great Chain of Being":[11] The One God generates the Mind, which generates the World-Soul, which generates the world, which exists in the World-Soul, which exists in the Mind, which exists in the One. Neoplatonism is panentheistic because everything exists within God in a series of concentric emanations. In Neoplatonism God is both the wholly

---

11. The term is from Arthur O. Lovejoy, *The Great Chain of Being: The History of an Idea* (Cambridge, MA: Harvard University Press, 1936; repr., 1964).

transcendent One, the Mind, and the World-Soul immanent in the world. Thus the Divine is both transcendent and immanent, eternal and temporal, changeless and changing, and so forth. This notion of Deity becomes the panentheist tradition that is still expressed by the process theologians Whitehead and Hartshorne in their concept of *dipolarity*, that God has two natures. This tradition has an unbroken history from Plato to Whitehead, who once observed that the history of Western philosophy is "a series of footnotes to Plato."[12] He could have made the same comment about theology. Much panentheism carries on the transcendent-immanent theology of Neoplatonism.

The other branch of panentheism equates God primarily with the World-Soul. It assimilates the transcendent aspects of the Neoplatonic divinity, the One and the Mind, into the World-Soul. It views God as the Life Force, the dynamic Spirit that generates life, intelligent order, and oneness in the universe. This version of panentheism is found, for example, in romanticism, Schleiermacher's Living God, New England transcendentalism's Over-Soul, Bergson's *élan vital* ("spark of life"), in the ecological feminism of Ruether and McFague, and in Wiccan neopaganism.

This book surveys the development and proliferation of panentheism from its roots in Neoplatonism to its many different branches in the twenty-first century. Almost all the modern alternatives to classical theism either are part of this family history or are influenced by it.

It is not, however, possible simply to equate Neoplatonism and panentheism, for three reasons. First, both the Western and the Eastern Christian traditions appropriated aspects of Neoplatonism without thereby being panentheistic. Augustine and Basil are examples. Second, a few philosophical influences on panentheism are not Neoplatonic. The ancient Stoics, Giordano Bruno, and Spinoza, for instance, were naturalistic pantheists who influenced the German romantic panentheists. Böhme's triadic Deity reflects Gnosticism. Third, panentheism is also found in religions beyond the range of Neoplatonism. For example, some Hindus, Buddhists, and animists who know Western theology identify their traditions as panentheistic.

With these qualifications, however, it is accurate to say that the history of panentheism is largely the history of Neoplatonism. Virtually all contemporary alternatives to classical theism stem from this tradition or have been shaped by it. If classical theism represents "the God of the philosophers," then panentheism counters with "the *other* God of the philosophers."

12. Alfred North Whitehead, *Process and Reality: An Essay in Cosmology* (New York: Macmillan, 1929); ed. David Griffin and Donald Sherburne, corrected ed. (New York: Free Press, 1978), 39. Citation is from the Free Press edition.

The Two Purposes of This Survey

The main goal of this survey is to present a historical overview of panentheism (chaps. 2–13). The second goal is a critical and apologetic response to panentheism (chap. 14). Let me make a few comments on each purpose and on their relationship.

As far as I know, this is the first survey of the history of panentheism as a whole, at least in English. Other books present important parts of this history. Reese and Hartshorne's *Philosophers Speak of God* includes a number of thinkers from ancient times to the twentieth century who anticipate Whitehead's process theology. Tillich's *A History of Christian Thought* includes important themes and figures.[13] John Macquarrie's *In Search of Deity* highlights several key figures between Plotinus and Heidegger.[14] Philip Clayton's *Problem of God in Modern Thought*, a detailed study of the emergence of panentheism in philosophical theology since Descartes, alludes to its precedents in medieval theology and Neoplatonism.[15] A recent anthology edited by Philip Clayton and Arthur Peacocke, *In Whom We Live and Move and Have Our Being*, contains many historical references but focuses on the diversity of contemporary panentheism.[16] The primary purpose of the present book is to outline the historical framework within which the materials from these other books form parts of a single narrative.

I emphasize that the account is an overview, not an exhaustive history. It considers the most important thinkers as well as representatives of particular kinds of panentheism. It does not pretend to be an encyclopedia of panentheists or even to include all the important contributors. It does not summarize theologians' entire systems but focuses on their panentheism.

The other purpose of this survey is critical and apologetic. It raises issues for all readers to consider, but especially for Christians who find the criticisms of classical theism persuasive and are inclined to adopt a contemporary relational theology instead. It will help them to look before they leap to the

13. Paul Tillich, *A History of Christian Thought: From Its Judaic and Hellenistic Origins to Existentialism*, ed. Carl Braaten (New York: Simon and Schuster, 1967, 1968).

14. John Macquarrie, *In Search of Deity: An Essay in Dialectical Theism*, Gifford Lectures, 1983 (New York: Crossroad, 1985), treats Plotinus, Dionysius, Eriugena, Nicholas of Cusa, Leibniz, Hegel, Whitehead, and Heidegger.

15. Philip Clayton, *The Problem of God in Modern Thought* (Grand Rapids: Eerdmans, 2000).

16. Philip Clayton and Arthur Peacocke, eds., *In Whom We Live and Move and Have Our Being: Panentheistic Reflections on God's Presence in a Scientific World* (Grand Rapids: Eerdmans, 2003). Michael Brierley's essay, "Naming a Quiet Revolution: The Panentheistic Turn in Modern Theology," ibid., 1–15, surveys panentheism's rise since the early nineteenth century. A number of essays in the collection contain historical references, but the overall history of panentheism is not presented.

conclusion that modern alternatives are more biblical and less philosophically problematic. The choice is much more complicated than typically presented. A full-blown response and critique of panentheism would take another long book. Only a single chapter is possible here; it presents and defends a fairly traditional version of classical theism.

I try not to confuse these two purposes. The apologetics is kept out of the history. The aim is to present an accurate, empathetic overview of panentheism that is helpful for all readers, including panentheists. I sometimes raise critical questions and contrast panentheism with classical theism in ways that other philosophers and theologians do, but I do not compare panentheism negatively with my own position. Caricatures are avoided because they are unprofessional, dishonest, and unhelpful for apologetics. A fair presentation of the history of panentheism will help clarify its philosophical meaning to all, whether or not they agree with my eventual evaluation.

For both purposes, readers deserve to know my position. I am a minister in the Christian Reformed Church and professor of philosophical theology at Calvin Theological Seminary, committed to historic biblical Christianity as stated in the Reformed confessional tradition. I am a classical theist who is not convinced that the traditional doctrines of divine eternity and immutability are biblically and philosophically untenable or incapable of generating an authentic account of God's relationship with his creatures. I can accept, however, minimal modifications of classical theism on some issues, including God's relation to time. Either way, I affirm God's sovereignty and knowledge of all times, places, creatures, and events. So I disagree with those who claim that God "learns," "grows," or "risks."

The last chapter spells out my commitments and my own theological views. I also make clear my respect for all positions and my willingness to affirm versions of relational theology and panentheism as authentically ecumenical Christian theologies even though I cannot endorse them. I do not think that my own perspective prevents me from understanding panentheism or presenting it fairly.

The Intended Readers: Theological Learners

This survey is intended for upperclass college and seminary students, clergy, and anyone interested in theology.[17] It is written for students because

---

17. Two excellent books of this sort are Diogenes Allen, *Philosophy for Understanding Theology* (Atlanta: John Knox, 1985); and Livingston, *Modern Christian Thought*.

awareness of the great panentheist tradition is crucial for understanding historical and contemporary theology. My own education was excellent, but it included only bits and pieces of this tradition. The same is probably true of most readers. My students have usually found this material almost entirely new.

Although the presentation is introductory, some acquaintance with philosophy and theology is an obvious advantage. Nonetheless, the basic ideas are presented clearly and without much technical jargon. Definitions of technical terms are supplied. Clear signs regularly mark the road. Frequent quotations keep the reader close to the primary sources and support the interpretations presented. Major themes are repeatedly noted. Regular summaries locate the many episodes within the ongoing story. These features should help make the book readable.

Still, the reader's task is challenging. Panentheism includes several combinations of complex philosophical and theological ideas, each with variations. Even a clear introduction is bound to be daunting. Another complication is the different levels of presentation. Some panentheists are introduced in a few paragraphs, others in a few pages, and some have entire chapters devoted to them. The book is introductory, but some parts are much more detailed than others. If a section is too dense, readers can skip to its conclusion and move on. One can follow the way through the woods without examining every tree.

A Preliminary Overview

A map showing the general features of this book can be useful. Chapter 2 takes us from Plato through Christian Neoplatonism. As already indicated, Plotinus recasts Plato's God-world dualism into the Neoplatonic Great Chain of Being: the One emanates the Mind, which emanates the World-Soul, which contains the world. Plotinus's student Proclus works out the dialectical process by which the world emanates from God. Dialectic remains important in most kinds of panentheism, most famously in Hegel's. Pseudo-Dionysius blends Neoplatonism with Christian theology and is the original source of Christian panentheism. Eriugena, Eckhart, and Nicholas of Cusa are three medieval Christian panentheists who work directly from Dionysius. Nicholas of Cusa elaborates a system of theology that concludes that God is the unity of all dialectical opposition. But he also asserts that humans cannot explain this unity in God. Jakob Böhme boldly explains what Nicholas of Cusa could not. He posits that God is the eternal dialectical unity of three oppositional potencies and that the world is the temporal outflow of this eternal dialectic. Böhme is the original source for theologians, such as Hegel and Moltmann, who understand the Trinity dialectically and view history as the dialectical reunification of the Trinity and the world.

Chapter 3 covers the Renaissance to romanticism. It begins with the pantheists Giordano Bruno and Spinoza because of their influence on the German romantic panentheists. The Neoplatonism of English Deism is introduced as the background of the American preacher Jonathan Edwards, whose philosophy is panentheist although his theology is Calvinist. In Germany the early romantics transform Spinoza's doctrine of God as Absolute Substance into the Living Spirit or Vital Force, much like Plato's World-Soul. This concept of God is clear in Schleiermacher's romantic philosophy and his theology in *The Christian Faith*.

Chapter 4 presents Schelling and Hegel, the two most important figures in panentheism between Plotinus and the present. They are the first to articulate the notion that God himself is developing in and through the world. Up to this point Plotinus's Great Chain of Being remained vertical: the One is the highest, emanates a hierarchy downward, and draws all things back up to itself. God is dynamic but does not change. Schelling and Hegel tip the hierarchy of being on its side so that the One is future, and they locate the existence of the One God within nature and history. Thus God's essence is changeless, but his existence develops in and through the world, encompassing the many within the One. The whole process is dialectical: Schelling and Hegel both adopt Böhme's dialectical ontology of God and the world. This general picture of the Trinity actualizing itself in world history until it completely includes the world is still represented by Moltmann and Pannenberg. There is a crucial difference between Schelling and Hegel, however. Hegel's dialectic is rational and deterministic. Schelling's is personal and historical, the interaction among nature, humanity, and God forging their common destiny. Schelling is therefore more appealing to post-Enlightenment panentheists, such as Coleridge, Peirce, James, Heidegger, Tillich, Macquarrie, Moltmann, and Clayton.

Chapter 5 illustrates the proliferation and diversification of panentheism during the nineteenth century by highlighting a number of influential thinkers from several countries. They include in Germany the theologian Isaak Dorner and the historian Ernst Troeltsch. The English representatives are Samuel Taylor Coleridge, several Gifford lecturers, Samuel Alexander, and William Inge, dean of St. Paul's Cathedral. Ralph Waldo Emerson, Charles Sanders Peirce, and William James are American panentheists. The philosopher Henri Bergson is the best-known example from France. These thinkers modify the theologies of Hegel, Schelling, and Enlightenment Neoplatonism to fit modern science and pass them on to twentieth-century panentheists.

Chapter 6 presents Teilhard de Chardin, a scientist and priest who synthesizes the evolutionary philosophy of Bergson with Roman Catholic theology. Teilhard views the evolution of the universe toward human existence as the progressive incarnation of God in the world. The incarnation is fully explicit in Jesus Christ. It culminates in an eschatological Omega point, the Cosmic Christ, where God and the human race, which has evolved into a completely spiritual mode of existence, reach full communion. Teilhard's vision has become well known around the world.

Chapter 7 surveys process theology, the main American form of panentheism, which draws more from English Neoplatonism than from Hegel and Schelling. This chapter introduces the philosophical ideas of Alfred North Whitehead and how they generate his doctrine of God. It then explains Charles Hartshorne's modifications and contributions to Whitehead's view of God. Both men emphasize that God is *dipolar*—God has two natures: eternal and temporal, changeless and changing, transcendent and immanent, potential and actual, and so forth. The chapter concludes with two leading Christian process theologians, John Cobb and David Griffin. A short appendix clarifies the similarities and key differences between process theology and open theism.

Chapter 8 introduces Paul Tillich's existential panentheism, which is mainly Schelling's theology modernized in terms of Heidegger's philosophy and stated in the language of Christian theology. Tillich argues that the tension between being and nonbeing at the core of human existence arises within the divine nature itself. Thus the human quest for authentic existence—"the courage to be," as Tillich puts it—is participation in the Ground of being/nonbeing, which is God. Participation in God makes "new being" possible; this is Tillich's doctrine of salvation. Tillich's existential panentheism has deeply impressed John Robinson, John Macquarrie, James Cone, and Rosemary Ruether, who are presented in later chapters.

Chapter 9 reveals the diversity of panentheism in the twentieth century by introducing representative philosophers, theologians, and religious thinkers from within and beyond the Christian tradition. Among philosophers, Martin Heidegger works from the Catholic tradition, Hans-Georg Gadamer from the Protestant tradition, and Nicholas Berdyaev from Russian Orthodoxy. Of the Christian theologians, William Temple, John Robinson, and John Macquarrie are Anglican, and Karl Rahner and Hans Küng are Roman Catholic. Beyond the Christian tradition, Martin Buber is a Hasidic Jewish rabbi, Muhammed Iqbal is a Sufi Muslim, Sarvepalli Radhakrishnan is Hindu, Alan Watts and Masao Abe are Zen Buddhists, and Miriam Starhawk is Wiccan. In spite of multiple diversities, all affirm that the world is ontologically within the Divine as they define it.

Chapter 10 presents Moltmann, a currently popular theologian who explicitly endorses "Christian panentheism." He continues to elaborate the broadly dialectical view of the Trinity and the world suggested by Böhme, Hegel, Schelling, and Berdyaev. Moltmann begins from the interaction of Father, Son, and Spirit during the crucifixion of Jesus, which includes the suffering of the world. He then expands the work of the Trinity to encompass the whole history of the world from creation to consummation, when it is fully included in the triune life. Moltmann's panentheism is *perichoretic*. *Perichoresis* refers to the relation of complete communion among the persons of the Trinity. Moltmann makes perichoresis his ontology, applying it not only to the Trinity but also to relations among creatures and to the relation between the world and the triune God.

Chapter 11 argues that Pannenberg is a panentheist in spite of his denial. It begins the case by surveying his philosophical method and his impressive philosophical theology of nature, humanity, history, and religion. His philosophy reflects Hegel's system in structure and scope, but his method is hermeneutical and much less rigid than Hegel's. Like Hegel, Schelling, and Moltmann, Pannenberg understands nature and history to involve God's progressive self-actualization toward the eschatological fulfillment of all things in God. Pannenberg's theology looks something like Plotinus's Great Chain of Being tipped horizontally, so that the transcendent One is not above the world but in the future. Pannenberg is a panentheist because he defines God as the infinite triune force field within which the universe is created and consummated.

Chapter 12 illustrates a variety of panentheisms in liberation, feminist, and ecological theology. In different ways, these theologies emphasize the liberation of specific groups of people as part of the reconciliation of the whole cosmos in God. James Cone's black theology borrows much from Tillich. The Latin American liberation theologians Gustavo Gutiérrez, Juan Luis Segundo, and Leonardo Boff draw significantly from Teilhard, and Boff from Moltmann as well. The ecological feminists Ruether and McFague combine aspects of Teilhard, Tillich, and process thought into theologies of the (maternal) divine Life Force reminiscent of the World-Soul. Matthew Fox's creation spirituality is Teilhardian in flavor and explicitly endorses panentheism.

Chapter 13 considers several contemporary experts in scientific cosmology and theology: Ian Barbour, Paul Davies, Arthur Peacocke, Philip Clayton, and John Polkinghorne. All affirm the contemporary scientific world picture, that the universe is an evolving system of increasingly complex systems and modes of existence. They argue that this world picture points to God and that panentheism is the most reasonable synthesis of science and theology. There are interesting differences among them as well. Barbour favors process theology whereas most of the others prefer the way Moltmann and Pannenberg relate God and the world. Clayton also identifies with Schelling's later theology. These thinkers are divided over whether the mind-body relation is a good model for the God-world relation. Polkinghorne stands apart from the others because, although he affirms panentheism for the world to come, he prefers dialectical theology for the present world. This chapter brings us up to date on the history of panentheism.

Chapter 14 challenges panentheism in comparison with classical theism based on a commitment to historic, biblical Christianity. This chapter acknowledges the significant biblical, theological, and philosophical questions that classical theism must address. Scripture itself speaks of being "in him [God]" and "in Christ." But the chapter argues that nuanced classical Christian theism is more biblically faithful, theologically adequate, and philosophically coherent than any kind of panentheism. If readers' theological deliberations are better informed, I am satisfied. If they are persuaded, I am delighted. If they disagree, I hope they find that the issues are presented fairly.

Basic Terms and Distinctions in Panentheism

Like classical theism, panentheism is not a single monolithic theology but a group of related views with common basic affirmations. Before beginning this history, it is important to identify these affirmations and introduce the issues on which there is variation.

Panentheism literally means "all-in-God-ism." This is the Greek-English translation of the German term *Allingottlehre*, "the doctrine that all is in God." It was coined by Karl Krause (1781–1832), a contemporary of Schleiermacher, Schelling, and Hegel, to distinguish his own theology from both classical theism and pantheism.[18] The term *panentheism* did not come into common usage, however, until Charles Hartshorne popularized it in the mid-twentieth century.[19] Since then it has acquired a commonly accepted generic definition:

18. See the section on Krause in chap. 5, below.
19. See Charles Hartshorne, preface to *The Divine Relativity: A Social Conception of God* (New Haven: Yale University Press, 1948), where he labels his view "surrelativism or panentheism." See also Hartshorne

"The Being of God includes and penetrates the whole universe, so that every part exists in Him, but His Being is more than, and not exhausted by, the universe."[20] In other words, God and the world are ontologically distinct and God transcends the world, but the world is in God ontologically.

Like all general terms, there are widely differing ways of understanding panentheism, in particular what "being in God" means and in what ways God's Being transcends the universe.[21] As a result, theologians who endorse panentheism do not agree on what it is or should be. Some virtually identify it with process theology. Some embrace versions much closer to classical theism than pantheism whereas others hold views close to pantheism. Some, such as Moltmann, gladly embrace the term *panentheism*. Others, such as Pannenberg, reject the term even though their theologies seem to fit the definition.

This diversity makes an introduction to panentheism more complicated. For the sake of clarity, it is important at the outset to identify five distinctions on basic issues that recur throughout this book: explicit and implicit panentheism; personal and nonpersonal panentheism; part-whole and relational panentheism; voluntary and/or natural panentheism; and classical (divine determinist) or modern (cooperative) panentheism.

The distinction between *explicit* and *implicit panentheism* is important. There are many thinkers whose theologies imply panentheism; that is, they meet the definition of panentheism even though they do not explicitly use the term. Obviously this is true of those who wrote before the word was coined. Thus we call Plotinus, Nicholas of Cusa, and Hegel panentheists because their theologies meet the qualifications, not because they owned the label. Strictly speaking, it is anachronistic to call them panentheists. But they are implicit panentheists.

Refinement of the distinction between panentheism and pantheism also enables us to discern implicit panentheism more precisely. Theologies that we now call panentheistic have traditionally been classified as species of pantheism.[22] Indeed Schleiermacher and Schelling endorsed positions that they termed pantheism.

---

and Reese, "Introduction: The Standpoint of Panentheism," in *Philosophers Speak of God*. Also Charles Hartshorne, "Pantheism and Panentheism," *EncRel* 11:165–71. Brierley, "Naming a Quiet Revolution," 1–15, details the history of the term.

20. F. L. Cross and E. A. Livingstone, eds., *The Oxford Dictionary of the Christian Church*, 3rd ed. (New York: Oxford University Press, 1997), 1213; see also E. R. Naughton, "Panentheism," in *Oxford Encyclopedia of the Reformation*, 4 vols. (Oxford: Oxford University Press, 1996), 1:943–45.

21. Again Clayton and Peacocke, eds., *In Whom We Live*, is recommended because it includes essays by panentheists of different kinds and several essays attempting to identify the core beliefs common to all types of panentheism. There is no consensus, however, on more refined technical issues.

22. C. A. Beckwith, "Pantheism," *Schaff-Herzog*, 8:328–32, and Alasdair Macintyre, "Pantheism," *EncPhil*, 6:31–35, include panentheism and panentheists such as Hegel and Schelling within pantheism.

So also did Teilhard de Chardin, and this brings us to contemporary theologians who are *implicit panentheists*. Some contemporary panentheists, such as Hartshorne and Moltmann, explicitly identify themselves as such. But others, such as Whitehead and Tillich, do not. A few—Pannenberg and perhaps Polkinghorne, for instance—criticize panentheism in spite of the fact that their own views meet the standard definition.

Clarity of definition and analysis is therefore crucial. This survey considers all thinkers who meet the conditions of panentheism without adopting the term to be implicit panentheists. I accept responsibility for showing whether and to what extent they meet the conditions of panentheism and for stating the results precisely. With respect to some, I conclude no more than that they are *probable* or *virtual* panentheists because their positions are not explicit enough to allow definite identification.

A second important distinction throughout the book is between *personal* and *nonpersonal* or *Ground-of-being panentheism*. For Plotinus, Fichte, Tillich, Ruether, Radhakrishnan, and Watts, the Divine is the Ground—the ultimate cause, source, and power—of personhood and interpersonal communion but is not itself personal. For Schelling, Teilhard, Buber, Hartshorne, and Moltmann, God is ultimately personal and creates for the sake of interpersonal relationship. Christians such as Berdyaev and Moltmann use (inter)personal panentheism as a basis for affirming the Trinity.

A third major issue is the meaning of "being in God" or "participating in God." Some panentheists view the world as part of the divine nature, an implicit part of God's Mind apart from creation and an explicit emanation of the divine Mind's Idea of the world in creation. Others view "being in God" more relationally or existentially, so that the mutual interaction between God and creatures in history involves God and the world so totally and intimately that they are one ontologically, analogously to the mind and body or symbiotic organisms. The history of panentheism displays variations of both positions, but the basic distinction between *part-whole* and *relational panentheism* persists.[23]

"Being in God" raises a fourth distinction: *voluntary* and/or *natural panentheism*. Could God exist without a world? Could God have chosen to

---

Paul Feinberg, "Pantheism," in *Concise Evangelical Dictionary of Theology* (Grand Rapids: Baker, 1991), 369, still identifies the notion of the World-Soul as "relativistic monistic pantheism."

Similarly, the term *pantheism* is anachronistic when applied to Spinoza and the Stoics because it was not coined until John Toland's *Socinianism Truly Stated* (1705) and *Pantheisticon* (1720). Pantheism holds that the world is divine, although God may also transcend the world in some way. It does not necessarily identify all of God with the world, but the world is an aspect or manifestation of God.

23. Philip Clayton, "Panentheism Today: A Constructive Systematic Evaluation," in *In Whom We Live*, ed. Clayton and Peacocke, 252–54, identifies more precisely several meanings of "in God" held by panentheists. The distinction described here is a useful generalization for present purposes.

create another world or no world at all? Some panentheists unabashedly assert the necessity of the world for God. Neoplatonism readily asserts that God naturally "overflows" or emanates into lesser kinds of being. Hartshorne insists that God must have some world or other. It is the divine nature to include a world. But most Christian panentheists affirm God's freedom and deny the necessity of the world.

The issue is more complicated, however. Although they affirm that God freely creates, almost all panentheists, including Christians, ultimately imply that a world is inevitable for God.[24] Their reasoning is this: God is love, and creation is the free expression of God's love, not the necessity of his nature; but God cannot love without having something other than himself to love; thus he cannot be God without creating something.

Those who make or imply this argument are adopting a *compatibilist* view of divine freedom. Compatibilism asserts the compatibility of freedom and necessity. It holds that an act is free if it is a self-determined expression of one's nature that is neither coerced by anything outside oneself nor involuntarily compelled by anything internal (e.g., a muscle spasm or psychological compulsion). According to this definition, God is self-determining and freely creates to express his love because that is his nature. By implication, however, it is impossible for God not to create a world to love. This topic will recur throughout this survey.

The fifth issue, the freedom of creatures to affect God, mainly divides *classical* from *modern panentheism*. Panentheism from Plotinus through Schleiermacher, like classical theism, affirms divine omnipotence and does not allow that creatures affect God even though they exist in him. Schelling is the first to posit human freedom correlative with divine freedom, so that God's existence is affected by human action. Almost all modern panentheists affirm divine-human cooperation. Hartshorne even makes creaturely autonomy the test of true panentheism: if ultimately God is the only determiner, then pantheism is true.[25] The libertarian freedom of creatures to act, shape history, and affect God is a basic principle of modern panentheism. Those, such as Pannenberg, who do not obviously affirm it are roundly challenged.

These five pairs of basic distinctions within panentheism—explicit or implicit, personal or nonpersonal, part-whole or relational, voluntary and/or natural, and classical (divine determinist) or modern (cooperative) panenthe-

---

24. Philip Clayton is an unusual exception, arguing that God could have refrained from creating anything without diminishing himself. See chap. 13, below.

25. Hartshorne, "Pantheism and Panentheism," *EncRel*, 11:165–71.

ism—are themes that endure and thus provide some framework throughout the long history that we now begin to recount. The last chapter addresses the variations on these themes as it inquires whether panentheism is biblically, theologically, and philosophically preferable to classical theism as a Christian doctrine of God.

2

Panentheism from Plato
through Christian Neoplatonism

Platonism: Source of Two Theological Traditions

Judaism, Christianity, and Islam are "religions of the book." They claim to be based on particular communications of God, written down by humans. Their teachings are believed to derive from divine revelation, not human reasoning. But Platonic philosophy has played a significant role in the theologies of all three religions. Philo of Alexandria used it to articulate Jewish monotheism even before the advent of Christian theology. Among Christians, Justin Martyr and Origen used Platonic categories in their formulations of doctrine. Platonism's grandchild, Neoplatonism, has been the philosophical background of Augustinian theology in the West and, in a slightly different way, of Eastern Orthodox theology since the fourth century. Thomas Aquinas's response to the Jewish theologian Maimonides and the Muslims Avicenna and Averroës highlights the fact that Neoplatonism was common to all three theological traditions during the Middle Ages.

Platonic categories have been crucial in the formulation of *classical* or *Anselmian theism*, the view that God is Perfect Being—simple, absolute, infinite, eternal, immutable, omnipotent, omniscient, perfectly good, and essentially independent of the world. Classical theism has been the position

31

of Western Christian orthodoxy—from Augustine, Aquinas, Scotus, Luther, Calvin, and their followers to the present. It is undeniable that although the Bible is its source and standard, traditional Christian theology has been shaped significantly by the legacy of Platonic philosophy.

But Plato also inspired another theological tradition, what is now called *panentheism*. Panentheism is the view that all things exist within the being of God but that God's being nevertheless transcends them. Although not explicitly named until the nineteenth century, it is suggested by Plato's *Timaeus*, elaborated in the Neoplatonic philosophy of Plotinus, and blended with Christian orthodoxy by Pseudo-Dionysius. Panentheism was a minority view, sometimes condemned, during the millennium of high orthodoxy guarded by the Church of Rome. With a few exceptions, most notably John Scotus Eriugena and Nicholas of Cusa, medieval theologians were classical theists in the line of Anselm. But panentheism reemerged as the Renaissance and Reformation weakened the constraints of the medieval church.

This chapter surveys the development of panentheism from Plato to the speculations of the post-Reformation mystic Jakob Böhme. Plotinus's Neoplatonism clearly elicits panentheism from the ambiguity in Plato's theology of the relation between the Divine and the world. Proclus systematizes Neoplatonic ontology, using Plato's method of dialectic. Pseudo-Dionysius elaborates a synthesis of Neoplatonism and Christianity that is the source of panentheism for medieval Christian theologians. John Scotus Eriugena's Christian panentheism is one of the few intellectual lights during the Dark Ages. Nicholas of Cusa's theology is a bridge from the Middle Ages to the Renaissance. He advocates "learned ignorance": all dialectical opposition is unified in God, but humans cannot comprehend how. Jakob Böhme boldly asserts that dialectic is the dynamic heart of God himself, eternally generating the Trinity and temporally generating the world. Böhme, then, is the origin of the dialectical panentheism we later encounter in Hegel, Schelling, Tillich, and Moltmann.

Plato

It is not clear that Plato (427–347 B.C.E.) is a panentheist. His theology developed over time and is somewhat ambiguous. For instance, in *The Republic* he relates God to the wholly transcendent Highest Good in the ideal world, but his later work *Timaeus* presents a creation myth in which God is the Maker of the world and the world has a divine Soul. For millennia scholars have debated the correct interpretation of Plato's theology, how to order his diverse assertions about God coherently. Regardless of the debate, his doctrine of the World-Soul has been a perennial favorite among panentheists as an analogy for the relationship between God and the cosmos.[1]

Plato's Dualistic View of Reality

To understand Plato's theology, it is necessary to introduce his philosophy.[2] Plato is a metaphysical dualist. He postulates that reality consists of two ultimate and different dimensions: the potentially chaotic material world of temporary, changing, contingent, imperfect, visible things; and the rationally ordered ideal world, a system of eternal, necessary, perfect, changeless Ideas or rational Forms.[3]

The material realm is readily apparent to the human senses. It consists of the basic elements (earth, air, fire, and water) and the things made from them that populate the universe (stars, trees, animals, human bodies, and human artifacts). Physical things come into existence, change, and eventually cease to exist. Matter without Form is pure chaos, disorder.

Conversely, the intelligible Forms in the ideal realm are accessible by the mind. The Forms are the archetypal patterns or prototypical designs of the things in the material world. They are the Ideas that define the nature, characteristics, and order of the world and everything in it. Yet they are independent of the physical cosmos. Circularity is an example of an ideal Form. There are many round things in the world, none of them perfectly circular. Yet there is an Idea or definition of perfect circularity that our minds can identify. This definition would be real and true even if there were no circular things and no human minds thinking of the definition. Thus the Idea is independent of the world. Although circular things change, the Idea

---

1. Alexander Pope, *Essay on Man*, Epistle 1 (London: Methuen; New Haven: Yale University Press, 1951), 267, "All are but parts of one stupendous whole, Whose body Nature is and God the soul"; Friedrich Schleiermacher, *On Religion: Speeches to Its Cultured Despisers*, trans. John Oman (New York: Harper Torchbook, 1958; repr., London: Routledge and Kegan Paul; Louisville: Westminster/John Knox, 1994), 40, who refers to "the holy, rejected Spinoza" as inspired by "the WorldSpirit"; Sallie McFague, "The World as God's Body," in *Models of God: Theology for an Ecological, Nuclear Age* (Philadelphia: Fortress, 1987); and Philip Clayton, *God and Contemporary Science* (Grand Rapids: Eerdmans, 1997), 101, "The world bears a relationship to God analogous to the body's relationship to the mind or soul."

2. The chapters on Plato in Diogenes Allen, *Philosophy for Understanding Theology* (Atlanta: John Knox, 1985), are a fine introduction for theology students. A fuller account is Copleston, *Hist. Phil.*, vol. 1, part 3. A detailed recent account is Giovanni Reale, *History of Ancient Philosophy*, ed. and trans. John Catan (Albany: State University of New York Press, 1985–), vol. 2.

3. Plato's most accessible account of the world of Forms and the human knowledge of them is his discussion of the education of philosopher-kings in *Rep.* 5.472 through bk. 7. References are to the standard pagination of Plato's works.

of circularity never does. It is eternal and immutable. It is also singular and universal because it is the one prototype of all circular things in the cosmos, such as the sun and metal rings. In sum, Plato asserts that Ideas or Forms are real, universal, changeless, and independent of the material cosmos, yet are somehow responsible for the order of the cosmos.

Plato identifies four kinds of Ideals or Forms. There are mathematical Forms, such as the number One and the shape Circularity. He also speaks of moral or value Forms, such as Truth, Beauty, and Justice,[4] which are the universal ideal standards for the earthly things that exemplify truth, beauty, or justice. A third category of Forms are kinds of natural things, such as Living Being,[5] and particular kinds, such as the ideal Tree or ideal Horse. Finally, there are Ideals for human artifacts and cultural objects, such as beds and houses.[6] The material world reflects a variety of complex combinations of the ideal Forms.

Plato further teaches that the Ideas are related to one another in a coherent, ultimately unified system because they are all generated by and reflect the Good, the Form of all Forms: "These derive from the Good not only their power of being known, but their very being and reality." The Forms emanate from the Good like light comes from the sun.[7]

Since the world reflects the Forms and the Forms reflect the Good, the path to knowledge and truth must lead from the world to the Good. Plato maps this route in *Rep.* 509–541, where "The Allegory of the Cave" illustrates how the human mind moves from sense perception of physical things to intellectual knowledge of the eternally true Forms. Mathematical reflection lifts the mind from sensory images of physical things to contemplation of the numerical and geometrical Forms. A similar process of abstraction gives one access to the universal Ideals, such as Justice and Beauty.

Finally, *dialectic* leads to knowledge of the ultimate unity of all the Forms, the Good itself. Dialectic is a method of thought that moves back and forth among the individual Forms, testing the truth of each and discerning how they collectively constitute a single coherent system that is grounded in and follows from the Good. The dialectician "must be able to distinguish the essential nature of Goodness, isolating it from all other Forms; he must fight his way through all criticism, determined to examine every step by the standard . . . of reality and truth." Only with attainment of the Good

4. Plato, *Rep.* 524–528, mathematical Forms; *Rep.* 478, Beauty and Justice.

5. Plato, *Tim.* 30–31.

6. Plato, *Rep.* 597, contrasts the ideal Bed as God's work with material beds made by human craftsmen and, even more remote from ideal reality, pictures of beds made by artists.

7. Plato, *Rep.* 508 (translated passages are from Plato, *Republic*, trans. Francis Cornford [New York: Oxford University Press, 1945, repr. 1968]).

by means of dialectic does knowledge of anything become certain. "The method of dialectic is the only one which takes this course, doing away with assumptions and traveling up to the first principle of all, so as to make sure of confirmation there."[8] Dialectical pursuit of absolute truth has remained a tantalizing but daunting challenge to philosophers ever since. The dialectical tradition culminated in the system of Hegel two millennia after Plato and continues to shape Marxist, existentialist, and postmodernist thought.

The Forms, the World, and God

In *Timaeus* Plato presents a figurative account, a "likely story," of how the Forms order the material world. He uses metaphor because he does not believe that earthly language, even philosophical language, can fully explain transcendent reality.[9] We can best understand the relation of worldly things to the Forms, he says, if we think of the cosmos as having been made by a *dēmiourgos kai patēr*, a Craftsman and Father, also called *ho theos*, the God. The Demiurge uses the eternal Forms as prototypes or paradigms: "The world has been fashioned on the model of that which is comprehensible by rational discourse and ... always in the same state."[10] The Demiurge fashions the world of things from pre-given matter, like a builder who makes a house of wood from a plan, or a sculptor who copies a model in clay.

The particular Form used by the Demiurge to make the cosmos as a whole is Living Being, the prototype of all living things, including humans and gods. Thus "this world came to be, by the god's providence, in very truth a living creature with soul and reason." The cosmos is a living being, "a single visible living creature, containing within itself all living things," "a body whole and complete, with complete bodies for its parts."[11] The universe is a single living thing that contains many living things.

As a living being, the most important part of the cosmos is its Soul. "In the center [the Demiurge] set a soul and caused it to extend throughout the whole and further wrapped its body round with soul on the outside ... to be the body's mistress and governor."[12] Thus the physical world is actually

8. Plato, *Rep.* 534bc, 533d.

9. Plato, *Tim.* 29d (translated passages are from Plato, *Timaeus*, trans. Francis Cornford [New York: Macmillan, 1959]).

10. Plato, *Tim.* 29a. Plato also compares God's making the Idea of a Bed, a craftsman making a bed, and an artist depicting a bed in *Rep.* 597.

11. Plato, *Tim.* 30c, 34b.

12. Plato, *Tim.* 34b–c. In *Philebus* 30a he also asserts that "the body of the universe ... happens to possess a soul" (trans. D. Frede, in Plato, *Complete Works*, ed. John M. Cooper [Indianapolis and Cambridge, UK: Hackett, 1997]).

in the Soul—a point most conducive to panentheism—rather than the Soul being in its body, the world.

Soul is the power by which the eternal Ideas are actualized in and govern the world, "as a soul having part in reason and harmony is the best of things brought into being by the most excellent of things intelligible and eternal." Soul is the means the Father-Craftsman uses to actualize the ideal Living Being in the world, thereby generating Time. "Now the nature of that Living Being was eternal . . . but he [the Demiurge] took thought to make, as it were, a moving likeness of eternity . . . to which we have given the name Time."[13] Soul is the Rational Life of the cosmos, the dynamic ordering of the eternal Ideals in matter and time. *Timaeus* offers an extensive account of how time, heaven and the heavenly bodies, the gods and human souls, the earth, ocean, and all living creatures are formed and infused by the World-Soul. The Demiurge made the souls of the stars (which are "gods") and humans from the same stuff as the World-Soul, and so they share its citizenship in both the eternal and the temporal realms. Plato regards humans as microcosms of the macrocosm, body-soul miniatures of the world who can knowingly participate in the rational patterns of the cosmic Life.

Is Plato's Theology Panentheism?

Plato is not a panentheist unless he places all things in God ontologically. And this depends on whether he regards the World-Soul, which contains all things, as God or part of God. There is little doubt that he identifies God with the Mind or Demiurge that fashions the universe. But the theological status of the World-Soul is ambiguous: is it part of "the God" or merely a creation of God?

In *Timaeus* Plato identifies "the God" as the Maker of the world, even designating him "Father." This Demiurge makes the world according to the Ideal as an artisan makes an object according to a model. *Republic* (597b) affirms the same view, that God is like a Craftsman, and it adds that he is the source of the Forms, a role that also belongs to the Good. This shared role implies the identity of the Creator God and the Good. Additionally, in *Philebus* (30c) God is the Mind or divine Reason [*Nous*] that orders the universe. This association takes us back to *Timaeus*, where ordering the universe is the job of the Demiurge, whose artifacts are likewise said to be "the works of Mind/Reason" (47e). In sum, Plato's developed view of

13. Plato, *Tim.* 37a, c–d.

God clearly includes the Good, Mind/Reason with the Forms, and the Demiurge.[14]

So far there is nothing panentheistic in his theology. The material cosmos as such does not exist in the Demiurge, the Good, or divine Reason. Earthly things are said to "participate in" the ideal Forms, but participation means only that they exemplify or are patterned according to the Ideal, not that they are immanent in it. Matter and change are never part of the ideal realm.

Timaeus does locate the world in the World-Soul. So, if the World-Soul is part of God, Plato is a panentheist. There are hints in this direction. *Timaeus* (34ab) refers to the World-Soul as "a god." Furthermore, in *Philebus* (30c) Plato asserts that the divine Mind who wisely orders the universe has a Soul: "There could be no reason and wisdom without a soul." If the Soul of eternal divine Reason can be identified with the World-Soul of *Timaeus*, then the World-Soul is an aspect of God, and Plato is a panentheist.

But caution is warranted. An essential difference remains between "the god" who is divine Reason and other beings Plato calls "gods." As mentioned, *Timaeus* 34ab refers to the World-Soul as a god, "the god who was sometime to be." But this god was planned and generated by the Demiurge, who is "the god who is forever." The World-Soul is more likely a quasi-divine creation of the Demiurge because *Timaeus* also explains the creation of the traditional Greek "gods" and even alludes to the physical universe as "a perceptible god."[15] Plato readily calls created things "gods." And he retains an absolute distinction between "the god" who is eternal and uncreated and the other "gods" who are generated and participate in time. The World-Soul is clearly in the latter category. The world's being "in" the World-Soul does not place the world in the eternal God who made the world. Thus Plato is not a straightforward panentheist.

Hartshorne and Reese identify Plato as an "ancient or quasi-panentheist." They acknowledge that he does not identify the eternal God and the World-Soul, but they argue that if he were logically consistent, he would not have regarded the eternal God as a "concrete nature." Instead he would have considered the eternal God and the World-Soul as correlative natures of one divine Being, which is "essentially the view of Whitehead."[16]

14. Copleston, *Hist. Phil.*, vol. 1, chap. 20, sec. 9, on Plato's theology in relation to the Forms. Also Reale, "The Demiurge (and Not the Idea of the Good) Is the God of Plato," in *History*, 2:113–15.

15. Plato, *Tim.* 40d–41a, 92c.

16. Charles Hartshorne and William Reese, *Philosophers Speak of God* (Chicago: University of Chicago Press, 1953), 38–57, quotes are from 55–56. Robert Whittemore, "The Proper Categorization of Plato's *demiurgos*," *TSP* 27 (1978): 163–66, and Leonard Eslick, "Plato as Dipolar Theist," *Process Studies* 12 (Winter 1982): 243–51, likewise argue that Plato is a proto-Whiteheadian. But in his preface to Plato, *Timaeus*, xiv, Cornford quips, "There is much more of Plato in [Whitehead's] *Adventure of Ideas* than there is of Whitehead in the *Timaeus*."

Plato cannot be identified as a panentheist even if Hartshorne and Reese are correct in their criticism. Nevertheless, his idea of the World-Soul has inspired panentheists up to the present.

Stoicism: Naturalistic Pantheism

The Stoics identify divine Reason with the Soul of the world, but they turn out to be naturalistic pantheists rather than panentheists. We consider them in order to highlight the difference between pantheism and panentheism and as forerunners of thinkers such as Spinoza.

Stoicism flourished periodically from Zeno (d. 264/263 B.C.E.) to the Roman emperor Marcus Aurelius (d. 180 C.E.).[17] It teaches that the physical universe is ordered and animated by an immanent Logos or divine Reason. The diversity of nature exists within a single unity. According to Aurelius, "all things are mutually intertwined, and the tie is sacred. . . . For there is both one Universe made up of all things and one God immanent in all things, and one Substance, and one Law, one Reason common to all intelligent creatures, and one Truth."[18] A "seed" of the divine Reason (*logos spermatikos* or *semen rationalis*) is in every individual being. It manifests itself as the life force in plants, desire in animals, and reason in humans. By using these capacities, creatures participate in God. Humans exercise all three—life, desire, and reason—and thus participate in God most fully. "You are a fragment of God; you within you a part of Him. . . . Whenever you mix in society, whenever you take physical exercise, whenever you converse, do you not know that you are nourishing God, exercising God? You are bearing God about with you."[19] The emphasis on participation in God is very strong.

Could this be panentheism? After all, God and the universe are distinguishable, and the universe exists in God as a body in its soul.[20] The famous lines Paul quoted on Mars Hill (Acts 17:28) are by a Stoic poet, Epimenides the Cretan: "in him we live and move and have our being."[21] Perhaps the Stoics are the original proto-Christian panentheists.

17. Copleston, *Hist. Phil.*, vol. 1, chaps. 36, 39–40, on the periods of Stoicism; Reale, *History*, vol. 3, pt. 3, on early and middle Stoicism; 4:53–103, on late.

18. Marcus Aurelius, *Meditations* 7.9, trans. G. Grube (Indianapolis: Hackett, 1983).

19. Epictetus, *The Discourses as Reported by Arrian* 2.8.11–13, trans. W. Oldfather, 2 vols. (London: Heineman; New York: G. Putnam's Son, 1926–1928).

20. Copleston, *Hist. Phil.*, vol. 1, chap. 36, sec. 3, p. 133: "When the world is in existence, God stands to it as soul to body, being the soul of the world."

21. F. F. Bruce, *The Book of Acts* (Grand Rapids: Eerdmans, 1977), 359–60; Allen, *Philosophy for Understanding Theology*, 69.

This conclusion is, however, unwarranted. Stoicism rejects the dualism between the ideal and the material realms that ensures the metaphysical God-world distinction for Plato. The primary reality for the Stoics is the living, rational universe itself. "The substance of God, Zeno says, is the entire cosmos and the heaven."[22] Again, Aurelius's "one Universe" and "one God" are not ontologically distinct beings but different aspects or dimensions of the "one Substance." Thus Stoicism is not panentheism but naturalistic pantheism.[23] It anticipates Bruno, Spinoza, John Toland's *Pantheisticon* (1720), and Einstein, not Schleiermacher, Schelling, and Hegel.

Neoplatonism

Neoplatonism is the genuine fountainhead of classical panentheism. Plotinus (204–270) is the seminal thinker of this movement,[24] which has exercised an enormous influence on Western thought.[25] Plotinus worked out the unresolved issues in Plato's philosophy and developed a unified account of reality in which the divine Mind/Demiurge, the World-Soul, and the universe emanate hierarchically from the Good, that is, the divine One. The One is both infinite and utterly transcendent, yet it includes or contains everything that emanates from it.[26]

Plotinus's Philosophy

Plotinus intentionally uses Plato's dialectical method to identify the Forms, analyze all that follows from them, and synthesize the results so that all truth leads to a single principle.[27] The principle attained by dialectic

22. Diogenes Laertius, *Lives of Eminent Philosophers* 7:148, trans. R. Hicks (London: Cambridge, 1958), quoted from Reale, *History*, 3:241.

23. "Epictetus . . . cannot abandon pantheism and Stoic materialism, because he lacked the theoretic conception of the supersensible and the transcendent" (Reale, *History* 4:83); "Marcus Aurelius admitted . . . a pantheistic conception of God, which contains and absorbs all into itself" (4:95).

24. Porphyry, Iamblichus, and others were also Neoplatonists. Except for Proclus, their modifications of Plotinus do not warrant inclusion in this overview. See Copleston, *Hist. Phil.*, vol. 1, chap. 46; and Reale, *History*, 4:400–450, for later Neoplatonism.

25. See Stephen MacKenna, "The Influence of Plotinus," appendix to *The Essence of Plotinus*, trans. Stephen MacKenna (New York: Oxford University Press, 1934), 249–71; and Dominic J. O'Meara, "Epilogue: Plotinus in Western Thought," in *Plotinus: An Introduction to the Enneads* (New York: Oxford University Press, 1993), 111–19.

26. Copleston, *Hist. Phil.*, vol. 1, chap. 45; Allen, *Philosophy for Understanding Theology*, 73–90; Elmer O'Brien, introduction to *The Essential Plotinus* (New York: New American Library, 1964); O'Meara, *Plotinus*; Reale, "Plotinus and Neoplatonism," part 3 of *History*, vol. 4.

27. Plotinus, *Enn.* 1.3.4 (*Plotinus*, trans. A. H. Armstrong, 7 vols. [Cambridge, MA: Harvard University Press, 1966–1988], 1:159): "[Dialectic enables one] to distinguish the Forms, and to determine the

is Plato's Good, which Plotinus emphasizes as the One Form that is the source of the many Forms.[28] Much more than Plato, however, Plotinus asserts the absolute transcendence of the One. It even transcends what Plato identifies as Mind, the Ideas, and Being. "There is 'no concept or knowledge' of it; it is indeed also said to be 'beyond being.'" In itself the One is utterly simple, containing no distinction of parts, aspects, attributes, or powers. "For there must be something simple before all things, and this must be other than all the things which come after it, existing by itself, not mixed with the things which derive from it."[29] The One is absolutely infinite—not just infinite in space, time, or number—because it is the incomprehensibly unlimited power that produces itself and everything else.[30]

Plotinus postulates that the infinite power of the One eternally "overflows" or emanates into what is other and less perfect than itself. But it does so without diminishing itself, like a limitless fountain or like the sun generating light. Each emanation or *hypostasis* emulates its source as closely as possible. And each in turn generates another level of being, a less perfect likeness of itself, which likewise strives to resemble its source. Thus reality is a hierarchical order of different levels of being that extends from the One on top to the unformed matter of the physical universe on the bottom. Everything comes from the One and seeks to return to the One.

The hierarchy proceeds from the One, which generates the Intellect (Mind), which produces the Soul: "Soul is an expression and a kind of activity of Intellect, just as Intellect is of the One."[31] Soul is the World-Soul, which animates the universe. We consider each in order.

The first emanation from the One is Intellect, an eternal but less perfect expression of the One itself. As Intellect, the One knows itself in terms of the diverse Platonic Ideas or Forms.[32] Thus the One is manifest both as mind and ideas, as thinking and thoughts, as subject and object, and as one and

---

essential nature of each thing, and to find the primary kinds, and weave together by the intellect all that issues from these primary kinds, till it has traversed the whole intelligible world; then it resolves again the structure of the world into its parts, and comes back to its starting point . . . having arrived at unity."

28. Plotinus, *Enn.* 2.9.1 (Armstrong, 2:225): "Whenever we say 'the One' and whenever we say 'the Good,' we must think that the nature we are speaking of is the same nature."

29. Plotinus, *Enn.* 5.4.1 (Armstrong, 5:141).

30. Plotinus, *Enn.* 6.9.6 (Armstrong, 7:323): "And it must be understood as infinite not because its size and number cannot be measured or counted but because its power cannot be comprehended."

31. Plotinus, *Enn.* 5.1.6 (Armstrong, 5:33).

32. Plotinus, *Enn.* 6.7.16 (Armstrong, 7:139): "Did Intellect, when it looked towards the Good, think that One as many, and because it was itself one being think him as many, dividing him in itself by not being able to think the whole at once?"

many. Intellect is therefore both the same as and different from the One. *Enneads* 5.1 identifies the divine Intellect with Plato's Demiurge.

Intellect in turn generates Soul: "Just as a thought in its utterance is an image of the thought in soul, so Soul itself is the expressed thought of Intellect, and its whole activity, and the life which it sends out to establish another reality."[33] Because it is less perfect than Intellect, Soul cannot possess all the Forms eternally, and so it expresses them progressively by incarnating itself in the cosmos.

Thus Soul is the World-Soul or "All-Soul." It includes all the individual rational souls of the gods and humans within itself.[34] It is also the Life Principle of the physical cosmos: "It made all living things itself, breathing life into them, those that the earth feeds and those that are nourished by the sea, and the divine stars in the sky; it made the sun itself, and this great heaven, and adorned it itself, and drives it round itself, in orderly movement."[35] The Soul has generated all things, and all things exist within the Soul. "And soul's nature is so . . . as to contain the whole of body in one and the same grasp; wherever body extends, there soul is. . . . The universe extends as far as soul goes; its limit of extension is the point to which in going forth it has soul to keep it in being."[36]

To summarize Plotinus's ontology: The physical world, with all that it contains, exists within a permanent structure consisting of a series of successive emanations that originate from the highest reality, the One. Reality is a vertical hierarchy, a "Great Chain of Being," with the most perfect and infinite on top and the least perfect and most limited (pure matter) at the bottom. This top-down hierarchy is simultaneously reinforced from the bottom up as all things constantly strive back toward the One. Physical things are empowered and arranged as a rationally ordered universe by the World-Soul. World-Soul strives to approximate Intellect, and Intellect seeks the One. Because they are rational, human souls are naturally drawn from physical existence toward God. The attractive power that holds all things together is Eros or love.[37] Some Christians even thought that Plotinus's emanation-return scheme echoes St. Paul: "from him and through him and to him are all things" (Rom. 11:36).

33. Plotinus, *Enn.* 5.1.3 (Armstrong, 5:19–20).
34. Plotinus, *Enn.* 6.4.4 (Armstrong, 6:289): "Souls were both many and one before the bodies. For the many are already in the whole, not in potency, but each and every one in active actuality."
35. Plotinus, *Enn.* 5.1.2 (Armstrong, 5:15).
36. Plotinus, *Enn.* 4.3.9 (Armstrong, 4:65).
37. Plotinus, *Enn.* 3.5 (Armstrong, 3:163–203).

Plotinus's Theology: Pantheism or Panentheism?

The emanation of all things from the One might suggest that Plotinus's theology is a form of monistic pantheism. All is divine because it is an extension of the one God. In addition, the emanation of the One is necessary. It is not a choice of the One, a voluntary act of creation from which it might have refrained. The One eternally and inevitably overflows by its own infinite nature, and so does each successive emanation. The One is free, but in the compatibilist sense that it is not necessitated by anything other than itself.[38] Thus the world is contingent because it depends on the One. But it is also necessary or inevitable, not in itself but as the natural expression of divine necessity. This position might sound like pantheism.[39]

Between pantheism and traditional theism, however, lies the middle ground now designated as panentheism.[40] Panentheism typically implies an inevitable divine emanation, but it also sustains a strong ontological difference between God and the world. Plotinus's doctrine of the World-Soul meets these conditions: it is divine, it includes the world, but it is distinct from and transcends the world.[41]

For Plotinus, Soul includes the physical cosmos and all things of which it consists. He explicitly appeals to Plato's World-Soul on this point: "Plato rightly does not put the soul in the body when he is speaking of the universe, but the body in the soul." But Soul is also distinct from the universe for Plotinus, for he affirms both the immanence and the transcendence of the World-Soul: "There is a part of the soul in which the body is and part in which there is no body."[42] By its very nature, Soul is the mediator of the Divine and the cosmos. It participates both in the eternal realm of the Intellect and in the sensible realm of the physical universe.[43] In *Enneads* 4.2.1 Plotinus

38. Compatibilist views of the will hold that freedom and complete determination or necessity are compatible: an agent is free provided that it can act according to its nature without internal compulsion or external coercion; freedom is self-determination. Noncompatibilist views of the will hold that freedom is not compatible with complete determination. Free choice requires, in addition to self-determination, that an agent have genuine options. The nature of God's freedom is a major issue among theists and panentheists.

39. Traditionally Neoplatonism has often been classified as a kind of pantheism. See, e.g., C. A. Beckwith, "Neoplatonism," *Schaff-Herzog*, 8:328–32.

40. Copleston, *Hist. Phil.*, vol. 1, chap. 45, sec. 2, p. 211, observes that Plotinus "tries to steer a middle course between theistic creation on the one hand and a fully pantheistic or monistic theory on the other hand."

41. Plotinus, *Enn.* 4.3.9 (Armstrong, 4:65): "If body did not exist, it would make no difference to soul as regards size; for it is what it is."

42. Plotinus, *Enn.* 4.3.22 (Armstrong, 4:103).

43. "Intellect, then, is always inseparable and indivisible, but soul is inseparable and indivisible There, but it is in its nature to be divided" (Plotinus, *Enn.* 4.2.1 [Armstrong, 4:21]). "It is better for the soul to

refers to the transcendent aspect of the World-Soul as "divine." Thus the universe is contained in, but is distinct from, the divine World-Soul. This is already a kind of panentheism.

But Plotinus's panentheism goes even deeper. The World-Soul and all that it contains are part of a higher unity grounded in the One. On the one hand, Plotinus makes clear ontological distinctions between finite physical beings, the universe as a whole, the World-Soul, the Intellect, and the ultimate One. On the other hand, all things emanate from the One, return to it, and are contained within it. Thus all things are within the divine One, which infinitely transcends all things. Reale succinctly summarizes Plotinus's inclusive hierarchy: "In a certain sense the world itself is in God, since the world is in the Soul, the Soul is in Mind (Nous), Mind is in the One, and the One is not in something else but encloses everything entirely within itself."[44] All things are not divine, but all participate in God, who infinitely transcends all. This is classical panentheism.

If being a person requires mind and soul, the One is not personal but is the suprapersonal Ground of all being and personhood, even divine personhood. This issue remains perennial in panentheism and is a challenge for the Christian doctrine of the Trinity: God in three persons is not a primordial One who generates three persons but three persons who eternally and fully share the primordial divine nature.

Plotinus's concept of participation in God also deserves comment. Plotinus overcomes Plato's ultimate dualism with his theory of emanation and participation in the One. It is important to note that this changes the meaning of the philosophical term *participation*. For Plato, things in the world participate in the divine Mind by reflecting or being patterned according to the Forms. But worldly things do not "take part" in the ideal existence of the divine Mind. For Plotinus, *participation* means not only reflecting the Divine but also "taking part" in it—directly in the World-Soul, mediately in the Intellect, and ultimately in the One. This is the meaning of *participation* that is characteristic of much panentheism: being part of God.

Proclus and Dialectical Ontology

Proclus (410–485) was an Athenian Neoplatonist most important for his elaboration of the dialectical structure of the emanations identified by

---

be in the intelligible, but all the same, since it has this kind of nature, it is necessarily bound to be able to participate in the perceptible . . ." (4.8.7 [Armstrong, 4:418]).

44. Reale, *History*, 4:370.

Plotinus.[45] He too begins with the One, "a cause ineffable . . . and incomprehensible, unfolding all things into light from itself, subsisting ineffably prior to, and converting all things to itself."[46] From the One proceed two opposing principles, infinity and delimitation, which in turn interact to constitute Being, Life, and Intelligence. These are the three "gods" or eternal principles that interact dialectically to generate subsequent emanations and thereby constitute the living universe.

Each level of reality below the One is generated dialectically and thus is dialectical in ontological structure. From "the triadic hypostasis of intelligibles . . . it is necessary that all things should be detained by a triadic progression."[47] Each new level of being that emanates from a higher level is both the same as its source and different from it: identity yields difference. (In language later popularized by Fichte and Hegel, a *thesis* generates its *antithesis*.) But the natural desire of the emanated level to resemble its source as fully as possible simultaneously draws it back toward that source. As a result, the emanated level is the union of its identity with and difference from its source (a *synthesis* of the *thesis* and *antithesis*). The process repeats itself all the way down the Great Chain of Being and back. Using dialectical reflection, Proclus articulates an entire system of triads from the highest to lowest reality, tracing the many from the One and returning to the One. Thus the basic structure of all being that emanates from the One is dialectical.

Proclus is the wellspring for the key role that dialectical ontology and logic play in the history of panentheism. It is worth noting that he and Plotinus regard the One itself as beyond dialectic. Only later was this tri-unifying dynamic projected into the inner life of God himself.

Pseudo-Dionysius and Christian Neoplatonism

Christian Evaluations of Platonism

Christians responded to the Platonic tradition in various ways.[48] Some, such as Tertullian, rejected it entirely as a pagan religion. Others, including

---

45. Proclus, *The Platonic Theology* [*Theologia platonica*], trans. T. Taylor, 2 vols. (1816; repr., Kew Gardens, NY: Selene, 1985–1986); and *Stoicheiosis theologike: The Elements of Theology*, ed. and trans. E. R. Dodds, 2nd ed. (Oxford: Clarendon, 1963). Also Copleston, *Hist. Phil.*, vol. 1, chap. 46, sec. 3; and Reale, *History*, 4:427–53.

46. Proclus, *Theol. plat.* 3.3 (Taylor, 1:165).

47. Proclus, *Theol. plat.* 4.2 (Taylor, 2:228).

48. Copleston, *Hist. Phil.*, vol. 2, chap. 2, provides an excellent summary of this interaction; also Étienne Gilson, *History of Christian Philosophy in the Middle Ages* (New York: Random House, 1955),

Justin Martyr and Origen, regarded Platonism as a largely true but incomplete anticipation of Christianity. The main Christian tradition engaged Greek philosophy critically, appropriating and adapting elements that could be used to explain and defend what was regarded as orthodox teaching while rejecting what conflicts with it. For example, Augustine, who was a Neoplatonist when he was converted, criticizes some aspects and approves of others.[49] Athanasius and Gregory of Nyssa used modified Neoplatonic categories to formulate the Nicene Creed's doctrine of the Trinity as well as to distinguish it from Neoplatonism. In the Creed, Father, Son, and Holy Spirit are each termed *hypostasis* (person). Although the Son and the Holy Spirit "proceed" from the Father, they are not emanations but eternally and fully share the one divine nature (*homoousios*) with the Father.[50] Furthermore, Christian thinkers viewed the world as the product of God's free act of creation, not an inevitable divine emanation. These examples illustrate how most Christians subordinated and modified Greek philosophy according to established doctrine.

Pseudo-Dionysius

Sometimes, however, a commitment to Neoplatonism stands in tension with orthodoxy. This is the case in aspects of Pseudo-Dionysius, writings traditionally but no longer attributed to Dionysius the Areopagite, Paul's first convert in Athens.[51] Much in these books is deeply Christian and orthodox, so that they were esteemed by such great theologians of the church as Bonaventure and Aquinas. But they are also the source of views condemned by the church, as we will see.

Pseudo-Dionysius is famous for articulating the dialectical method of theology, which has been widely used in Christian tradition: The *via positiva* (positive way) attributes creaturely categories to God; the *via negativa* (negative way) then denies that creaturely categories apply to God; and the *via eminentiae* (way of eminence) finally attributes creaturely categories to God as the source of creaturely categories but not as defined by those categories.

parts 2–3; and Leo Scheffczyk, *Creation and Providence*, trans. R. Strachan (New York: Herder and Herder, 1970), chap. 2.

49. Augustine, *The City of God against the Pagans*, ed. and trans. R. W. Dyson (New York: Cambridge University Press, 1998), esp. bks. 8 and 10.

50. J. N. D. Kelly, "The Doctrine of the Trinity," chap. 10 in *Early Christian Doctrines*, rev. ed. (New York: Harper and Row, 1978).

51. Pseudo-Dionysius, *The Complete Works*, trans. Colm Luibheid (New York: Paulist, 1987), esp. *The Divine Names* [*De divinis nominibus*] and *The Celestial Hierarchy* (translated passages of *De divinis nominibus* are from Luibheid); Copleston, *Hist. Phil.*, vol. 2, chap. 9.

Thus, when we say, "God is good," we cannot simply mean that God is good as a human is good, because God's goodness is infinite and perfect. So we must also deny that God is good. The resolution, according to this method, is this: "God is good" means that God is the source of creaturely goodness. Thus the assertion is appropriate but not definitive of God's goodness.[52] The method is dialectical in that it affirms something, then denies it, then reconciles what it affirms and denies: a thesis, antithesis, and synthesis.

Pseudo-Dionysius's dialectical method is heavily indebted to the theology of Plotinus and Proclus. For instance, his *via eminentiae* presupposes that the One is beyond all being and reason.[53] Given his Neoplatonism, some of Dionysius's formulations express Nicene orthodoxy on the Trinity while others are ambiguous or unorthodox. For example, his assertion that God is "the inexpressible Good, this One, this Source of all Unity, this supra-existent Being"[54] is typical of Neoplatonism. It is consistent with the following orthodox statement about the Trinity: "The Father is the only source of that Godhead which in fact is beyond being and the Father is not a Son nor is the Son a Father."[55] But Dionysius's Neoplatonism prevails when he refers to God as "a monad or henad" and the three persons of the Trinity as "manifestations."[56] This statement implies, contrary to the Nicene Creed, that the persons are emanations of the One.[57]

Likewise ambiguously, Pseudo-Dionysius construes the biblical doctrine of creation in terms of the Neoplatonic hierarchy of emanation and return. Accordingly, God is "for all things the creator and originator, the One who brings them to completion ... the power which returns them to itself ... [which] actually contains everything beforehand within itself."[58] The world is the natural, free, but inevitable overflow of God's superabundant intellect, goodness, and love.

Although Pseudo-Dionysius strongly distinguishes the world from God, he emphasizes the inclusion of all things in God. "The name 'One' means

52. The method is spelled out and applied in Pseudo-Dionysius, *The Mystical Theology*.

53. Aquinas uses this method also, but he affirms that our language for God is analogical in the sense that there is some finite likeness of the Creator in the creature. This assumes that being and reason are intrinsic to God. See *ST*, Ia, q. 13.

54. Pseudo-Dionysius, *Div. nom.* 1.1.

55. Pseudo-Dionysius, *Div. nom.* 2.5.

56. Pseudo-Dionysius, *Div. nom.* 1.4.

57. "The Pseudo-Dionysius meant to harmonize the two elements, to express Christian theology and Christian mysticism in a neo-Platonic philosophical framework and scheme; but it can scarcely be gainsaid that, when a clash occurred, the neo-Platonic elements tended to prevail" (Copleston, *Hist. Phil.*, vol. 2, chap. 9, sec. 7, p. 115).

58. Pseudo-Dionysius, *Div. nom.* 1.7.

that God is uniquely all things through the transcendence of the one unity and that he is the cause of all without ever departing from that oneness. Nothing in the world lacks its share of the One. Just as every number participates in unity ... so everything, and every part of everything, participates in the One. By being the One, it is all things."[59] Recognizing his conceptual dependence on Neoplatonism, it is reasonable to construe this statement as panentheism, not pantheism. Neoplatonism posits an infinite difference between the One and creatures, as well as the inclusion of creatures in the One.

John Scotus Eriugena

John Scotus Eriugena (810–877) was steeped in Christian Neoplatonism and translated the writings of Pseudo-Dionysius.[60] He sought to demonstrate that all Christian truth is consistent with, and can be formulated in terms of, sound philosophy, by which he meant Neoplatonism.

Eriugena's Philosophical Theology

His major work, *On the Division of Nature*, begins by defining Nature as "all things, whether or not they have being" and distinguishing four species of Nature that reflect its own self-division: "The first is the division into what creates and is not created; the second into what is created and creates; the third, into what is created and does not create; and the fourth, into what neither creates nor is created."[61] The first and last categories of Nature refer to God. As the source of all, God is uncreated Creator. As the final consummation of all, he is the uncreated that does not create. The creatures that create are the "primordial causes," the Neoplatonic archetypal Ideas or Principles in the divine Mind. The creatures that do not create are the finite things that collectively constitute the living world. In sum, Nature is God and all that proceeds from him.

Defining God in terms of Nature should not be construed as naturalistic pantheism. By "Nature" Eriugena means something like "Reality" rather than

59. Pseudo-Dionysius, *Div. nom.* 13.2.

60. Copleston, *Hist. Phil.*, vol. 2, chaps. 12–13; Jean Potter, introduction to John Scotus Eriugena, *Periphyseon: On the Division of Nature [De divisione naturae]*, trans. Myra Uhlfelder (Indianapolis: Bobbs-Merrill, 1976); John O'Meara, *Eriugena* (Oxford: Clarendon, 1988); Dermot Moran, *The Philosophy of John Scottus Eriugena* (Cambridge: Cambridge University Press, 1989); Dierdre Carabine, *John Scottus Eriugena* (Oxford: Oxford University Press, 2000).

61. Eriugena, *Div. nat.* 1.1. This and the following quotations are from Uhlfelder.

the mere physical universe.[62] God is the real source of the natural world, not a dimension of it. Repeatedly quoting Proclus, Eriugena takes the standard Neoplatonist position that God in himself is the Absolute Infinite Supra-essential One, the transcendent source of all thought, being, categories, and differentiations.[63] Book 2 of *On the Division of Nature* clearly affirms the God-world distinction and explains creation from nothing as the work of the Trinity. Eriugena identifies God's ideal self-expression as the eternal Logos, the Son, and God's presence in the world as the Spirit. The Christian intention and content of his views are clear.

But aspects of Eriugena's theology are in tension with Christian doctrine because they seem to compromise the difference between God and the world. He often speaks as though God is all of Nature, not just its uncreated divisions: "If there is one and the same Nature whose simplicity is inviolable and whose unity is inseparable, then surely it will be granted that God is Everything everywhere, Whole in the whole." Accordingly, God has both divine and creaturely characteristics: "Maker and made, Seer and seen, Time and Place, Essence and Substance of all, Accident, and to put it simply, Everything that Truly Is and Is Not, superessential in essences, supersubstantial in substances, Creator above all creation, created within all creation . . . beginning to be from Himself . . . infinitely multiplied in Himself through genera and species, not deserting the simplicity of His nature, and recalling the infinity of His manifoldness to Himself. For in Him all things are one."[64] In this passage, God is all of Nature or Reality, not just its uncreated aspects. Pantheism seems to be the most obvious implication.

Eriugena holds that God is both Creator and creature because he creates himself in creating other things. "We should not therefore understand God and creation as two different things, but as one and the same. For creation subsists in God, and God is created in creation in a remarkable and ineffable way, manifesting Himself." By creating, God gives himself nondivine attributes: "Though . . . lacking form and species, endowing Himself with form and species; though superessential . . . [he is] essential; though supernatural . . . natural; though simple . . . compound; though infinite . . . finite; . . . though above time . . . temporal; . . . though creating everything, making himself created in everything. The Maker of all, made in all, begins to be eternal and, though motionless, moves into everything and becomes all things in all things."[65] God creates himself as he creates the world. The

62. Copleston, *Hist. Phil.*, vol. 2, chap. 13, sec. 1, p. 133.
63. Eriugena, *Div. nat.* 1.75–78.
64. Eriugena, *Div. nat.* 3.16.
65. Ibid.

theology that results is clearly dialectical: God is both x and not-x, yet he is the source of x; he is both y and not-y, yet the source of y.

Eriugena's theology entails that without the world God is not God and cannot exist or know himself. The world is in God eternally. It is the natural manifestation of the divine One, a theophany. Consider his account of creation *ex nihilo*. With Neoplatonism, Eriugena identifies the "nothing"—nonbeing, the "*darkness . . . the abyss*"—out of which creation was made with "the Superessential Good . . . supernal excellence . . . indivisible unity . . . [and] simplicity" of God.[66] Creation *ex nihilo* therefore means creation *from God himself*, not simply creation without raw material. Since God in himself is not Being, he is Non-being, No-thing, and he does not have being or existence without creation. In creation he moves "from nothing to something" (*ex nihilo in aliquid*).[67] Thus God is self-creating. Furthermore, God in himself is unknowable, not just to humans but also to himself because in himself is Nothing for him to know. Thus God also comes to self-knowledge through creation. In sum, God must make something of himself to exist and know himself, and the nothing from which he creates is himself. For Eriugena, the dialectical relationship of nothingness, being, and becoming something is intrinsic to the divine life. This view is also held by Tillich and Moltmann.

Pantheism or Panentheism?

Perhaps Eriugena's theology is pantheistic. The church condemned it in the thirteenth century for failing to distinguish God and creation strongly enough. Some statements do seem pantheist: "We should not therefore understand God and creation as two different things, but as one and the same."[68] In equating God with Nature, Eriugena's language anticipates Spinoza's famous epithet *Deus sive natura* (God or Nature) and his distinction between *Natura naturans* and *Natura naturata* (Nature making nature and Nature being made nature).

Yet Eriugena does distinguish God and world as uncreated and created, locating the world in God: "God contains and comprehends the nature of all sensible things in Himself, not in the sense that He contains within Himself anything beside Himself, but in the sense that He is substantially all that He contains, the substance of all visible things being created in

---

66. Eriugena, *Div. nat.* 3.2. The reference to nonbeing as darkness and abyss is in 2.7. Divine nonbeing becomes a crucial theme in, e.g., Böhme, Hegel, Schelling, and Moltmann.

67. Eriugena, *Div. nat.* 3.19.

68. Eriugena, *Div. nat.* 3.16.

Him."[69] God eternally and infinitely transcends the world as the Simple, Infinite, and Supernatural One to the complex, finite, and natural many; yet the world exists within God. This position is consistent with Neoplatonic panentheism, but it borders on pantheism.[70]

John Scotus Eriugena's dialectical theology was appreciated by some later medieval thinkers, such as Nicholas of Cusa, and much later by German idealists such as Schelling and Hegel.[71]

Meister Eckhart

Johannes Eckhart (ca. 1260–1327) was a devout priest and mystical theologian influenced both by such great doctors of the church as Augustine, Anselm, and Aquinas and by the doctrinally ambiguous tradition of Pseudo-Dionysius.[72] There is no doubt of Eckhart's commitment to the doctrine of the church and the soundness of many of his formulations. But some of his statements on the Trinity and the God-world relation reflect the tension between Christianity and Neoplatonism and suggest that his views are panentheistic.

Eckhart follows the Neoplatonic tradition in asserting the absolute transcendence of the One beyond all categories of being and knowledge: "God is something that must necessarily be above being."[73] Consequently, he sometimes separates the divine nature [Godhead] from the Triune God: "God and the Godhead are as different as heaven and earth."[74] And he sometimes

69. Eriugena, *Div. nat.* 3.18, cited from Copleston, *Hist. Phil.*, vol. 2, chap. 13, sec. 6, p. 142.

70. Scholars lean both ways. For example, Gordon Leff, *Medieval Thought: St. Augustine to Ockham* (Baltimore: Penguin Books, 1958, 1962), 72: "Although it would be quite unfounded to regard his outlook as pantheism, it led to a blurring of the line between uncreated and created." But Carabine, *John Scottus Eriugena*, 65: "Eriugena's continual assertion that God is all things . . . is finally shown to be inadequate in light of the truth that God is none of the things." Philip Clayton regards him as a precursor of modern panentheism; see *God and Contemporary Science* (Grand Rapids: Eerdmans, 1997), 88.

71. Copleston, *Hist. Phil.*, vol. 2, chap. 13, sec. 6, p. 142: "If we want to call John Scotus an Hegelian before Hegel, we must remember that it is extremely unlikely that he realized what he was doing." Also O'Meara, *Eriugena*, 217–19; and Moran, "Eriugena and German Idealism," in *Eriugena*, 89–91.

72. E. Colledge and B. McGinn, introduction to *Meister Eckhart: The Essential Sermons, Commentaries, Treatises, and Defense,* trans. E. Colledge and B. McGinn (New York: Paulist, 1981). Also Copleston, *Hist. Phil.*, vol. 3, chap. 12, sec. 2; Armand Maurer, "Master Eckhart and Speculative Mysticism," in *Medieval Philosophy* (New York: Random House, 1962); Gilson, *History of Christian Philosophy*, 438–42; and James Clark, "Introduction to His Life and Work," in *Meister Eckhart: An Introduction to the Study of His Work with an Anthology of His Sermons,* ed. and trans. James Clark (New York: Thomas Nelson and Sons, 1957).

73. Eckhart, *Serm.* 17 (Clark, 205).

74. Eckhart, *Serm.* 12 (Clark, 183).

speaks as though the Godhead, the wholly transcendent One, is a deeper reality from which the Trinity emanates. He preaches, for example, that the pure soul "wants nothing but its naked God, as he is in himself. . . . It wants to know the source of this essence, it wants to go into the simple ground, into the quiet desert, into which distinction never gazed, not the Father, nor the Son, nor the Holy Spirit."[75] In this statement the One transcends and grounds the Three, a view found in Pseudo-Dionysius but contrary to the Nicene Creed.

The inevitability of creation follows the generation of the Trinity from the Supra-essential One. "The beginning" of Genesis 1:1 is "the first simple now of eternity . . . in which the emanation of the divine Persons eternally is." But the eternal generation of the Word includes the eternal generation of the world. "In one and the same time in which he was God and in which he begat his coeternal Son as God equal to himself in all things, he also created the world."[76] For Eckhart, creation is an inevitable expression of the eternal triune God.

Thus, all of creation participates in God. The human soul is the part of creation that participates most fully in the divine nature. Indeed, Eckhart repeatedly suggests that the soul shares the same divine Ground that gives rise to the Trinity. For example, he says of the pure soul that "nothing but the Simple One suffices him." He then refers to "the ground of the soul, where God's ground and the soul's ground are one ground."[77] This seems to be a straightforward pantheistic identification of the soul with the divine Ground, the Godhead.

It is not surprising, then, that some of Eckhart's statements on the Trinity and the God-creation relation were condemned as heretical soon after his death.[78] Taken alone, they are heterodox. But two considerations can soften that judgment—factors that suggest panentheism.

First, Eckhart's theological method is dialectical. He intentionally juxtaposes apparently contradictory propositions in seeking the whole truth. He asserts, for example, that God is the world and that God is not the world; that God is all things and that God is Nothing. Thus his theology, as a synthetic

75. Eckhart, *Serm.* 48 (Colledge and McGinn, 198).

76. Eckhart, *Commentary on Genesis* 1:1, sec. 7 (Colledge and McGinn, 84–85). His evocative term for the generation of the Trinity is *bullitio* (bubbling or boiling); *ebullitio* (bubbling or boiling over) refers to the generation of the world; see Colledge and McGinn, *Meister Eckhart*, 38–39.

77. Eckhart, *Serm.* 15 (Colledge and McGinn, 192).

78. *In agro dominico*, papal bull, March 27, 1329, in Colledge and McGinn, *Meister Eckhart*, 77–81. Copleston, Maurer, and Clark defend his orthodoxy. Gilson argues that Neoplatonism prevails.

whole, is not simple pantheism.[79] Dialectical theology implies something more like panentheism: the world is in God and yet not in God insofar as he transcends the world.

Second, specific evidence for panentheism appears in a sermon in which Eckhart uses the soul-body analogy for the relation of God, himself, and the world: "My body is in my soul more than my soul is in my body. My body and my soul are more in God than they are in themselves."[80] Maurer explains: "This analogy helps us to understand how Eckhart avoids pantheism. . . . As the body is not the soul, so the universe is not God. And yet the universe is contained in God and exists through his presence to it, as the body is contained in the soul and exists with its existence."[81] Eckhart's appeal to the soul-body analogy for the Creator-creatures relation suggests Neoplatonic panentheism rather than pantheism.

Although his views were condemned, Eckhart had supporters, especially in the tradition that leads through Schleiermacher, Schelling, and Hegel to Heidegger.[82]

Nicholas of Cusa

Nicholas of Cusa (Nicolaus Cusanus, Nikolaus Krebs of Kues, 1401–1464), who became a cardinal of the church, admired and quoted Eckhart. He was strongly influenced by Eriugena and Neoplatonism in general.[83] Nicholas wished to place Christian theology on a rational basis and to reconcile the divisions between the competing scholastic traditions. He regarded the Aristotelian logic they used, governed by the law of noncontradiction, as exclusivistic. By that logic, a proposition is either true or false; God is either infinite or finite; if one theologian is right, the other must be wrong. Nicholas embraced the dialectical method as a pastoral means of reconciling theological opponents.

79. Clark, "Introduction to His Life and Work," 36: "If Eckhart . . . seems to be using pantheistic language, we must remember that he is only stating one aspect of reality. What he says must be placed beside his teachings about the Divine transcendence."

80. Eckhart, *Serm.* 16 (Clark, 198).

81. Maurer, *Medieval Philosophy*, 298.

82. Scheffczyk, *Creation and Providence*, 167, observes that Eckhart presents "a new grasp of the created world which fused creature and Creator in one and coloured the minds of Giordano Bruno, Spinoza, . . . Jakob Boehme, and Fichte." Heidegger studied Eckhart and credits him for his concept of *Gelassenheit*, yieldedness to Being's self-revelation.

83. Jasper Hopkins, *A Concise Introduction to the Philosophy of Nicholas of Cusa* (Minneapolis: University of Minnesota Press, 1978); Copleston, *Hist. Phil.*, vol. 3, chap. 15; Gilson, *History of Christian Philosophy*, 534–40; James Collins, *God in Modern Philosophy* (Chicago: Henry Regnery, 1959), 2–11; and Maurer, "Nicholas of Cusa," in *Medieval Philosophy*.

God as All-Inclusive Infinite Being

On Learned Ignorance, the title of Nicholas of Cusa's best-known treatise, is the fruit of his dialectical theology. Learned ignorance is knowing that we cannot know God in himself. But if we recognize our limitations, Nicholas thought it possible to form a legitimate concept of God.

His theological project begins thus: "Since I am going to discuss the maximum learning of ignorance, I must deal with the nature of Maximality. Now I give the name 'Maximum' to that than which there cannot be anything greater." Thus he deftly moves from ignorance to "that than which there cannot be anything greater," Anselm's definition of God in the ontological argument. He then connects maximal greatness to the One: "But fullness befits what is one. Thus, oneness—which is also being—coincides with Maximality. . . . Thus, the Maximum is the Absolute One."[84] Note that Nicholas identifies "being" and "oneness." The One is Being, not the reality beyond being: "Absolute Maximality is Absolute Being" (1.2.6). So God is the One Absolute Maximal Being. By equating God with Being, Nicholas aligns himself with Augustine, Anselm, and Aquinas, not with Neoplatonism.[85]

Following Duns Scotus, he then conjoins Being and Infinity:[86] "Such a Maximum is infinite" (1.3.9). It is absolutely without limitation, opposition, or "otherness" of any kind. "But if such oneness is altogether free from all relation and contraction, obviously nothing is opposed to it, since it is Absolute Maximality." But then it must include all things—both ideal distinctions and actual beings. "Thus the Maximum is the Absolute One which is all things. And all things are in the Maximum" (1.2.5). In other words, true Infinity must include all of reality, for if it did not, some reality would be outside and other than Infinity. But that would limit Infinity, which is impossible by definition. As Infinite Being, God must include all beings and all differences.

Nicholas's argument from Maximal Infinity is repeated by later panentheists, including Hegel, Tillich, Pannenberg, and Clayton. Whereas classical theism protects the God-world distinction by opposing the infinite and finite, the absolute and relative, and other such antithetical qualities, Nicholas argues

---

84. Nicholas of Cusa, *On Learned Ignorance* [*De docta ignorantia*] 1.2.5 (translated passages are from Nicholas of Cusa, *Complete Philosophical and Theological Treatises*, trans. Jasper Hopkins, 2 vols. [Minneapolis: A. J. Banning, 2001], vol. 1).

85. The debate over whether God is Being or the One beyond Being continues to the present, as we shall see. Paul Tillich attempts to have it both ways.

86. Maurer, *Medieval Philosophy*, 314. Duns Scotus (1266–1308) should not be confused with Scotus Eriugena.

that *the truly infinite must include both sides of these polarities.* For example, the Maximum must include the Minimum: "Since nothing is opposed to it, the Minimum likewise coincides with it." This is dialectical theology par excellence. "God is Absolute Maximality and Oneness, who precedes and unites absolutely different and separate things—i.e., contradictories—between which there is no middle ground" (2.4.113). Nicholas's Maximum One is the *coincidentia oppositorum,* the Unity of opposites, the Identity of differences in a way that is beyond human comprehension.[87]

The implications of this conclusion upon his view of God's relation to creation are clear and represent classical Neoplatonic emanation theory. "Just as Absolute Maximality is Absolute Being, . . . so from Absolute Being there exists a universal oneness of being which is spoken of as 'a maximum deriving from the Absolute [Maximum]'—existing from it contractually and as a universe." In other words, the universe is essentially in God as a maximum that is a "contraction," a specification or self-delimitation of the Maximum. The maximal universe in turn is an infinity that includes a maximal plurality of finite beings. "This maximum's oneness is contracted in plurality, and it cannot exist without plurality. Indeed, in its universal oneness this maximum encompasses all things so that all the things which derive from the Absolute [Maximum] are in this maximum and this maximum is in all [these] things" (1.2.6). In this way Nicholas distinguishes between God's Absolute Infinity and the mathematical, temporal, and spatial infinities that characterize the universe. "Only the absolutely Maximum is negatively infinite. . . . But since the universe encompasses all things which are not God, it cannot be negatively infinite, although it is unbounded and thus privatively infinite" (2.1.97). Absolute Infinity includes all other infinite/finite polarities.

The universe "unfolds" and is "enfolded" in God. "Therefore there is one enfolding of all things . . . substance, quality or quantity, and so on. . . . For there is only one Maximum, with which the Minimum coincides and in which enfolded difference is not opposed to enfolding identity." The whole process of unfolding is dialectical: a mode of being posits its opposite only to be reunited. "Just as oneness precedes otherness, so also a point . . . [precedes] magnitude, . . . rest [precedes] motion, identity . . . difference, equality . . . inequality, and so on. . . . These are convertible with Oneness, which is Eternity itself. . . . Therefore, God is the enfolding of all things in that all

---

87. Nicholas of Cusa, *Doc. ign.* 1.2; 2.1. The pre-Socratic Greek philosopher Heraclitus first stated the coincidence of opposites. Nicholas reaches his conclusion using the dialectical method of theology developed by Proclus and Pseudo-Dionysius.

things are in Him; and He is the unfolding of all things in that He is in all things" (2.3.107).[88]

By identifying the One and Being, Nicholas of Cusa does not face the Neoplatonic temptation of explaining the Trinity as a generation of the One. Indeed he argues that the One itself is "trine": "there cannot be more than one eternal thing. But since oneness is eternal, equality eternal, and union also eternal: oneness, equality, and union are one. And this is that trine One-ness which Pythagoras . . . affirmed to be worthy of worship" (1.7.21). Thus philosophy provides a concept of the Triune God. "Oneness is called Father, Equality is called Son, and Union is called Love or Holy Spirit" (1.9.26).

Nicholas's philosophy likewise shapes his Christology. Having distin-guished the universe as "contracted maximum" from the Absolute Maximum, he dialectically deduces "a maximum of a third sort": "This maximum . . . is both contracted and absolute and which we name Jesus, blessed forever." As Maximum and maximum, Jesus is both God and creature. He is also the mediator of creation, "the one maximum in which the universe actually exists most greatly and most perfectly as in its goal" (1.2.7). Book 3 of *On Learned Ignorance* fully elaborates Nicholas's Christology.

Pantheism or Panentheism?

Johannes Wenck, professor of theology at Heidelberg, charged Nicho-las of Cusa with the heresy of identifying God and creation.[89] Seemingly pantheistic statements are easy to find: "Absolute Maximality is, absolutely, that which all things are: in all things it is the Absolute Beginning of things, the [Absolute] End of things, and the [Absolute] Being of things; in it all things are—indistinctly, most simply, and without plurality—the Absolute Maximum, just as an infinite line is all figures" (2.4.113). This statement does seem to identify God and the world. Nicholas also seems to affirm the eternity of the world, "since—in the Maximum—being, making, and creat-ing are the same things: creating seems to be not other than God's being all things. Therefore . . . how can we deem the creation not to be eternal, since God's being is eternal?" (2.2.101). Practicing learned ignorance, however,

---

88. Nicholas's dialectical language is a striking anticipation of Hegel, who honored him. A crucial difference is "learned ignorance." Nicholas concedes, "You will have to admit that you are thoroughly ignorant of how enfolding and unfolding occur and that you know only that you do not know the manner, even if you do know that God is the enfolding and unfolding of all things" (*Doc. ign.* 2.3.111). But Hegel believed that philosophy can transcend religion to attain Absolute Knowledge of Absolute Spirit. See chap. 4, below.

89. Hopkins, introduction to *Philosophy of Nicholas of Cusa*, 12–15.

Nicholas does not answer his question. But his reasons for posing it anticipate Spinoza's pantheism.

Nevertheless, Nicholas's Christian confession of creation and his denial of pantheism must be respected. It is more accurate to consider him a
panentheist. Like Eriugena and Eckhart, he thinks dialectically, infinitely
distinguishing God and creation as well as identifying them. Only God
is Absolute—Maximum, Being, One. The universe is a "contracted maximum"—an infinite maximal unity of plural, diverse, and finite beings. All
is in God—in him all differences are unified—but his Maximum Oneness
transcends all things infinitely and absolutely. Furthermore, Nicholas distinguishes God as Being from creatures as beings. God is the Being of all
beings. And all beings participate in Being.[90] Because he regards dialectic
as ontological, Nicholas's both–and view of God and the world implies
panentheism, not pantheism.

Like Eckhart, Nicholas's adoption of the World-Soul is further evidence
of his panentheism. On Learned Ignorance 2.9 is an extensive treatment of the
Platonic doctrines of the divine Mind and World-Soul. Nicholas notes that
they lack the benefit of revelation: "The philosophers were not adequately
instructed regarding the divine Word and Absolute Maximum" (2.9.150).
But he does identify the World-Soul with the Christian God. "For Plato
referred to the world as an animal. If you take God to be its soul, without
intermingling, then many of the points I have been making will be clear to
you" (2.12.166). God is the Soul of the world, but he is not "intermingled"
with it.

This assertion of divine transcendence confirms that Nicholas of Cusa
is not a pantheist but a panentheist. In many ways he anticipates German
romanticism and idealism, as shown below in other chapters.[91] Philip Clayton,
a contemporary panentheist, regards him as an ancestor: "Nicholas may be

90. Hopkins, introduction to The Complete Philosophical and Theological Works of Nicholas of Cusa,
1:xi. "This distinction between being and beings Nicholas draws from Meister Eckhart; and it is one of
the distinctions that influences both Paul Tillich and Martin Heidegger."

91. Robert Williams, "Cusanus' Panentheism," in Schleiermacher the Theologian (Philadelphia:
Fortress, 1978), 64–68, argues Schleiermacher's similarity to Nicholas of Cusa.

Copleston, Hist. Phil., vol. 3, chap. 15, sec. 9, p. 52: "His insistence on negative theology, for
example, and his doctrine of God as the coincidentia oppositorum can be assimilated to Schelling's
theory of the Absolute as the vanishing-point of all differences and distinctions, while his view of
the world as the explicatio Dei can be regarded as a foretaste of Hegel's theory of Nature as God-in-
His-Otherness as the concrete manifestation or embodiment of the abstract Idea."

Maurer, Medieval Philosophy, 324: "Hegel makes an effort similar to that of Nicholas of Cusa to
surmount the principle of non-contradiction and to reach the absolute in which all differences disappear.
The interest shown by the nineteenth-century German idealists in Nicholas of Cusa is indicative of the
affinity they felt between his thought and their own."

taken as an early precursor of the theology of *panentheism*, which under-stands the world as within God at the same time that God also transcends the world."[92]

Jakob Böhme

Nicholas of Cusa professed ignorance of how all opposites coincide in God. Jakob Böhme (1575–1624) claims to explain it precisely: God himself is the primordial instance of dialectical triunity.[93] Böhme blends Protestant Christianity with mysticism, Neoplatonism, Gnosticism, alchemy, and the hermetic and kabbalistic traditions.[94] Although uneducated, he has inspired generations of followers, including such eminent panentheists as Schelling, Hegel, Heidegger, Berdyaev, Tillich, and Moltmann.[95]

92. Philip Clayton, *The Problem of God in Modern Thought* (Grand Rapids: Eerdmans, 2000), 149.

93. Jakob Böhme, *The Aurora*, ed. D. Hehner and C. Barker, trans. John Sparrow (1656) (London: J. M. Watkins, 1914; repr., 1960); *The Way to Christ*, trans. P. Erb (New York: Paulist, 1978); excerpts grouped by topic are found in John Joseph Stoudt, *Jacob Boehme: His Life and Thought* (New York: Seabury, 1968); Jakob Böhme, *Essential Readings*, ed. Robin Waterfield (Wellingborough, UK: Aquarian, 1989).

Accessible introductions are Ernest Koenker, "Musician in the Concert of God's Joy: Jacob Boehme on Ground and Unground," chap. 3 in *Great Dialecticians in Modern Christian Thought* (Minneapolis: Augsburg, 1971); Copleston, *Hist. Phil.*, vol. 3, chap. 17, sec. 5; and Waterfield, "Part One: The Background," in Böhme, *Essential Readings*; Arlene Adrienne Miller, "Jacob Boehme: From Orthodoxy to Enlightenment" (Ph.D. diss., Stanford University, 1971); Andrew Weeks, *Boehme: An Intellectual Biography of the Seventeenth-Century Philosopher and Mystic* (Albany: State University of New York Press, 1991); Cyril O'Regan, *Gnostic Apocalypse: Jacob Boehme's Haunted Narrative* (Albany: State University of New York Press, 2002).

94. Miller, "The Occultist Heritage," chap. 2 in "Jacob Boehme"; Waterfield, "The World of Boehme's Writings," and "The Sacred Sciences," chaps. 3 and 4 in Böhme, *Essential Readings*; Weeks, *Boehme*, 48–51; O'Regan, introduction to *Gnostic Apocalypse*.

Gnosticism was a competitor of early Christianity. It posited a primal One that divides into a series of dyads—male and female, good and evil, etc.—and emanates into the physical world. Salvation is return to the spiritual realm through gnosis, secret wisdom made available by a Savior, often the Primal Man.

The *Corpus hermeticum* is a body of writings from the period 100–300 C.E., supposedly authored by Hermes Trismegistus, an Egyptian magician and priest of Hermes. The texts mix magic, the occult, astrology, and alchemy with Neoplatonism and thus preserved a non-Christian Neoplatonic tradition during the Christian centuries in Europe. Hermeticism resurfaced in the Renaissance and was appropriated as part of the rebirth of Platonism by such prominent thinkers as Marsilio Ficino and Pico della Mirandola.

The Kabbalah are Jewish mystical texts that (among other things) adapt Neoplatonism and hermeticism. They view God as the unity of polar forces and regard the spiritual and physical worlds as emanations of God. Significant for panentheism is the kabbalist doctrine of *Tsim-Tsum*, that God negates or contracts himself to make space within himself for the world. Moltmann appeals to this notion for his own view of creation "in" God.

95. Koenker, *Great Dialecticians*, 53: "Schelling was to turn to Boehme for his positing of 'first potency' as dialectical nonbeing in God. In his *Lectures on the Philosophy of History*, Hegel was to acknowledge his own deep indebtedness to the *teutonicus philosophus*. . . . In our own day his influence is

Böhme was not content with his mystical visions. For years he struggled for the words to express the intuition of the God-world complex that came to him in a flash of light:

> For I saw and knew the Being of all Beings, the Byss (the ground or original foundation), and the Abyss (that which is without ground, or bottomless and fathomless); also the birth or eternal generation of the Trinity; the descent and origin of this world, and of all divine creatures, through the divine wisdom. ... And thirdly, the external, and visible world, being a procreation. Or extern birth; or a substance expressed, or spoken forth, from both the external and spiritual worlds; ... and likewise how the pregnant mother (*genetrix* or fruitful bearing womb of eternity) brought forth ...[96]

In this Neoplatonic-gnostic vision, the world is a progressive extension of the same eternal process that generates the Trinity out of the divine depths. We consider this picture from the depths out.

God as Dialectical Triunity

Böhme begins with the standard Neoplatonic assertion that God in himself is "the hidden God, as the Eternal One," beyond Being, and therefore Nonbeing or No-thing.[97] Like Nicholas of Cusa, he affirms that God is the One in whom the opposing forces and contrary qualities are harmonized.

But Böhme goes beyond Neoplatonism toward Gnosticism by assimilating God along with everything else into the dialectical unification of contrary forces, positive and negative "potencies."[98] His own summary is worth quoting at length:

> The reader should know that in Yes and No all things consist, whether it be divine, or demonic, earthly, or whatever may be named. The One, as the Yes, is pure power and life, and is the truth of God, or God himself. He would be unknowable in himself, and there would be no joy, or exaltation, or feeling, in Him without the No. The No is the counterstroke of the Yes, or the Truth, in

---

traceable as well in the panpsychism of Charles Hartshorne, in Tillich's 'Ground of Being,' in the meontic freedom of Berdyaev, and in the primordial *Nichts* of Heidegger." Miller, "Jacob Boehme," 1, lists "Hegel, Coleridge, Novalis, Schelling, von Baader, Fichte, Schopenhauer, Schleiermacher, Kierkegaard, Berdyaev, Heidegger and Tillich."

96. Jakob Böhme, "A Letter to an Inquirer [Caspar Lindner]," in *Essential Readings*, 62–81, quote at 64.

97. Böhme, *The Way to Christ*, 7.3.1. All references are to the Erb translation.

98. O'Regan's thesis in *Gnostic Apocalypse* is that Böhme is more a Valentinian Gnostic than a Neoplatonist where these traditions differ.

order that the Truth might be manifest and a something, in which there might be a *contrarium*, in which the eternal love might be active, feeling, willing, and something to be loved. And yet one cannot say that the Yes is separated from the No and that they are two things distinct from one another, for they are but One Thing, but themselves divide into two Beginnings (*Principia*) and form two Centra, since each works and wills in itself. Without these two, which stand in perpetual conflict, all things would be a Nothing, and would stand still without movement."[99]

In this famous quote it is evident that God and all things consist as the union of contrary positive and negative powers.

Böhme explains his vision in philosophical terms. The primordial principle in God is *Ungrund* (Non-ground, Groundlessness), which is his term for Non-being or No-thing—what Neoplatonists call the Abyss, the divine depths. This is "the No," the negative potency of nonbeing, chaos, darkness, and wrath. But *Ungrund* is not the absolute negation of being. It contains infinite potential, the absolute freedom to be, and even the will or desire to be. "The unground is an eternal nothing, but makes an eternal beginning as a craving. For the nothing is a craving after something. But as there is nothing that can give anything, accordingly the craving itself is the giving of it, which yet is also nothing, or merely desirous seeking."[100] In other words, the negative potency in *Ungrund* is a "will" to be, a longing for unification with its opposite, the *Urgrund* (Primal Ground). *Urgrund* is the second ground or principle that arises from the first. It is the positive potency, "the Yes," the power of being, reason, light, goodness, life, and love. In themselves, however, the negative and positive potencies do not amount to anything. To exist, God must include a third potency that eternally synthesizes the negative and positive potencies of irrationality and reason, freedom and necessity, darkness and light, wrath and love. This unitive power is divine Spirit.

The eternal divine self-generation from the Abyss "gives birth" to the Trinity. In *Four Tables of Divine Revelation* Böhme provides a diagram as well as an explanation.[101] The first table treats "What God is without Nature and Creature." The highest level is "the Abyss, Nothing and All," what is elsewhere termed *Ungrund*. The next level is "the will of the Abyss," also designated as the Father. The third level is "delight or impression of the Will,"

99. Jakob Böhme, *Reflection on Divine Revelation*, Question 3, Responses 2 and 3, as translated by Koenker, *Great Dialecticians*, 61–62.

100. Jakob Böhme, *Concerning the Earthly and Heavenly Mystery, First Text*, as translated by Koenker, *Great Dialecticians*, 59.

101. Böhme, in his Appendix to *Four Tables of Divine Revelation*, in *Essential Readings*, 214–39; the diagram is on 216.

which is "procreation out of itself, where God begetteth God." This is the *Urgrund* and designated as the Word or Son. The fourth level is "Science or Motion," which "is the attraction of the *Will* to the place of God; . . . by which outbreathing is understood the Spirit of God. And here is understood . . . the Tri-une Being."[102] The three trinitarian persons, in other words, are the three potencies or principles that eternally arise from the divine depth and co-constitute the One God.

Previous Neoplatonism located dialectic in what flows from the One, not in the One itself. Nicholas of Cusa locates dialectical unity in the One but cannot explain it. Böhme boldly places it in the heart of the One and explains it in detail. God himself is Eternal Dialectic.

The World as Externalization of the Triune God

Generating the Trinity does not, however, exhaust the divine potency. According to Böhme, God as Word and Spirit has the impulse to reveal and know himself in the world. Words are by nature expressive. Thus intrinsic to the eternal Word is "Wisdom, signifying the outspoken Word, as the power of Divine Contemplation; wherein God to himself is Intelligible, Perceptible, and Revealed."[103] Like Eriugena, Böhme thinks that God must create to exist and know himself. God's Word uttered as Wisdom naturally generates the world. Böhme even refers to God as a "pregnant mother (*genetrix* or fruitful bearing womb of eternity)" who births the world.[104] The generation of the world is "the Divine Extrication or Revelation, how God introduceth himself in the eternal Nature, in Love and Wrath."[105] God's eternal nature, unifying its positive and negative potencies, is manifest in all creation.

Like the Trinity, God's generation of nature is dialectical. "He brings Himself out of Himself into divisibility, into *centra*, so that contrariety arises in the outflow."[106] Böhme explains the flow of the world from God by means of gnostic, hermetic, and alchemical categories.[107] Seven energies or qualities operate in two triads: a higher triad (love, expression, and harmonization)

102. Ibid., 217.

103. Ibid.

104. Böhme, "A Letter to an Inquirer," 64. Feminist theologians frequently appeal to this tradition, mediated by Tillich, to legitimate the use of maternal language for God. See chap. 12, below.

105. Böhme, Appendix to *Four Tables*, 217. Wisdom as Sophia and the Pregnant Womb image are gnostic theological themes embraced by Böhme. Gnosticism affirmed male-female as a universal polarity. Thus Böhme's Adam before the fall is androgynous.

106. Böhme, *The Way to Christ*, 7.1.14.

107. Böhme, in his Appendix to *Four Tables*, 217–39; Waterfield provides a summary, 28–31, 33–34.

and a lower (contraction, diffusion, and rotation or oscillation), conjoined or synthesized by the seventh energy, "flash" or "spark" (*Blitz, Fünkelein*). He associates the higher triad with the persons of the Trinity; in this context love is Father, expression is Son, and harmonization is Spirit. The higher triad overflows into the lower, thus producing the world and the individual things of which it consists. The "flash" (like static electricity) is the reconciliation generated by the opposition of the triads. It is the work of the Spirit in creatures, bringing the kingdom of God, where the Trinity and nature are ultimately reconciled and united. In cosmic history "the three-fold godhead, like everything else in nature, goes through a seven-stage process to fulfillment."[108] In sum, the Triune God naturally generates a world that reflects in time and space the same process of tri-unification that is eternal in God. The actualization of the Trinity in world history is also basic for Hegel, Schelling, Berdyaev, Tillich, and Moltmann, all of whom intentionally embrace the legacy of Jakob Böhme.

Böhme likewise treats the necessity and freedom of God's creative action dialectically. On the one hand, creation is necessary because it is God's nature to generate the world. God's will to create is a striving for full actualization of the divine potential: "If the hidden God ... had not led Himself by His will out of Himself ... to a natural and creaturely life, ... how then could the hidden will of God, which in itself is one, have been revealed to itself?"[109] On the other hand, creation is free in two senses: because God wills it without any limitation or imposition and because God endows creatures with the power of self-creativity. "The Eternal One ... leads itself out ... into plurality. ... Each spiritual characteristic has its own *Separator*, divider and maker in it. ... Thus the *Separator* of each will, will again bring characteristics out of itself from which the endless plurality rises."[110] Because God wills creatures' self-creativity, Böhme sometimes speaks of the origination of the actual world as a free and spontaneous "leap" or "fall" of creatures from the Creator. His view of creation as "fall" recurs in Hegel, Schelling, Heidegger, and Tillich.

The divine dialectic also shapes Böhme's treatment of evil, which is as gnostic as it is Neoplatonic. God himself is intrinsically oppositional—Yes and No, Byss and Abyss, Light and Dark, Love and Wrath. Yet he is essentially good in that he perfectly harmonizes the polarities within himself. As God generates the contingent world, however, the polarities are not necessarily balanced, and possible evil becomes actual. But the actuality of evil turns

---

108. Miller, "Jacob Boehme," 56. Böhme, Appendix to *Four Tables*, 218–32.
109. Böhme, *Way to Christ*, 7.1.10.
110. Ibid., 7.3.10–11.

out to be good because evil can eventually be eliminated and the good alone fulfilled in God: "We can philosophize and say concerning the single good will of God, that . . . He brings Himself out of Himself into divisibility . . . so that the good might become perceptive, working and willing in the evil, that is, desiring to divide itself from evil and desiring to go again into the single will of God."[111] History is the coming of God's kingdom, where all finite oppositions are progressively actualized and reconciled in God. Without the actuality of finite evil, neither creation nor redemption is possible. God makes evil possible, but creatures make it actual. Schelling was deeply influenced by Böhme's account of God, freedom, and evil. Berdyaev, Tillich, and Moltmann follow Schelling.

Böhme's Panentheism

Böhme is important primarily because of his influence on subsequent panentheists, but there is sufficient reason to classify him with them. Böhme's God is self-generating and self-contained, but it is his nature to actualize himself in the world. Yet God and world are distinct: Word and Spirit in God are distinct from their manifestation in Wisdom and the World-Soul. Böhme explicitly invokes the World-Soul as an aspect of God, "the Soul of the external world . . . the life of all creatures of the visible world by which the Separator or Creator of this world forms Itself and makes an image of the spiritual world in which the power of the inner spiritual world forms, images and sees itself."[112] The world is comprehended by its Soul, which is a dimension of God. This amounts to panentheism.[113]

Conclusion

The history of panentheism thus far is, in large measure, the story of Neoplatonism, which recasts Plato's doctrine of the Good, the Ideas, the Demiurge, and the World-Soul into a comprehensive account of how the spiritual, natural, and human worlds emanate from, and are encompassed by, the divine One. Pseudo-Dionysius was the main conduit of Neoplatonism

---

111. Ibid., 7.1.14.

112. Ibid., 7.3.18.

113. Miller, "Jacob Boehme," 56, does not use the term *panentheism* but places Böhme between pantheism and exclusively transcendent theism: "With his concept of a self-enclosed Godhead, Boehme is, on the one hand, dangerously close to pantheism, of which he has often been accused, and, on the other, of a transcendent God wholly divorced from creation and creature. But Boehme steers a sturdy course between the Scylla and Charybdis of these two positions; his God is both transcendent and immanent."

into Christian theology. Although most medieval Christian thinkers appreciated Pseudo-Dionysius, some, such as Eriugena, Eckhart, and Nicholas of Cusa, embraced his Neoplatonism more fully than did Anselm, Aquinas, and Scotus in the mainstream tradition of classical theism.

Two features of Neoplatonism are conducive to panentheism. One is the notion that the world is a divine emanation. Not only is the idea of the world eternally in God's mind; it is also God's nature to actualize and comprehend the world as "other" than himself. God is not the sort of being who exists without a world. Creation is the natural phase of the divine life. The generation and completion of the world are essential to the maximal greatness of God. The world is thus ontologically implicit in, and part of, the divine nature. *Creatio ex nihilo* really amounts to *creatio ex Deo*. This position is different from the Christian doctrine that God is completely perfect whether or not he creates the world and that creation *ex nihilo* is an act of God's sovereign free choice whether or not to create.

The second factor nurturing panentheism is the rise of dialectical theology, the generation and reconciliation of contraries in God. God in himself is viewed as the unity beyond all polarity, the One in whom being and non-being, infinity and finitude, immanence and transcendence, contingency and necessity, freedom and determination are included and reconciled. To the extent that the world is characterized by these polarities, it must be included in God but not be identical with God, who also remains the transcendent One.

These factors, emanation and dialectic, are closely related. Dialectic is ontological—it is the form and structure of the process of emanated being. Thus the ideas of dialectic and emanation cooperated historically in promoting panentheistic theologies. The relationship between dialectic and God became progressively tighter as the tradition developed. Original Neoplatonism emphasized the absolute transcendence of the One to dialectic, but Nicholas of Cusa identified God as the One Infinite Being in whom all opposites are unified, and Böhme projected dialectic into the very heart of God himself, as the form of his own eternal self-generation, not just the generation of the world.

3

Pantheism and Panentheism
from the Renaissance to Romanticism

The last chapter traced the history of panentheism from Plotinus through Christian Neoplatonism to the post-Reformation mysticism of Jakob Böhme. This chapter begins with the non-Christian post-Renaissance pantheisms of Giordano Bruno and Baruch Spinoza because they exercise a significant influence on subsequent panentheists. It then notes some evidence of panentheism among the seventeenth-century Cambridge Platonists and focuses on the philosophical theology of Jonathan Edwards. Next it shifts back to Germany, where modern panentheism begins to take shape in the confluence of Christianity, Neoplatonism, and early romanticism. The chapter concludes with Friedrich Schleiermacher, who combines Spinoza and Neoplatonism into a panentheistic theology of Christian romanticism.

Giordano Bruno

Giordano Bruno (1548–1600) was influenced significantly by Nicholas of Cusa, as well as the non-Christian Neoplatonic traditions.[1] His philosophi-

1. On the influence of Nicholas of Cusa, see Copleston, *Hist. Phil.*, vol. 3, chap. 16, sec. 6. Like Böhme, Bruno was conversant with hermetic and kabbalistic thought. See Frances A. Yates, *Giordano*

cal theology developed in ways that anticipate Spinoza's pantheism partly because, unlike Nicholas of Cusa, he was not committed to the church's doctrine of the Creator-creature relation.

God as the Infinite Immanence of Nature

In his two major works, *Concerning the Cause, Principle, and One* and *On the Infinite Universe and Worlds*, Bruno begins from an emphasis on the cognitive transcendence of the divine One as the source of Nature and all things in it.[2] Like Eriugena and Nicholas of Cusa, he distinguishes God and Nature and views the cosmos as the manifestation of God. He also gives a prominent role to the World-Soul in explaining the principles and causes of the world: "the soul of the world . . . the divine essence which is all in all, filleth all, and is more intrinsically pervasive of things than is their very own essence, because it is the essence of essences, the life of lives, the soul of souls."[3] At first glance, Bruno seems to follow the God-emanation-world scheme of Neoplatonism.

But his position is in fact closer to the naturalistic pantheism of ancient Stoicism. The World-Soul is not a higher reality that generates the physical world but the rational causal agent immanent in the world.[4] "Just as the soul is in the whole form to which it giveth being, and is at the same time individual; and is thus similarly in the whole and in every individual; so the essence of the universe is One in the infinite and in every part or member thereof so that the whole and every part become One in substance."[5] In other words, there is just one substance that is both World-Soul and universe, both Form and matter. The divine essence is the productive force immanent in the universe. God is not a distinct supernatural reality but the infinite depths of Nature itself.

Bruno and the Hermetic Tradition (Chicago: University of Chicago Press, 1964); and Karen Silvia de Leon-Jones, *Giordano and the Kabbalah: Prophets, Magicians, and Rabbis* (New Haven: Yale University Press, 1997).

2. Giordano Bruno, *Concerning the Cause, Principle, and One*, trans. Sidney Greenburg, in Sidney Greenburg, *The Infinite in Giordano Bruno* (New York: King's Crown, 1950; repr., New York: Octagon, 1978); *On the Infinite Universe and Worlds*, trans. D. W. Singer, in D. W. Singer, *Giordano Bruno: His Life and Thought* (New York: Schuman, 1950). See also Copleston, *Hist. Phil.*, vol. 3, chap. 16, sec. 6; and James Collins, *God in Modern Philosophy* (Chicago: Henry Regnery, 1959), 20–29.

3. Bruno, *On the Infinite*, dialogue 1 (Singer, 267).

4. Bruno, *Concerning the Cause*, dialogues 2 and 3; *On the Infinite*, dialogue 1 (Singer, 264–69); Greenburg, "Universal Soul and Universal Form," in *The Infinite*, 28–30; see Singer, *Giordano Bruno*, 98–99.

5. Bruno, *Concerning the Cause*, dialogue 5 (Greenburg, 164).

The coincidence of God and world is reinforced by Bruno's analysis of infinity. He recasts Nicholas of Cusa's distinction between absolute divine Infinity and relative worldly infinity (mathematical, temporal, spatial, etc.) so that God possesses both. The world is relatively or extensively infinite (*tutto infinito*) because it is also finite.[6] "I call the universe *tutto infinito*, because it has no margin, limit or surface. I do not call the world *totalmente infinito*, because any part that we take is finite." God, however, is both absolutely and relatively infinite. "I call God *tutto infinito* because He excludes of Himself all limits and because each of His attributes is one and infinite; and I call God *totalmente infinito* because He is wholly in the whole world and infinitely and totally in each of its parts, in distinction from the infinity of the universe, which is totally in the whole but not in the parts."[7] Thus God's Infinity both transcends and includes the infinite-finite polarities of the world, as Nicholas of Cusa argued. Bruno's distinction between God and world amounts to a partial difference in the kind of infinity that characterizes God's immanence in the world. It does not imply the supernatural transcendence of God's Being.

The ontological overlap of God and the world is confirmed in *De triplici minimo et mensura* [*On the Threefold Minimum and Measure*]. Bruno asserts that God is *natura naturans* (nature generating nature) when regarded as distinct from his particular manifestations in the universe. And God is *natura naturata* (nature being generated) when regarded as his manifestation in the world.[8] This terminology echoes Eriugena's approach to God from the divisions of Nature and is adopted by Spinoza.

Bruno's Pantheism

Although Bruno affirms a God-world distinction that superficially sounds Neoplatonic, his account of the World-Soul, his analysis of infinity, and his definition of God as *natura naturans* all suggest that God is the infinite dynamic depths of nature, not a supernatural reality that generates and includes nature. Thus Bruno is reminiscent of Stoic pantheism and anticipates Spinoza and Toland instead of implying panentheism.[9]

6. Philip Clayton, *The Problem of God in Modern Thought* (Grand Rapids: Eerdmans, 2000), 152: "Where Nicholas spoke of [the world's] privative infinity, . . . Bruno distinguishes between extensive and intensive infinity." For Bruno, the world is extensively infinite and God is infinite in both senses.

7. Bruno, *On the Infinite*, dialogue 1 (Singer, 261).

8. I rely on Copleston, *Hist. Phil.*, vol. 3, chap. 16, sec. 6, as there is no English translation.

9. Greenburg, *The Infinite*, 76, regards Bruno as a pantheist: "God, Nature, Intellect, Form, Matter and Soul, are one." So does Collins, *God in Modern Philosophy*, 22: "God is one with substantial nature. . . . There is no real, substantial transcendence of God to sensible nature, but there is an endless progress of human intelligence and love toward the infinite substance of nature itself." Clayton, *The Problem of*

He is significant in this history nonetheless. "An unbroken line leads from at least Plotinus via Pseudo-Dionysius to early medieval thinkers such as John Eriugena, through the Renaissance rediscovery of the Neoplatonic thinkers (and the Hermetic tradition) to Nicholas of Cusa and Bruno." The young Schelling chose Bruno as his own voice in his dialogue *Bruno: On the Natural and Divine Principle in Things* (1802).[10]

Baruch Spinoza

For most readers, the name Baruch Spinoza (1632–1677) is associated with pantheism, not panentheism. Including him here is not intended to alter that judgment, although the classification is debated. In any case, thinkers who have admired Spinoza but modified his views have significantly shaped modern panentheism. Clayton argues that Spinoza's pantheism, though untenable, "when worked out systematically in Western philosophy, has invariably turned into *panentheism*."[11] Lessing, Herder, Schleiermacher, Fichte, Schelling, and Hegel all admired and modified Spinoza's views.

Spinoza was raised in the Jewish faith but was expelled from the synagogue as a young man for his unorthodox views. The immediate stimulus for his theological reflections was the work of René Descartes (1596–1650), commonly regarded as the father of modern philosophy.

Although Descartes holds some traditional opinions and religious beliefs, he brackets them in order to see whether they qualify as genuine knowledge. He defines knowledge as possession of clear and distinct ideas that are known with certainty to be true because they are either self-evident or derived by valid deductive reasoning from self-evident truths. He holds that all knowledge must be constructed entirely upon the foundation of such truths. And he thinks that at least generic belief in a transcendent God can be justified as genuine knowledge.[12]

Spinoza's Monistic Philosophy

Although he begins from Descartes's philosophy and endorses his theory of knowledge, Spinoza's conclusions contradict Descartes's metaphysics.

God, 151–52, classifies him as monist/pantheist, leading directly to Spinoza. Copleston, *Hist. Phil.*, vol. 3, chap. 16, sec. 6, p. 69, is more cautious: "His philosophy may be a stage on the road from Nicholas of Cusa to Spinoza; but Bruno himself did not travel to the end of that road."

10. Clayton, *The Problem of God*, 215–16. See the next chapter on Schelling.
11. Ibid., 389.
12. René Descartes, *Meditations on First Philosophy* (1641).

Descartes is a thoroughgoing metaphysical dualist. He posits an irreducible difference between thinking substance (God, angels, and human minds) and extended substance (human bodies, animals, and material things). Within the category of thinking substance, he makes an even more basic distinction between independent (God) and dependent substance (creatures).

Spinoza's metaphysics is just the opposite—the most explicit and consistent monism (one substance) in Western thought. The seeds of his monism were probably planted during his early reading of Jewish mystical and kabbalistic writings and were likely nurtured by familiarity with Giordano Bruno.[13]

The charge of pantheism arises because Spinoza concludes that there is only one substance, which he regularly calls God and occasionally "God or Nature." This leaves the impression that he either denies the reality of finite beings other than God or regards God as identical with the totality of things that constitute Nature. In either case, his philosophy seems to imply that "all is God"—straightforward pantheism. But his position is more subtle.[14]

Spinoza's Philosophy of God and Nature

Spinoza posits his concept of substance by adapting Descartes's definition: "By substance I understand what is in itself and is conceived through itself, that is, that whose concept does not require the concept of another thing, from which it must be formed." He concludes from this definition that one self-sufficient substance necessarily exists and that it must be absolute, eternal, self-causing, and infinite. In short, it is God. "By God I understand a being absolutely infinite, that is, a substance consisting of an infinity of attributes, of which each one expresses an eternal and infinite essence."[15] Thus far Spinoza's philosophical definition of God sounds traditional and uncontroversial.

The issue of pantheism immediately arises, however, because his definition of substance implies that there can be only one substance: that which

---

13. Copleston, *Hist. Phil.*, vol. 4, chap. 10, pp. 214–15. Spinoza also studied Moses Maimonides (1135–1204), from whom he learned Neoplatonic monotheism. He mentions several Jewish kabbalistic thinkers as sources. Although he never mentions Bruno by name, apparently paraphrased passages in his early writings and his use of the terms *Natura naturans* and *Natura naturata* indicate that he most likely knew Bruno's philosophy.

14. Ibid., chap. 10; Collins, *God in Modern Philosophy*, 69–79; Étienne Gilson and Thomas Langan, "Benedictus Spinoza," chap. 9 in *Modern Philosophy* (New York: Random House, 1963); Roger Scruton, *Spinoza* (New York: Oxford University Press, 1986); and Richard Mason, *The God of Spinoza: A Philosophical Study* (Cambridge: Cambridge University Press, 1997).

15. Baruch Spinoza, *The Ethics*, I, D6, in *A Spinoza Reader*, trans. and ed. Edwin Curley (Princeton, NJ: Princeton University Press, 1994), 85.

is self-contained and self-sufficient. "Except God, no substance can be nor can be conceived."[16] A corollary of this definition is that "a substance cannot be produced by anything else."[17] It follows that finite beings are not individual mental and/or physical substances created by and dependent on God, as Descartes proposes, following the whole Christian tradition. Indeed Spinoza turns away from the main tradition of Western philosophy since Aristotle, which understands contingent individual entities as substances. Spinoza's move can leave the impression that finite things are unreal and that God is the only reality.

In fact, however, Spinoza views individual things in the world neither as unreal nor as individual substances but as modifications of the One Infinite Substance. Whereas Descartes infers the reality of mental (thinking) substance and physical (extended) substance from our experience of mental and physical properties, Spinoza regards mental and physical properties as finite appearances of two of the infinity of attributes of the divine Substance. Because there is just one Substance, finite mental and physical entities must be modifications of that Substance, regarded from a finite point of view.

What Spinoza means becomes clearer when applied to the human body and mind. Descartes posits mind and body as two distinct substances conjoined in each human being. Spinoza views body and mind instead as two mutually irreducible aspects of one finite thing, an individual human being. The mind is the person regarded according to the category of thought, and the body is the person regarded according to the category of extension. Each individual human being is the extended (physical) actuality of a particular idea in the eternal mind of God, not the conjunction of two substances. Analogously, each individual entity in the world is a finite modification and exemplification of one or two of the eternal and necessary attributes of the one Substance. In this way individual things are actual, but they are not distinct substances.

Another reason Spinoza's position seems pantheistic is that he sometimes identifies God and Nature, calling the Infinite Substance *Deus sive natura* (God or Nature).[18] This way of speaking has a long, nuanced history. Eriugena's *Division of Nature* gives *God* and *Nature* correlative meanings. Nicholas of Cusa speaks of God as being created through his creating, and Bruno expresses this idea with the terms *natura naturans* and *natura naturata*. Spinoza inherited this tradition of viewing Nature as God's self-

16. Ibid., I, P14 (Curley, 93). In these citations, P = proposition.
17. Ibid., I, P6 (Curley, 87).
18. Ibid., IV, preface (Curley, 198). This expression is used only occasionally.

generation and God as being caused in that he is self-causing. He retains and consolidates these ideas in his own account of the two ways in which God or Nature can be regarded. *Natura naturans* is "God insofar as He is considered as a free cause." *Natura naturata* is "whatever follows from the necessity of God's nature, or from any of God's attributes, that is, all the modes of God's attributes insofar as they are considered as things which are in God, and can neither be nor be conceived without God."[19]

What we have here is a complex picture presenting a clear God-creature distinction with necessary unilateral relations between them. God is not simply identical with Nature as the sum total of individual things in the world. God is properly *Natura naturans*: "God as free cause." This is the Substance whose infinite, eternal, self-sufficient, active nature produces the things in the world. *Natura naturata* is "everything that follows from the necessity of the nature of God." But the individual things that collectively follow from the divine necessity, constituting *Natura naturata*, are not eternal, infinite, necessary, or self-causing. Thus they are not divine. So we do have a divine/nondivine distinction between the Infinite Substance and the individual entities that make up the world.

But God and the world are necessarily connected. Without *Natura naturata* "God cannot be or be conceived." *Natura naturata* "follows from the necessity of the nature of God." It too is eternal and necessary. Even though *Natura naturans* is "God as free cause," God's freedom is not the freedom of choice but the freedom (compatible with necessity) of not being determined by anything else. For Spinoza, it is absolutely impossible that God not manifest himself in the world exactly as he does: "All things, I say, are in God, and all things that happen, happen only through the laws of God's infinite nature and follow . . . from the necessity of his essence."[20] In other words, Spinoza continues to work with an idea we see in Stoicism, Neoplatonism, Eriugena, Nicholas of Cusa, and Bruno, that the world necessarily but finitely manifests or actualizes the infinite ideal possibilities in God.[21]

This position also implies that everything that happens is absolutely determined, including human choices and actions, that all the evil in the world must occur, and that it is caused by God. *"In nature there is nothing contingent, but all things have been determined from the necessity of the divine*

---

19. Ibid., I, P29, scholium (Curley, 104–5).
20. Ibid., I, P15 [VI] (Curley, 97).
21. Ibid., I, P16 (Curley, 97). *"From the necessity of the divine nature there must follow infinitely many things in infinitely many modes (i.e., everything which can fall under an infinite intellect)."* The worldly *plenum* (fullness) of Neoplatonic philosophy is alive and well.

nature to exist and produce an effect in a certain way."[22] Discomfort with these views motivated Spinoza's admirers in later generations toward pan-entheisms with more creaturely self-determination. Schelling is foremost among them.

Finally, the necessary relationship between God and world, according to Spinoza, is divinely constituted inherence. God determines that the world be in God and God in the world. Proposition 15, "On God," locates the world in God: *"Whatever is, is in God, and nothing can either be or be conceived without God."* And Proposition 18 asserts that God's relation to the world is exclusively immanent: *"God is the immanent, not the transitive, cause of all things."*[23] Bruno had already worked out the notion of divine activity in nature as infinite immanence.

The Debate about Spinoza's Pantheism

Because Spinoza is commonly regarded as a pantheist, it may be surprising to learn that this label is disputed. If pantheism simply identifies God and world whereas panentheism posits a God-world distinction while locating the world in God, then Spinoza might be a panentheist.[24]

But the situation is more complex. Although Spinoza distinguishes God and the world, the key point is whether he provides an adequate account of the ontological difference between them, whether the finite things in *Natura naturata* have an actuality of their own. His doctrine of One Substance entails that the individual entities in the world are nothing more than temporary self-modifications of God/*Natura naturans*. Even human minds or souls exist only as long as their bodily correlates.[25] In the final analysis, entities are no more than finite, temporary, passive manifestations of God. Spinoza may assert that God and creatures are different actualities, but his

22. Ibid., I, P29 (Curley, 104).

23. Ibid., I, P15 (Curley, 97); I, P18 (Curley, 100).

24. See Mason, *The God of Spinoza*, 28–38. E. M. Curley, *Spinoza's Metaphysics* (Cambridge, MA: Harvard University Press, 1969), and Alan Donagan, *Spinoza* (Chicago: University of Chicago Press, 1989), 90, deny that he is a pantheist because he affirms the ontological distinctness of creatures from God. M. P. Levine, *Pantheism* (London: Routledge, 1994), 137, 361–62 n.7, is ambivalent. Clark Butler, "Hegelian Panentheism as Joachimite Christianity," in *New Perspectives on Hegel's Philosophy of Religion*, ed. David Kolb (Albany: State University of New York Press, 1992), 138, claims that "Spinoza is properly a panentheist, since finite things—the intelligible modes and attributes of the infinite substance—are not illusory; they are contained as finite in the infinite, which they reveal."

25. Spinoza, *Ethics*, V, P23, notes, "our mind can only be said to endure, and its existence can only be defined by a fixed time, insofar as it involves the actual existence of the body." Spinoza, *The Ethics* (Malibu, CA: Joseph Simon, 1981). A human soul is eternal only in the mind of God, not in actual individual existence. There is no personal afterlife.

philosophy does not quite justify this claim. Because he lacks a sufficiently strong ontological distinction between God and Nature, it is proper to retain the view that he is one kind of pantheist.[26] But most of his admirers have adapted his ideas in the direction of panentheism.

Seventeenth-Century Neoplatonism

The history of panentheism thus far virtually coincides with the history of Neoplatonism. This correlation continued from the Renaissance into the Enlightenment. The classical Neoplatonism of Dionysius, Eriugena, and Nicholas of Cusa was reinvigorated by Pico della Mirandola and by Marsilio Ficino's translation of Plotinus's *Enneads* in 1492, which shaped the so-called Christian humanism of the Renaissance. John Colet brought the New Platonism to England about 1500, where it eventually grew into the Cambridge Platonism of the seventeenth century. This revival of Neoplatonism mediated its implicit panentheism to the early Enlightenment, where it appeared in philosophy, theology, science, and literature.[27] We will consider some significant examples.

The Cambridge Platonists were a group of seventeenth-century English Neoplatonists who resisted Puritan Calvinism, on the one hand, and Thomas Hobbes's materialism, on the other.[28] In his writings, the founder of the group, Benjamin Whichcote (1609–1683), expresses a strong sense of living in God's Spirit "as in a house" and regularly quotes from St. Paul's sermon "in him we live and move and have our being."[29] John Smith (1618–1652) implies panentheism more philosophically, writing of "that Omnipresent Life that penetrates and runs through all things, containing and holding fast together within himself; and therefore, the ancient philosophy was wont rather to say that the world was in God, than that God was in the

26. Nondual Hinduism is extreme pantheism: only God is real. Spinoza has been understood as identifying God and Nature, but this identification has been understood both as Absolute Theism and Naturalistic Atheism by a vast majority of scholars and devotees from his own time to the present. See Copleston, *Hist. Phil.*, vol. 4, chap. 15, sec. 6; T. L. S. Sprigge, "Spinoza," in *The Oxford Companion to Philosophy*, ed. Ted Honderich (Oxford, NY: Oxford University Press, 1995), 845–48.

27. Arthur O. Lovejoy, chaps. 5–9 in *The Great Chain of Being: The History of an Idea* (Cambridge, MA: Harvard University Press, 1936; repr., 1964), is a detailed account of Neoplatonism in all aspects of seventeenth- and eighteenth-century thought.

28. Ernst Cassirer, *The Platonic Renaissance in England*, trans. James Pettegrove (Edinburgh: Nelson, 1953); J. Deotis Roberts, *From Puritanism to Platonism in Seventeenth Century England* (The Hague: Martinus Nijhoff, 1968).

29. W. C. Pauley, *The Candle of the Lord: Studies in the Cambridge Platonists* (London: SPCK; New York: Macmillan, 1937), 8–9.

world."[30] Ralph Cudworth (1617–1688) argues for a divine World-Soul by whose agency material atoms are woven into the one harmonious system of the universe.[31] The philosophy and theology of the Cambridge Platonists clearly asserts the Neoplatonic doctrine of existence in God.

This perspective also shaped their philosophy of nature. Henry More (1614–1687), who studied Plotinus, adapts the doctrine of World-Soul to seventeenth-century science as the Spirit of Nature, the divine agency operative in the world-machine. He reasons that since God is infinite and since we exist in God, infinite extension or space must be an attribute of God.[32] Later his doctrine was adopted by the great scientist Isaac Newton (1642–1727), who believed time and space to be divine attributes, implying that the universe literally exists within God.[33]

The idea of the World-Soul was widespread enough in the eighteenth century that Alexander Pope (1688–1744) set it to verse: "All are but parts of one stupendous whole, Whose body Nature is and God the soul."[34] The implicitly panentheistic themes of Neoplatonism continue to recur in Enlightenment England.

In addition to the writings of Plotinus, those of Jakob Böhme also became popular in England during the 1640s, and the themes of Neoplatonism and "Behmism," as it was called, sometimes converged.[35] This is evident in the writings of the Anglican theologian and mystic William Law (1686–1761), who studied and embraced both Cambridge Platonism and Böhme as well as Pseudo-Dionysius and Eckhart.[36]

30. John Smith, "The Existence and Nature of God," in *Select Discourses* (London, 1660), 145, quoted from Douglas Elwood, *The Philosophical Theology of Jonathan Edwards* (New York: Columbia, 1960), 100.

31. Pauley, *The Candle of the Lord*, 108.

32. Basil Wiley, *The Seventeenth Century Background* (New York: Columbia University Press, 1962), 167: "As is well known, this infinite extension or space became with More, by a very analogy, an attribute of God, the Infinite Spirit. In this making space the divine ground of the universe he was followed by Locke and Newton."

33. E. J. Dijksterhuis, *The Mechanization of the World Picture* (New York: Oxford University Press, 1961), 487; also William Lane Craig, *Time and Eternity: Exploring God's Relation to Time* (Wheaton, IL: Crossway, 2001), 32–35, 44–47. Newton held that "God's infinite being has as its consequence infinite time and space, which represent the quantity of his duration and presence" (ibid., 46). According to Clayton, *God and Contemporary Science*, 89, "Newton did see that, theologically, space must be understood also as an attribute of God, and hence as part of God."

34. Alexander Pope, *An Essay on Man* (New Haven: Yale University Press, 1951), Epistle I, p. 267.

35. Jacob Behmen [Jakob Böhme], *Forty Questions concerning the Soul*, trans. John Sparrow (London: Matthew Simmons, 1647); *Letters* (London: Matthew Simmons, 1649).

36. Erwin Rudolf, *William Law* (Boston: Twayne, 1980), 49, 62–63, 69–76, 82–90; Caroline Spurgeon, "William Law and the Mystics," chap. 12 in *Cambridge History of English and American Literature*, 15 vols. (New York: G. P. Putnam's Sons, 1907–1921), vol. 9.

These examples illustrate that all the ingredients of panentheism, if not explicitly stated, were close to the surface in the intellectual and spiritual life of the English Enlightenment.

Jonathan Edwards

Although the history of panentheism does not often overlap with traditional Protestant orthodoxy, the two converge in America's first great theologian, Jonathan Edwards (1703–1758). Edwards's heart, soul, mind, and strength were devoted to biblical Christianity and Calvinist theology.[37] But his philosophical formulations, influenced by the Cambridge Platonists, Newton, and Locke, have affinities with pantheism and panentheism long recognized by scholars.[38]

God and the World

Edwards's philosophical doctrine of God is traditional classical theism. He argues that God is the eternal, infinite, necessary, perfect, self-sufficient Being who is the cause of everything else that exists. The question of panentheism arises with respect to his ontology of creatures and their relation to God. He clearly affirms the immanence of all things in God: "God is the sum of all being, and there is no being without his being; all things are in him, and he in all."[39] But since Aquinas, a classical theist, and Spinoza, a pantheist, also affirm immanence in God, more evidence is necessary to determine whether Edwards is a panentheist.

Several themes indicate that his view of "in-ness" is ontological—that things actually exist in the divine Being. Consider his view of substance. He

37. George Marsden, *Jonathan Edwards: A Life* (New Haven: Yale University Press, 2003).

38. Colin Brown, *Christianity and Western Thought* (Downers Grove, IL: InterVarsity, 1990–), 1:273. Robert Whittemore, "Philosopher of the Sixth Way," *Church History* 35 (March 1966): 60–75, argues that Edwards is a mystical pantheist, not a panentheist. Elwood, *Philosophical Theology of Jonathan Edwards*, claims that he is a panentheist who in some ways anticipates Whitehead and Hartshorne. John Gerstner, "An Outline of the Apologetics of Jonathan Edwards," *Bibliotecha sacra* 133 (1976): 3–10, 99–107, 195–201, 291–98, argues that he is a Christian panentheist by intention but a pantheist by implication. Robert Jenson, *America's Theologian: A Recommendation of Jonathan Edwards* (New York: Oxford University Press, 1988), implies but does not clearly affirm that Edwards is a panentheist (see the index entry "panentheism," ibid., 223). Sang Hyun Lee, *The Philosophical Theology of Jonathan Edwards* (Princeton: Princeton University Press, 1988), challenges the diagnosis of pantheism but does not finally decide between classical theism and panentheism.

39. Jonathan Edwards, "Entry 880.1," in *The Works*, vol. 20, *The "Miscellanies," 833–1152*, ed. Amy Plantinga Paauw (New Haven: Yale University Press, 2002), 121–23.

insists that those who use this term "must apply it to the divine Being."[40] He reasons, like Spinoza, that a substance is by definition self-sufficient and thus that the concept of a dependent substance is incoherent. Only God is substance, and God is the only substance. Creatures are not substances. Instead Edwards equates the actuality of creatures with God's power, which is identical to his knowledge. His ontology of creatures comes to this: to be is to be thought by God to be.

Edwards explains matter accordingly. Regarding physical atoms, he writes that "the very substance of the body itself" is "nothing but the divine power, or rather the constant exertion of it."[41] An atom is an extended divine power burst. Put another way, an atom is God's thinking of an actual atom.

Edwards's view of space correlates with his view of substance. Space is a mode of God's presence to what he has created. He adopts Newton's view that God's omnipresence is the absolute space in which the universe exists: "I have already said as much as that space is God."[42] Edwards's philosophy of nature hovers between pantheism and panentheism.

A human soul, in Edwards's view, is not a spiritual substance but a consciousness that is immediately actualized, sustained, and filled by the mind of God. Jenson's summary is accurate: minds, "as continuing entities, have their substantiality only in God's mind, they exist only in that God forms and communicates a coherent 'series' of ideas."[43] Like physical things, human minds are God's thinking of them as actual.

Edwards combines his ontology of physical objects and human souls into an account of how God thinks of the whole creation's culmination in humans, who think God's thoughts after him. "That which truly is the substance of all bodies is the infinitely exact and precise and perfectly stable ideas in God's mind, together with his stable will that the same shall gradually be communicated to . . . other minds, according to . . . established laws."[44] In other

---

40. Jonathan Edwards, *The Works*, vol. 6, *Scientific and Philosophical Writings*, ed. Wallace Anderson (New Haven: Yale University Press, 1980), 215. Edwards was aware that the notion of substance was under suspicion in the seventeenth century. See Jenson, *America's Theologian*, 25–27. One problem is the idea that substance entails self-sufficiency, a view held by the Greeks, Spinoza, and the materialists, which made it impossible for theists to regard creatures as substances. On another front, Locke's empiricism implied that if substance is simply that in which properties inhere, it is an unknowable, empty x because we only ever experience things with properties.

41. Jonathan Edwards, "On Atoms," in *Scientific and Philosophical Writings* (New Haven: Yale University Press, 1980), 351–52.

42. Ibid., 342–43.

43. Jenson, *America's Theologian*, 29–33, quote at 33.

44. Edwards, "On Atoms," 344. Jenson, *America's Theologian*, 32: "The world of bodies is what God thinks in order to think a *communal plurality* of consciousnesses, who are to think and feel each other's thoughts and feelings while yet remaining plural." This position is similar to the philosophy of George

words, God's constant thinking and willing order and populate the universe, fill human minds with ideas of the universe, and animate and order human thinking and communication about the universe. God's thinking about nature culminates in human thinking about nature. Man is "the consciousness of the creation, whereby the universe is conscious of its own being," and all of this is "the actions of the Creator."[45] The whole creation is a reality in God's mind, and individual beings, both physical and mental, are particular thoughts of God within his coherent knowledge of the whole. Jenson summarizes Edwards's view of the God-universe relation: "God contains, envelops, all other reality . . . as a consciousness contains that of which it is conscious."[46] In this way, all things are in God.

The Neoplatonism of Edwards's theology is especially evident in his famous treatise "Concerning the End for Which God Created the World." He invokes the analogy of the World-Soul for God: "The whole universe . . . should proceed . . . with a view to God . . . as if the whole system were animated and directed by one common soul: or, as if such an arbiter . . . possessed of perfect wisdom and rectitude, became the common soul of the universe."[47] He also regards creation as an inevitable emanation of the divine nature, not a divine choice: "We may suppose *that a disposition in God, as an original property of his nature, to an emanation of his own infinite fullness, was what excited him to create the world; and so that the emanation itself was aimed at by him as a last end of the creation.*"[48] Edwards denies that this implies any deficiency or lack in God. "'Tis no argument of the emptiness or deficiency of a fountain that it is inclined to overflow." He affirms that God is free in being unconstrained: "He is independent on any other that should hinder him." Yet by nature God cannot fail to overflow in love and self-glorification by generating creatures that love and glorify him. "God would be less happy, if he was less good, or if he had not that perfection of nature which consists in a propensity of nature to diffuse his own fullness."[49] For Edwards, God's sovereignty does not include the choice whether to create the world.

Berkeley, although it is unclear whether Edwards read him. It is also similar to themes in Malebranche, who taught that God does not need physical things to produce their effects in the human soul.

45. Jonathan Edwards, "Entry 1," in *The Works*, vol. 13, *The "Miscellanies," Entry Nos. a–z, aa–zz, 1–500*, ed. Thomas A. Schafer (New Haven: Yale University Press, 1994), 197. Emerson could have written this statement. See chap. 5, below.

46. Jenson, *America's Theologian*, 21.

47. Jonathan Edwards, "Concerning the End for Which God Created the World," in *The Works*, vol. 8, *Ethical Writings*, ed. Paul Ramsey (New Haven: Yale University Press, 1989), 424–25.

48. Ibid., 435.

49. Ibid., 447–48.

Pantheism or Panentheism?

It is clear why scholars debate whether Edwards is a panentheist or pantheist. Like Spinoza, he regards God as the only substance and embraces a deterministic view of God's relation to the world. Creatures are simply direct projections of God's mind and power, individual divine thoughts and acts. This sounds like pantheism.

Yet Edwards affirms God's transcendence of creation in ways impossible for Spinoza. He cannot say that *God* and *Nature* are two terms for the same substance. He does not regard the productivity of nature (*Natura naturans*) as divine. Moreover, although he agrees with Spinoza that humans are not substances, Edwards affirms that humans retain their individual existence everlastingly, a doctrine that Spinoza denies. These factors point away from pantheistic monism. But Edwards lacks the robust ontological Creator-creature distinction of classical theism. For him, creatures are divine thoughts. All things considered, his affirmation that "the whole is *of* God, and *in* God, and *to* God"[50] is best construed philosophically as a panentheism that borders on Spinozan pantheism.

There is no doubt of Edwards's Christian faith and Calvinist orthodoxy. But some of his philosophical statements, aimed against granting the universe independence from God, do not sufficiently recognize its distinctness from God. Edwards's philosophy, taken out of the context of his Christian theology, anticipates Emerson and the New England transcendentalists.

Early German Romanticism: Lessing and Herder

In late eighteenth-century Germany, the Sturm und Drang (storm and stress) movement was an early expression of the romantic reaction against Enlightenment rationalism. Although panentheism was not absent from the Age of Reason, the new trend was much more amenable to it. The cultured elite began turning away from the Enlightenment's quest for universal rational truth, focusing instead on historical development, cultural diversity, intuitive knowledge, and nondoctrinal, noninstitutional spirituality. The universe was increasingly viewed as a spiritually energized organism rather than a divinely designed machine.[51]

---

50. Ibid., 531.
51. James Livingston, "Christianity and Romanticism," chap. 4 in *Modern Christian Thought: From the Enlightenment to Vatican II* (New York: Macmillan, 1971), is an excellent short introduction. See also Oskar Walzel, *German Romanticism*, trans. A. E. Lussky (New York: Putnam's Sons, 1932; repr., New York: Capricorn, 1966); Lovejoy, "Romanticism and the Principle of Plenitude," chap. 10 in *The*

The spirit of romanticism, however, was not entirely new. It involved the resurgence of older traditions that had been overshadowed during the height of Protestant orthodoxy and the Age of Reason. Chief among these were Christian mysticism and Neoplatonism. In his classic study, *German Romanticism*, Oskar Walzel traces this heritage from Plotinus through medieval theology and mysticism to Renaissance Italy, post-Reformation Germany, and Cambridge Platonism. Romanticism, he observes, "resuscitated the ancient fusion of the Neoplatonic and the Germanic ... which carried on the legacy of Plotinus."[52] The tradition of Christian Neoplatonism already had a long history in Germany through Eckhart, Nicholas of Cusa, and Böhme.

The playwright and religious thinker Gotthold Lessing (1729–1781) stands as a transitional figure between the Enlightenment and romanticism. In *The Education of the Human Race* (1780), he draws on ancient and recent Christian Neoplatonism in arguing that God's revelation is not primarily in the Bible or in any book but in God's progressive self-manifestation in nature, history, and especially in human religious experience.[53] Lessing's Neoplatonism is evident in his idea that the finite world progressively manifests the self-articulation of the Infinite God in time. His view that the history of world religions follows a pattern of progressive divine self-revelation was adopted and developed much more fully by Schleiermacher, Hegel, Schelling, and Troeltsch.

The other source of Romantic panentheism is Spinoza.[54] Some thinkers reacted thoroughly against him. Gottfried Leibniz (1646–1716) regarded Spinoza's identification of God and Nature as atheism and reintroduced the notion of finite individual substances as "monads" to secure their ontological distinctness from God. Following Leibniz, Christian Wolff (1679–1754) elaborated a rather classical natural theology that strongly emphasizes divine transcendence.

But Lessing and others embraced Spinoza. Lessing spent his career promoting religious progressivism and toleration, but not as a typical Deist like Voltaire. Before his death he confided to Friedrich Jacobi (1743–1819) that

Great Chain of Being; John Herman Randall, "The Romantic Protest against the Age of Reason," chap. 16 in *The Making of the Modern Mind* (Boston: Houghton Mifflin, 1940; repr., New York: Columbia University Press, 1976); and Isaiah Berlin, *The Roots of Romanticism* (Princeton, NJ: Princeton University Press, 1999).

52. Walzel, *German Romanticism*, 7; see 4–8.

53. Gotthold Lessing, *The Education of the Human Race*, in *Theological Writings: Selections in Translation*, ed. and trans. Henry Chadwick (Stanford, CA: Stanford University Press, 1957).

54. Clayton, "The Temptations of Immanence: Spinoza's One and the Birth of Panentheism," chap. 7 in *The Problem of God*.

he was a Spinozist.[55] He also adopted Spinoza's term for God, "the One and All." In his 1763 essay "On the Reality of Things outside God," he claims not to be able to conceive of anything outside God's mind: "Why should we not say that the ideas which God has of real things are those real things themselves? They are still sufficiently distinct from God, and their reality becomes in no sense necessary because they are real in him."[56] Similarly in *The Education of the Human Race*, Lessing writes that God's oneness is a "unity which does not exclude a sort of plurality" and that God's self-knowledge "contains everything which is in him."[57] If contingent things are sufficiently distinct from God yet in God as his thoughts, then this theology implies a form of panentheism that is close to pantheism.[58] Lessing's Spinozism generated the "pantheism controversy," which stimulated various forms of panentheism for two generations.[59]

Another early romantic Spinozan is the historian and linguist Johann Gottfried Herder (1744–1803). He conceives of the universe not as a machine but as the nexus of living forces that functions organically. Herder rejects Spinoza's concept of God as Infinite Substance because it suggests that God is a static thing. He shifts instead to view God as "Infinite Substantial Force," a dynamic living power that underlies and permeates all particular forces. Like Spinoza, Herder distinguishes God and Nature, but not by way of supernatural ontological transcendence.[60] The Infinite Life Force is entirely immanent in nature and history. The literary genius Johann Wolfgang Goethe (1749–1832) was likewise a Spinozan, regarding Spinoza as "the most theistic, indeed the most Christian of thinkers."[61]

The conjunction of Neoplatonism and Spinozism in German romanticism forged the main link between traditional and modern panentheism. "Pantheism, thanks to its contact with Spinozism, progressed from its traditional manifestation as Neoplatonic emanation to a concept of evolution, which in

---

55. Henry Chadwick, introduction to Lessing, *Theological Writings*.

56. Gotthold Lessing, "On the Reality of Things outside God" (Chadwick, 102–3).

57. Lessing, *The Education of the Human Race*, par. 73 (Chadwick, 94).

58. Clayton, *The Problem of God*, 413, concurs: "Lessing's writings clearly espouse some form of panentheism."

59. Leo Scheffczyk, *Creation and Providence*, trans. R. Strachan (New York: Herder and Herder, 1970), 203: "This pantheist or panentheist cast of mind was to have a forcible effect on the religious and philosophical outlook of the educated classes in the nineteenth century."

60. Johann Gottfried Herder, *God, Some Conversations*, trans. Frederick Burkhardt (New York: Veritas, 1940; repr., Indianapolis: Bobbs-Merrill, 1962); Julia Lamm, "Spinoza and Spinozism in Germany," in *The Living God: Schleiermacher's Theological Appropriation of Spinoza* (University Park: University of Pennsylvania Press, 1996), 16–24.

61. Kurt Weinberg, "*Pantheismusstreit*," *EncPhil* 6:35, quoting a letter Goethe wrote to Jacobi in 1785.

Hegel's philosophy (and in the twentieth century, that of Bergson) entails the development of the Absolute in and with the world."[62]

Friedrich Schleiermacher

Friedrich Schleiermacher (1768–1834) is commonly regarded as the father of liberal theology and the most important theologian since Calvin.[63] Like Edwards, he is better known for his theology than for the philosophical categories that shaped it. Although it is clear that his account of the God-world relation does not represent classical theism, it is more difficult to decide between pantheism and panentheism. He was deeply influenced both by Spinoza and by Neoplatonism and always sought a third way between an anthropomorphic, "personal" view of God and merely identifying God with nature.

God and World in On Religion

Romantic spirituality is the heart and mind of Schleiermacher's first major work, *On Religion: Speeches to Its Cultured Despisers* (1799).[64] He defends religion in general and Christianity in particular as the fullest expression of our deepest human intuition of the Infinite in and through the finite, fallible world. He acknowledges his debts to Spinoza and Neoplatonism.

Schleiermacher's admiration for Spinoza was deep and abiding. As a student he wrote two essays that sketch a post-Kantian Spinozism.[65] *On Religion* again pays homage to "the holy, rejected Spinoza. The high World-Spirit pervaded him; the Infinite was his beginning and his end; the Universe was his only and his everlasting love. . . . He was full of religion, full of the Holy Spirit."[66] The book is peppered with Spinozan references to God. At the outset he refers to the Deity both as "the eternal and holy Being that lies beyond the world" and as "the Universe that made you."[67] This parallel reflects Spinoza's "God or Nature." Schleiermacher also invokes Spinoza's epithet "the One in All, and

62. Ibid., 37. Weinberg's "pantheism" is implicit panentheism.

63. Stanley J. Grenz and Roger E. Olson, *Twentieth-Century Theology: God and the World in a Transitional Age* (Downers Grove, IL: InterVarsity, 1992), 39–51, provide an excellent introduction.

64. Schleiermacher, *On Religion*.

65. Richard Brandt, "The Influence of Spinoza," in *The Philosophy of Schleiermacher* (New York: Harper and Row, 1941; repr., Westport, CT: Greenwood, 1962), 35–41; Lamm, "The Early Essays on Spinoza, 1793–1794," chap. 1 in *The Living God*.

66. Schleiermacher, *On Religion*, 40.

67. Ibid., 1–2.

All in One."[68] In the "Second Speech" he asserts, "There lives immediately in you the eternal unity of Reason and Nature, the universal existence of all finite things in the Infinite."[69] He also refers to God as the Whole, which is the highest unity of the diversity in the world: God is the "Uni-" of the "-verse," so to speak. It is not surprising that Schleiermacher's contemporaries took him for a Spinozist, a charge he later rejected.[70]

But the Infinite One and All is not simply the legacy of Spinoza. It goes back to Parmenides through Plato and Plotinus.[71] Schleiermacher was a lifelong student of Plato and edited the Berlin Academy's Greek text of Plato's dialogues. His lectures on dialectic, a course at the University of Berlin, explicitly follow Plato's method of moving toward the absolute.[72]

Schleiermacher's Platonism is clearly Neoplatonic. The world is generated as the All inexorably emanates from the divine One according to a dialectical pattern of opposition and unification. "The Deity, by an immutable law, has compelled Himself to divide His great work even to infinity. Each definite thing can only be made up by melting together two opposite activities. Each of His eternal thoughts can only be actualized in two hostile yet twin forms, one of which cannot exist except by means of the other. The whole corporeal world . . . appears . . . a never-ending play of opposing forces." Finite spirits are likewise governed by the coincidence of opposites: "The spirit also, in so far as it manifests itself in a finite life, must be subject to the same law. The human soul . . . has its existence chiefly in two opposing impulses."[73] This dialectical ontology echoes Plotinus, Proclus, Nicholas of Cusa, and Böhme.[74] *On Religion* also identifies the World-Spirit as the agent of world formation.[75]

68. Ibid., 7, and several times throughout the book.

69. Ibid., 39.

70. In the 1821 edition of *On Religion* (ibid., 104), he denied ascribing "the Holy Spirit to Spinoza in the special Christian sense of the word." He claimed to admire Spinoza but "never defended his system."

71. Lamm, *The Living God*, 125; Copleston, *Hist. Phil.*, vol. 7, chap. 8, sec. 1, p. 184: "He shared the general romantic concern with the totality, and he had a profound sympathy with Spinoza. At the same time, he had been attracted from an early age by Plato's view of the world as the visible image of the ideal realm of true being." See also Robert Williams, "The Platonic Background of Schleiermacher's Thought," chap. 2 in *Schleiermacher the Theologian* (Philadelphia: Fortress, 1978).

72. John Thiel, *God and the World in Schleiermacher's* Dialektik *and* Glaubenslehre (Las Vegas: Peter Lang, 1981), 14–15: "Clearly it was Schleiermacher's life-long devotion to Plato's philosophy that most influenced his own understanding of *Dialektik*. . . . For Schleiermacher, as for Plato, all thinking is relative and this relativity points to, and requires as its ground, a final consummate unity beyond thinking."

73. Schleiermacher, *On Religion*, 3.

74. Williams, "How Schleiermacher Resembles Cusanus," in *Schleiermacher the Theologian*, 68–71.

75. He backs off from the World-Spirit in the 1821 edition: "No one will confuse it with *World-Soul*. It neither expresses reciprocal action between the World and the Highest Being, nor any kind of

On Religion likewise envisions a Neoplatonic eschatology. The goal of creation is that the One be fully in the All, and the All fully in the One. Thus nature and history move from less unity, harmony, and Godlikeness to greater unity, harmony, and Godlikeness as they develop from simple to more complex and more beautiful forms of existence in God.

The history of religious experience is the vanguard of this pilgrimage. "The whole of religion is nothing but the sum of all relations of man to God, apprehended in all the possible ways in which any man can be immediately conscious in his life."[76] Since no individual believer or religion can express all modes of God-consciousness, there must be a progressive variety of religions. "The whole of religion can only be actually given in the sum of all the forms possible in this sense."[77] Christianity is the highest religion because Jesus Christ possessed perfect God-consciousness in himself and mediated it to others.[78] Schleiermacher's view of Christianity and other religions is shaped more by Neoplatonism's eschatology of dialectical synthesis than by the traditional Christian view of final judgment and separation.

In sum, *On Religion* blends themes of Spinozism, Neoplatonism, and Christianity into a dynamic romantic view of God and the cosmos.

God and World in The Christian Faith

Scholars debate whether Schleiermacher's youthful romanticism continued to define his Christianity or whether his deepest allegiance was to the historic Christian faith in spite of its tension with his philosophy.[79] No one disputes that his philosophy is Neoplatonic romanticism. Our interest is whether *The Christian Faith* (1820–1821) is pantheistic or panentheistic.

First an overview. *The Christian Faith* begins by eliciting "the feeling of absolute dependence" in contrast to our experience of relative freedom and dependence in the world. Schleiermacher identifies this fundamental intuition

---

independence of the World from Him" (Schleiermacher, *On Religion*, 111). But the Platonic World-Soul never connoted reciprocity or dependence, which first occurs in modern panentheism.

76. Ibid., 217.

77. Ibid., 223.

78. Ibid., 247: "This consciousness of the singularity of His knowledge of God and of His existence in God, of the original way in which this knowledge was in Him, and of the power thereof to communicate itself and awake religion, was at once the consciousness of His office as mediator and of His divinity."

79. Brandt, *Philosophy of Schleiermacher*, 252, wonders whether the theistic language of his Christian writings is anything more than rhetoric for his philosophical views. Hendrikus Berkhof, *Two Hundred Years of Theology* (Grand Rapids: Eerdmans, 1989), 32–40, defends Schleiermacher's Christianity and relativizes his philosophy to it.

as true piety, and God is its "whence" and cause in us.[80] He then traces this intuition through the history of religions to its culmination in Christianity. There is nothing in Scripture or in true Christianity that does not derive from and cannot be explained by the experience of absolute dependence. Reflection on God as Absolute Cause of the world yields definitions of the divine attributes of eternity, omnipresence, omniscience, and omnipotence. Moving beyond creation, Schleiermacher unpacks the experience of absolute dependence in redemption through Jesus Christ to explain God's personal attributes of holiness, mercy, and grace. On this basis he explains the person and work of Jesus Christ, the work of the Holy Spirit, the life of the church in the world, Scripture, and the last things. *The Christian Faith* culminates with God's love, the attribute that most fully expresses the divine essence. In this way Schleiermacher derives his entire dogmatics from the intuition of absolute dependence.

Our interest is the God-world relation, beginning with Schleiermacher's treatment of pantheism. *The Christian Faith* defends pantheism but does not mention Spinoza. Schleiermacher asserts that pantheism is compatible with true piety, provided that it expresses "some variety or form of Theism, and that the word is not simply and solely a disguise for a materialistic negation of Theism."[81] This statement is not an affirmation of classical theism but merely an insistence that pantheism is not atheism.[82] Schleiermacher then defends the legitimacy of pantheism. First, pantheists base their theology on the same feeling of absolute dependence as theists. "Such states of mind can scarcely be distinguished from the religious emotions of many a Monotheist." Second, pantheism does distinguish God and the world: "Let us hold Pantheism fast to the usual formula of One and All: then God and world will remain distinct at least as regards function." Third, it is not clear that theism more adequately acknowledges divine transcendence than pantheism. "The distinction (always rather a curious one, and, if I may say so, roughly drawn) between a God who is outside of and above the world, and a God who is in the world, does not particularly meet the point."[83] Schleiermacher does not challenge pantheism. He defends the formula "One and All" and makes it basic to his theology,

---

80. Friedrich Schleiermacher, *The Christian Faith*, ed. H. R. Macintosh and J. R. Stewart (Edinburgh: T&T Clark, 1989), par. 4, p. 16. I summarize the book without further references.

81. Ibid., par. 8, postscript 2, p. 39.

82. Spinoza was commonly accused of atheism, as was John Toland, who coined the term *pantheism* in *Pantheisticon* (1720). See Thomas McFarland, "Toland and the Word *Pantheism*," in *Coleridge and the Pantheist Tradition* (Oxford: Clarendon, 1969), 266–68.

83. Schleiermacher, *The Christian Faith*, par. 8, postscript 2, p. 39.

which is derived entirely from absolute dependence on the One intuited in and through the All.[84]

God and world are not identical. The All is in the One and the One in the All, but they are distinct. "God and world will remain distinct at least as regards function."[85] God and Nature are not just two words for the same thing. In fact Schleiermacher regards identification of God with nature as untenable: "I leave it to you to say whether the World can be conceived as a true All and Whole without God."[86] He certainly distinguishes the All from the One.

But they cannot be separated. "There is no God without the world, just as there is no world without God."[87] One reason is the impossibility of conceiving of God in himself apart from our experience, as Kant argues. Schleiermacher acknowledges the validity of Kant's theological agnosticism but attempts to overcome it in a most un-Kantian way—by rooting knowledge of God in our immediate experience. *All attributes which we ascribe to God are to be taken as denoting not something special in God, but only something special in the manner in which the feeling of absolute dependence is to be related to Him.*[88] Our concepts of God and his attributes are not of God in himself but of our relation to him. Thus Schleiermacher concedes that there is no basis for asserting that God in himself exists beyond the world. *"The Absolute Causality to which the feeling of absolute dependence points back can only be described in such a way that, on the one hand, it is distinguished from the content of the natural order and thus contrasted with it, and, on the other hand, equated with it in comprehension."*[89] The range of the One is not known to extend beyond the All. As Lamm comments, "Divine activity does not occur over and apart from natural causality; God is not found outside of the totality of finite things."[90] Like Spinoza, Schleiermacher asserts that divine causality is entirely immanent and never supernatural. We cannot even form a concept of God himself apart from the world, much less affirm its truth. And we cannot affirm the reality of supernatural miracles.

84. Lamm, "Limits and Method: The Coincidence of Divine Causality and the Natural System," chap. 4 in *The Living God*.

85. Schleiermacher, *The Christian Faith*, 39.

86. Schleiermacher, "Explanations," in *On Religion*, 104 (commentary written about the same time as *The Christian Faith*).

87. "Kein Gott ohne Welt, so wie keine Welt ohne Gott" was Schleiermacher's motto. See Thiel, "The Philosophical Formulation of the God-World Relationship in the 'Dialektik,'" in *God and the World*, 144–59.

88. Schleiermacher, *The Christian Faith*, par. 50, p. 194.

89. Ibid., par. 51, p. 200.

90. Lamm, *The Living God*, 150.

Schleiermacher's inability to affirm God's ontological independence of the world is also apparent in his treatment of the doctrine of creation. He cannot justify the notion of creation *ex nihilo* as a voluntary act by which God originates finite beings with time. He can affirm only creation as the constant absolute dependence of finite beings on God. Thus he cannot distinguish the doctrine of creation from the doctrine of preservation. "Our self-consciousness, in its universality, as both these doctrines relate to it, can only represent finite being in general so far as it is a continuous being; for we only know ourselves in this manner but have no consciousness of a beginning of being."[91] Schleiermacher can neither affirm nor deny the eternity of creation or the transcendence and aseity of God implied by creation *ex nihilo*. "The controversy over the temporal or eternal creation of the world (which can be resolved into the question whether it is possible or necessary to conceive of God as existing apart from created things) has no bearing on the content of the feeling of absolute dependence, and it is therefore a matter of indifference how it is decided."[92] He sees no important difference between Christianity, Spinoza, and Neoplatonism with respect to the origin of the world.

Schleiermacher holds a compatibilist view of the divine freedom to create. God is free in creating the world because he is self-determining, not coerced or limited by anything outside himself. "But if we . . . interpret freedom as meaning that God might equally well have not created the world (because we think that there must have been this possibility, otherwise God was compelled to create), we have then assumed an antithesis between freedom and necessity, and, by attributing this kind of freedom to God, have placed Him within the realm of contradictions."[93] Schleiermacher cannot affirm that creation is God's free choice. His reason is standard dialectical theology: in God all antitheses of finite existence, including free choice versus necessity, are unified and transcended. God is both free and determined in that he is self-determining. "For if He wills Himself, He wills Himself as Creator and Sustainer, so that in willing Himself, willing the world is already included."[94] Schleiermacher follows the Neoplatonists and Spinoza in counting the cosmos as an essential expression of the divine nature.

Schleiermacher intentionally distances himself from pantheism on the question of cooperation between divine and creaturely causality. "This expression ['cooperation'] requires at least to be treated very cautiously if the

91. Schleiermacher, *The Christian Faith*, par. 39, p. 148.
92. Ibid., 155.
93. Ibid., par. 41, postscript, p. 156.
94. Ibid., par. 54, p. 217.

differences of finite being are not to be placed within the Supreme Being and thus God Himself appear as the totality, a view which can scarcely be differentiated from that of Pantheism."[95] He wishes to affirm the reality and activity of finite creatures *in addition to* God and not to view them as merely passive modifications of divine being and power. This is more like panentheism than Spinoza's pantheism. It is crucial to note, however, that "cooperation" does not mean that creatures have an effect on God or co-determine the course of history, as it does in modern panentheism. Human agency is intraworldly and remains absolutely dependent on divine causality. But they do operate together—cooperate.

Schleiermacher holds that God's nature, which is evident in creation, is more fully revealed in redemptive history and eschatology. The goal of all things is "the union of the Divine Essence with human nature," which is the kingdom of God. Thus God's governance of world history is redemptive, aiming to reconcile all things with him. Redemption manifests God's wisdom and love. "*The divine causality presents itself to us in the government of the world as* Love *and as* Wisdom."[96] God's love is "divine self-impartation," the manifestation of the essence of God in and for the world. Schleiermacher regards love as the attribute by which all other divine attributes must be understood.[97]

This definition of love and wisdom do not commit Schleiermacher to the view that God is a person (or three persons)[98] with a mind and will who operates on the world from outside. He rejects such anthropomorphism: "But whosoever insists . . . that the highest piety consists in confessing that the Highest Being thinks as a person and wills outside the world, cannot be far traveled in the region of piety." He proposes instead a Living God. "As it is so difficult to think of a personality as truly infinite and incapable of suffering, a great distinction should be drawn between a personal God and a Living God. The latter idea alone distinguishes from materialistic pantheism and atheistic blind necessity."[99] The Living God is Schleiermacher's way of steering among anthropomorphism, pantheism, and atheism. It is highly reminiscent of Herder's Vital Force, which was a modification of Spinoza's

95. Ibid., 192.

96. Ibid., par. 165, p. 726.

97. Ibid., par. 167, pp. 730–32. He appeals to 1 John 4:16.

98. Schleiermacher regarded the Trinity as "the coping-stone of Christian doctrine." The church's historic doctrine of the Trinity, however, "is not an immediate utterance concerning Christian self-consciousness, but only a combination of several such utterances" that have not been coherently formulated (ibid., par. 170). The Trinity is treated in an appendix.

99. Schleiermacher, *On Religion*, 99, and "Explanation of the Second Speech," number 19, p. 116, written when *The Christian Faith* was already published. See Lamm, *The Living God*, 101–9.

Substance.[100] Schleiermacher identifies Absolute Vitality as the best way of conceiving God's presence in the world.[101] The Neoplatonic notion of the World-Soul as the Life Force lives on in his theology.

In sum, Schleiermacher's Living God is the infinitely productive power whose essence exemplifies itself in the world, dialectically generating an infinite variety of creatures and drawing them into harmony with one another as it progressively encompasses them within itself. This Living Force does so most explicitly by generating humans with the capacity for self-consciousness and thus with consciousness of the Force itself. The Deity has actualized, exemplified, and communicated the self-conscious, God-conscious harmony of all things most fully in Jesus Christ, who is the perfect human realization and mediating source of God-consciousness in the communion of all with all. Sin is the failure of humans to value and take part in the communion of All in One. Salvation is inclusion and participation in it. God's wisdom is his ordering of all things to himself. His love is his self-impartation in all things in order to draw them to himself. From this summary it is evident how Schleiermacher's mature theology ingeniously combines aspects of Neoplatonism and Spinozism into a romantic version of *The Christian Faith*.

Pantheism or Panentheism?

Schleiermacher is obviously not a classical theist in the tradition of Augustine, Aquinas, and Calvin. But scholars are not agreed on what he is. Grenz and Olson, for example, think he is a panentheist.[102] But most prominent process panentheists view him as a pantheist.[103]

100. When Schleiermacher wrote, "I had never defended his system" (*On Religion*, 104), he did not repudiate Spinoza entirely. He explained the difference: "Anything philosophic that was in my book ... had quite a different basis than the unity of substance." In other words, he did not follow Spinoza in basing his system on God as *the unity of substance*. But he did adopt Spinoza's general perspective, reconceived in terms of God as the Absolute Vital Force. In this way Schleiermacher is a neo-Spinozan. See Lamm, "Spinozism, Pantheism, and Christian Dogmatics: Explanations and Revisions, 1821–30," chap. 3 in *The Living God*.

101. Schleiermacher, *The Christian Faith*, 203. Lamm, *The Living God*, argues at length that Absolute Vitality is the key notion in Schleiermacher's appropriation of Spinoza. See esp. chap. 5, "The First Part of the *Glaubenslehre* and Schleiermacher's Post-Kantian Spinozism."

102. Grenz and Olson, *Twentieth-Century Theology*, 50, conclude, "Schleiermacher's doctrine of God is best described as *panentheistic* in that it correlates God and the world, making them inseparable."

103. Lamm, *The Living God*, 2–4, summarizes the range of scholarly opinion on Schleiermacher's view of God. Note 9 observes that John Cobb, Charles Hartshorne, William Reese, and Schubert Ogden view Schleiermacher as a pantheist. The issue is Schleiermacher's absolute determinism. Hartshorne regards creaturely freedom as necessary for ontological distinctness from God. Lamm, 6, claims that Schleiermacher's "notion of a *living God* ... is free from the charges of pantheism commonly made against it." She does so in spite of her thesis that he is an "organic monist."

All things considered, Schleiermacher is best classified as a panentheist who is close to pantheism. He certainly distinguishes God and the world. His Spinozan use of divine terms in *On Religion* to refer to the Universe is absent from *The Christian Faith*. He argues that the All cannot be the same reality as the One, because the One is the Absolute Cause of the All. In addition, he asserts that finite beings have their own power of causality, although he does not offer a metaphysical explanation of their individual reality. For Schleiermacher, God and world are distinct.

Yet they are inseparable. In fact, a self-sufficient Being without the world is inconceivable for Schleiermacher. It is God's nature and will to generate and fill the world. He does so freely yet necessarily. Furthermore, the world is in God and God is in the world: *All in One, and One in All*. Schleiermacher holds that God and the world are asymmetrically but ontologically co-inherent.

It is Schleiermacher's more robust view of individuals that distinguishes him from Spinoza. Like Edwards, he is a Christian who takes individual creatures, especially humans, with ultimate seriousness in his ethics and eschatology, even though he does not work out an ontology of finite beings.[104] He regards humans as enduring, irreducible, creative, active, and responsible beings, not merely temporary modifications of the One.[105] This difference is enough to locate Schleiermacher on the panentheist side of the border with Spinozan pantheism.

Conclusion

The development of panentheism from the Renaissance to romanticism becomes more diverse and nuanced as rejuvenated Neoplatonism and post-Reformation Christianity encounter Enlightenment philosophy and science. Reconceiving the relationship between God and the universe as understood by Galileo, Kepler, and Newton becomes a top priority during this period.

Pantheists come to view the universe as an aspect of God. Bruno locates the infinity of nature within the Absolute Infinity of God and defines God's transcendence as the absolute immanence of Nature. Spinoza defines God

---

104. Copleston, *Hist. Phil.*, vol. 7, part 1, p. 192: "The pantheistic elements in his metaphysics were offset by his emphasis on the individual in his theories of moral conduct and of society." I add the weight of his eschatology to this argument.

105. In *The Christian Faith*, par. 163, Schleiermacher affirms personal immortality with God but finds no coherent way to define it, which leaves its meaning uncertain (p. 720). He also defends "a universal restoration of all souls," so that no one is finally lost (p. 722).

as Absolute Substance and views Nature as the finite manifestation of the divine attributes of thought and extension. Most theologians of this period, however, resist pantheism.

The Cambridge Platonists adapt the Neoplatonic doctrine of the divine World-Soul to the mechanistic picture of nature being elaborated in the seventeenth century. They consider divine Spirit to be the force that generates the universe as a machine-like system out of primitive material atoms. Preeminent scientists such as Newton share this implicitly panentheistic theology of nature. In large measure, Edwards affirms this view as well.

The early German romantics adapt the Platonic World-Soul to a more organic view of nature. They replace Spinoza's definition of God as Absolute Substance with God as Absolute Life Force. The organic connotation of this theology is, much more than the mechanical model, in keeping with Plato's idea that the world is a living body animated by a Soul. Schleiermacher's theology, in large part, is an elaboration of this sort of panentheism.

But emphasis on divine immanence and rejection of the traditional metaphysical category of dependent substance makes the difference between God and the world a challenge to maintain. Spinoza regards finite beings as modifications of God, Edwards as divine thoughts, and Herder as individuations of the Life Force. In retrospect, what distinguishes the pantheists from the panentheists is how energetically they emphasize the distinctness of creatures from God. Perhaps Edwards and Schleiermacher do not provide ontologies quite sufficient to secure completely distinct creaturely existence. But it is fair to conclude that they are panentheists if only because, much more than Spinoza, they emphasize the responsive relationship of humans to God. And unlike Spinoza, they affirm continuing human existence after death. These tenets imply that humans are effectually and permanently distinct from God.

The panentheism of Edwards and Schleiermacher raises another issue: the relation between religion and philosophy. Edwards was first and last a traditional biblical Christian and orthodox Calvinist. Whatever the tensions between them, his philosophy must be understood in terms of his religion. But Schleiermacher is different. The evangelical biblical pietism he left as a youth is much like Edwards's mature faith. Schleiermacher's mature faith is Christianity recast in terms of romanticism.

4

~~~~~~~~~~~~~~~~~~~~~~~~~~~~~~~~~~~~~~

Schelling and Hegel

The Godfathers of Modern Panentheism

This chapter focuses on the transition from classical to modern panentheism—the shift from a God who contains the world but remains immutable to a God whose existence indeed changes within the developing world. Schleiermacher was progressive in his romantic attempt to ground theology in religious experience, but his theology itself was rather traditional. His Living God is still an Unmoved Mover—a Dynamic Life Force that is absolutely unaffected by the world because the world is absolutely dependent on it.

The German idealists Schelling and Hegel are the first to articulate panentheisms in which God himself actually develops in and through the world—nature, history, and the human quest for transcendence. This shift to a dynamic God is the watershed in the history of panentheism, the key change from its classical to its modern form. Schelling and Hegel are the godfathers of modern panentheism because they have influenced all subsequent adaptations of this theological tradition. This includes the variety of Christian panentheisms because both men elaborated trinitarian theologies in the manner of Jakob Böhme. The legacy of Hegel has continued, fluctuating in breadth, throughout the nineteenth and twentieth centuries and is currently evident in the theologies of Küng, Moltmann, and Pannenberg.

Ironically, Schelling's influence is more widespread but lesser known. He has inspired Coleridge, Peirce, James, Bergson, Heidegger, Tillich, Hartshorne, Moltmann, and Clayton.

Background: Kant and Fichte

Schelling and Hegel developed their theologies in response to the master philosophers of the previous generation in Germany: Kant, who is not a panentheist, and Fichte, who is. We therefore highlight the ideas of Kant and Fichte that motivated Schelling and Hegel.

Kant's Unresolved View of God and World

Immanuel Kant (1724–1804) is an Enlightenment deist who interprets Christianity accordingly.[1] Two aspects of his philosophy, however, are conducive to panentheism. Negatively, his system leaves a number of unresolved oppositions or "antinomies," including a chasm between God and the world, that tantalizes dialectical thinkers, panentheists among them, to resolve. Positively, Kant proposes a doctrine of "transcendental subjectivity" from which Fichte, Schelling, and Hegel develop various forms of panentheism.

First, the unresolved antinomies. David Hume (1711–1776) had concluded that, since all knowledge is derived from experience, we have no basis for claiming that we know nature, our souls, or God as they are in themselves apart from experience.[2] Hume "awakened" Kant from his "dogmatic slumbers." To ground knowledge of these realities, Kant distinguishes between theoretical reason, which explains what things are, and practical reason, which tells us how we should live. In the *Critique of Pure Reason* (1781), he concedes that theoretical knowledge does not explain things in themselves but only our experience of them (*phenomena*). Experience, however, generates

1. Kant's *Religion within the Limits of Reason Alone* (1793) interprets the Bible and the basic doctrines of Christianity according to his moral philosophy. On Kant's religious ideas, see Emil Fackenheim, "Kant's Philosophy of Religion," in *The God Within: Kant, Schelling, and Historicity*, ed. John Burbidge (Toronto: University of Toronto Press, 1996), 3–19; James Livingston, *Modern Christian Thought: From the Enlightenment to Vatican II* (New York: Macmillan, 1971), 63–76; and Alan Wood, "Rational Theology, Moral Faith, and Religion," in *The Cambridge Companion to Kant*, ed. Paul Guyer (New York: Cambridge University Press, 1992), 394–416. Diogenes Allen, "Kant and the Limits of Knowledge," chap. 9 in *Philosophy for Understanding Theology* (Atlanta: John Knox, 1985), is an excellent short introduction to Kant. Copleston, *Hist. Phil.*, vol. 6, part 2, is more detailed.

2. Hume's skeptical conclusions are worked out in *An Inquiry concerning Human Understanding* (1748). His challenge to knowledge of God is developed in *Dialogues concerning Natural Religion*, which was not published until 1779, after his death.

legitimate ideas (*noumena*) of nature, our souls, and God, and we can have *practical* knowledge that they are real.[3] Kant makes his case in the *Critique of Practical Reason* (1788).[4] In brief, we humans know with certainty our moral obligation to attain the highest good. But the highest good is not attainable unless we are immortal and unless God exists as the Moral Judge and the Author of the world. Thus our moral nature gives us sufficient practical reason to believe in God, the soul, and nature even though we cannot prove them theoretically.

Kant's response to Hume is ingenious, but it leaves a significant gap between theoretical and practical knowledge, phenomenal and noumenal reality, determinism and freedom, and the world and God. Most readers at the time found his attempt to reconcile these dualities in his *Critique of Judgment* (1790) to be unsuccessful. Kant's unresolved antinomies enticed Neoplatonic and romantic dialecticians to try their hand at a solution.[5]

The second incentive toward panentheism in Kant's philosophy is his doctrine of the Transcendental Ego. Pondering the human soul, Kant postulates a transcendental subject or ego (*a noumenon*) behind the experience of the self and world (*phenomena*). In this preconscious dimension of subjectivity, Reason and the Understanding constitute, order, and unify our experience of self, nature, and morality.[6] The Transcendental Ego orders reality. But Kant also suggests that God, as the Author of the world and Moral Lawgiver, is a Transcendental Ego.[7] In "The Conflict of the Faculties" (1798), he also refers to "the God within us who speaks with us through our own intellect and reason"—closely linking God and human reason.[8] Kant's correlation of God, human subjectivity, and Transcendental Subjectivity raises questions: How many Transcendental Egos are there? Is God a Rational-Moral Ego distinct from human subjectivity? If not, then atheism is implied. Conversely, is each human an individual transcendental ego? If

3. Immanuel Kant, *Critique of Pure Reason*, trans. N. K. Smith (New York: Macmillan, 1929; repr., 1965). "The Canon of Pure Reason," chap. 2 of part 2, "The Transcendental Doctrine of Method," is a succinct summary of his whole philosophical project.

4. The arguments for immortality, God, and the coherence of nature and morality are in Immanuel Kant, *The Critique of Practical Reason*, trans. L. W. Beck (Indianapolis: Bobbs-Merrill, 1956), bk. 2.

5. Romantic and idealist responses to Kant's dualism are detailed by Emil Fackenheim in the first two sections of "Schelling in 1800–1801: Art as Revelation," in *The God Within*, ed. John Burbidge, 50–74; also Steve Wilkens and Alan G. Padgett, *Christianity and Western Thought* (Downers Grove, IL: InterVarsity, 2000), 2:16–18, 24.

6. Kant, "The Paralogisms of Pure Reason," chap. 1 of "Second Division: Transcendental Dialectic," bk. 1, in *Critique of Pure Reason*.

7. Kant, *Critique of Practical Reason*, bk. 2, chap. 2, sec. 7.

8. Quoted by Hendrikus Berkhof, *Two Hundred Years of Theology* (Grand Rapids: Eerdmans, 1989), 15–16.

not, then each of us is merely a bit of the One Transcendental Ego, which amounts to pantheism.

"Kant's readers were inclined to reinterpret his great undertaking either in a pantheistic or in an atheistic direction. Fichte was the first to attempt the former."[9] But panentheism is a third possibility. By affirming finite subjects within the Infinite Subject, one can appropriate Kant's philosophy in a way that preserves individuality against pantheism and God against atheism. This is Fichte's eventual solution.

Fichte's Panentheism

Johann Gottlieb Fichte (1762–1814) develops Kant's emphases on the Transcendental Ego and the moral will in order to overcome his dualisms.[10] In *The Science of Knowledge* (1794), he argues that it is unnecessary to postulate the soul and nature as things in themselves beyond experience, because Ego posits the world in relation to itself within experience.[11] Ego is not an entity—a thing or substance—but rational-moral activity, the unity of knowing and doing. By a preconscious act of rational-moral will, Ego posits itself in experience as distinct from, limited by, and acting upon Non-ego—the things that constitute the world of experience—and does so in order to have a realm for rational-moral activity. The positing process is dialectical: Ego posits itself (thesis: *A*) as Non-ego (anti-thesis: *not-A*) in order to achieve synthesis (*A and not-A*) by practical-rational activity. Fichte is the first to use the terms *thesis*, *antithesis*, and *synthesis*. He hereby appropriates traditional Neoplatonic dialectic and passes it to Schelling and Hegel.[12]

But what about God, Kant's third thing in itself? Fichte in "On the Foundation of Our Belief in a Divine Government of the World" (1798) argues that Ego must be Infinite and Absolute because the rational-moral activity that posits the world of individual egos and finite things cannot itself be finite and relative.[13] Further, since God is Infinite and Absolute Ego, he cannot

9. Ibid., 17.

10. Wilkens and Padgett, *Christianity and Western Thought*, 2:66–72, is a good short introduction to Fichte. Philip Clayton, "Excursus: Limits of Divine Personhood: Fichte and the Atheism Debate," chap. 8 in *The Problem of God in Modern Thought* (Grand Rapids: Eerdmans, 2000), is an excellent exposition of Fichte's theology in relation to pantheism and panentheism.

11. Johann Gottlieb Fichte, *Science of Knowledge* (*Wissenschaftslehre*), ed. and trans. Peter Heath and John Lachs (New York: Apple-Century-Crofts, 1970).

12. For a fuller explanation of dialectic, see "Dialectic: God's Nature and Way in the World" in the section on Hegel later in this chapter.

13. Johann Gottlieb Fichte, "On the Foundation of Our Belief in a Divine Government of the World," trans. Paul Edwards, in *Nineteenth-Century Philosophy*, ed. Patrick Gardiner (New York: Free Press, 1969), 19–26.

be personal because persons are essentially responsive and interrelate with other persons, which makes them finite. God is identical with the eternal rational-moral activity immanent and manifest in the human ego.

In *The Vocation of Man* (1800) Fichte reiterates God as "the One Eternal Infinite Will . . . the creator of the world, in the only way in which it can be and in which alone a creation is required: *infinite reason*."[14] The Infinite Will necessarily manifests itself through the finite ego in a plurality of finite beings unified within itself. "This will unites me with itself; it unites me with all finite beings like me and is the general mediator between all of us . . . *a world or a system of a number of individual wills: that union and direct interaction of a number of autonomous and independent wills with each other*." In other words, all of us are part of the one Will, but it is more than we are, even when taken all together. "All our life is Its life. We are in Its hand and remain there, and no one can tear us out of it. We are eternal because It is."[15]

Fichte's philosophy is often regarded as a kind of pantheistic idealism in which God is the Absolute Ego that posits everything finite, both minds and physical things. In fact his view is similar to Spinoza's, with the significant substitution of Absolute Ego/Will for Spinoza's Infinite Substance. Fichte, however, strongly distinguishes finite egos from Absolute Ego even though he locates all finite entities within Absolute Ego. He also stresses individual moral responsibility so emphatically that individual egos cannot simply be determined by Absolute Ego. Some level of individual autonomy is entailed. Fichte's modifications of Spinoza have convinced some scholars that his mature theology is panentheism. Copleston labels it "dynamic panentheistic idealism."[16] Hendrikus Berkhof considers him a "mystical panentheist."[17] Philip Clayton classifies him as a "mystical or metaphysical panentheist."[18]

Schelling

Fichte's dialectical attempt to explain reality from Absolute Ego was regarded by most of his contemporaries as one-sided and incomplete. In response, both Friedrich Wilhelm Joseph von Schelling (1775–1854) and

14. Johann Gottlieb Fichte, "Faith," bk. 3 in *The Vocation of Man*, trans. Peter Preuss (Indianapolis: Hackett, 1987), 110.

15. Ibid., 107–8, 111.

16. Copleston, *Hist. Phil.*, vol. 7, part 1, chap. 4, sec. 4, p. 109.

17. Berkhof, *Two Hundred Years of Theology*, 25–29, esp. "Panentheism as the End of the Road."

18. Clayton, *The Problem of God*, 445: "What makes Fichte's position panentheistic is that it combines the irreducible existence of individuals with the overarching unity of all things supplied by the One."

Georg Friedrich Wilhelm Hegel (1770–1831) developed more comprehensive systems. They were friends and roommates during their student days. Schelling was the first to publish his philosophy, became famous immediately, and initially influenced Hegel. And so we consider him first. Hegel took longer to develop his system, but once he did, he quickly eclipsed Schelling in reputation and influence. Schelling retreated into bitter obscurity, but he outlived Hegel and had the last word.

From his youth on, Schelling shared the romantic preoccupation with the One and took on the challenge of constructing a comprehensive philosophy that would resolve all dualisms and polarities. He was at home in the philosophical tradition from Plato through Eckhart, Nicholas of Cusa, Böhme, and Spinoza.[19] A prolific thinker, he developed three philosophical perspectives during his lifetime: a philosophy of the Absolute that identifies God and world, a personalism that emphasizes the freedom and cooperation of God and humans in history, and a philosophy of religion as divine revelation.[20] All his life Schelling defended "true pantheism," which turns out to be modern (dynamic, cooperative) panentheism. His early system of absolute identity states it inconsistently. His philosophy of personal freedom, on which we mainly focus, works it out. His mature philosophy of religion, which we briefly acknowledge, refines and applies it. We consider the development of his panentheism through each of these phases of his thought.

Schelling's Philosophy of Absolute Identity

Schelling's first approach aims at explaining all things in terms of the Absolute One. In *Philosophical Letters on Dogmatism and Criticism* (1795), he compares the Ground of the world as conceived by Spinoza (dogmatism) and Fichte (criticism).[21] Both thinkers move from Infinite to finite, and both

19. Friedrich Schelling, *On the History of Modern Philosophy*, trans. Andrew Bowie (Cambridge: Cambridge University Press, 1994), locates himself in this tradition. Also Copleston, *Hist. Phil.*, vol. 7, part 1, chap. 7, sec. 5: "Plato, the Neo-Platonists, Giordano Bruno, Jacob Boehme, Spinoza and Leibniz, not to mention Kant and Fichte, were all used as sources of inspiration."

20. Paul Tillich, *A History of Christian Thought: From Its Judaic and Hellenistic Origins to Existentialism*, ed. Carl Braaten (New York: Simon and Schuster, 1968), 437–48, and Wilkens and Padgett, *Christian and Western Thought*, 2:71–76, are short summaries. Copleston, *Hist. Phil.*, vol. 7, part 1, chaps. 5–7, and Alan White, *Schelling: An Introduction to the System of Freedom* (New Haven: Yale University Press, 1983), are excellent accounts of his whole project, including his views of God. Rowland Gray-Smith, *God in the Philosophy of Schelling* (Philadelphia: University of Pennsylvania Press, 1933), is dated but still illuminating.

21. Friedrich Schelling, *Philosophical Letters on Dogmatism and Criticism*, trans. Fritz Marti, in *The Unconditional in Human Knowledge: Four Early Essays, 1794–96* (Lewisburg, PA: Bucknell University Press, 1980).

eventually lose the finite subject—Spinoza to Absolute Object (Substance) and Fichte to Absolute Subject or Ego. Neither is adequate, but Schelling prefers Fichte's freedom to Spinoza's determinism.

He states his own view of the Absolute in *Ideas for a Philosophy of Nature* (1797). In the Absolute itself there is no difference between objective nature and subjective knowledge of nature: "The absolute contains neither Nature as Nature nor ideal world as ideal world, but both are as one world." Yet the Absolute posits itself as Nature both subjectively and objectively. "Nature in itself, or eternal Nature, is just Mind born into objectivity, the essence of God introduced into form." Schelling's language is Spinozan: the Absolute's subjective knowledge of Nature is *Natura naturans*. *Natura naturata* is objective nature, "Nature, in so far as it appears as Nature . . . *external* to the absolute."[22] Like the German romantics, he blends Spinoza with Platonism: *On the World Soul* (1798) identifies the World-Soul with *Natura naturans*.

Schelling's *System of Transcendental Idealism* (1800) seeks to justify the assumption from which his philosophy proceeds, that knowledge of the Absolute is possible. The first parts extend his philosophy of nature into theoretical philosophy, deriving the metaphysical categories of nature, such as space and causality. He eventually concludes with Kant and Fichte, however, that the primary interest of Ego is not theoretical but practical. Because the activity of Ego is basic in both, he asserts that "the beginning and ending of this philosophy is freedom."[23] Thus Schelling's search for the Absolute shifts to practical philosophy.

Here we glimpse the theme of Schelling's dynamic panentheism for the first time. He first argues that unless moral agents are autonomous—determining morality as well as being subject to it—we are mere objects of another kind of determinism in addition to the laws of nature. To ground individual moral autonomy, he follows Fichte and locates humans in God: "Every individual intelligence can be regarded as a constitutive part of God, or of the moral world-order."[24] As parts of God, we are like him in having freedom—moral *self*-determination.

22. Friedrich Schelling, introduction to *Ideas for a Philosophy of Nature as Introduction to the Study of This Science* (1797), trans. Errol Harris and Peter Heath (New York: Cambridge University Press, 1988), 50. Also Joseph Esposito, *Schelling's Idealism and Philosophy of Nature* (Lewisburg, PA: Bucknell University Press, 1977); and Dale Snow, *Schelling and the End of Idealism* (Albany: State University of New York Press, 1996), chap. 3, "Philosophy of Nature."

23. Friedrich Schelling, *System of Transcendental Idealism*, trans. Peter Heath (Charlottesville, VA: University Press of Virginia, 1978), 33.

24. Ibid., 206.

He then argues that God must be dynamic. Freedom entails that the complete unity of object and subject, the identity of nature and morality in the Absolute, and therefore God's relation to the world, cannot be a static, fully actual reality. The reason is this: If the full existence of God were already actual and perfectly fulfilled, then everything related to God would also already be completely determined. Humans would not be free and thus would not be human. In short, "if he existed thus, then we should not." So God must present himself gradually and progressively in human history.

A third implication follows. Because we humans participate in divine freedom—we are in God—God cannot exist without free human action. "If he *does* not exist independently of us, but reveals and discloses himself successively only, through the very play of our own freedom, so that without this freedom even he himself *would not be*, then we are collaborators of the whole and have ourselves invented the particular roles we play."[25] Therefore God and humans codetermine the course of their mutual self-actualization. God determines the end and general trajectory of history; humans determine the details of the journey. For Schelling, God does not even fully exist until the historical epoch of human freedom. "When this period will begin . . . God also will then *exist*."[26] In this way Schelling clearly states the twin themes of modern panentheism, that God's existence is essentially historical and that God and humans cooperate in their common existential quest to fulfill their destiny and actualize their essence in history.

Schelling also draws an epistemological conclusion. Because history is progressive, knowledge of the Absolute is no more than partial and provisional, and philosophy cannot achieve absolute knowledge. What, then, is the foundation for *Transcendental Idealism*, the question from which the book began? Kant and Fichte claimed to access the Absolute in morality, and Schleiermacher appealed to religion. Young Schelling delights the romantics by pointing to art: "An absolutely simple and identical [Reality] cannot be grasped or communicated through description, nor through concepts at all. It can only be intuited. . . . This intuition is the aesthetic."[27] Only art reveals the Absolute. Artistic creativity is the clearest manifestation of God. Philosophy is based on what the great artists intuit and represent.

In sum, Schelling's first philosophy is an aesthetically grounded idealism that asserts the progressive unity of Ego and Non-ego, humanity and nature, God and the world, regarding them as manifestations of the self-identical

---

25. Ibid., 210.
26. Ibid., 212.
27. Ibid., 229.

Absolute. Schelling still holds this position in *Bruno* (1802): "The absolute itself appears divided into difference and indifference, into the finite and the infinite . . . nature within God and God within nature."[28]

Schelling's theology at this stage seems ambivalent between pantheism and what we now call panentheism. His view of the world as the necessary manifestation of God recalls Spinoza: all creatures are within the living God, and this God is identical with the Soul—*Natura naturans*—that constitutes the human world. At the same time, his claim that free human action is partially constitutive of God's self-actualization anticipates modern panentheism. This theological ambivalence reflects the instability, if not incoherence, of his philosophy of absolute identity. For if identity is absolute—if God is utterly simple, without distinctions within himself—then how are the finite human perspective, the world of multiple polarities, and divine and human freedom even possible, much less necessary? Absolute identity and freedom are logically incompatible.

Schelling's Personalism: The Turn to Böhme

To relieve this tension, Schelling developed a more personalistic view of God, borrowing significantly from Jakob Böhme. Hints of this shift appear already in the 1804 essay *Philosophy and Religion*.[29] To ground the world in the Absolute without determinism, Schelling continues to emphasize the freedom of both: It is "distinctively characteristic of Absoluteness that it endows its counterpart with its own Being and also with independence. This being-in-itself, this true and genuine reality of the primal object of vision, is Freedom."[30] But if God and creatures are both truly free, then reason cannot fully explain the world's existence. It is an irrational leap: "The origin of the world of the senses is thinkable only as a complete breaking off from absoluteness through a leap . . . a *distancing*, in a *fall* from the absolute."[31] In his *System of Philosophy* (1804), Schelling even calls the actuality of finite enti-

28. Friedrich Schelling, *Bruno: On the Natural and the Divine Principle of Things*, ed. and trans. Michael Vater (Albany: State University of New York Press, 1984), 222. Schelling chooses Giordano Bruno as his own voice in this dialogue.

29. See James Gutman, introduction to Friedrich Schelling, *Philosophical Inquiries into the Nature of Human Freedom*, trans. James Gutman (Chicago: Open Court, 1936), xl–xliii; Copleston, *Hist. Phil.*, vol. 7, chap. 7, sec. 1; and White, *Schelling*, 97–101. Hereafter referred to as *Of Human Freedom*.

30. Friedrich Schelling, *Philosophy und Religion* [*Philosophy and Religion*], in *Sämtliche Werke*, ed. K. Schelling, 14 vols. (Stuttgart: Cotta, 1856–1861), 6:39–40, quoted in English from Gutman, introduction to Schelling, *Philosophical Inquiries*, xli. Heidegger's *Being and Time* develops Schelling's ideas of human existence (*Dasein*) as "being fallen," as "a leap," and as "thrown into the world."

31. Schelling, *Philosophy und Religion*, 6:38, quoted from White, *Schelling*, 98.

ties "a Fall—a *defectio*—from God . . . this is sin."[32] Here he adapts Böhme's notion of creation as cosmic fall and the groundless, irrational spontaneity in God himself (*Ungrund*) from which it springs.[33]

Philosophical Inquiries into the Nature of Human Freedom (1809) is Schelling's most important contribution to panentheism, what he calls "true pantheism" that affirms "the liveliest sense of freedom."[34] Spinoza's error, he writes, is not that "he posits *all things in God*, but . . . the abstract conception of . . . eternal Substance."[35] Schelling agrees that "man exists not outside God but in God, and that man's activity itself belongs to God's life." But in the divine Being are "man and his freedom."[36] Just as humans are free because they are in God, so God's self-actualization requires free human action. "The procession of things from God is God's self-revelation. But God can only reveal himself in creatures who resemble him, in free, self-activating beings."[37] These ideas were stated already in Schelling's *Transcendental Idealism*.

The main interest in *Of Human Freedom* is the problem of evil. Schelling poses the dilemma as follows: "Either real evil is admitted, in which case it is unavoidable to include evil itself in infinite Substance or in the primal Will, and thus totally disrupt the conception of an all-perfect Being; or the reality of evil must in some way or other be denied, in which case the real conception of freedom disappears at the same time."[38] Either evil is unreal or God is its cause. Schelling's solution to this perennial problem is to view God's freedom as the ground of the *possibility* of evil and human freedom as responsible for the *actuality* of evil.

He explains divine freedom in terms of the dialectic inherited from Nicholas of Cusa and Böhme: God's personal existence is the eternal self-unification of two opposing principles in the divine nature. Schelling's own "dialectical exposition" is dense but revealing: "The essence of the basis [*Grund*], or of existence, can only be precedent to all basis [*Urgrund*], that is, the absolute viewed directly, the groundless [*Ungrund*]. But . . . it cannot

32. Friedrich Schelling, *System der gesamte Philosophie und der Naturphilosophie inbesondere* [*System of Philosophy in General and of Nature in Particular*], in *Sämtliche Werke*, 6:552, quoted in English from Thomas O'Meara, "'Christianity Is the Future of Paganism': Schelling's Philosophy of Religion, 1826–1854," in *Meaning, Truth, and God*, ed. Leroy Rouner (Notre Dame, IN: University of Notre Dame Press, 1982), 235 n. 18.

33. Recall the section on Böhme in chap. 2, above. See also Copleston, *Hist. Phil.*, vol. 7, chap. 7, sec. 1.

34. Schelling, *Of Human Freedom*, 10.

35. Ibid., 22.

36. Ibid., 11.

37. Ibid., 19.

38. Ibid., 26.

be this in any other way than by dividing into two equally eternal beginnings. .... But the groundless divides itself into the two equally eternal beginnings only in order that the two . . . should become one through love; that is, it divides itself only that there may be life and love and personal existence."[39] In sum, two eternal principles in God are unified by a third factor, love.

Thus there are three divine "potencies." One eternal principle is "the abyss," "emptiness," "non-being," "nothingness," "pure potentiality," "contingency," "the darkness in the heart of God," "the unconscious," "will," "the longing which the eternal One feels to give birth to itself," "the non-ground (*Ungrund*) which is the primal ground (*Urgrund*)" of God's personal existence. The other principle is "God's essence, a light of life shining in the dark depths," "the principle of being," "reason," "order," "positivity," or the principle of "love."[40] God's actuality—his personal existence or life—is the eternal, necessary, self-generated synthesis of these two principles by the third, actualizing love. In this account, there is a truly free, indeterminate, spontaneous, creative dimension in God. Thus the necessity of the divine nature does not fully determine everything in God or in what proceeds from God. Schelling's theogony and cosmogony, involving the three divine principles or potencies, virtually reiterate Böhme's gnostic vision.

In the openness of divine indeterminacy, Schelling finds room for creation as spontaneous cosmic fall, for the possibility of evil, and for human freedom as the source of actual evil. The possibility of evil, we have seen, lies in the freedom of God—in the dark abyss beyond love and reason. But God's self-actualization eternally and necessarily unifies the two aspects of his nature in perfect harmony. God by nature freely wills the good. "But if God is essentially love and goodness, that which is morally necessary in him also follows with a genuinely metaphysical necessity."[41] Goodness is not, however, necessary in humans. In humanity, nature, freedom, and goodness are related contingently and can separate: "That unity which is indissoluble in God must be dissoluble in man—and this constitutes the possibility of

---

39. Ibid., 88–89.

40. Schelling uses all these Böhmian terms and more, ibid., 32–98. See Robert F. Brown, *The Later Philosophy of Schelling: The Influence of Boehme on the Works of 1809–1815* (Lewisburg, PA: Bucknell University Press, 1977). After hearing Schelling lecture in Berlin in 1841, Heinrich Heine quipped, "Once the cobbler Jacob Boehme talked like a philosopher; now the philosopher Schelling talks like a cobbler" (Heinrich Heine, *Die romantische Schule*, in *Sämtliche Werke* [Leipzig: Insel, 1910–15], 5:294, quoted in English by Fackenheim, "Schelling's Philosophy of Religion," in *The God Within*, ed. Burbidge, 209 n. 3).

41. Schelling, *Of Human Freedom*, 77.

good and evil."[42] Thus God's nature makes evil possible but not actual. Only humans can make it actual, and we inevitably do.

But could God not have created the world and prevented evil? Schelling is forthright: if God exists, then the world, freedom, and evil are inevitable. He agrees with Leibniz that "just as there is only one God, so there is but one possible world."[43] The only way God could have avoided the fallen world is by choosing not to exist: "In order that evil should not be, God himself would have not to be." But God rejects nonexistence because he is good. "God's self-revelation should be regarded ... as an act morally necessary, in which love and goodness triumphed over absolute inwardness."[44] God, freedom, and evil are necessary because a good God wills to exist. Evil must become actual in order to be eliminated. This is the very purpose of God's existence: "The good is to be raised out of darkness to actuality in order to dwell with God everlastingly; and evil is to be separated from goodness in order to be cast out eternally into non-being. For this is the final purpose of creation."

Thus world history is God's history, and it is redemptive history. It actualizes the good, incorporates it into God, and ultimately renders evil impossible. This process not only saves humanity and the world; it also culminates in the full existence of God. "Thus in its freedom the basis [*Grund*] effects the separation and the judgment [of evil] and in this very way accomplishes God's complete actualization."[45] Böhme's gnostic dialectic of good and evil lives on in Schelling.

Unlike Fichte's God, Schelling's is personal. The same dialectical self-generation that triumphs over evil makes God personal, just as humans acquire personhood and personality as they mature by integrating their competing rational-moral and physical-emotional natures. "We have explained God as the living unity of forces; and if personality consists ... in the connection of an autonomous being with a basis which is independent of it, in such a way namely that these two completely interpenetrate one another and are but one being, then God is the highest personality."[46] The unity of the three

---

42. Ibid., 39.

43. Ibid., 78.

44. Ibid., 83. The idea that God is free not to exist might seem implausible or absurd, but it is a given in Schelling's theology. See Robert Brown, "Schelling and Dorner on Divine Immutability," *JAAR* 53/2 (1985), 241–42: "Schelling's God is a voluntary duality-in-unity. On the one hand, this God's being is freely willed; the freedom pole need not dominate the trio of powers, and if it does not, there is no actual God. On the other hand, he has to have the structure he does have.... Hence God freely wills (and does not have to will) *that* he is, but in so willing God does not (in a capricious sense) will *what* he is."

45. Schelling, *Of Human Freedom*, 85.

46. Ibid., 74. "Because there is in God an independent basis of reality, and hence two equally eternal beginnings of self-revelation, therefore God with respect to his freedom, must also be viewed

potencies in God already makes him personal in his eternal essence. In actuality, moreover, God grows through suffering just as humans do. "God is a life, not a mere being. All life has a destiny and is subject to suffering and development. God freely submitted himself to this too, in the very beginning, when, in order to become personal, he divided light and the world of darkness. For being is only aware of itself in becoming."[47] Thus God's essence is eternal and immutable, but his existence involves growth, change, and suffering. God in himself is personal, but God in actual existence acquires personhood by developing in and through the world, especially its conflict and suffering.

Schelling follows Böhme in detailing how God's dialectical self-generation actualizes the Trinity through nature and history. "There is born in God himself . . . the first stirring of divine Being. . . . God sees himself in his own image . . . the God-begotten . . . and the eternal Spirit which feels within it the eternal Logos and the everlasting longing. This Spirit . . . utters the Word which then becomes creative and omnipotent Will . . . which informs nature."[48] In other words, the One reflects itself as Word, which it empowers as Spirit. Nature, Schelling explains, is the initial way in which God actualizes his triune essence. Nature expresses the divine Word, but Nature does not use language. "Only in man is the Word completely articulate, which in all other creatures was held back and left unfinished. But in articulate Word the spirit reveals itself, that is God as existing, in act."[49] Schelling continues to identify the world with God's self-actualization, human freedom with God's freedom, human language with the divine Word, and religion with divine self-knowledge. In all of this, the triune essence of God becomes actually triune in and through nature and human history.[50]

Schelling concludes *Of Human Freedom* still linking his theology with pantheism: "Since all antitheses disappear with respect to the Absolute when regarded as such, whoever wishes to call this system pantheism should have

---

in relation to both. The first beginning of creation is the longing of the One to give birth to itself, or the will of the depths. The second is the will of love through which the Word is pronounced in nature and through which God first makes himself personal." Recall that Fichte and Schleiermacher denied that God is personal.

47. Ibid., 84.

48. Ibid., 35–36. Gray-Smith, "The Triune God," chap. 7 in *God in the Philosophy of Schelling*, details Schelling's elaboration of the Trinity in terms of the "three potencies": $A1 = -A$ (nonbeing), $A2 = +A$ (the principle of being), and their synthesis, $A3 = (-A \text{ and } +A)$.

49. Schelling, *Of Human Freedom*, 39.

50. This is a common assertion in Rahner, Moltmann, and Pannenberg.

the privilege."[51] But he insists that his emphasis on humanity and freedom distinguishes him from Spinoza's "God or Nature." "Only man is in God, and through this very being-in-God is capable of freedom. . . . In him [man] all things are created, just as it is also only through man that God accepts nature. . . . Man is the beginning of the new covenant . . . as mediator . . . the redeemer of nature . . . the Word."[52] In this passage Schelling's correlation of God and humanity is so strong that Man is Christic—God is in him and he is in God—incarnate, living, acting, and suffering for the salvation of the world. Schelling's earlier language of absolute identity is no longer present. All things considered, his "pantheism" is more accurately understood as a cooperative personal panentheism.

His final work of this period, *The Ages of the World* (1811–1815), is a dense poetic elaboration of his Böhmian theology of freedom.[53] Its original conception was grand: a three-volume account of the dialectic of God in himself (God's past), God's generation of nature (God's present), and God's self-revelation in human history (God's future). But Schelling completed only book 1 on God in himself and God in nature.[54]

His panentheism of personal freedom, to the extent that it is developed, is even more elaborate and striking than in *Of Human Freedom*. God's existence is the synthesis of his nature and freedom: The "Godhead is whole and undivided, the eternal Yes and the eternal No, the Godhead is again neither one nor the other, but the unity of both."[55] The Godhead first actualizes itself in nature as a world-embodying Soul. "This soul has its ectype in an external spiritual-corporeal being . . . the first actual existence of God."[56] But the central purpose of God's life is his redemptive participation in human history, especially in its suffering. "Suffering is universal . . . also with respect to the creator . . . God leads human nature down no other path than that down which God Himself must pass. Participating in everything blind, dark, and evil, the suffering of God's

51. Schelling, *Philosophical Inquiries*, 91.

52. Ibid., 92.

53. Friedrich Schelling, *The Ages of the World* (3rd version, 1815), trans. Jason M. Wirth (Albany: State University of New York Press, 2000); also *The Ages of the World* (2nd draft, 1813), trans. Judith Norman, in Slavoj Zizek, *The Abyss of Freedom/Ages of the World* (Ann Arbor: University of Michigan Press, 1997); and Paul Collins Hayner, "The History of Mankind," chap. 5 in *Reason and Existence: Schelling's Philosophy of History* (Leiden: E. J. Brill, 1967). Charles Hartshorne and William Reese, *Philosophers Speak of God* (Chicago: University of Chicago Press, 1953), 233–43, excerpt passages from *Ages of the World* to exhibit Schelling as "the first modern panentheist."

54. Wirth in Schelling, *Ages of the World*, trans. Wirth, xxxiii–xxxiv, presents the "Synoptic Table of Contents" developed by Schelling's son, Karl, and published in the original edition. It clearly outlines the layers of dialectical and subdialectic in Schelling's theogony and cosmogony.

55. Ibid., 74.

56. Ibid., 88.

nature is necessary in order to elevate God to the highest consciousness."[57] God actualizes himself by involving himself in the world and saving it. Schelling concludes *Ages of the World* by reiterating his claim to "true pantheism."[58] In retrospect, it is the first articulation of modern panentheism.

Schelling's "Positive" Philosophy of Religion

Schelling did not finish *Ages of the World*. Perhaps he realized that because God's future is open, his history cannot yet be written.[59] Even God cannot predict the course of human freedom in history or know the particularities of his own destiny. For this reason, humans must take God's presence in history as it comes. Thus philosophy must be "positive," beginning from what is so far revealed in history. Reason can neither justify nor fully explain revelation. This is why Schelling turned to "positive philosophy" and "revealed" religion.[60] But he had emphasized the limited basis of philosophy ever since *Transcendental Idealism* in his first period.

It is important to stress that Schelling's final philosophy of religion does not depart from his panentheism of divine-human freedom but builds on it. If anything, the Böhmian language of "three potencies" becomes more prominent.[61] What changes is his focus on precisely where God actualizes himself in and through humanity.

Religion is where the general self-actualization of God in history is most explicit. God exists in nature and human history, but religion, particularly in its myths and symbols, is where humans become aware of the God who personalizes himself in nature and humanity. Correlatively, the personal self-consciousness of God emerges through his self-manifestation in human religion. Thus the history of revelation and the history of religion are two sides of the same coin.[62] Because revelation is progressive, religion and its

---

57. Ibid., 101.

58. Ibid., 104–8.

59. Schelling, ibid., 45, translates the divine name in Exod. 3:14 as "I will be that I will be," anticipating many twentieth-century theologians who think that God develops.

60. Fackenheim, "Schelling's Philosophy of Religion" and "Schelling's Conception of Positive Philosophy" in *The God Within*, ed. Burbidge, 92–108 and 109–21; O'Meara, "Christianity Is the Future of Paganism," 216–36.

61. Edward Allen Beach, *The Potencies of God(s): Schelling's Philosophy of Mythology* (Albany: State University of New York Press, 1994).

62. Schelling is the main source of Tillich's theology, including his theory that religious symbols do not describe but "participate" in God. See Paul Tillich, "Religious Symbols and Our Knowledge of God," *Christian Scholar* 38/3 (1955): 189–97; and *The Construction of the History of Religion in Schelling's Positive Philosophy: Its Presuppositions and Principles*, trans. Victor Nuovo (Lewisburg, PA: Bucknell University Press, 1974).

symbolism develop in stages: mythology in natural religion, positive revelation in supernatural religion, and finally philosophical religion. But contrary
to Hegel, Schelling denies that philosophy can dispel the mystery of God,
which is rooted in divine-human freedom.[63]

Schelling's Panentheism: A Summary

Throughout his life Schelling regarded himself as the champion of "true
pantheism," what we now term modern or dynamic panentheism. His "God
or Freedom" is different than Spinoza's "God or Nature." Even his early
philosophy of absolute identity strongly distinguishes God and creatures,
grants both freedom, and locates humanity "in God." His panentheism gains
clarity with his Böhmian theology of divine and human personhood. God's
essence is the eternal self-generating union of opposites. But his existence
is a progressive self-actualization of his essence in and through the action
of free creatures, their suffering, and eventual triumph.

A number of scholars regard Schelling as a panentheist. His emphasis
on divine-human interaction and its implication that God has two natures
(eternal and temporal) move Hartshorne and Reese to feature him as the first
truly modern panentheist, "the most radical to be met with in all philosophy
prior to Whitehead."[64] Wilkens and Padgett conclude that "Schelling's view
is not so much pantheistic as it is panentheistic. God is unified with his
creation but is also its Creator."[65] Clayton adopts Schelling's later theology
as the basis for his own. "The most adequate position is what Schelling calls
'true theism' . . . the view that I am here labeling *panentheism.*"[66]

Although Schelling was overshadowed by Hegel, his influence remained
a strong current in nineteenth- and twentieth-century theology. Indeed,
contemporary theologians, such as Tillich and Moltmann, who combine
trinitarian panentheism with human freedom in a nondeterministic view
of history, reflect more of Schelling than Hegel.

---

63. Friedrich Schelling, *Philosophie der Mythologie* [*Philosophy of Mythology*], 2 vols. (Darmstadt: Wissenschaftliche Buchgesellschaft, 1957); *Philosophie der Offenbarung* [*Philosophy of Revelation*] (Darmstadt:
Wissenschaftliche Buchgesellschaft, 1966), a photo reproduction of the handwritten text.

64. Hartshorne and Reese, *Philosophers Speak of God*, 233–34. Arthur O. Lovejoy, *The Great Chain of
Being: The History of an Idea* (Cambridge, MA: Harvard University Press, 1936; repr., 1964), 323, points
out that Schelling is the first thinker to develop a truly evolutionary theology in which God himself
actually develops. He does not, however, use the term *panentheism*.

65. Wilkens and Padgett, *Christianity and Western Thought*, 2:73.

66. Clayton, *The Problem of God*, 479–80. "True theism" is a later term for the same theology that
Schelling earlier called "true pantheism."

Hegel

Georg Wilhelm Friedrich Hegel (1770–1831) and Schelling were youthful friends in seminary at the University of Tübingen. Schelling quickly gained a reputation as a promising philosopher. Hegel adopted some of his central ideas but concluded that Schelling's philosophy of identity utterly fails to explain the unity of diversity. He regarded Schelling's lifelong belief that art and religion provide the surest access to the Absolute as an admission of failure. In contrast, he claimed that his own philosophy is God's path to absolute self-knowledge.

Hegel's Theological-Philosophical Project

Hegel accepts the same challenge as Schelling and other Romantic thinkers: to give a comprehensive account of the relative and the Absolute, the many and the One, the world and God.[67] He agrees with Schelling that Fichte's philosophy absolutizes Ego and reduces nature to an opportunity for morality. But he sides with Fichte against Schelling and Schleiermacher that philosophy, not aesthetic or religious intuition, must justify our claims about the Absolute.

Unlike Schelling, Hegel does not shift perspectives during his career. His constant preoccupation—the dialectical self-actualization of the Absolute (God, Spirit) in and through the world—is sketched already in *Fragments of a System* (1800) and *The Difference between Fichte's and Schelling's Systems of Philosophy* (1801). Each subsequent publication works out his vision in greater detail. His philosophy and theology can be distinguished but never separated.

His first major work, *Phenomenology of Spirit* (1807), explicates the dialectical appearance of Spirit through increasingly complex levels of human consciousness—from individual sense impressions of nature, through various kinds of social consciousness, to morality, art, and religion. In philosophy, he

67. Georg Hegel, *Lectures on the History of Philosophy*, trans. H. S. Haldane, 3 vols. (London: Kegan Paul, Trench, Trübner, 1892–1896; repr. with introduction by Frederick C. Beiser; Lincoln: University of Nebraska Press, 1995).

Eric Rust, "The Absolute Spirit and Process—From Being to Becoming," chap. 2 in *Evolutionary Philosophies and Contemporary Theology* (Philadelphia: Westminster, 1969); Robert Solomon, "Hegel and the Apotheosis of Self as Spirit," chap. 4 in *A History of Philosophy since 1750* (New York: Oxford University Press, 1988); Allen, "Hegel and the Restoration of Optimism," chap. 10 in *Philosophy for Understanding Theology*; and Wilkens and Padgett, *Christianity and Western Thought*, 2:76–86, are theologically oriented overviews of Hegel. Copleston, *Hist. Phil.*, vol. 7, part 1, chaps. 9–11, is a clear exposition of his entire system. A fine book-length treatment is Charles Taylor, *Hegel* (Cambridge: Cambridge University Press, 1975).

asserts, Spirit can finally reach absolute self-knowledge, the "unity of Being and Thought. . . . Here, therefore, God is *revealed as He is*; He is immediately present as He is *in Himself*, i.e., He is immediately *present* as Spirit."[68] *The Science of Logic* (1812–1816) is Hegel's dialectical deduction of the basic logical and metaphysical categories of reality, beginning from Being itself: "This content is the exposition of God as he is in his eternal essence before the creation of nature and a finite mind."[69]

Hegel begins *The Encyclopedia of Philosophical Sciences* (3 editions: 1817, 1827, 1830) by stating that philosophy and religion "both hold that *God* and God *alone* is the truth. Both of them also go on to deal with the realm of the finite, with *nature* and the *human spirit*, and with their relation to each other and to God as their truth."[70] The *Encyclopedia* is a comprehensive justification of this claim. In addition to his books, Hegel repeated several series of lectures at the University of Berlin on politics, history, art, religion, and philosophy that further elaborate his theological-philosophical system with relentless logic and great detail.

The 1827 *Lectures on the Philosophy of Religion* concludes that philosophy "is the justification of religion, especially of the Christian religion, the true religion; it knows the content in accord with its necessity and reason." Further, "philosophy is to this extent theology. It presents the reconciliation of God with himself and with nature, showing that nature, otherness, is implicitly divine, and that the raising of itself to reconciliation is on the one hand what finite spirit implicitly is, while on the other hand it arrives at this reconciliation, or brings it forth, in world history."[71] When Hegel died of cholera in 1831, his system was largely complete. His philosophy is not just theological; it is also a wholesale reconstruction of the Christian faith as dialectical historical panentheism.[72]

68. Georg Hegel, "Revealed Religion," in *The Phenomenology of Spirit*, trans. A. V. Miller (Oxford: Oxford University Press, 1977), par. 761, p. 461.

69. Georg Hegel, introduction to *Science of Logic*, trans. A. V. Miller (London: Allen and Unwin, 1969; repr., Atlantic Highlands, NJ: Humanities Press International, 1989), 50.

70. Georg Hegel, introduction to *The Encyclopedia of Logic, with the Zusätze: Part I of the Encyclopedia of Philosophical Sciences with the Zusätze*, trans. T. F. Geraets, W. A. Suchting, and H. S. Harris (Indianapolis and Cambridge, UK: Hackett, 1991), par. 1, 24.

71. Georg Hegel, *Lectures on the Philosophy of Religion*, ed. P. Hodgson, 1-vol. ed. (Berkeley: University of California Press, 1988), 487, 489.

72. It is astounding that Hegel's religious and theological interests were largely ignored for more than a century, at least by English-speaking philosophers. This began to change in the 1960s. See, e.g., Stephen Crites, "The Gospel according to Hegel," *JR* 46 (1966): 246–63, and Emil Fackenheim, *The Religious Dimension in Hegel's Thought* (Bloomington: Indiana University Press, 1967).

Dialectic: God's Nature and Way in the World

Hegel likely obtained from his friend Schelling the idea that the Absolute progressively actualizes itself through nature and history. But he rejected Schelling's philosophy of absolute identity because it cannot explain how it is possible to derive polarity (A and not-A) and diversity ($B, C, D, \ldots N$) from absolute identity ($A = A$). Hegel judged that Schelling left an unintelligible chasm between God and the world, and he dismissed his notion of absolute identity as "the night in which . . . all cows are black."[73]

To succeed where Schelling failed, he proposed that the Absolute in itself is not simple identity in distinction from the diversity and polarities of the world but must include them within itself. "The Absolute itself is *absolute identity*; this is its *determination*, for in it all manifoldness of the world-in-itself and the world of Appearance, or of inner and outer totality, is sublated."[74] His reason is the familiar argument from Infinity. "If God has the finite only over against himself, then he himself is finite and limited. Finitude must be posited in God himself."[75]

The nature of the Absolute is three-dimensional: self-identity, otherness, and their perpetual unification within itself. In Hegel's own rather difficult terminology, the Absolute is "*Spirit*. . . . The spiritual alone is the *actual*; it is essence, or that which has *being in itself*; it is that which *relates itself to itself* and *is determinate*, it is *other-being* and *being-for-self*, and in this determinateness, or in its externality, abides within itself; in other words, it is *in and for itself*."[76] In other words, the "in itself," "for itself," and "in and for itself" are not just abstract dimensions of a static Absolute. They are dynamic correlates in the reality of its life: "The *triadic form* must not be . . . reduced to a lifeless schema . . . degraded into a table of terms." For "[it is] the life of the Notion itself . . . ; the self-moving soul of the realized content."[77]

The Absolute posits itself as other than itself in order to constitute a self-conscious unity of the differences within itself. It exists according to the "Heraclitean principle," that is, dialectic, in order to attain absolute knowledge.

The essence of each thing lies in determination, in what is the opposite of itself. . . . Its essence as this identity is . . . to pass over into its opposite, or to

---

73. Hegel, *Phenomenology*, preface, par. 16, p. 9.

74. Hegel, "The Absolute," chap. 1 in *Science of Logic*, vol. 1, bk. 2, sec. 3, p. 531.

75. Hegel, *Lectures on the Philosophy of Religion* (1988), 406. This is Hegel's version of the argument from the True Infinite, developed by Eriugena and Nicholas of Cusa and still used by Pannenberg and Clayton.

76. Hegel, *Phenomenology*, preface, par. 25, p. 14.

77. Ibid., par. 50, 53, pp. 29, 31–32.

realize itself, to become for itself something different; and thus the opposition in it is brought about by itself . . . ; the true reconciliation of the opposition is the perception that this opposition, when pushed to its absolute extreme, resolves itself; as Schelling says . . . eternal life consists in the very process of continually producing the opposition and continually reconciling it. To know opposition in unity, and unity in opposition—this is absolute knowledge.[78]

By locating dialectic not only in the world but also in the essence of the Absolute itself, Hegel claims to solve Schelling's problem and to provide a coherent account of the many in One, the finite in the Infinite, the relative in the Absolute, that is, the world in God.[79]

A fuller explanation of dialectic might be helpful.[80] Dialectical logic moves beyond the polarities and contradictions—the positions and counterpositions, or *theses* and *antitheses*—that exist on particular levels of knowledge. It demonstrates that they are components of a higher unity—a *synthesis* that preserves the essential truth of each in a noncontradictory way. We see this sort of rationality at work in ordinary conversation when people who initially disagree engage in dialogue until they find common ground consistent with both of their initial positions. Put formally, a thesis A elicits its antithesis *not-A*. In ordinary logic, this is a contradiction: *A or not-A, but not both*. In dialectical logic, however, both A and *not-A* are shown to be true when preserved in a higher, more complex synthesis, B. Thus B is the truth of (*A and not-A*).

Hegel argues that absolute knowledge can be attained by reasoning dialectically until all antitheses are elicited and preserved in a single comprehensive synthesis. Formally stated, A elicits *not-A*; A and *not-A* are reconciled in B; B (*A and not-A*) elicits *not-B*, and B and *not-B* are reconciled and preserved in C; C (B [*A and not-A*] and *not-B* [*A and not-A*]) implies *not-C*, which are combined in D; and so forth. In principle this line of thought can continue until Y and *not-Y* are reconciled in Z, and Z generates no *not-Z* because it contains all previous polarities, leaving nothing outside of itself to oppose it. In that case, the massively complex concept Z will contain the truth of all

78. Georg Hegel, *Lectures on the History of Philosophy: The Abridged Student Edition*, trans. H. S. Haldane, ed. Tom Rockmore (Atlantic Highlands, NJ: Humanities, 1996), 701–2.

79. Recall that Schelling also moved beyond his philosophy of identity to a personalism that followed Böhme and included dialectic in God. But Hegel's 1807 *Phenomenology* far surpassed Schelling in applying dialectic to God and the world.

80. Michael Forster, "Hegel's Dialectical Method," in *The Cambridge Companion to Hegel*, ed. F. C. Beiser (Cambridge: Cambridge University Press, 1993), 130–70, is helpful. Michael Kosok, "The Formalization of Hegel's Dialectical Logic," in *Hegel: A Collection of Critical Essays*, ed. A. MacIntyre (Notre Dame, IN: Notre Dame University Press, 1976), 237–88, is more technical.

lesser truths in a single coherent unity without any of the contradictions or opposition between them that obtains on lower levels: Z is ([Y and not-Y], Y is [X and not-X], X is [W and not-W] . . . and B is [A and not-A]). Thus Z is shown to be the one, infinite, absolute, and necessary proposition, but it includes all the many, finite, relative, and contingent propositions. If Z is not merely an idea but the self-comprehending mind of God, then all things are in God and panentheism is fully real and fully rational.

God Comprehending the World in Himself

Hegel asserts that the Absolute as Spirit does actualize itself in the world dialectically in order to comprehend itself. No place is this more clearly stated than in the "Final Result" of his *Lectures on the History of Philosophy*.[81] His detailed explanation of how the Absolute actualizes itself through the dialectical relationship Nature, Spirit, and Reason far surpasses Schelling. It is worth parsing this typically dense passage.

First he asserts their distinctness and correlation: "The sides of [the Absolute's] diremption, Nature and Spirit, are each of them recognized as representing the totality of the Idea. . . . Nature, and the world or history of spirit, are the two realities; what exists as actual Nature is an image of divine Reason; the forms of self-conscious Reason are also the forms of Nature." Then he explains the unity of Nature and Spirit in the Absolute as a manifestation of Reason, grasped and justified by philosophy: "In apprehension the spiritual and the natural universe are interpenetrated as one harmonious universe, which withdraws into itself, and in its various aspects develops the Absolute into a totality, in order, by the very process of so doing, to become conscious of itself in its unity, in Thought. Philosophy is thus the true theodicy."[82] The same rational Spirit that is implicit in Nature articulates itself with increasing self-consciousness through the human spirit in society, state, culture, and especially in theoretical knowledge: "Spirit produces itself as Nature, [and] as the State; nature is its unconscious work, in the course of which it appears to itself something different, and not spirit; but in the State, in the deeds and life of History, as also of Art, it brings itself to pass with consciousness; it knows very various modes of its reality, yet they are only modes. In scientific knowledge alone it knows itself as absolute spirit; and this knowledge, or spirit, is its only true existence."[83] In human knowledge, Spirit explicates the Reason that is implicit in all of nature and humanity.

81. Hegel, *Lectures on the History of Philosophy* (1996), 696–705.
82. Ibid., 696–97.
83. Ibid., 703.

Hegel boldly asserts that philosophy not only is the clearest and most comprehensive human knowledge but is also God's cumulative self-knowledge. "To this point the World-spirit has come, and each stage has its own form in the true system of Philosophy; nothing is lost, all principles are preserved, since Philosophy in its final aspect is the totality of forms." The history of philosophy is God's own quest. "This work of the spirit to know itself . . . is the life of the spirit and the spirit itself. . . . The history of Philosophy is a revelation of what has been the aim of spirit throughout its history . . . one Philosophy in its development, the revelation of God, as He knows Himself to be." Hegel was not shy about asserting his own crucial role in this history: "A new epoch has arisen in the world. It would appear as if the World-spirit had . . . succeeded in . . . apprehending itself at last as absolute Spirit. . . . Finite self-consciousness has ceased to be finite. . . . This is the whole history of the world in general up to the present time, and the history of Philosophy in particular. . . . At this point I bring this history of Philosophy to a close."[84] Like the Virgin Mary, Hegel is the humble servant of the Lord, pregnant with God's own self-knowledge.

Hegel's divine-human system deserves a straightforward summary: The Absolute in itself is essentially dialectical. Thus it does not exist in itself but naturally posits itself as other than itself. The One Infinite Absolute appears first in Nature as many finite, relative entities. At this stage, Spirit is the Life Force of Nature. From Nature, which is unconscious and unspiritual, Spirit posits itself as other than Nature in finite Spirit. It posits subjective Spirit by generating humanity with the capacities for knowledge, communication, and practical activity. Through these capacities Spirit posits itself objectively in the cultural artifacts, political communities, forms of morality, and intellectual constructs that humans develop in history. But although Spirit is active and conscious in human culture and society, it is still finite and not yet explicitly aware of itself as Spirit—the One, Infinite, Absolute. Its crucial turn toward self-consciousness occurs in the history of religion, the progressive awareness of Spirit's "otherness," universality, and creative power as God. But ultimate self-knowledge is acquired only through philosophy, where the true nature and history of Spirit as Absolute are set forth completely, both conceptually and systematically.[85] In sum, world history is God's self-actualization, self-liberation, and self-comprehension. "The Truth is the whole. But the whole is nothing other than the essence consummating itself through its

84. Ibid., 697–98, 702–3.

85. Hegel agreed with Schelling that the Absolute is accessible in art and religion, but he insisted, against Schelling and Schleiermacher, that philosophy discloses it most fully and clearly.

development. Of the Absolute it must be said that it is essentially a *result*, that only in the *end* is it what it truly is."[86]

Divine Freedom and Historical Determinism

Divine freedom is crucial for Hegel because world history is God's self-liberation. Freedom is "the absolute end and aim of the world."[87] God is free in that he is absolutely rational and self-consciously self-determining. His action intentionally expresses his nature without any internal compulsion or external coercion. But God's action is also completely determined, albeit by himself, that is, by his nature. It is the Absolute's nature to posit itself in order to become completely one with itself. Not having a world is not an option for God. "It belongs to his being, his essence to be the creator."[88] Thus God is not free not to posit the world and not free not to realize himself dialectically in and through the world. "Without the world God is not God."[89] What is must be.

Hegel therefore holds a *compatibilist* view of God's freedom: freedom and determination are compatible—two sides of one coin. God does not have *libertarian* freedom—the choice whether to create the world, or which world to create, or how to relate to the world. God necessarily determines the world and the course of history as it is.

But Hegel's view requires only general divine determination, not determination of every detail in nature and history. The kinds of societies, civilizations, political institutions, religions, and philosophies must develop more or less as they have. But the existence of each individual person, the actions they each engage in, and even the events of particular nations and cultures need not be thought of as divinely determined in meticulous detail. The wisdom of Spirit inexorably weaves the lives of individuals and nations and the events of history into the grand dialogue of its own inevitable self-fulfillment. Therefore Hegel's view of human freedom is also compatibilist. A person is truly free who intentionally acts without coercion or compulsion in accordance with his rational nature and destiny in world history. Here Hegel is closer to Spinoza than Schelling.

---

86. Hegel, *Phenomenology*, par. 20, p. 11.

87. Georg Hegel, *Philosophy of Right*, trans. T. M. Knox (Oxford: Clarendon, 1942), sec. 129. See Richard Schacht, "Hegel on Freedom," in *Hegel: A Collection of Critical Essays*, ed. MacIntyre, 289–328.

88. Hegel, *Lectures on the Philosophy of Religion* (1988), 417.

89. Georg Hegel, *Lectures on the Philosophy of Religion*, trans. E. Haldane and F. Simpson, 3 vols. (London: Routledge and Kegan Paul, 1955), 1:200.

Philosophy Explicates the Trinity and the Incarnation

Hegel regards his philosophy to be the definitive explication of the Christian faith, not merely of religion in general.[90] He values Christianity as the culmination of world religions, "the absolute religion," "the revealed religion," "the consummate religion,"[91] because he thinks its doctrines of the incarnation and the Trinity most fully symbolize ultimate philosophical truth.

The Christian affirmation of the incarnation of Jesus Christ as the God-man, according to Hegel, is the religious representation of the truth that God actualizes himself in humanity, beginning as an individual. He holds this view already in the *Phenomenology*: "God is sensuously and directly beheld as a Self, as an actual individual man; only so is this God self-consciousness. . . . This incarnation of the divine Being . . . is the simple content of the absolute religion."[92] He affirms it again in *Lectures on the Philosophy of Religion*: "The unity of divine and human nature comes to consciousness for humanity in such a way that a human being appears to consciousness as God, and God appears to it as a human being."[93] Indeed, this mature work of Hegel's provides a philosophical interpretation of Jesus's incarnation, ministry, death, resurrection, and mission of the Holy Spirit as dialectical steps in God's self-deployment in the world—"divine history," "redemptive history," "the coming of God's Kingdom."[94]

The incarnation involves the Trinity, for Christ is the Son of God, the Word made flesh. Throughout his philosophical career, Hegel regards the Christian doctrine of the Trinity as the religious representation—"the picture-thinking of the religious community"[95]—of the conceptual truth that the Absolute is essentially dialectical in nature, both in itself and in the world.[96] In *Phenomenology* he notes "three distinct moments: essence, being-for-self

90. Crites, "The Gospel according to Hegel," and Livingston, *Modern Christian Thought*, 143–57, are excellent summaries of Hegel's philosophical account of Christianity. Also Philip M. Merklinger, *Philosophy, Theology, and Hegel's Berlin Philosophy of Religion, 1821–1827* (Albany: State University of New York Press, 1993); and Stephen Crites, *Dialectic and Gospel in the Development of Hegel's Thinking* (University Park: University of Pennsylvania Press, 1998).

91. Hegel, *Phenomenology*, par. 759, pp. 459–60; *Lectures on the Philosophy of Religion* (1988), part 3, "The Consummate Religion."

92. Hegel, *Phenomenology*, par. 758–59, p. 459.

93. Hegel, *Lectures on the Philosophy of Religion* (1988), 454.

94. Ibid., part 3, "The Consummate Religion," 452–89.

95. Hegel, *Phenomenology*, par. 771, p. 465.

96. Crites discusses manuscripts even earlier than *Phenomenology* in which the dialectical elaboration of the Trinity is well articulated. See "The Eternal Triangle," in *Dialectic and Gospel*, 220–23. Also Dale M. Schlitt, *Hegel's Trinitarian Claim: A Critical Reflection* (Leiden: E. J. Brill, 1984); and Patricia Marie Calton, *Hegel's Metaphysics of God: The Ontological Proof as the Development of a Trinitarian Divine Ontology* (Burlington, VT: Ashgate, 2001).

which is the otherness of essence . . . and being-for-self, or the knowledge of
the self *in the 'other.'*" He identifies *"essence's knowledge of its own self"* as the
Word, and the Spirit as "the immanent circular movement . . . that resolves
the distinctions as soon as they are made." Here Hegel implies that the first
moment, essence, is the unnamed Father.[97]

Lectures on the Philosophy of Religion works out his trinitarianism more
fully. God as living Spirit is dialectically three-in-one. "He is absolute activity . . . and his activity is to posit himself in contradiction, but eternally
to resolve and reconcile this contradiction: God himself is the resolving of
these contradictions." Hegel then distinguishes the three aspects of the divine life of Spirit: "First . . . God in his eternity before creation; . . . Second,
God creates the world and posits the separation; . . . In the third place . . .
spirit has reconciled with itself what it distinguished from itself."[98] In other
words, these three aspects of Spirit are God in himself, God for himself, and
God in and for himself. He considers each aspect in turn, both in essence
and in actuality.

We begin with God in himself apart from creation. The very idea of
God in himself is triune: "The eternal idea is expressed in terms of the holy
Trinity: it is God himself, eternally triune." Spirit in itself is the union or
"sublation"—*"the Holy Spirit is eternal love"*—of two primordial dimensions
in God, the Father and the Son. "The Father, the One, the ὄν [Greek], is
the abstract element . . . the abyss, the depths . . . the inexpressible, the inconceivable." "The second moment, other being, the action of determining,
self-determining activity as a whole, is, according to the broadest designation, *logos*—rationally determinative activity, or precisely the word. . . . This
second moment is also defined as *sophia*, wisdom, the original and wholly
pure human being, an existing other."[99] Thus God's essence is triune—the
eternal unification of identity and otherness. This is the *ontological, essential,*
or *intrinsic Trinity*.

It is crucial to recognize that, for Hegel, the Triune God in himself is an
Idea, a Notion abstracted by theologians and philosophers from the living
God as Spirit. God in himself apart from the world does not actually exist.
The actual God always has a world. Creation is therefore not an originating
event. "It belongs to his being, his essence to be the creator. . . . His creative
role is not an *actus* that happened once." Creation is "an eternal determination of the Idea." Thus God the Father, the Creator of heaven and earth, is

97. Hegel, *Phenomenology*, par. 770, 771, p. 465.
98. Hegel, *Lectures on the Philosophy of Religion* (1988), 413, 415–16.
99. Ibid., 417–18, 430.

an abstraction: "If we say, 'God the Father,' we speak of him as the universal, only abstractly."[100]

And so the dialectic must shift to the second aspect, God for himself in the world. God actually exists only as Spirit, as the process of his self-realization in the finite world of nature and spirit. Thus the ontological Trinity actually exists only as *economic* or *extrinsic Trinity*, the Trinity as it unfolds in and enfolds the world.[101] The Son as Word likewise does not exist apart from the world but only in the world as Wisdom in God's self-othering: "The primal division of the idea is to be conceived in such a way that the other, which we have also called 'Son,' obtains the determination of the other as such—that this other exists as a free being for itself, and that it appears as something actual, as something that exists outside of and apart from God."[102] The Son as Logos is the rational (dialectical-teleological-eschatological) order of the entire creation; as Wisdom he is the presence of the image of God in humans;[103] as the complete "self-othering" of the Father, he is the unique God-man, Jesus Christ.[104]

The third aspect, God in and for himself, is the Holy Spirit, who exists explicitly as the presence of God in the church after the death of Christ. (Spirit is more than the Holy Spirit.) With the indwelling of the Spirit in the church, God's self-identification with a human individual, Jesus, has dialectically transformed itself into communal identification: "The community itself is the existing Spirit, the Spirit in its existence, God existing as community."[105] Now the church has literally become "the body of Christ," the locus of the resurrected life of Jesus, the actuality of God in the world.

In sum, Hegel views his entire philosophy as the articulation of the Christian doctrine of the Trinity, both ontological and economic Trinity. God/Spirit is ontologically triune in that his essence is the eternal process of distinguishing and reconciling his identity. But God actually exists as economic Trinity, as Spirit progressively distinguishing and reconciling himself through every aspect and epoch of world history, culminating in the church and Christendom.[106] Hegel positions himself as the ultimate Christian philosopher

100. Ibid., 417, 421.

101. Pannenberg and Moltmann both hold that the Trinity is not actual without history and not fully actual until the eschaton. They follow "Rahner's Rule": that the ontological Trinity is identical with the economic Trinity.

102. Hegel, *Lectures on the Philosophy of Religion* (1988), 434.

103. Ibid., 438.

104. Ibid., 452–58.

105. Ibid., 473.

106. Like Joachim of Fiore and Schelling, Hegel designated historical epochs and developmental stages of religion as *ages* and *kingdoms* of the Father, the Son, and the Holy Spirit. See Hegel, *Lectures*

and identifies the ubiquitous dialectic as the presence of the Triune God actualizing itself throughout the world.

Orthodox Christians counter that Hegel does not preserve historic Christianity at all. Instead he alters it significantly and assimilates it into a philosophy that contradicts the Christian affirmation of God's independence of the world, the actuality of the ontological Trinity, the nature of the incarnation and atonement, and the manner of God's relation to the world.[107]

Hegel is as aware of the specific source of dialectical trinitarianism as he is of the entire history of philosophy. "Jacob Boehme was the first to recognize . . . the presence of the Trinity in everything and everywhere."[108] Its importance in Hegel makes this history worth summarizing. Plato uses dialectic to gain knowledge of the Good. Proclus discerns dialectic in the emanations of the Mind, the Soul, and the world from the One. Eriugena, Eckhart, and Nicholas of Cusa view God as the One in whom all the oppositions of finite existence are reconciled. But Jakob Böhme locates dialectic in the heart of the eternal divine essence, in the very triune nature of God himself, as well as in the world. Böhme thereby introduces a principle of Gnosticism into Christian theology that Hegel and Schelling mediate to the nineteenth and twentieth centuries.

Hegel's Panentheism

In response to theologian Friedrich August Tholuck's charge of pantheism, Hegel rejects the label. He dismisses simple identification of One and All as a "thoughtless, shoddy, unphilosophical view. . . . For in the doctrine that 'the All is God,' if God were the All there would be only one God; in the All the singular things are absorbed, they are merely accidental, or are only shadows or phantoms."[109] He even defends Spinoza: "Spinozistic philosophy was the philosophy of substantiality, not of pantheism; 'pantheism' is a poor expression because of . . . possible misunderstanding." Like Fichte and Schelling, Hegel goes beyond Spinoza: "God is the one and absolute substance; but at the same time God is also subject, and that is something

---

on the Philosophy of Religion (1988), 416–17 n. 67; and Raymond Williamson, Introduction to Hegel's Philosophy of Religion (Albany: State University of New York, 1984), 163–78, on the kingdoms of Father, Son, and Spirit.

107. Cyril O'Regan, The Heterodox Hegel (Albany: State University of New York Press, 1994), is a thorough treatment of Hegel's interpretation of Christianity; see also William Desmond, Hegel's God: A Counterfeit Double? (Burlington, VT: Ashgate, 2003).

108. Hegel, Lectures on the Philosophy of Religion (1988), 431.

109. Ibid., 261.

more. Just as the human being has personality, there enters into God the character of subjectivity, personality, spirit, absolute spirit."[110]

This "something more"—subjectivity, personality, spirit—implies that Hegel is a panentheist, not a pantheist. God is always other and more than the world, even though it is part of him. All things are in God, both ideally and actually, but finite things, even taken collectively as the world, are not the entirety of God; God is always both in the world and other than the world. The ontological distinction between Spirit and world, the distinctions among Spirit's eternal identity, its self-differentiation in the world, and its self-comprehension as Absolute Spirit are consistently maintained throughout Hegel's system.

This entire exposition of Hegel's system has implied panentheism. His initial alternative to Schelling's philosophy of identity locates the many in the One, the finite in the Infinite, and the relative in the Absolute. Hegel's dialectic formally includes all in one: $Z (Y \text{ and not-}Y [X \text{ and not-}X] \ldots)$. His whole account of Spirit's career in world history intends to show the synthesis of Infinite and finite, One and many, Absolute and relative, freedom and necessity. His interpretation of Christianity corroborates this reading: the Triune God incorporates the world into himself as he dialectically actualizes himself in the world.

The complexity of Hegel's philosophy and the ambiguity of terms such as pantheism have fueled debate for generations. But recent scholarship has increasingly favored the side of panentheism.[111] The most thorough treatment of this issue is Raymond Williamson's *Introduction to Hegel's Philosophy of Religion*. He offers an extensive analysis of the arguments that Hegel is a theist, an atheist, or a Spinozan pantheist, and he concludes that Hegel is a panentheist,[112] as does Philip Merklinger.[113] Cyril O'Regan has recently refined the diagnosis as narrative dialectical panentheism,[114] which is similar to my own term, *dialectical historical panentheism*.

110. Ibid., 263. See Daniel Jamros, *The Human Shape of God: Religion in Hegel's Phenomenology of Spirit* (New York: Paragon House, 1994).

111. Robert Whittemore, "Hegel as Panentheist," *TSP* 9 (1960): 134–64, is the first extensive case for this judgment. See also Clark Butler, "Hegelian Panentheism as Joachimite Christianity," in *New Perspectives on Hegel's Philosophy of Religion*, ed. David Kolb (Albany: State University of New York Press, 1992); and Wilkens and Padgett, *Christianity and Western Thought*, 2:85.

Bernard M. G. Reardon, "Theism or Pantheism?" in *Hegel's Philosophy of Religion* (New York: Barnes and Noble, 1977), 100–104, and Quentin Lauer, "The Question of Pantheism," chap. 6 in *Hegel's Concept of God* (Albany: State University of New York Press, 1982), locate Hegel between pantheism and theism but do not use the term *panentheism* explicitly.

112. Williamson, "Ambiguity of Hegel's God," part 3 in *Introduction*, esp. chap. 12, "A Medial View: Hegel as a Panentheist."

113. Merklinger, *Philosophy, Theology*, 160, 232 n. 70.

114. O'Regan, *The Heterodox Hegel*, 296–98.

Conclusion

Schelling and Hegel are the patriarchs of contemporary panentheism because they are the first to affirm that God, though eternal in essence, develops in existence by involving himself in the world and the world in himself. Thus they moved beyond the Neoplatonic and Spinozan traditions, still evident in Schleiermacher, which affirm the full actuality of the eternal, immutable God and regard the changing world as his temporal projection or manifestation. Both Schelling and Hegel therefore distinguish God's essence from his existence and imply duality in the divine nature: God is eternal and temporal, potential and actual, infinite and finite, immutable yet developing. Both of these thinkers rely on dialectic as the key to understanding God's nature and way in the world, and both focus God's activity in humanity, not primarily in nature. In parallel ways, Schelling and Hegel both influence subsequent philosophy significantly.

They also shape theology. Both regard themselves as Christian philosophers. Both adapt Jakob Böhme's dialectical speculations to articulate dynamic doctrines of the Trinity: the intrinsic triunity of the divine essence and its extrinsic self-actualization in history. Both Schelling and Hegel classify epochs of history and religion as ages of the Father, Son, and Holy Spirit. Both offer ontological accounts of the incarnation as God's explicit historical self-actualization in humanity, beginning in Jesus Christ. And both regard world history as redemptive history—God's explication and elimination of evil as he reconciles all in One. The shape of much contemporary theology was outlined by Schelling and Hegel.

In spite of the striking similarity of their projects, however, significant differences stem from a fundamental disagreement over the nature and role of reason in history and knowledge of God. Ironically, on this point Schelling is more forward-looking although Hegel is more famous.

Hegel boldly affirms that reason is fundamental and ultimate for God and humanity: "What is real is rational, and what is rational is real."[115] The very essence of God is rational dialectic, as is his self-realization in history. Since philosophy is the ultimate rational discipline, it is the medium through which God comes to absolute knowledge in, of, and for himself. Hegel confidently elaborates the dialectical intricacies and interrelationships of the divine life in every aspect of its earthly career. Art, religion, and the human quest for freedom are all aspects and functions of Divine Reason's self-comprehension. Hegel believes that he writes the definitive biography of God. He is

115. Hegel, preface to *Philosophy of Right*.

the most ambitious thinker of the long rationalist tradition that stretches back to Aristotle, Plato, and Parmenides. He is also the last.

Schelling always held a more modest view of reason, which earned him Hegel's scorn. His early idealism grounds a philosophy of the Absolute in art. He bases his mature philosophy on religion, where he thinks God is most fully actual. Schelling's modesty about human reason reflects his doctrine of God. He recognizes the *Ungrund*—the groundless, nonrational, spontaneous, fully free element in the divine nature. In this he is more faithful to Böhme than to Nicholas of Cusa (and Hegel), who define God's essence as dialectical reason. The rationally open nature of God means that the creation of the world and the reality of evil cannot be explained fully and that human history cannot be predicted. God's freedom entails human freedom because humans participate in God. History is a genuine adventure in which God and humanity cooperate in mutual enrichment and fulfillment. Nothing is predetermined except that evil and suffering will ultimately be eliminated when God and the fully humanized world are all in all.

It is important to note, however, that the freedom of Schelling's God is, like Hamlet's, either "to be or not to be." It is not fully libertarian freedom. God can choose to exist or not to exist. But if he exists, which he chooses because it is the right thing to do, he is not free to choose whether to create the world, or whether to create humans free to determine the course of history, or whether to allow evil. If God exists, the world that actually exists must necessarily exist. In his own way, Schelling too is a compatibilist. His notion of divine freedom is not an alternative equal to the classical theistic notion of divine sovereignty, in which God freely chooses among alternatives.

Schelling's modest view of reason based on revelation can claim continuity with the Christian tradition more easily than Hegel can, although his views of Scripture and core doctrines are far from historic Christian orthodoxy. He is appreciated by many post-Enlightenment thinkers—romantics, historicists, pragmatists, existentialists, and postmodernists—who do not regard reason as ultimate, God as comprehensible, or human history as predictable by God. Schelling has contributed more than Hegel to modern panentheism even though he is less known. Whatever their relative importance, the combined influence of Hegel and Schelling on subsequent philosophical theology is massive.

5

Nineteenth–Century Proliferation

Readers familiar with twentieth-century theology are no doubt aware of the importance of Teilhard de Chardin, Alfred North Whitehead, and Paul Tillich, perhaps even of their respective panentheisms. Acquaintance with their background in the philosophical theology of the nineteenth century, however, is less common. Apart from this background, Teilhard, Whitehead, and Tillich seem to be radical innovators who suddenly appear on the theological scene. But this is not so. Although they are creative thinkers, they are just another generation in a long family history that reaches back to antiquity through Hegel, Schelling, and Neoplatonism.

This chapter is not a complete account of nineteenth-century panentheism. Instead it highlights a few of the most interesting and influential figures in Germany, England, the United States, and France who adapted and modified the panentheistic theologies of Schelling and Hegel and mediated them to the twentieth century. Some, such as Coleridge, Emerson, Peirce, James, and Bergson, are famous figures in literature or philosophy, although their panentheism may not be common knowledge. Other names are not familiar outside academic circles. Either way, panentheism diversified and proliferated significantly during the nineteenth century and so had become a major theological option by the twentieth century.

120

Developments in the natural and human sciences were particularly stimu-lating to this proliferation. In the natural sciences, Darwinian evolution became a basic paradigm for biology and indirectly suggested that the entire universe is evolving. This new view of nature continued the organic metaphor preferred by the Platonic tradition, but it replaced the romantic dialectic of polarities with empirical science. For panentheists, God's body became an evolving organism. In the human sciences, the more empirical approach corroborated the romantic belief in the historical diversity and pluriformity of cultures, worldviews, and religions. Panentheism could present itself as the common-denominator view of divinity amid human diversity, much as Deism was the generic position in the Enlightenment. The emerging dis-cipline of psychology proposed new theories of the human mind and spirit consistent with evolutionary biology, theories that replaced the body-soul dualism of the Platonic tradition. For panentheists, this suggested a new model for the World-Soul: *panpsychism*, the view that "everything is soul," a Life Force that is conscious in higher beings.

In addition to developments in science and human studies, some nine-teenth-century panentheists remained committed to historic Christianity. The challenge for them was to maintain adequate doctrines of divine tran-scendence; the Trinity; creation; the incarnation, atonement, and resurrection of Christ; and the ultimate distinctiveness of the Christian gospel as they integrated theology with the intellectual outlook of their times.

Germany

Karl Krause

Karl Krause (1781–1832) is noteworthy because he coined the term *panentheism* (*Allingottlehre*, literally "the doctrine that all is in God") in an attempt to distinguish his position from traditional theism and pantheism.[1] Following Fichte, he begins with ego. Just as the human ego discovers itself to be a developing, organic unity of body and mind, so God, an absolute unity in himself, is manifest as the dynamic coincidence of nature and reason.

1. Karl Krause, *Vorlesungen über die Grundwahrheiten der Wissenschaft* (Göttingen, 1829), 484; see Thomas MacFarland, "Panentheism," excursus 4 in *Coleridge and the Pantheist Tradition* (Oxford: Clar-endon, 1969), 268–70. See also Karl Krause, *The Ideal of Humanity and Universal Federation*, trans. W. Hastie (Edinburgh: T&T Clark, 1900), translation of *Das Urbild der Menschheit* (1812); Arnulf Zweig, "Krause, Karl Christian Friedrich," *EncPhil* 4:363–65; Charles Hartshorne, "Pantheism and Panenthe-ism," *EncRel* 11:165–71, especially 169; and David Pailin, *Probing the Foundations: A Study in Theistic Reconstruction* (Kampen, Neth.: Kok Pharos, 1994), 116–17.

This unity is most fully actualized, both actively and passively, in humanity. Humanity in all of its self-expressions is the highest manifestation of God in nature and history.

Krause conceives of God as "the one infinite ideal Being." God in himself is primordial Being, the absolutely self-identical One, the unity of all that is. But there is a polarity intrinsic to God's essence that manifests itself in the existence of the All, the world. "The One in itself and through itself also is the All."[2] The All is essentially distinct from the One because, unlike the One, the concept of All contains the idea of many. Arnulf Zweig explains Krause's view of God and world: "Though [God] contains the world, he is nevertheless other than and superior to it. The distinction between God and the world is that of whole and part."[3] This is the original definition of panentheism. Krause describes the manner of God's relating to the world in terms of both love and monarchial power. Thus it is not clear whether he affirms that creatures are free, determined by God, or both in a compatibilist sense.[4]

Although Schelling and Hegel better articulated the philosophical intuitions that Krause expressed, he certainly deserves recognition for coining the term *panentheism*.

Isaak Dorner

Isaak Dorner (1809–1884) was a Lutheran theologian famous for his work on the history of Christian doctrine, especially the incarnation of Christ. Less known are his revision of the doctrine of divine immutability[5] and an influential essay on Schelling.[6]

Dorner is thoroughly familiar with the leading role of contemporary German philosophy in promoting a dynamic-historical view of God. "The idea of God's becoming man was brought to acceptance through the philosophy of Schelling and Hegel, in the third and fourth decades of the century," he

---

2. Karl Krause, *Vorlesungen über das System der Philosophie* (Göttingen, 1828), 255–56, quoted from McFarland, 268.

3. Zweig, "Krause," 4:364.

4. Pailin, *Probing the Foundations*, 117.

5. Isaak Dorner, "Dogmatic Discussion of the Doctrine of the Immutability of God" (1856), trans. Claude Welch, in *God and Incarnation in Mid-Nineteenth Century German Theology*, ed. Claude Welch (New York: Oxford University Press, 1965), 115–80. Part 2 of Dorner's *System of Christian Doctrine: The Doctrine of Christ* is also found ibid., 181–284.

6. Isaak Dorner, "Über Schellings neues System" (1860). See Robert F. Brown, "Schelling and Dorner on Divine Immutability," *JAAR* 53/2 (1985): 237–49. Brown, 238, also documents Dorner's appreciation of Böhme's theology.

observes. He does not agree with Schelling's or Hegel's account of Christ's divinity.[7] But he does embrace their panentheistic argument from infinity. "The recognition that finite and infinite do not exclude each other may be designated as a gain of recent scientific thought since Schelling. . . . If the divine had to maintain itself exclusively in opposition to the human . . . then the finite would be an unsurpassable dualistic limit for God, as Hegel has shown. And God would thereby be finitized forthwith."[8] Dorner takes the same general philosophical approach as the godfathers of modern panentheism.

His treatment of divine immutability dialogues directly with Schelling's mature theology. Schelling, following Böhme, views God as eternally self-generating—free yet self-determining. Following Schelling, Dorner's view of divine immutability is not static sameness but the unchanging self-generating dynamic of the living God. "God is to be conceived as eternally both absolute potentiality and absolute actualization by virtue of the eternally self-rejuvenating divine life-process."[9]

Dorner sides with Hegel on the issue of God's necessary goodness, however. Schelling's notion of divine freedom asserts that although God in fact always wills the good, he could will not to be good because he could will not to exist at all. Thus God is good by choice, not by the necessity of his nature. But Dorner states that his own view, following Hegel, "mediates these antitheses [necessity and freedom] into the eternal absolute actuality of the ethical divine personality."[10] He concludes that the living God exists necessarily and is immutably good.

Dorner intends for his view of the God-world relation to avoid both pantheism and deism, and so he endorses the "recent theology" that postulates both God's immutable transcendence and his living immanence in the world.[11] This places him in the conceptual location of panentheism, as Brown observes: "Dorner finds more congenial Schelling's idea of a world existing within God that is nevertheless not identical with, nor exhaustive of, God. . . . Schelling calls this 'the true pantheism.' Today we might call it 'panentheism.'"[12] Using this concept of God and world, Dorner outlines a

7. Dorner, *System of Christian Doctrine*, 197.

8. Ibid., 182.

9. Dorner, "Dogmatic Discussion," 121.

10. Ibid., 150–62, quote at 158; Brown, "Schelling and Dorner," 245–48, elaborates Dorner's position in detail.

11. Dorner, "Dogmatic Discussion," 146: "Certain recent theology . . . does very well to repudiate deism and pantheism. . . . Recent theology postulates both God's immutability, which is often confused with transcendence, and God's livingness, which is often identified with his immanence in the world."

12. Brown, "Schelling and Dorner," 243–44.

philosophy of nature. Time, space, and all forms of creaturely finitude are eternally, essentially, and immutably in God conceptually and potentially. Any world he creates must conform to his nature. As the living God participates in the world, he therefore actualizes these categories. He is not immutable in relation to the world, but he is so in his eternal nature. "The whole historical life of God in the world takes place, not at the expense of the eternal perfection of God himself, but precisely by virtue of this permanent perfection."[13]

Dorner's dynamic panentheism is likewise fundamental to his Christology. In classical theism, the incarnation is difficult to reconcile with the eternity and immutability of God because the eternal Son takes a human nature in time. But Schelling and Hegel taught that becoming human is intrinsic to God's very essence. Dorner follows them: "The objective fundamental fact of Christianity, the incarnation of God, is the factual solution of the problem of the uniting of God's immutability and livingness."[14] The incarnation does not negate the divine nature but in fact manifests its inner dialectical dynamic.

Dorner was a theologian committed to historic Christianity who concluded that dynamic panentheism is more adequate than classical theism for articulating the doctrines of God, the world, and Christ as God incarnate. In this he anticipates Pannenberg and Moltmann.

Gustav Fechner

Gustav Fechner (1801–1887) successively taught physics, psychology, and philosophy at Leipzig.[15] His experiments and temporary blindness persuaded him that all entities—"plants as well as planets"—possess parallel psychic (sensitive) and physical states in varying proportions. He thus endorsed philosophical *panpsychism*, the view that "soul" is the basic reality in all things, even matter, which is the most condensed form of soul.[16]

Fechner does not hesitate to extend his panpsychist metaphysics to God, who is thus the soul of the world. "Instead of contrasting the world with God, we rather treat it as the other side of the divine existence, as something belonging to God, in the same manner as we view a man's body. . . . The spirit

13. Dorner, "Dogmatic Discussion," 145.

14. Ibid., 149.

15. A. Zweig, "Fechner, Gustav Theodor," *EncPhil* 3:184–86; Copleston, *Hist. Phil.*, vol. 7, chap. 20, sec. 2; Charles Hartshorne and William Reese, *Philosophers Speak of God* (Chicago: University of Chicago Press, 1953), 243–57; Johann Erdmann, *A History of Philosophy*, trans. W. S. Hough, 2nd ed., 3 vols. (New York: Macmillan, 1890–1892), 3:282–98.

16. Gustav Fechner, *Elemente des Psychophysik*, 2 vols. in 1 (Leipzig: Breitkopf und Härtel, 1860). See Paul Edwards, "Panpsychism," *EncPhil* 6:22–31.

of God stands not, any more than the human soul, in a dead, external fashion above the bodily world, but manifests itself, rather, as a living essence immanent in it, or else . . . nature itself is an expression of God which remains immanent in him."[17] Because nature is in God, "all space and all time and all reality are included within him, and in him find their basis, truth, and essence."[18] Fechner's panpsychism is consistent with romantic panentheism.

According to Fechner, God is present in all parts of his body and sustains their existence, but he does not determine or predict their behavior. Creatures possess the freedom of self-determination analogous to God's. Thus God's existence is conditioned and partly determined by the creatures who constitute his body. As the universe grows, God also grows in actuality, consciousness, knowledge, and power. Yet Fechner notes an important difference between God and humans. Unlike a human person who develops from infancy to maturity and from instinct and sensuality to rationality and morality, "God's primordial reason governed his physical nature from the beginning as today."[19]

Fechner's "growing personal God" is highly reminiscent of Schelling's personalism but is expressed in the more scientific language of developmental psychology. Fechner did not have a huge following, but his work was taken seriously by his peers. William James appreciated both his panpsychism and panentheism.[20]

Hermann Lotze

Hermann Lotze (1817–1881) studied medicine and was a student of Fechner who became more widely recognized as a philosopher than his teacher.[21] But he did not adopt Fechner's panpsychism or his type of panentheism.

Lotze argues that the mechanistic explanations of physics and chemistry are sufficient for biology and that they are not incompatible with the genuinely

17. Gustav Fechner, *Zend-Avesta; oder, Über die Dinge des Himmels und des Jenseits* [*Zend-Avesta: Things of Heaven and the World to Come*] (1851), 2 vols. (Leipzig: Leopold Voss, 1922), 1:200–201 (Hartshorne and Reese, 244).

18. Fechner, *Zend-Avesta*, 1:222–23 (Hartshorne and Reese, 249).

19. Fechner, *Zend-Avesta*, 1:242 (Hartshorne and Reese, 253).

20. William James, "Concerning Fechner," lecture 4 in *A Pluralistic Universe* (1909). Reprinted in *Essays in Radical Empiricism* (New York: Longmans, Green, 1947).

21. Hermann Lotze, *Metaphysic, in Three Books: Ontology, Cosmology, and Psychology* (1841), ed. and trans. Bernard Bosanquet (Oxford: Clarendon, 1884); *Microcosmos: An Essay concerning Man and His Relation to the World* (1856–1864), trans. E. Hamilton and E. E. Constance Jones (New York: Scribner and Welford, 1886); *Outlines of the Philosophy of Religion: Dictated Portions of the Lectures*, ed. and trans. George T. Ladd (Boston: Ginn, Heath, 1885; repr., New York: Kraus, 1970). See also Copleston, *Hist. Phil.*, vol. 7, chap. 20, sec. 3; Rubin Gotesky, "Lotze, Rudolf Hermann," *EncPhil* 5:87–89; and Erdmann, *History of Philosophy*, 3:298–327.

goal-directed behavior of living things. He therefore concludes that positing a mysterious "vital force" to explain life is unnecessary. However, he finds that physical-chemical explanations cannot account for the data of consciousness, which include the unity of individual consciousness and the possibility of communication among conscious beings. He therefore concludes that the unity of consciousness suggests the reality of the soul, and that communal interaction presupposes a common "organic" field of operation. Furthermore, both the individual soul and the community of souls point to a deeper reality that makes them possible, a personal God. In spite of this theistic evidence, however, Lotze holds that the final ground of our belief in God is not metaphysical, but moral—the experience of value and obligation in personal existence.[22]

Lotze's theology is panentheistic. God is infinite and absolute, yet personal. Since God is infinite, he contains all finite beings. All finite persons are immanent in the infinite person. God is absolute, but since he is morally good and (inter)personal, he does not absolutely determine finite persons (and other beings) but allows them to share the genuine individuality and freedom of response that he has. Although Lotze locates all finite beings in God, he believes that affirming their genuine responsiveness enables him to avoid pantheism: "we do not share the inclination which commonly governs the pantheistic imagination to suppress all that is finite in favor of the infinite."[23] This assertion implies panentheism.

Lotze's philosophy remained influential into the twentieth century. William James and Josiah Royce in the United States studied it, as did the idealists in England. He had a significant impact on the young Ernst Troeltsch in Germany. In addition, his neo-Kantian epistemology and argument for a personal God based on moral experience were highly influential in the theology of Albrecht Ritschl, the great proponent of liberal Protestantism.[24]

Otto Pfleiderer

Otto Pfleiderer (1839–1908) was a theologian at the University of Berlin who was influenced by Hegel, Schelling, and Fechner. Reese and Hartshorne embrace him as a modern panentheist because he criticizes classical theism and emphasizes that God must be both eternal and temporal, both transcendent and immanently active in the world.[25] "The idea of God as living and

22. Lotze follows the Kantian tradition at this point. Kant based belief in God on morality. The neo-Kantians defined morality in terms of value rather than law, as Kant did.

23. Lotze, *Microcosmos*, bk. 9, chap. 4, sec. 3, quoted from Copleston, *Hist. Phil.*, vol. 7, chap. 20, sec. 3.

24. James Livingston, *Modern Christian Thought: From the Enlightenment to Vatican II* (New York: Macmillan, 1971), 248–49.

25. Hartshorne and Reese, *Philosophers Speak of God*, 269–71.

self-conscious spirit absolutely requires the admission of a temporal alter-ability in the content of the divine knowing and acting, despite the eternal immutability characterizing his essence and the form ... of his thinking and willing." In addition, Pfleiderer invokes a classic panentheistic model of God, "the relation of God to the entire physical world as analogous to that of the human mind to its physical organism."[26] God is Mind and the world is his body. What happens in the world is the activity of God's mind, but it also changes his mind. This is dynamic personal panentheism.

Ernst Troeltsch

Ernst Troeltsch (1865–1923) was one of the most brilliant German in-tellectuals of his time, a philosopher, theologian, and historian of religion. His historical methodology and religious pluralism have had an enormous impact on higher critical biblical scholarship.[27]

Troeltsch's view of God's immanence in history is inherited from Schlei-ermacher, Hegel, and Schelling. For much of his career, he follows them in defending Christianity as God's most advanced self-revelation among the world religions. His argument is Kantian—that Christianity holds the high-est, most noble view of divine and human personhood.[28] But World War I shattered his confidence in the superiority of Western civilization and the Christianity upon which it is based. His final theology is culturally relative and religiously pluralistic. At the end of his life he writes, "The Divine Life within history constantly manifests itself in always-new and always-peculiar individualizations," so that "its tendency is not toward unity or universality at all." Therefore "it is quite impossible to characterize Christianity as the reconciliation and goal of all the forces of history."[29] Christian commitment is a matter of historical faith, not reason.

26. Otto Pfleiderer, *Grundriss der christlichen Glaubens- und Sittenlehre* [*Outline of Christian Faith and Ethical Doctrine*] (Berlin: G. Reimer, 1888), 69–71, (Hartshorne and Reese, 270). See also Otto Pfleiderer, *The Philosophy of Religion on the Basis of Its History*, trans. Alexander Stewart and Allen Menzies, 4 vols. (London: Williams and Norgate, 1886–1888); and *Philosophy and Development of Religion*, Gifford Lectures, 1894 (Edinburgh: W. Blackwood, 1894).

27. Walter Wyman Jr., *The Concept of Glaubenslehre: Ernst Troeltsch and the Theological Heritage of Schleiermacher* (Chico, CA: Scholars Press, 1983); Sarah Coakley, *Christ without Absolutes: A Study of the Christology of Ernst Troeltsch* (Oxford: Clarendon, 1988); Hendrikus Berkhof, *Two Hundred Years of Theology* (Grand Rapids: Eerdmans, 1989), 150–59. All these authors regard Troeltsch as a panentheist.

28. Ernst Troeltsch, *The Absoluteness of Christianity and the History of Religions* (1902), trans. David Reid (Richmond, VA: John Knox, 1971).

29. Ernst Troeltsch, *Christian Thought: Its History and Application* (1923), ed. F. von Hügel (London: University of London Press, 1923; repr., New York: Meridian, 1957), 44–45. Citation is from the Meridian edition.

In spite of this shift, a panentheistic theology is discernible throughout Troeltsch's career. His doctrine of God in *The Christian Faith* develops in dialogue with Spinoza, Leibniz, Schleiermacher, Hegel, and James.[30] Reminiscent of Hegel, Troeltsch posits that God is the Infinite Spirit in which there is an "inner separation" that generates the world. Nature and finite spirits emanate from God and subsist in him. God is the immanent Life Force that perpetually manifests itself in new forms of existence. To avoid Spinozan pantheism, Troeltsch invokes Leibniz's doctrine of monads: God is the ultimate monad that contains all finite monads, which are distinct from God. He also appeals to James's pluralism: not only are creatures distinct from God; they also possess an element of genuine freedom and responsiveness. In sum, the world proceeds from the divine Life but is distinct from it. Creatures are included in God by way of "participation," which involves God's ultimate transformation of nature into spirit, working in and through the activity of his creatures.

Troeltsch points out the Neoplatonic scheme of his own theology: the emanation and return of all things to God.[31] Even more striking is the fact that he explicitly adopts the term *panentheism* in *The Christian Faith* and other works.[32] His later religious pluralism does not alter this position. *Christian Thought: Its History and Application* asserts a "metaphysical faith" and affirms a divine Spirit, the Ground of history and the immanent historical source of all religions.[33] "The similarities of this concept of God to Troeltsch's quest for a panentheistic alternative in the *Glaubenslehre* are obvious."[34]

England

Samuel Taylor Coleridge

Samuel Taylor Coleridge (1772–1834) is most famous as a romantic poet, but he had a lifelong interest in philosophy and theology as well. John Stuart Mill and John Henry Newman regarded him as one of the great minds of

---

30. Ernst Troeltsch, *The Christian Faith: Based on Lectures Delivered at the University of Heidelberg, 1912–1913*, trans. Garret Paul (Minneapolis: Fortress, 1991). I rely on the summary and quotations of Wyman, "Fundamental Theology: The First Distinctive Mark," chap. 2 in *Concept of Glaubenslehre*.

31. Wyman, *Concept of Glaubenslehre*, 44.

32. Ibid., 44, 191, 202, 245; Michael Brierley, "Naming a Quiet Revolution: The Panentheistic Turn in Modern Theology," in *In Whom We Live and Move and Have Our Being: Panentheistic Reflections on God's Presence in a Scientific World*, ed. Philip Clayton and Arthur Peacocke (Grand Rapids: Eerdmans, 2003), 4 n. 83.

33. Ernst Troeltsch, *Christian Thought: Its History and Application* (London: University of London Press, 1923).

34. Wyman, *Concept of Glaubenslehre*, 191.

his era. He was an important conduit of the philosophies of Kant, Hegel, and Schelling to the English-speaking world. In theology he is best known for his epistemology—which aims to reconcile reason, intuition, and the imagination—and his application of it to the relation of reason, revelation, and the proper interpretation of Holy Scripture.[35]

But Coleridge also pondered questions about God and the world.[36] His views changed with his religious beliefs. Raised an Anglican, he journeyed through Deism, Unitarianism, and a brief period of materialism before settling on trinitarian Christianity.[37] His ideas also depended heavily on contemporary German philosophy and its roots. Plato, Plotinus, Proclus, Eriugena, Eckhart, Nicholas of Cusa, Bruno, Böhme, and Spinoza, as well as Kant, Hegel, and Schelling, all contributed to Coleridge's thought.[38]

Young Coleridge was enamored of Schelling's philosophy of nature and identity because it claims to overcome the traditional dualisms of God and cosmos, One and many, subject and object. He follows Schelling and the Neoplatonic tradition in embracing a philosophy of nature that accounts for all levels and aspects of the cosmic order—astrological, physical, chemical, and organic—as the interplay of polarities. Light, magnetism, color, sound, the dynamics of vitality—all of nature manifests the One God in an infinite diversity of forms and combinations that constitute a dialectical hierarchy culminating in human life.[39] But Coleridge eventually takes distance from Schelling's philosophy, which he perceptively regards as "Behmenism . . . reduced at last to a mere Pantheism" and as "Plotinised Spinozism."[40]

Instead he adopts the Christian Trinity as his first principle. He gives several reasons: it is a personal "I AM"; it is interpersonal; it unifies reason,

35. Livingston, *Modern Christian Thought*, 87–96, and Steve Wilkens and Alan G. Padgett, *Christianity and Western Thought* (Downers Grove, IL: InterVarsity, 1990–), 2:40–49, are fine introductions.

36. John Muirhead, *Coleridge as Philosopher* (New York: Macmillan, 1930); James Boulger, *Coleridge as Religious Thinker* (New Haven: Yale University Press, 1961); Thomas McFarland, *Coleridge and the Pantheist Tradition* (Oxford: Clarendon, 1969); Raimonda Modiano, *Coleridge and the Concept of Nature* (Tallahassee: Florida State University Press, 1985); J. Robert Barth, *Coleridge and Christian Doctrine* (Cambridge, MA: Harvard University Press, 1987); and Mary Anne Perkins, *Coleridge's Philosophy: The Logos as Unifying Principle* (Oxford: Clarendon, 1994).

37. Wilkens and Padgett, *Christianity and Western Thought*, 2:41–42.

38. All are exposited in Samuel Taylor Coleridge, *Philosophical Lectures* (1819), ed. Kathleen Coburn (London: Routledge and Kegan Paul, 1949). He appropriated some of their ideas in his own writings and wrote notes in the margins of his copies of their works. See McFarland, *Coleridge*, 242–51; Perkins, *Coleridge's Philosophy*, 10–13, 113–15.

39. See chap. 4, above, on Schelling's early philosophy. See also McFarland, *Coleridge*, 148–52; Modiano, "Origins of Coleridge's System of *Naturphilosophie*," in *Coleridge and the Concept of Nature*, 151–85; Perkins, *Coleridge's Philosophy*, 113–32.

40. Samuel Taylor Coleridge, *Collected Letters*, ed. E. L. Griggs, 6 vols. (Oxford: Oxford University Press, 1966–1971), 4:883; Perkins, *Coleridge's Philosophy*, 120.

will, and love; and it grounds all otherness and polarity.[41] With the Trinity as his basic principle, Coleridge incorporates themes from Böhme and Schelling that he would otherwise reject. He keeps much of their philosophy of nature. He also retains aspects of their doctrine of the Trinity, as is evident in this rather obtuse formulation:[42] "God is one, but exists or manifests himself to himself, at once in a three-fold Act, total in each and one in all. Prothesis = God, Thesis = Son, Antithesis = Spirit, Synthesis = Father. Hence in all things the Synthesis images what in God only absolutely is, the Prothesis manifested—it is a return to the Prothesis, or re-affirmation. Thus the Monas, the Dyas, the Trias, and the Tetractys are one."[43] In this passage, Coleridge affirms Böhme and Schelling's doctrine that the depth of God is a self-positing Will that acts to posit itself eternally as a triadic unity (Father) of Reason (Logos, Son) and Love (Spirit). This picture suggests that the Trinity is the eternal product of a deeper dimension in God, which is contrary to historic Christian orthodoxy. But Coleridge apparently believes that his view fits the Nicene Creed.[44]

Is Coleridge a panentheist? He almost certainly was during his pretrinitarian period. In a marginal note in his copy of Böhme's *Aurora*, he admits affirming "the dim distinction, that tho' God was = the world, the world was not = God—as if God were a Whole composed of Parts, of which the world was One!"[45] This statement is very close to Krause's panentheism, in which the world is "part of God." But Coleridge subsequently took distance from Böhme and Schelling's "pantheism," which is actually panentheism. It is more difficult to verify that he remains a panentheist after he becomes a trinitarian, although the evidence supports this conclusion.[46] He believes that his trinitarianism is creedal orthodoxy, but he retains dialectical elements of Böhme and Schelling's doctrine of God and nature that imply

41. McFarland, "The Trinitarian Resolution," chap. 4 in *Coleridge*; Modiano, "*Naturphilosophie* and Christian Orthodoxy in Coleridge's View of the Trinity," in *Coleridge and the Concept of Nature*, chap. 4.

42. Modiano, in *Coleridge and the Concept of Nature*, 189: "His marginalia to Boehme or Oken, as well as various notebook entries, present strong evidence that Coleridge extracted a philosophical model for the Trinity from the *Naturphilosophen*, especially from Schelling."

43. Samuel Taylor Coleridge, *The Notebooks*, ed. Kathleen Coburn (Princeton, NJ: Princeton University Press, 1957–), vol. 3, para. 4427 (August–September 1818).

44. See Barth, *Coleridge and Christian Doctrine*, 92–95, 100–104, on the tension between Coleridge's affirmation of orthodoxy and the "fourness" in his view of God.

45. Marginal note on p. 127 in his copy of Böhme's *Aurora*, ed. W. Law (1764); McFarland, *Coleridge*, 250–51.

46. McFarland addresses his shift in perspective most directly, but he too easily concludes that Coleridge is a traditional theist, on the ground that "'panentheism' cannot be distinguished from 'pantheism'" (*Coleridge*, 269), which is false. Thus panentheism remains the most likely result.

panentheism. With respect to God and the world, the mature Coleridge regularly refers to *participation* of the Logos and Spirit in creation and the world's *participation* in them. Although he does not explicitly state whether participation is ontological or merely relational, all the German romantic and Neoplatonic philosophers from whom he draws define it ontologically. Most likely Coleridge follows them.[47]

All things considered, therefore, Coleridge is most likely a Christian panentheist.[48] In any case, he belongs in this history because he is the primary conduit of German philosophy, with its panentheistic tendencies, to England and the United States.

But Coleridge is not the only source of German philosophy in English thought. Most English philosophers read the German idealists. We consider a few prominent figures.

Thomas Hill Green

Oxford philosopher Thomas Hill Green (1839–1882) worked directly from Hegel and is a rather straightforward panentheist. In his *Prolegomena to Ethics*, Green begins from human knowledge of nature and morality. He concludes that we must conceive the finite mind as participating in the life of an infinite eternal consciousness or intelligence that "partially or gradually reproduces itself in us."[49] Thus God manifests himself in us, and we participate in him, but God and creatures remain distinct. Green's strong view of human freedom in relation to God, however, is closer to Schelling than to Hegel.[50]

John and Edward Caird

The brothers John (1820–1898) and Edward (1835–1908) Caird are both Hegelian philosophers who gave Gifford Lectures.[51]

Edward Caird's Gifford Lectures of 1891–1892, in *The Evolution of Religion*, argue that religion is essential to human existence because the

---

47. See Barth, "Creation and Sinful Man," chap. 5 in *Coleridge and Christian Doctrine*; Perkins, *Coleridge's Philosophy*, 117–18.

48. In particular, his doctrine of the Logos in creation anticipates Teilhard de Chardin's evolutionary cosmology as incarnation of the Cosmic Christ. See Barth, *Coleridge and Christian Doctrine*, 137, 197; Perkins, *Coleridge's Philosophy*, 279–82.

49. Thomas Hill Green, *Prolegomena to Ethics*, ed. A. C. Bradley (Oxford: Clarendon, 1899), 38; Copleston, *Hist. Phil.*, vol. 8, chap. 7, sec. 2.

50. Copleston, *Hist. Phil.*, vol. 8, chap. 7, sec. 3.

51. Livingston, *Modern Christian Thought*, 161–68.

history of religion is the history of the human search for reconciliation of the tensions between human subjectivity and objective existence. Correlatively, religion is also God's immanent historical revelation of that reconciliation. Caird closely follows Hegel's stages of the history of religion: "objective religion" (God objectified in nature or particular deities), "subjective religion" (God as absolute subject, especially in Judaism), and "absolute religion" (Christianity). In Christianity's doctrine of the incarnation, Caird claims, God is no longer conceived as a spiritual being standing above nature and humanity but as "the ultimate unity of our life and of the life of the world."[52] He virtually asserts panentheism: "We cannot think of the infinite Being as a will which is external to that which it has made . . . least of all to the spiritual beings who, as such 'live and move and have their being in Him.' This idea of the immanence of God underlies the Christian conception."[53] Following Hegel, he also holds that God's knowledge of his own actuality is realized in and through human knowledge of God. And he emphasizes that the historical realization of the unity of God and humanity at the same time includes and preserves their distinctness. All of this implies panentheism.

John Caird's Gifford Lectures, in *The Fundamental Ideas of Christianity*, set out to resolve the dilemma between pantheism and deism. For pantheism, "the contradiction thus involved in its thought forces it onwards in quest of an Infinite which contains and accounts for the finite instead of annulling it." Deism, in contrast, posits God's "transcendent opposition to the world," and therefore "the gulf between the infinite and the finite remains unbridged."[54] To resolve this dilemma, Caird posits God as "Infinite Mind or Intelligence which constitutes the reality of the world, not simply as its external Creator, but as the inward Spirit in and through which all things live and move and have their being."[55] Against pantheism he affirms the distinctness and conditional freedom of creatures from God, which implies panentheism.

The brothers Caird are clearly dynamic panentheists who are part of the British intellectual background of Whitehead's process philosophy.[56]

52. Edward Caird, *The Evolution of Religion*, 2 vols., Gifford Lectures, 1890–1891, 1891–1892 (Glasgow: MacLehose and Sons, 1893), 1:140; also *Hegel* (Edinburgh: W. Blackwood and Sons, 1883); Copleston, *Hist. Phil.*, vol. 8, chap. 7, sec. 4.

53. Caird, *The Evolution of Religion*, 1:195–96.

54. John Caird, *The Fundamental Ideas of Christianity*, 2 vols., Gifford Lectures, 1892–1893, 1895–1896 (Glasgow: J. MacLehose, 1899), 1:141–42.

55. Ibid., 1:143–44.

56. Livingston, *Modern Christian Thought*, 164: "Caird develops a doctrine of God similar in ways to that of twentieth-century Panentheism." Livingston points to Whitehead and Hartshorne.

James Ward

James Ward (1843–1925), a Cambridge philosopher and psychologist, was a student of Lotze. His 1896–1899 Gifford Lectures, in *Naturalism and Agnosticism*, argue against materialism and dualism in favor of panpsychism. Similarly to William James, he concludes that reality consists in a plurality of centers of activity, although not all are conscious. His 1907–1910 Gifford Lectures, in *The Realm of Ends*, argue for a theology in which God is the personal, transcendent-immanent source and fulfillment of the finite world. God limits himself in order to cooperate with the free subjectivity of his creatures.[57] Ward admits that the existence of God cannot be proven, but he argues that affirming the existence of a personal God who grounds and is involved with the cosmic community of creatures is a more intuitive, plausible, and meaningful belief than the ultimate plurality of finite material beings. His theology is a dynamic personal panentheism in which God himself grows as he works with creatures to realize love and goodness and to overcome evil.

Andrew Seth Pringle-Pattison

The Scottish philosopher Andrew Seth Pringle-Pattison (1856–1931) likewise develops a panentheism in which the personal God cooperates with autonomous creatures. In his Gifford Lectures, in *The Idea of God*, he suggests that nature, humanity, and God constitute a God-generated organic whole. Finite subjects "have no independent subsistence outside of the universal Life which mediates itself to them in a world of objects." God in turn "becomes an abstraction if separated from the universe of his manifestation."[58] Creatures are distinct from, inseparable from, and exist in God. Because he is personal, God naturally generates a world because full personhood is possible only through interaction with other persons. The God-world totality, although dynamic, does not, however, create genuinely new levels of existence through this interaction. Interaction actualizes what is present in God from the beginning.

Samuel Alexander

Samuel Alexander (1859–1938) taught philosophy at the University of Manchester and is best known for his theory of emergent evolution: "Within

57. James Ward, *Naturalism and Agnosticism*, 4th ed., Gifford Lectures, 1896–1898 (London: A. & C. Black, 1915); *The Realm of Ends; or, Pluralism and Theism*, Gifford Lectures, 1907–1910 (Cambridge: Cambridge University Press, 1911).

58. Andrew Seth Pringle-Pattison, *The Idea of God in the Light of Recent Philosophy*, 2nd ed., rev., Gifford Lectures, 1912–1913 (New York: Oxford University Press, 1920), 314.

the all-embracing stuff of Space-Time, the universe exhibits an emergence in Time of successive levels of finite existences."[59] Even the Divine emerges; it is the level beyond mind. "Deity is thus the next higher empirical quality to mind, which the universe is engaged in bringing to birth."[60] God is emerging from the evolution of the universe, but only one aspect of God.

The other aspect of God is one with Space-Time and the material universe from which his other aspect is emerging. "God is the whole world as possessing the quality of deity. Of such a being the whole world is the 'body' and deity is the 'mind.' But this possessor of deity is not actual but ideal. As an actual existent, God is the infinite world with its nisus towards deity."[61] God is the whole universe, which eventually actualizes its implicit potential to produce God. God as the whole is both body and mind. The cosmic mind is the emerging aspect of God. Because it is embodied, however, this mind is always growing but can never actualize absolute infinity, which thus remains ideal.

Alexander's God has two natures, one actual and dynamic, the other abstract, ideal, and potential. As we shall see, Whitehead is deeply indebted to Alexander for this dipolar view of God and his strategy for deriving theology from the scientific world picture.

Alexander's speculations are fascinating. They adapt the old Platonic notion of the divine Soul of the world to modern naturalistic evolutionism. The world is not the self-actualizing emanation of its Soul; divine Soul is the self-actualizing emanation of the primordially divine world. Alexander's vision is a naturalistic inversion of Hegel, Schelling, and Fechner. The Divine posits itself as nature and then humanity in order to actualize itself fully. If God were only the Space-Time Universe, Alexander would be a naturalistic pantheist. He is a panentheist because he asserts that although "God includes the whole universe," there is a metaphysical distinction between the emerging God and the world.[62]

William Ralph Inge and Anglican Theology

The panentheistic tendency of Neoplatonism exercised an impact on Anglican theology during this time as well. Coleridge was one important

59. Samuel Alexander, *Space, Time, and Deity*, 2 vols., Gifford Lectures, 1916–1918 (New York: Macmillan, 1920; repr., New York: Dover, 1966), 2:345.
  60. Ibid., 2:347.
  61. Ibid., 2:353.
  62. Hartshorne and Reese, *Philosophers Speak of God*, 365–72, classify him instead as an "extreme temporalistic theist" because he is not sufficiently strong on divine transcendence and eternity.

source of this influence. But the legacy of Cambridge Platonism had remained strong since the seventeenth century.

William Inge (1860–1954), longtime dean of St. Paul's Cathedral in London, chose the philosophy of Plotinus for his Gifford Lectures. During the chaos of World War I, he warns, "We cannot preserve Platonism without Christianity, nor Christianity without Platonism, nor civilization without both."[63] In his famous work *Christian Mysticism*, he clearly identifies his own position in the tradition of Christian Platonism: "the belief in the *immanence* of a God who is also transcendent. This should be called *Panentheism*, a useful word coined by Krause, and not Pantheism. In its true form it is an integral part of Christian philosophy, and, indeed, of all rational theology."[64] This is the most explicit and knowledgeable endorsement of panentheism in the English language before Charles Hartshorne.

William Temple, John Robinson, and John Macquarrie are among the Anglican theologians who elaborate panentheism in the twentieth century.

The United States

Ralph Waldo Emerson and Transcendentalism

The transcendentalists, according to Perry Miller, are "children of the Puritan past who, having been emancipated by Unitarianism from New England's original Calvinism, found a new religious expression in forms derived from romantic literature and from the philosophical idealism of Germany."[65] The Puritan ancestors of such transcendentalist luminaries as Ralph Waldo Emerson (1803–1882), Henry David Thoreau (1817–1862), Amos Bronson Alcott (1799–1888), and Orestes Brownson (1803–1876) "had early exhibited a mystical strain and an ability to find God in nature." In addition, their philosophical preferences were clearly Neoplatonic. "Puritan philosophic thinking had favored the Platonic tradition with its idealism and its system of analogy between the material world and the spiritual realm."[66]

---

63. William Inge, *The Philosophy of Plotinus*, 3rd ed., 2 vols., Gifford Lectures, 1917–1918 (New York: Longmans, Green, 1929), 2:228; see John Macquarrie, *Twentieth-Century Religious Thought* (London: SCM Press, 1963), 148–50.

64. William Inge, *Christian Mysticism* (London: Methuen, 1899), 121.

65. Perry Miller, forward to *The American Transcendentalists: Their Prose and Poetry* (Garden City, NY: Doubleday, 1957; repr., Baltimore: Johns Hopkins University Press, 1981), ix. See also Donald Koster, "Major Influences," chap. 2 in *Transcendentalism in America* (Boston: Twayne, 1975).

66. Catherine L. Albanese, introduction to *The Spirituality of the American Transcendentalists* (Macon, GA: Mercer University Press, 1988), 3.

Jonathan Edwards typifies this perspective. His philosophy isolated from his theology is quite conducive to transcendentalism.

The transcendentalists were not American provincials. They traveled and studied in Germany, where they read Kant, Fichte, Schleiermacher, Hegel, and Schelling.[67] They also learned German philosophy from the works of Coleridge. More broadly, transcendentalists considered Jakob Böhme and Emanuel Swedenborg (1688–1772) as "spiritual heros."[68] Some even meditated on works of Hindu and Confucian spirituality.[69] The movement's intuitive ethos encouraged transcendentalism to embrace a diverse community of kindred spirits and sometimes incompatible ideas.

Ralph Waldo Emerson is a seminal figure. In "Nature" he asserts, "Philosophically considered, the universe is composed of Nature and the Soul."[70] Thus he introduces the "Over-Soul," the most famous doctrine of transcendentalism.[71] He summarizes this perspective: "Man is conscious of a universal soul within or behind his individual life, wherein, as in a firmament, the natures of Justice, Truth, Love, Freedom, arise and shine. This universal soul he calls Reason. . . . That which intellectually considered we call Reason, considered in relation to nature, we call Spirit. Spirit is the Creator. Spirit hath life in itself."[72] Soul or Spirit is an emanation of the divine One, it animates the whole world, and it is manifest in each individual soul: "Within man is the soul of the whole; the wise silence; the universal beauty, to which every part and particle is equally related; the eternal ONE."[73] The Soul's presence enlightens each soul to perceive the world as truly manifesting the One and to understand the One as the transcendental essence of the world. Indeed, the world is the manifestation of the One through the Soul in each soul.

---

67. Ibid., 6–7. See Octavius Frothingham, "Transcendentalism in Germany," chap. 2, and "Theology and Literature—Schleiermacher, Goethe, Richter, etc.," chap. 3 in *Transcendentalism in New England* (New York: Putnam's, 1876; repr. (Gloucester, MA: Peter Smith, 1965). Frothingham is a transcendentalist and discusses the transcendentalists' ongoing dialogue with imported German philosophy. See also Joseph Esposito, "Schelling's Influence in Nineteenth-Century America," chap. 7 in *Schelling's Idealism and Philosophy of Nature* (Lewisburg, PA: Bucknell University Press, 1977); and Henry Pochmann, *New England Transcendentalism and St. Louis Hegelianism* (New York: Haskell House, 1970).

68. Albanese, *Spirituality of the American Transcendentalists*, 7. Swedenborg was a Christian Neoplatonic mystic who affirmed emanation instead of creation *ex nihilo*. Yet he distinguished God from creation and disavowed pantheism. A good case can be made that he is a panentheist. Emerson was an enthusiastic devotee.

69. Ibid., 8; also Arthur Christy, *The Orient in American Transcendentalism: A Study of Emerson, Thoreau, and Alcott* (New York: Columbia University Press, 1932; repr., New York: Octagon, 1972).

70. Ralph Waldo Emerson, "Nature," in Albanese, *Spirituality of the American Transcendentalists*, 46–75, quote at 47.

71. Ralph Waldo Emerson, "The Over-Soul," ibid., 92–105.

72. Emerson, "Nature," 55.

73. Emerson, "Over-Soul," 93.

The Soul "passes into and becomes that man whom it enlightens . . . it takes him to itself."[74] Elsewhere Emerson expresses it more poetically: "I become a transparent eyeball; I am nothing; I see all; the currents of the Universal Being circulate through me; I am part or parcel of God."[75]

Although Emerson's assertions are not always precise, he is clearly a pan-entheist. He views himself and all creatures as "part or parcel of God." Yet he also distinguishes God and nature, affirming that God is the transcendent One manifest as the Soul of the World. Emerson's appeals to Plotinus, Böhme, and Swedenborg in his essays explicitly invoke the Neoplatonic tradition in an American romantic mode.

Transcendentalism shapes the American perspective in diverse ways. The prominent pastor and theologian Horace Bushnell (1802–1876), "America's Schleiermacher," reflects it in his *Nature and the Supernatural*.[76] It finds poetic expression in Walt Whitman's *Leaves of Grass*, particularly "Song of Myself." It is the intellectual and spiritual environment in which Charles Sanders Peirce and William James were raised.

Charles Sanders Peirce

Charles Sanders Peirce (1839–1914) is the father of American pragmatism.[77] He is thoroughly familiar with his intellectual heritage: "I was born and reared in the neighborhood of Concord—I mean Cambridge—at the time when Emerson, Hedge, and their friends were disseminating the ideas that they had caught from Schelling, and Schelling from Plotinus, from Boehme, or from God knows what minds stricken with the monstrous mysticism of the East. . . . Now, after long incubation, it comes to the surface, modified by mathematical conceptions and by training in physical investigations."[78] Peirce identifies with Schelling in a letter to William James: "If you were to call my philosophy Schellingism transformed in the light of

74. Ibid., 98.
75. Emerson, "Nature," 48.
76. Horace Bushnell, *Nature and the Supernatural: As Together Constituting the One System of God* (New York: Scribner's, 1864).
77. Wilkens and Padgett, *Christianity and Western Thought*, 2:217–26, provide a helpful introduction to his philosophy. Also Copleston, *Hist. Phil.*, vol. 8, chap. 14; Bruce Kucklick, "Charles Sanders Peirce," chap. 6 in *The Rise of American Philosophy* (New Haven: Yale University Press, 1977); and Robert Neville, "C. S. Peirce as a Non-Modernist Thinker," chap. 1 in *The Highroad around Modernism* (Albany: State University of New York Press, 1992).
78. Charles Sanders Peirce, *The Collected Papers*, ed. C. Hartshorne and P. Weiss, 8 vols. (Cambridge, MA: Harvard University Press, 1931–1935), vol. 6, par. 102–3.

modern physics, I should not take it hard."[79] Peirce modernizes romantic
Neoplatonism with scientific precision and Yankee practicality.

Peirce shares with Hegel and Schelling the view that the metaphysical
structure of reality is triadic. He distinguishes *firstness*, *secondness*, and
thirdness as the basic categories of logic and metaphysics. "First is the
conception of being or existing independent of anything else. Second
is the conception of being relative to, the conception of reaction with,
something else. Third is the conception of mediation, whereby a first
and second are brought into relation. . . . Chance is First, Law is Second,
the tendency to take habits is Third. Mind is First, matter is Second,
Evolution is Third."[80] Peirce insists that each category by itself is a mere
abstraction. Actually existing things are constituted by and exemplify all
three. Entities are triadic unities.

Correlated with firstness, secondness, and thirdness is a triad of basic
factors or forces that co-constitute the universe of actual beings: *tychasm,
ananchasm,* and *agapasm.*[81] *Tychasm* refers to the element of spontaneity or
chance in firstness. *Ananchasm* reflects secondness, the element of necessity
that orders and structures chance without completely eliminating it. *Agapasm*
is the factor that provides continuity, direction, and final purpose to the
spontaneity, order, and structure of things. The evolution of the universe as
a whole is thus constituted by the interplay of chance, determination, and
purpose in all things relative to other things.[82] The similarity of Peirce's triads
to the three potencies of Böhme and Schelling is not accidental.

The constitution of the universe as a whole naturally raises the question
of God. Peirce does not believe that the existence of God can be proven,
but he holds that our deep-seated intuitive belief in a personal deity is
justified by our awareness of the purposefully evolving order of nature.[83]
What we humans can know of God is limited and developing, and so a
definitive philosophical theology is beyond our reach. But Peirce does offer
general suggestions. He speaks of God the Creator as the "Absolute First"

79. Charles Sanders Peirce, letter to William James, January 28, 1894, in Ralph Barton Perry, *The
Thought and Character of William James*, 2 vols. (Boston: Little, Brown, 1935), 2:416.

80. Peirce, *Collected Papers*, vol. 6, sec. 32, pp. 25–26.

81. Ibid., 6:302.

82. Peirce, "Evolutionary Love," ibid., 6:287–317. Peirce is closer to Schelling than to Hegel in
two ways. His notion of dialectic, like Schelling's, is much broader and looser than Hegel's. And his
affirmation of spontaneity as an irreducible aspect of all reality reflects Schelling's later philosophy of
freedom. He criticizes Hegel for overemphasizing ananchasm.

83. Peirce, "A Neglected Argument for the Reality of God," ibid., 6:452–92; "Answers to Questions
concerning My Belief in God," ibid., 6:494–519, esp. 500, where he offers "an apology for resting the
belief [in God] upon instinct as the very bedrock on which all reasoning must be built."

and God the Terminus of all things as the "Absolute Second."[84] Similarly, he identifies the agapasm that draws the evolving universe into a community of love as the power of God.[85] Analogously to creatures, the divine nature itself exemplifies firstness, secondness, and thirdness as spontaneity, orderly determination, and purpose. Peirce suggests that God is like a "mind" or "vast consciousness" that constitutes the deep, dynamic structure of the purposefully evolving psychophysical universe.[86] One can see why he considered his view "a Schelling-fashioned idealism which holds matter to be mere specialized and partially deadened mind."[87] Plotinus's view of matter as the most remote emanation echoes in the background.

Like Schelling, Peirce is a panentheist. Firstness, secondness, and thirdness are clearly reminiscent of Schelling's three potencies. Like Schelling, he cannot posit the actuality of God in himself without the universe, for that would be Absolute Firstness alone. In fact the evolving universe, together with the divine agape to which it responds, is the Third that necessarily mediates God as First and Second, the first and final cause. Although the universe is an aspect of and thus "in" the divine Mind, Peirce strongly distinguishes God and creatures, affirming that God is more than the material universe. Furthermore, creatures are not merely extensions of the divine essence, as in pantheism, because they possess their own actuality and spontaneity. Though not fully systematized, Peirce's view of God and the world is a clear case of modern panentheism.

William James

Like Peirce, William James (1842–1910) was raised in transcendentalist New England. His father, Henry, was an ardent Swedenborgian. Trained in medicine, he turned to philosophy after years of teaching psychology at Harvard.

James embraces pragmatism as a methodology that does not automatically entail particular philosophical positions.[88] Pragmatism determines the meaning of propositions and tests their truth by their practical consequences—whether they clarify our experience, remove dissonance between our beliefs and experience, and enable us to live better. Shaped by science,

---

84. Ibid., 1:362.
85. Peirce, "Evolutionary Love."
86. Peirce, "My Belief in God," in *Collected Papers*, 6:501–3.
87. Ibid., 6:102.
88. William James, *Pragmatism: A New Name for some Old Ways of Thinking together with Four Related Essays Selected from The Meaning of Truth* (New York, London: Longmans, Green, 1948).

James's epistemology is a radical pragmatic empiricism that bases all knowledge on experience.

Radical empiricism yields two metaphysical consequences for James—panpsychism and pluralism.[89] *Panpsychism* is a position reached by a series of inferences. Because all distinctions between mental and physical reality are derived from experience, there must be an experiential reality more basic than either mind or matter that variously appears as one or the other or both. This position is *neutral monism*. James then qualifies this monism as *vitalism*, the view that the primordial reality is the powerful force of life in the universe.[90] Following Fechner, he further characterizes this vital force as a "stream of consciousness," thereby bridging the gap between life and sentience.[91] This position is equivalent to panpsychism, the doctrine that "all is psychic."

The second consequence of James's empiricism is the irreducible plurality of existent things. What we experience is not one reality, and it does not entail only one reality. Thus he endorses a metaphysical pluralism completely contrary to the monistic idealism of his contemporaries Josiah Royce and F. H. Bradley.

Combining both conclusions, James's metaphysics is a *panpsychic pluralism*. The basic reality is a conscious living force that is diversified in and contains an irreducible plurality of individuals, some of which are conscious and some not.[92]

This basic reality is God. "I will call this higher part of the universe by the name God." James argues that belief in God is rationally justified by its significant consequences in human life, even though God's existence cannot be demonstrated.[93] The preconscious awareness of the power of life deep in each human being is the seed of religion in all its diverse forms. "Transcendentalists are fond of the term 'Over-soul,'" he notes, but they think of God only as "a medium of communion." He counters, "'God' is a causal

89. Kucklick, "Jamesean Metaphysics," chap. 17 in *The Rise of American Philosophy*, is a clear summary.

90. James's vitalism was confirmed and strengthened by his study of, and correspondence with, the French philosopher Henri Bergson, whom we encounter later in this chapter. See Perry, "James and Bergson," chap. 36 in *Thought and Character of William James*.

91. James, "Concerning Fechner." James holds that the basic stuff is "psychic" but not that rocks and plants have a hidden psychic life.

92. William James, *Essays in Radical Empiricism* (1912) and *A Pluralistic Universe* (1909), published together in one volume (New York and London: Longmans, Green, 1947). Whitehead's panentheism also affirms panpsychism and pluralism.

93. William James, "The Will to Believe" (1896) in *The Will to Believe and Other Essays in Popular Philosophy* (New York and London: Longmans, Green, 1911).

agent as well as a medium of communion, and that is the aspect which I wish to emphasize."[94]

But God cannot be the sole causal agent for two reasons: the universe is genuinely pluralistic, and it contains evil as well as good. James concludes that the best way of relating God and the world is "to accept, along with the superhuman consciousness, the notion that it is not all-embracing, the notion, in other words, that there is a God, but that he is finite, either in power or in knowledge, or in both at once."[95] Similar to Schelling, he affirms creaturely freedom by limiting divine power and thereby absolves God of responsibility for evil.

Although James is often called a finite theist and at least one commentator labels him a pantheist,[96] the evidence indicates that he is a panentheist. He distances himself from the "pantheistic idealism" and "monism" of Hegel, Bradley, and Royce, but he affirms that creatures are within God.[97] "We are indeed internal parts of God and not external creations, on any possible reading of the panpsychic system. Yet because God is not the absolute, but is himself a part when the system is conceived pluralistically, his functions can be taken as not wholly dissimilar to those of the other smaller parts."[98] In James's view, reality is one system that includes God and creatures, where God and creatures are metaphysically distinct and plural and yet creatures are part of and thus "in" God. James's God is finite—not absolute, infinite, or all-determining. But his theology is finite panentheism, not just finite theism.[99]

The panentheistic legacy of Peirce and James is preserved in twentieth-century American philosophy by thinkers such as Alfred North Whitehead (who moved from England to Harvard), Edgar Brightman, William Hocking, and Charles Hartshorne, all of whom read Peirce and James carefully.

France

Jules Lequier

Jules Lequier (or Lequyer, 1814–1862) was a French philosopher and sincere Roman Catholic who emphasized human freedom to the point of

---

94. William James, *The Varieties of Religious Experience* (New York: Longmans, Green, 1911), 512–19, quotes from 516–517 n. 2.

95. James, "Conclusions," section VIII of *A Pluralistic Universe*, 311.

96. Kucklick, *The Rise of American Philosophy*, 333.

97. Essays in James, *A Pluralistic Universe*, deal with each of these thinkers.

98. Ibid., "Conclusions," 318.

99. James Collins, *God in Modern Philosophy* (Chicago: Henry Regnery, 1959), 440 n. 28: "Today his standpoint would perhaps be catalogued as an instance of 'panentheism' or the presence of everything in God."

relativizing God.[100] Influenced by Fichte's philosophy of the ego as will, Lequier asserts that humans are endowed by God with irreducible libertarian freedom. Since this is so and since free actions are uncaused and undetermined, God's omniscience does not include eternal or predictive knowledge of what humans will freely choose to do. "You are free to do something. God does not know that you will do it, since you are able not to do it, and God does not know that you will not do it, since you can do it."[101] God only knows what we will do when we do it. Therefore God grows in knowledge as history unfolds. God changes in other ways as well, because "the relation of God to the creature is as real as the relation of the creature to God. . . . The act of the man makes a spot in the absolute which destroys the absolute. God, who sees things change, changes also in beholding them, or else he does not perceive that they change."[102] Lequier asserts that God is both absolute and changing.

Lequier is not attempting to subvert Christian doctrine but to argue that Christianity truly preserves human freedom as no other philosophy can. His claims—that God does not know the future, that he learns by observing our actions, and that he therefore changes—echo the Socinians and anticipate the open free-will theism currently debated by American evangelicals.[103]

Lequier may not be a full panentheist because he does not explain how creatures are "in" God. But he does state that free human acts put "a spot in the absolute which destroys the absolute." This assertion implies panentheism if being "in" the Absolute is understood as God's internalization of all the effects that creatures have on him. If creatures significantly shape what God knows and does, then they do become part of the divine life while retaining their ontological distinctness. The existence and history of God and his creatures are completely intertwined. In this way Lequier's position at least suggests relational panentheism.[104]

100. Jules Lequier, *Oeuvres complètes* (Neuchâtel: Baconnière, 1952); *Translation of the Works*, ed. Donald Wayne Viney, Studies in the History of Philosophy 48 (Lewiston, NY: Edwin Mellen, 1998). See Étienne Gilson, Thomas Langan, and Armand A. Maurer, *Recent Philosophy: Hegel to the Present* (New York: Random House, 1962), 736–37; Hartshorne and Reese, *Philosophers Speak of God*, 227–30; and Donald Wayne Viney, "Jules Lequyer and the Openness of God," *Faith and Philosophy* 14/2 (1997): 212–35.

101. Jules Lequier, *La recherche d'une première verité* [*The Search for a Primary Truth*], ed. Charles Renouvier (Saint-Cloud, France: Belin, 1865), 253 (Hartshorne and Reese, 230).

102. Lequier, *Recherche*, 141–42 (Hartshorne and Reese, 229).

103. See the discussions of open theism in chaps. 7 and 14, below.

104. Hartshorne and Reese, *Philosophers Speak of God*, 228, classify Socinus and Lequier as temporalistic theists but state that "perhaps they could be shown to have been panentheists as well." For the same reasons, open or free-will theists might be panentheists even though they reject the label.

Lequier was not a major figure. But he did influence his student Charles Renouvier and, through him, William James, who met Renouvier and carried on a lifelong correspondence.[105]

Charles Renouvier

Charles Renouvier (1815–1903) was a respected philosopher even though he never held a university post.[106] Influenced by Kant's critique of metaphysics and Comte's positivism, he insists that phenomena or empirical data are the foundation of knowledge. Like Kant, he argues that some phenomena of human existence cannot be reduced to the categories of nature because humans experience themselves as free personal and moral agents as well. Following Kant and Lequier, Renouvier's moral philosophy emphasizes human freedom as a necessary condition of moral responsibility.[107]

Renouvier's theology is strikingly similar to James's. Affirming human freedom, he rejects Spinozism, absolute idealism, and classical Christian theology because he finds their views of God as infinite, omniscient, and omnipotent to be deterministic. He does not reject God altogether, however, but posits instead a personal God who, though great, is finite in knowledge and power. God must be regarded as personal, because personhood is the highest ontological status known to humans. Renouvier's theology not only preserves human freedom but also absolves God from the evil that humans commit. The existence of God cannot be proven but is suggested by moral experience in addition to grounding it. Belief in God, as belief in general, requires an element of will. We will to believe in a personal God because this belief arises from and enhances the experience of personal existence in the world. In Renouvier's own words, God is "the permanent personality in the world."[108] James shares all these views.

Renouvier is not an explicit panentheist because he does not assert directly that creatures are in God ontologically. Like Lequier, however, his interactive view of the relation between human persons and the divine person in the cosmos is readily conducive to panentheism. It surely implies that God has two natures. His similarity to James strengthens the case. But even if he is

---

105. Perry, *Thought and Character of William James*, 152–53.

106. George Boas, "Renouvier, Charles Bernard," *EncPhil* 7:180–82; Copleston, *Hist. Phil.*, vol. 9, chap. 7, sec. 2; Gilson, Langan, and Maurer, *Recent Philosophy*, 318–21.

107. Charles Renouvier, *Science de la morale*, 2 vols. (Paris: Librairie Philosophique de Ladrange, 1869); and *Philosophie analytique de l'histoire* (Paris: Laroux, 1896–97).

108. Gilson, Langan, and Maurer, *Recent Philosophy*, 321, referring to Renouvier's *Philosophie analytique de l'histoire*.

not a panentheist, he influenced some who are, including Henri Bergson and James.

Henri Bergson

Henri Bergson (1859–1941) was professor of philosophy at the Collège de France from 1900 to 1924. He developed a unique metaphysical system that attempts to reconcile two trends: French positivism's interest in empirical facts and the theory of evolution, and idealism's concern to avoid materialism and to preserve room for human personality, culture, morality, and religion.[109]

Bergson begins with the data of human consciousness and the process by which we come to distinguish ourselves from objects in the world.[110] The basic datum is the immediate stream of consciousness of our own inner experience or psychic life. All our ideas and language, including math and science, arise from experience. Even metaphysics must be derived from intuition. Science and philosophy ought never to subvert the primacy of experience. In fact, science is inadequate to express all that we experience. The basic reality for Bergson is the experiential movement of life. This position is akin to the vitalism and panpsychism of Fechner and James.

Creative Evolution is Bergson's elaboration of an intuitive metaphysics that incorporates the evolutionary world picture of science.[111] From experience we notice that we are both determined and free, he argues. We are constrained by the conditions of life and by other beings as well as by our own limited capacities. But we also have the powers of choice and action by which we shape our world. Bergson posits that his intuitive approach to philosophy is "the coincidence of human consciousness with the living principle whence it emanates, a contact with the creative effort." "The creative effort" is the cosmic power that generates life and human creativity. Awareness of our capacity for limited creativity, in turn, gives humans direct access to this power. Bergson's philosophy claims to articulate this relationship explicitly: "The impetus of life . . . consists in a need of creation. It cannot create ab-

---

109. Copleston, *Hist. Phil.*, vol. 9, chaps. 9–10. Gilson, Langan, and Maurer, *Recent Philosophy*, 306–17; Daniel Herman, *The Philosophy of Henri Bergson* (Washington, DC: University Press of America, 1980); Alan R. Lacey, *Bergson* (New York: Routledge, 1989); John Mullarkey, *Bergson and Philosophy* (Notre Dame, IN: University of Notre Dame Press, 2000).

110. Henri Bergson, *Time and Free Will: An Essay on the Immediate Data of Consciousness*, trans. F. L. Pogson (London and New York, 1910), translation of *Essai sur les données immediates de la conscience* (1889).

111. Henri Bergson, *Creative Evolution*, trans. Arthur Mitchell (New York: Henry Holt, 1911), translation of *L'évolution creatrice* (1907).

solutely, because it is confronted with matter, that is to say with the movement that is the inverse of its own. But it seizes upon this matter, which is
necessity itself, and strives to introduce into it the largest possible amount
of indetermination and liberty."[112] Here the life-impetus shapes matter like
Plato's Demiurge.

In the "creative effort" or "impetus of life" we encounter Bergson's famous
élan vital, the Vital Force manifest in the evolution of the world. This force
is creative because it generates the emergence of new levels of existence and
new kinds of being that are not preformed or predetermined in previous
states of the world. In evolution there are genuine chance, spontaneity, and
novelty, as well as the causal determination and structural limitations implicit
in nature. The Vital Force is purposive: it aims at realizing higher forms of
existence. But precisely what forms they take, including the particular spiri-
tual-rational-moral characteristics that humans happen to have, is open to
the creative process.

Creative Evolution criticizes traditional views of God but is hesitant to
deify the Vital Force. Bergson does not wish to push his conclusions beyond
the limits of intuition. Yet the natural theology implicit in the book is obvious. It is highly reminiscent of Neoplatonism and German romanticism. As
Copleston observes, "the concept of the élan vital bears some resemblance
. . . to that of the soul of the world as found in ancient philosophy and in
some modern philosophers such as Schelling."[113]

In a much later work, *The Two Sources of Morality and Religion*, Bergson
does extend the conclusions of *Creative Evolution* into religion and theology.[114]
He focuses on "dynamic religion," which is the mystical consciousness that
has evolved as a capacity of the human species. "In our eyes, the ultimate
end of mysticism is the establishment of a contact, consequently of a partial
coincidence, with the creative effort which life itself manifests."[115] In mystical
experience humans enjoy immediate participation in the Vital Force that
has generated them. Mystical experience provides Bergson a way of moving
beyond the merely philosophical conclusions of *Creative Evolution*: "There is
nothing preventing the philosopher from following to its logical conclusion

---

112. Ibid., 251.

113. Copleston, *Hist. Phil.*, vol. 9, chap. 9, sec. 5, p. 223. Gilson, in Gilson, Langan, and Maurer,
Recent Philosophy, 314, observes that "the active power behind Bergson's creative evolution still had a
long way to go before joining the God of Christian theology."

114. Henri Bergson, *The Two Sources of Morality and Religion*, trans. R. Ashley Audra and Cloudes-
ley Brereton (New York: Henry Holt, 1935), 244; translation of *Les deux sources de la morale et de la
religion* (1932).

115. Ibid., 209.

the idea which mysticism suggests to him of a universe which is the mere visible and tangible aspect of love and of the need of loving, together with all the consequences entailed by this creative emotion."[116]

Bergson concludes that the Creative Force is divine: "This effort is of God, if it is not God himself."[117] God has a special, correlative relation with his human creatures. "Beings have been called into existence who were destined to love and be loved, since creative energy is to be defined as love. Distinct from God, Who is this energy itself, they could spring into being only in a universe, and therefore the universe sprang into being."[118] In other words, God had to create the world in order to create humans so that some of them might directly know and love him in return. Mystical participation in God is the ultimate purpose of the evolution of the world.

Bergson's own summary is worth quoting:

> The mystical love of humanity . . . lies at the very root of feeling and reason, as of all other things. Coinciding with God's love for His handiwork, a love which has been the source of everything, it would yield up, to anyone who knew how to question it, the secret of creation. . . . What it wants to do, with God's help, is to complete the creation of the human species and make of humanity what it would have straightaway become, had it been able to assume its final shape without the assistance of man himself. Or to use words which mean . . . the same thing in different terms: its direction is exactly that of the vital impetus; it *is* this impetus itself, communicated in its entirety to exceptional men.[119]

For Bergson, mysticism is the evolutionary means toward the divine end, which is complete human evolution and communion with God.

Bergson's theology is a species of modern dynamic panentheism. God is the creative power of the evolving universe. He needs a world and is immanent in the cosmos as the Vital Force in which all creatures live, move, and have their being. Although they are in God, creatures are ontologically distinct from God and partially free in how they evolve. And although all things are in God, he has generated human creatures with a special capacity for mystical experience: direct, self-conscious, reciprocal participation in the Vital Force itself.

Bergson's mystical vitalism is unique. But the general similarities of his cosmological and theological ideas to thinkers such as Schelling, James, and

116. Ibid., 244.
117. Ibid., 209.
118. Ibid., 245–46.
119. Ibid., 223.

Alexander are unmistakable. He is widely read but has had few close disciples. In the twentieth century, his countryman, Pierre Teilhard de Chardin, carried on his synthesis of religion and cosmic evolution.[120]

Conclusion

This chapter highlights the proliferation of panentheism since the great systems of Hegel and Schelling, whose influence can be traced not only in Germany but also in England, the United States, and France (as well as Italy and Spain, which are not included). Innovative thinkers refine Neoplatonic and romantic panentheism in various ways as they engage natural science, psychology, social science, philosophy, theology, and religion during the nineteenth century. Their numerous, sophisticated, and diverse contributions provide the context in which more famous twentieth-century panentheists, such as Teilhard, Whitehead, and Tillich, forge and refine their ideas.

120. Teilhard acknowledges his debt to Bergson at several points in his spiritual autobiography, Pierre Teilhard de Chardin, "The Heart of Matter" (1950), in *The Heart of Matter*, trans. René Hague (New York: Harcourt Brace Jovanovich, 1979).

6

Teilhard de Chardin's
Christocentric Panentheism

The cosmic evolutionary spirituality of Pierre Teilhard de Chardin (1881–1955) is heir to the legacy of Christian Neoplatonism and is shaped by the philosophy of Henri Bergson. Teilhard has had a broader impact than any other twentieth-century panentheist. Far beyond academic theologians and intellectual devotees, his perspective has inspired progressive forces in the Roman Catholic Church since Vatican II.[1] Much liberation, feminist, and ecological theology builds on his panentheistic vision. He is widely regarded in interreligious and non-Christian circles as a model for integrating spirituality with current postmodern worldviews.[2] Indeed, in 1984 the United Nations sponsored a Teilhard Colloquium.[3]

Teilhard's spiritual autobiography recounts the development of his religious worldview.[4] Raised in a devout Roman Catholic family, he sensed

---

1. David Lane, *The Phenomenon of Teilhard: Prophet for a New Age* (Macon, GA: Mercer University Press, 1996), esp. chap. 3, "'Patron Saint' of 'New Age' Catholicism?"

2. See, e.g., references to Teilhard by New Age proponent Marilyn Ferguson, *The Aquarian Conspiracy: Personal and Social Transformation in the 1980's* (Los Angeles: J. P. Tarcher, 1980).

3. Leo Zonneveld, ed., *Humanity's Quest for Unity: A United Nations Teilhard Colloquium* (Wassenaar, Neth.: Mirananda, 1985).

4. Pierre Teilhard de Chardin, "The Heart of Matter," in *Heart of Matter*, trans. René Hague (New York: Harcourt Brace Jovanovich, 1979). Ursula King, *Spirit of Fire: The Life and Vision of Teilhard de*

the presence of God in matter already in early childhood. The scholastic philosophy and theology he learned as a Jesuit novitiate did not always fit with his study of paleontology and evolutionary biology. It was Bergson's *Creative Evolution* that first enabled him to accept cosmic evolution, to move from a "static Cosmos to the organic state and dignity of a *Cosmogenesis* . . . an 'evolutive' Universe."[5] As a generalization, Teilhard's entire project is a progressive Roman Catholic modification and augmentation of Bergson's philosophy, which views cosmic love and mystical experience as the culminating coincidence of human evolution and the divine Vital Force.[6] Teilhard articulates a perspective in which the evolution of the universe strives toward life, and life toward the human mind, which generates a universal community of love that eventually reaches a climax, an Omega point in union with Christ. In his own unique language: "Cosmogenesis reveals itself . . . first as Biogenesis and then Noogenesis [genesis of Mind], and finally culminates in the Christogenesis which every Christian venerates." The entire process centers on Christ. "The *Christ of Revelation* is none other than the *Omega of Evolution*."[7] Thus Teilhard synthesizes his devotion to Christ, his understanding of Roman Catholic theology, and his evolutionary cosmology into a grand scientific-metaphysical-mystical vision.

This chapter begins with Teilhard's account of cosmic evolution toward its ultimate state, then considers his theological interpretation of this process, and concludes with observations about his panentheism.

Cosmic Evolution to the Omega Point

The Human Phenomenon is Teilhard's fullest account of cosmic and human evolution. He insists that the book is scientific. It "must not be read as a metaphysical work, still less as some kind of theological essay, but solely and

---

Chardin (Maryknoll, NY: Orbis, 1996), is a sympathetic biography. Doran McCarty, *Teilhard de Chardin* (Waco: Word, 1976), is a good introduction to his thought. Henri de Lubac, *The Religion of Teilhard de Chardin,* trans. René Hague (New York: Desclee, 1967); Émile Rideau, *The Thought of Teilhard de Chardin,* trans. René Hague (New York: Harper and Row, 1967); and Donald Gray, *The One and the Many: Teilhard de Chardin's Vision of Unity* (New York: Herder and Herder, 1969), are more extensive studies.

5. Teilhard, "Heart of Matter," 25–26.

6. Recall the section on Bergson in chap. 5, above. In "Creative Union" (1917) Teilhard explains that his view is the converse of Bergson's: for Bergson, the cosmos radiates from a center of emission; for Teilhard, it concentrates upward toward a center of attraction. See de Lubac, *Religion of Teilhard,* 198. Teilhard also studied others in the panentheist tradition, such as Emerson and James; see King, *Spirit of Fire,* 59.

7. Teilhard, "The Christic," in *Heart of Matter,* 94, 92.

exclusively as a scientific study."[8] Briefly summarized, the book reflects on standard scientific accounts of the origin and development of the universe in order to understand the basic elements, dynamics, and patterns of cosmic evolution that eventually produced the human race with its current social, cultural, intellectual, and spiritual achievements. Following the trajectory of past evolution into the future, Teilhard projects a culmination, or "Omega point," of human evolution—a community of spiritual persons. It appears to him that the whole universe has existed and developed over billions of years in order to actualize humanity in this ultimate state. Teilhard regards this conclusion as scientific. Only in the epilogue does he interpret cosmic evolution in the light of Christian revelation.

Evolution from Energy to Humanity

The Human Phenomenon begins with matter, but not as a purely material substance. Teilhard learned from Bergson that "Matter and Spirit . . . were no longer two things, but two states or two aspects of one and the same cosmic Stuff."[9] Like James, Bergson, and Whitehead, Teilhard adopts panpsychism: "All energy is essentially psychic." Matter and spirit are different forms of psychic energy: "This fundamental energy is divided into two distinct components: a *tangential energy* . . . and a *radial energy*."[10] Tangential energy is the material principle, the "outside" of things, which is organized into relatively stable patterns and structures and distributed centrifugally on constant levels of being. Tangential energy is evident in the regularity of physical, chemical, and biological entities and functions. Radial energy is the spiritual principle, the "inside" of things that pulls them together centripetally and reorganizes them in novel ways so that new levels of being emerge. The emergence of life from chemicals and consciousness from life are effects of radial energy. Teilhard's term for the emergence of new kinds of being is "Transformism."[11]

He then outlines how the interaction of tangential and radial energy generated the cosmos, the earth and its crust, and their life-supporting environments: the "barysphere, lithosphere, hydrosphere, atmosphere, and stratosphere."[12] He explains that life began as a result of the interplay of the

8. Pierre Teilhard de Chardin, *The Human Phenomenon*, trans. Sarah Appleton-Weber (Portland, OR: Sussex Academic Press, 1999), 1. It was completed in 1947 and first published in 1955. An earlier translation (1959) is entitled *The Phenomenon of Man*.

9. Teilhard, "Heart of Matter," 26.

10. Teilhard, *Human Phenomenon*, 30.

11. Teilhard, "Notes on the Essence of Transformism," in *Heart of Matter*, 107–14. Lane, "Transformism and Cosmogenesis," in *Phenomenon of Teilhard*, 37–44.

12. Teilhard, *Human Phenomenon*, 34.

tangential distribution of chemical complexity with radial energy's concentration of chemicals into new forms. "The cell is the *natural grain of life* just as the atom is the natural grain of unorganized matter."[13]

Teilhard's overview of the biosphere and the development of the various branches of the tree of life tracks evolution toward consciousness. "Life is at the head—with the whole of physics subordinate to it. And at the heart of life, to explain its progression, is the driving force of a rise of consciousness."[14] Thus the biosphere strains toward the psychosphere, the realm of sensation and awareness. From simple worms to higher primates, animals share these capacities for life and consciousness in many different forms.

Only in humans, however, has radial energy transformed consciousness into intelligence, the capacity for reflection, which is consciousness turned upon itself. "Psychogenesis has led us to ... *noogenesis*" (genesis of mind). This development gives humans tremendous abilities in relating to the world that animals do not enjoy. It also gives us self-awareness, which is personhood. "The cell has become 'someone.' After the grain of matter, after the grain of life, here, finally constituted, is the *grain of thought!*"[15] The evolution of humanity continues to strive toward completion. In Teilhard's technical terms: "Hominization ... is the individual instantaneous leap from instinct to thought, but which also in the wider sense is the progressive phyletic spiritualization in human civilization of all the forces contained in animality."[16] In other words, evolution transforms bodies into minds and nature into culture.

Teilhard traces the development and history of Homo sapiens. His reading of world history is unabashedly Eurocentric: "The principal axis of anthropogenesis has passed through the West.... It has taken on its definitive human value only by becoming incorporated into the system of European ideas and occupations."[17] He explains all the fruits of modern civilization—social organization, technology, political justice, and high culture—as evolutionary transformations of previous levels of existence by radial energy: "Are not the artificial, moral, and juridical quite simply the natural, physical, and organic, *hominized*?"[18] Cultural development and progress are possible because human heredity is augmented by communal education and learned behavior is enriched by intellectual innovation. With culture, the course of

13. Ibid., 43.
14. Ibid., 96.
15. Ibid., 123, 117.
16. Ibid., 122.
17. Ibid., 146.
18. Ibid., 155.

evolution becomes subject to human action: "To a fundamental extent *we hold it in our own hands*: responsible for its past to its future."[19]

Such power has been a bane as well as a blessing. Mixed with the advances and benefits of modern civilization are its problems and dark sides: new diseases, masses of urban poor, social and labor unrest, environmental degradation, and technological warfare. "What is forming and swelling beneath our modern uneasiness is nothing less than an organic crisis in evolution," Teilhard warns. The human race faces an ultimate dilemma: "Either nature is closed to what we require of the future; in which case thought, the fruit of millions of years of effort, will suffocate, still-born, aborting on itself, in an absurd universe. Or else an opening does exist—of supersoul above our souls."[20] Evolution will burn out if it does not continue upwards toward spirit.

At this point Teilhard steps beyond purely rational reflection: "the observations of science must cede to the anticipations of faith." He offers an argument for faith in the future, based on the evolutionary history of the past: "Fundamentally, the best guarantee that something will happen is that it seems to us to be vitally necessary."[21] For the human race to survive and achieve its full potential, he argues, it must act on the sure belief that it will continue to evolve in the same direction as it has to the present. It must believe and live toward the future. In addition, future flourishing requires human solidarity, which excludes individualism, tribalism, and racism. "The gates of the future, the entry into the superhuman, will not open ahead to some privileged few, or to a single people. . . . They will yield only to the thrust of *all together* in the direction where all can rejoin and complete one another in a spiritual renewal of the Earth."[22]

Evolution from Humanity to the Superpersonal Omega

Teilhard is aware that the monstrous collectivisms of National Socialism and Communism, along with all the other evils in history, leave him vulnerable to charges of utopianism. He even raises the possibility that humans will fail to adapt and will die out. But he points to the deep dynamics of evolution itself to justify his hope. "Evolution must culminate ahead in some kind of supreme consciousness" because "structurally the noosphere and in a more general sense, the world represent an ensemble that is not merely

19. Ibid., 158.
20. Ibid., 161, 163.
21. Ibid., 163.
22. Ibid., 173.

closed, but *centered* . . . in a point—call it *Omega*—which fuses them and consummates them integrally in itself."[23] He explains that the same radial energy as originally produced human persons continues to concentrate and center them on a point that must be superconscious and superpersonal, or "hyperpersonal." In order to be personal, this Center must not absorb other persons but commune with them: "Omega in its ultimate principle *can only be a distinct Center radiating at the core of a system of centers* . . . a grouping in which the personalization of the whole and the elementary personalization of each reach their maximum simultaneously, and without blending."[24] The Omega point must be a Superperson in community with all individual persons.

The only way this community can evolve is through love, not random association or coercion. Teilhard argues that it is cosmic evolution, not romantic utopianism, that gives him reason for hope. "Love (namely, the affinity of one being for another) . . . represents a general property of all life. . . . If some internal propensity to unite did not exist, even in the molecule . . . it would be physically impossible for love to appear higher up, in ourselves, in the hominized state."[25] Cosmic evolution generates human love and a sense of cosmic solidarity. But neither the cosmos nor the human race as such can be the highest object of human love because both are impersonal aggregates. The evolving trajectory of personal love points to an ultimate Person. Cosmic evolution "will only end by plunging us back into supermatter if it does not lead to Someone."[26]

Teilhard now argues that this Someone is not just future but has existed all along. Someone is the "*already present* reality and radiation of that mysterious Center of our centers . . . called 'Omega.'"[27] He points out that science recognizes a mysterious "something more" in each level of being from which newer and higher levels have emerged, but science cannot explain it. Thus a "Soul of souls" is not an unreasonable, antiscientific idea.

Teilhard gives two arguments for postulating the transcendence and preexistence of Omega. The first appeals again to love, the fact that attraction has been present throughout cosmic evolution. "To be supremely attractive, Omega must be already supremely present." The second is a kind of "unmoved mover" argument, that the evolution of life must depend on a "superlife" that is not subject to death. To have elicited the cosmos contain-

23. Ibid., 183–84.
24. Ibid., 186–87.
25. Ibid., 188.
26. Ibid., 190.
27. Ibid., 191.

ing human life and love, "Omega must be independent of the collapse of the powers with which evolution is woven."[28] For these reasons, Teilhard claims, a truly scientific overview of cosmic evolution concludes that Spirit is fundamental, the *"Prime Mover ahead."* In more technical terms: "In its radial nucleus, the world finds its shape and natural consistency by gravitating . . . toward a divine focal point of Spirit that draws it forward." In sum, scientific cosmology implies that the principle of love and life must be both within and beyond the cosmos. "In its evolutionary aspect Omega still only shows *half* of itself. At the same time that it is the term of the series, it is also *outside* the series."[29]

A quote in the previous paragraph refers to the Spirit as "divine," thus introducing religious language at this point in *The Human Phenomenon*. Teilhard's reflections on human evolution turn out to be a natural theology, a rational argument for God's existence from the nature and order of the universe. He is even able to deduce some divine attributes from the Goal of his scientific projection: "Autonomy, actuality, irreversibility, and finally, therefore, transcendence are the four attributes of Omega."[30]

The Superlife that is the Soul of cosmic evolution also enables human souls to survive death. Although plants and animals die, personhood is an "irreversible unification. . . . In the human, the radial escapes the tangential and is freed from it. . . . One by one . . . 'souls' break away around us, carrying their incommunicable charge of consciousness toward what is above."[31] The evolution of matter into individual spirits is permanent.

The ultimate future will inevitably complete the evolution of matter into mind and spirit in union with God. Eschatologically, all becomes spirit with Spirit: "The end of the world: the reversal of equilibrium, detaching the spirit, complete at last, from its material matrix, to rest from now on with its whole weight on God-Omega." There are two possible ways of ending, "ecstasy in concord or discord."[32] One is peaceful, the other a violent apocalyptic clash with fully developed evil. It is impossible to predict which will occur, but both culminate at Omega.

Teilhard summarizes his whole project: "To make a place for thought in the world, I have had to interiorize matter; to imagine an energetics of spirit; to conceive a noogenesis rising counter to entropy; to provide a direction, an arrow, and critical points for evolution; and to make all

28. Ibid., 192.
29. Ibid., 193.
30. Ibid.
31. Ibid., 194.
32. Ibid., 206–7.

things finally turn in on Someone."[33] Scientific reflection on nature has led to a Person.

Teilhard's Theology: Omega Is God in the Cosmic Christ

Natural Theology and Apologetics

In Catholic tradition, natural theology is interpreted and completed by revealed theology. Accordingly, the epilogue of *The Human Phenomenon* offers a brief apologetics indicating Christian doctrine's rich comprehension of cosmic evolution.[34] Christian truth and Christian love are Teilhard's evidence that the Omega is already present in world history: "God, the Center of centers. Christian dogma culminates in this final vision—exactly and so clearly the Omega point." God achieves the ultimate unity of all things "by partially immersing himself in things ... and then, from this base found interiorly at the heart of matter, by taking on the leadership and head of what we now call evolution." This "redemptive incarnation" of God in all things culminates in Jesus Christ: "Christ, who is the principle of universal vitality, has sprung up as man among us ... aggregating the entire psyche of the Earth to himself."[35] In this way Teilhard argues that the Christian faith not only fits with contemporary science but also strongly affirms it. He even claims that it is necessary for the completion of human evolution. "Christianity represents the only current of thought bold and progressive enough to embrace the world. ... It *alone* ... on the modern Earth shows itself capable of synthesizing the whole and the person in a single vital act."[36] Christianity and evolution are not antithetical but in fact need each other.

Overview of Teilhard's Theology

Because Teilhard did not write a systematic theology, his theology must be reconstructed from various sources.[37] His "last and supreme definition of the Omega point," in "Outline of a Dialectic of Spirit," is a summary of his

---

33. Ibid., 208.
34. Teilhard, "My *Phenomenon of Man*: An Essential Observation," in *Heart of Matter*, 150: "It is precisely classical apologetics—but (in conformity with modern views) transposed from a static Universe to a Universe in movement—from a Cosmos to a Cosmogenesis."
35. Teilhard, *Human Phenomenon*, 211.
36. Ibid., 212.
37. Rideau, *The Thought of Teilhard*, esp. chap. 6, "Theology," is an excellent account.

comprehensive theological vision.[38] Omega is the center of a single complex whole (Pleroma) that consists of three concentric and progressively deeper centers. The outermost center is the natural culmination of the humanized cosmos. Within this center is the natural-supernatural culmination of Christ's union with the church. The innermost center is the transcendent Triune God. Christ involves all three, binding them together. In other words, the Triune God and the humanized creation, mediated by the Cosmic Christ in the church, constitute one complex Whole. Let us look at the parts, beginning with God.

God's Transcendence and Immanence

"Outline of a Dialectic of Spirit" reaffirms "the Existence of a Transcendent God,"[39] which Teilhard had argued for in *The Human Phenomenon*. Responding to charges of pantheism and naturalism, he points out that the cosmic Omega presupposes "behind it, and deeper than it, a transcendent—a divine—nucleus." It is "necessarily an *auto*-center.... In virtue of this center of himself he subsists in himself, independently of time and space."[40] Thus God is transcendent.

God's transcendence is also defended in "My Fundamental Vision." Here Teilhard reiterates his "metaphysics of union," which defines Being as Union: For active being, "to be is to unite oneself, or to unite others." Passive being is "to be united and unified by another."[41] The first phase of the metaphysics of union is to posit the existence of "the irreversible and self-sufficient presence of a 'First Being' (our Point Omega)."[42] Teilhard clearly affirms God's transcendence and aseity.[43]

---

38. Pierre Teilhard de Chardin, "Outline of a Dialectic of Spirit" (1946), in *Activation of Energy*, trans. René Hague (New York: Harcourt Brace Jovanovich, 1970), 149. Omega is "the center, at once one and complex, in which, bound together by the person of Christ, may be seen *enclosed one within the other* (one might say) *three* progressively deeper *centers*: on the outside, the immanent ('natural') apex of the humano-cosmic cone; further in, at the middle, the immanent ('supernatural') apex of the 'ecclesial' or Christic cone; and finally, at the innermost heart, the transcendent, triune, and divine center: The complete Pleroma coming together under the mediating action of Christ-Omega."

39. Ibid., 141.

40. Ibid., 145–46.

41. Pierre Teilhard de Chardin, "My Fundamental Vision" (1948), in *Toward the Future*, trans. René Hague (New York: Harcourt Brace Jovanovich, 1973), 193. In the appendix, 207, he modifies this statement, so that "being and union" are not identical but form "a natural pair, the two terms of which, while each equally primordial and fundamentally irreducible, are nevertheless ontologically inseparable." This does not, however, change the implications for God's self-unification or his unification of the world in himself. Teilhard's metaphysics of union was outlined as early as 1917 in "Creative Union."

42. Teilhard, "My Fundamental Vision," 193.

43. See Rideau, *Thought of Teilhard*, 148–50 and notes with several quotations of Teilhard's affirmations of divine transcendence.

The second phase of the metaphysics of union is the triunity of the transcendent God. "To be is to unite." As First Being, therefore, God must be self-uniting, which entails his triunity: "If this initial and final center is to subsist upon itself . . . we are obliged to represent it to ourselves as, in its triune nature, containing its own self-opposition. . . . God exists only by *uniting himself*."[44] God in himself is therefore the unity of identity and otherness—Three in One.

The third phase of the metaphysics of union involves the world. If "to be = to unite oneself or to unite others,"[45] then Complete Being includes both. God's being himself is the very same activity that generates the world. The God beyond space and time is "the transcendent aspect of Omega." But transcendence is only one aspect of God, "the most central part of himself."[46] The other aspect is immanent in cosmic evolution.

Many texts confirm that Omega-God is both transcendent and immanent, eternal and temporal, being and becoming, immutable and changing. In "The Heart of Matter," for example, Teilhard writes, "God, eternal Being-in-himself, is everywhere, we might say, in process of formation *for us*." God is "a Being which mingled with things yet remained distinct from them; a Being of a higher order than the substance of things with which it was adorned, yet taking shape within them."[47] Elsewhere he writes that God is "the true Spirit of Matter."[48] Teilhard is aware that his view of God's transcendence and immanence is different than in the tradition of Anselm and Aquinas. His aim is to combine the transcendent God of classical orthodoxy with the God immanent in cosmic evolution: "An exact conjunction is produced between the old God of the Above and the God of the Ahead."[49]

The Necessity of the World for God

Since Being is Union, creation and God's immanence in the world are in some sense necessary or inevitable for God. Teilhard is inclined against regarding creation as God's free, gratuitous choice. "In making God personal and free, Non-being absolute, the Creation gratuitous, and the Fall accidental, are we not in danger of making the Universe *intolerable* and the value

44. Teilhard, "My Fundamental Vision," 193–94.

45. Ibid., 193.

46. Teilhard, "Outline of a Dialectic of Spirit," 146.

47. Teilhard, "Heart of Matter," 66, 74.

48. Pierre Teilhard de Chardin, letter to Lucile Swan, January 22, 1951, quoted by King, *Spirit of Fire*, 217.

49. Teilhard, "The Christic," in *Heart of Matter*, 99.

of souls . . . inexplicable?"[50] He affirms that "God is entirely self-sufficient: nevertheless the universe brings him something that is vitally necessary."[51] Again: "I see in the World a mysterious product of completion and fulfilment for the Absolute Being himself."[52] He also appeals to "Duns Scotus's views on the necessity of *some* form of [cosmic] Incarnation."[53] Teilhard even states that "the 'triune' is now seen not as a higher continuation, but as the very heart of the 'Christic,'"[54] which implies that there is no Trinity without the cosmic incarnation. Both Trinity and incarnation are essential to God. Consequently, God cannot be without the world. Regarding God's freedom to create, Teilhard can concede only that "our minds are completely unable to distinguish supreme necessity from supreme freedom."[55]

Teilhard's explanation of the necessity of creation makes clear that his metaphysics of union is traditional Neoplatonic dialectic applied to the Being of God himself, much like Nicholas of Cusa's.[56] God's internal self-unification necessitates an external unification of multiplicity. We have seen that Teilhard's dialectic first posits God as self-sufficient Being. God's triunity is the second step. The third is God's positing what is other than himself. Thus, "by the very fact that he unifies himself upon himself in order that he may exist, the First Being *ipso facto* stimulates the outbreak of another type of opposition, not in the core of his being but at the very opposite pole from himself (*phase three*)." An ultimate polarity of the One Being and the many nonbeings results. "The self-subsistent unity, at the pole of being: and as a necessary consequence, surrounding it on the circumference, the multiple—the *pure* multiple . . . or creatable *nil*, which is nothing." But this nothing is not absolutely nothing. It pulls God almost irresistibly to create. It is "a possibility of being, a prayer for being . . . which it is just as though God had been unable to resist."[57] The nothingness posited opposite God is so full of desire and potential for being that God, the Ultimate Unifier, cannot resist actualizing. Hence the fourth phase of unification. God does not stop until all possibilities are actualized. "Once the reduction of the multiple

50. Teilhard, "Note on the Presentation of the Gospel" (1919), in *Heart of Matter*, 219.

51. Pierre Teilhard de Chardin, "Christianity and Evolution" (1945), quoted from Rideau, 508.

52. Teilhard, "Heart of Matter," 54.

53. Teilhard, "Outline of a Dialectic of Spirit," 150. In this passage Teilhard speaks of the cosmic incarnation. Scotus thought that perhaps the Word would have become flesh to complete God's relation to creation even if humans did not sin, but he did not think that the creation of the world or the incarnation are necessary or inevitable for God. They are God's free choices.

54. Teilhard, "From Cosmos to Cosmogenesis," in *Activation of Energy*, 263 n. 5.

55. Teilhard, "My Fundamental Vision," 194.

56. See Gray, *The One and the Many*.

57. Teilhard, "My Fundamental Vision," 194.

has been effected, no form of still unsatisfied opposition (either interior or exterior) subsists for the 'pleromized' being."[58] God must become all in all—completely full. All of these themes are characteristically Neoplatonic and resonate in Böhme, Schelling, and Hegel as well.

The Incarnation and God-World Reciprocity

God's presence in the cosmos is best conceived as incarnation or embodiment.[59] Teilhard prays that the Lord God will bless the whole universe with the reality of the sacramental words "*hoc est Corpus meum*" (This is my body).[60] Teilhard's cosmic "transformism," the evolutionary emergence of higher levels of being, is literally *transubstantiation*, the progressive sacramental divinization of matter, a "Mass on the World."[61]

More precisely, the divine presence is the cosmic incarnation of Christ: "It is God himself who rises up in the heart of this simplified world. And the organic form of the universe thus divinized is Christ Jesus."[62] The incarnation of Christ animates cosmic evolution from the beginning: "In a *physical* sense, the Energy of Incarnation was to flow into . . . a cosmic Center which was positively attributed to Evolution."[63] The conception of the human individual, Jesus, in Mary's womb is the highest concentration of a process that has gone on from the beginning. "Christ, who is the principle of universal vitality, has sprung up as man among us . . . superanimating the general rise of consciousness into which he has inserted himself."[64] As the whole creation participates in his incarnation, so it also participates in his crucifixion and resurrection. Every kind of death found in the cosmic process is transformed into new and everlasting life. God in Christ is not only reconciling the world to himself but literally incorporating himself into it. Christ is the divine Soul of the world, and the world is his body.[65]

God's organic immanence in the world also means that the world has an effect on him. As God forms the world, so he is formed by it. "As God 'metamorphized' the World from the depths of matter to the peaks of Spirit, so in addition the World must inevitably and to the same degree 'endomorphize'

---

58. Ibid., 196.

59. Rideau, *Thought of Teilhard*, 162–69.

60. Pierre Teilhard de Chardin, "Pensée 17," in *Hymn of the Universe*, trans. Simon Bartholomew (New York: Harper and Row, 1965), 90.

61. The title of a piece Teilhard wrote in 1923.

62. Teilhard, "Pensée 46," in *Hymn of the Universe*, 119.

63. Teilhard, "Heart of Matter," 48–49.

64. Teilhard, *Human Phenomenon*, 211.

65. Gray, "Christ: the Soul of Evolution," chap. 6 in *The One and the Many*.

God." We humans effect change in God, especially by how we consciously relate to him. "All around us, and within our own selves, God is in process of 'changing,' as a result of the coincidence of his magnetic power and our own Thought."[66] Christ himself receives redemptive benefits from his own cosmic incarnation. "It is Christ in very truth, who saves—but should we not immediately add that at the same time it is Christ who is saved by Evolution?"[67] The incarnation makes the effects of the God-world relation reciprocal.

Although the cooperation of creation is necessary for God to attain the fullness of his being, Teilhard's view of creaturely freedom is less open than Schelling's or Whitehead's with respect to the inevitable goal of history. Teilhard's God intentionally and irresistibly realizes himself in and through the actions of his creatures. Creatures are not fully autonomous and do not codetermine with God how things will develop and turn out. Their actions inevitably advance the cosmic march toward a specific Omega.

In sum, Teilhard models his theology of the Omega as three concentric circles forming a "complete Pleroma." The heart of Omega is "the transcendent, triune, and divine center." The outside circle is the cosmos focused in humanity, "the immanent ('natural') apex of the humano-cosmic cone." Between them are those humans who know Christ explicitly, love him, and participate in his body through the sacrament. This is the church, "the immanent ('supernatural') apex of the 'ecclesial' or Christic cone." The whole Pleroma is "bound together by the person of Christ . . . the mediating action of Christ-Omega."[68]

Teilhard's Panentheism: "Christian Pantheism"

Teilhard repeatedly identifies himself as a "Christian pantheist" while rejecting other forms of pantheism and monism.[69] He rejects the identification of God with nature and the absorption of nature into God because both eliminate love: "Pantheism of identification, at the opposite pole from love: 'God is all.' And pantheism of unification, beyond love: 'God all in all.'" Teilhard's alternative, a Christian "pantheism of differentiation," aims to avoid both mistakes and to recognize that love is essential: "Christianity has

---

66. Teilhard, "Heart of Matter," 52–53.

67. Teilhard, "The Consummation of Christ by the Universe," in "The Christic," 92.

68. Teilhard, "Outline of a Dialectic of Spirit," 149.

69. Gray, "Pantheism," in *The One and the Many*, 149–54; de Lubac, *Religion of Teilhard*, 154–60; Rideau, *Thought of Teilhard*, 149–52.

... equilibrium ... of unification and synthesis: God finally becoming *all in all* within an atmosphere of pure charity. In that magnificent definition of the pantheism of differentiation is expressed ... the very essence of Christ's message."[70] Similarly, *The Human Phenomenon* expresses "a very real 'pantheism,' if you will (in the etymological sense of the word), but absolutely legitimate, since ultimately, if the reflective centers of the world are really 'one with God,' this state is not obtained by identification (God becoming all), but by the differentiating and communicating action of love (God all *in all*)—and this is fundamentally orthodox and Christian."[71] Ultimately humans commune in God but are not absorbed by him.

Teilhard is a panentheist precisely because his "pantheism of differentiation" includes a sufficient ontology of the many within the One. Creatures are distinct from God because, according to his metaphysics of union, for creatures, "to be is to be unified." Thus they are distinct from God, the Unifier. All the creatures in the cosmos, not just humans, are real beings—individuations of tangential and radial energy—distinct from God. In addition, the future Omega will consist of human persons participating permanently in the ultimate Person. At the same time, creatures literally exist in God. From the beginning of creation, the God who transcends the world generates prime matter and embodies himself in the emerging cosmos. In Christ, God is in all things, and all things are in God. But the immanent God also transcends the world. From Alpha to Omega, God as Christ is the One in whom All exist. Teilhard's "pantheism" is clearly panentheism even though he does not use the term.[72]

With an initial qualification, Teilhard's panentheism is a modern version of standard Neoplatonism.[73] The qualification is his identification of God with Being, as in Nicholas of Cusa, and not with the Super-essential One, as in Pseudo-Dionysius, Eriugena, and Eckhart. The rest of his theology is typical: Creation is a natural expression or generation from God, not a sovereign choice. God's being is unitive, so he not only unifies himself but also posits multiplicity other than himself in order to unify all in the Pleroma, the fullness of being. The process by which he does so is dialectical. The One Being eternally tri-unifies himself; the One Being also posits multiplicity other than itself in order to achieve unity by synthesis. In other words, Being

70. Teilhard, "Two Converse Forms of Spirit," in *Activation of Energy*, 223, 225.

71. Teilhard, *Human Phenomenon*, 223.

72. King, *Spirit of Fire*, 59, 86; Stanley J. Grenz and Roger E. Olson, *Twentieth-Century Theology: God and the World in a Transitional Age* (Downers Grove, IL: InterVarsity, 1992), 142; Lane, *Phenomenon of Teilhard*, 59, 134.

73. Jacobus Oosthuizen, *Van Plotinus tot Teilhard de Chardin* (Amsterdam: Rodopi, 1974).

posits nonbeing in order to become all that can be. Omega-God is not only the unifier of the many but also the coincidence of opposites. Further evidence of Teilhard's Platonism is his view that God in Christ is the Soul of the world.[74] As a soul permeates yet is other than its body, so God incarnate both includes and transcends the cosmos.

Teilhard's panentheism is Christian Neoplatonism wedded to the modern evolutionary world picture. He echoes Eriugena in holding that by creating and completing nature, God creates, reveals, and fulfills himself. His system is very much like Nicholas of Cusa's, given the substitution of Cosmogenesis for Nicholas of Cusa's infinite Cosmos. Aside from Teilhard's significant insistence that "part of God" is primordially and ontologically transcendent, his dialectical view of the God-world relation and its inevitable outcome is similar to Hegel's in many ways.

Teilhard's panentheism is typically modern when it asserts that creatures affect God. But it is not typically modern in the degree to which he affirms divine determination of the course of cosmic evolution toward its inevitable union with God. Creatures have freedom, and some humans may even choose to resist the inevitable. But the destiny of history is not codetermined by God and creatures as it is for Schelling and Whitehead.

Conclusion: From Heretic to Prophet

Teilhard is opposed to Hegel on a fundamental issue. Whereas Hegel intended to assimilate Christianity into his philosophy, Teilhard strives to be a faithful Christian and to incorporate his evolutionary philosophy into Roman Catholic theology.

Nevertheless, Teilhard criticizes traditional theology and promotes a "transformed" version of Christianity.[75] It is not surprising that some of his views stand in tension with historic Christian doctrines.[76] Three that have attracted criticism are the relation between nature and the supernatural, the origin of sin and evil, and the scope of salvation. We briefly consider each.

Teilhard's philosophy goes a long way toward rendering his faith reasonable. "In a metaphysics of union, the three fundamental 'mysteries' of Christianity [God, creation, and redemption] are seen to be simply the three aspects of one and the same mystery of mysteries, that of pleromiza-

---

74. Cf. Pierre Teilhard de Chardin, "L'âme du monde" ["The Soul of the World"] (1918). I did not find a translation.

75. See, e.g., Teilhard, "The Religion of Tomorrow," in "The Christic," in *Heart of Matter*, 96–99.

76. Lane, "Teilhard's Transformation of Christian Doctrines," in *Phenomenon of Teilhard*, 71–80.

tion (or unifying reduction of the multiple)."[77] If pleromization is so natural and necessary for God, it is hard to see anything supernaturally gratuitous in the existence of the world, the incarnation of Christ, or the salvation of the world. Teilhard seems to have lost significant aspects of supernatural transcendence and divine grace.[78]

Fallibility and evil are natural and integral in evolutionary Neoplatonism, but they are a nonessential intrusion in Augustinian Christianity. The Neoplatonic One creates by way of positing dialectical polarities that necessarily include negativity and nonbeing. Thus sin and evil are inevitable by-products of cosmic evolution and human existence. The negative polarities are actually necessary for good, because the One saves the world by dialectically synthesizing the antitheses. In contrast, Augustinian Christianity regards sin and evil as the negative but just consequences of divinely permitted free human choice that in principle could have been otherwise. Sin and evil are not ontologically inevitable and integral to creation. In fact, there is an irreconcilable antithesis between good and evil. The tension between Neoplatonism and Augustinianism becomes acute with respect to the creation and fall of humans: are sin and death natural evolutionary inheritances or consequences of avoidable disobedience? Teilhard tries unsuccessfully to have it both ways.[79] In fact, he is decidedly Neoplatonic at times: "Evil is an inevitable by-product. It appears as a forfeit inseparable from Creation." Even more sinister: "God is forced into war with evil."[80] His views on original sin are what first brought the censure of church authorities in the 1920s.

Finally, the Neoplatonic Pleroma leaves no room for hell—angels and humans enduring eternal punishment. In the end, all things not united in God cease to exist. Teilhard allows for possible resistance to Omega that might result in an apocalyptic confrontation and separation. And he affirms belief in hell. But hell is inconsistent with the all-inclusive logic of Christogenesis, according to which the entire creation is evolving into spiritual union with God.[81] His progressively positive view of the world religions became a major support to the notion of "implicit" or "anonymous Christianity" that was promoted at Vatican II: Christ is drawing humanity to himself through the non-Christian religions even though they do not know his name.

77. Teilhard, "My Fundamental Vision," 198.

78. Eulalio Balthazar, *Teilhard and the Supernatural* (Baltimore: Helicon, 1966); Rideau, *Thought of Teilhard*, 152–54, 167–68, 245–51; de Lubac, *Religion of Teilhard*, 200–203; and McCarty, *Teilhard*, 134–35.

79. McCarty, *Teilhard*, 135–36; Rideau, *Thought of Teilhard*, 169–71.

80. Teilhard, "My Fundamental Vision," 198, 196.

81. Rideau, *Thought of Teilhard*, 187–88 and notes.

Given these and other tensions with traditional orthodoxy in Teilhard's writings, even a sympathetic commentator such as Rideau concludes that the warning of the Roman Catholic authorities "was justified by the danger presented to uninformed Christians by reading Teilhard and becoming familiar with his thought."[82]

In spite of these tensions, many regard Teilhard as a spiritual genius who intelligently and effectively expresses the essence of Christianity for the contemporary world. In full conformity with church teaching or not, his God is actually transcendent, personal, and triune, unlike the emerging Deity of Samuel Alexander, the Vital Force of Bergson, or the all-inclusive Actual Occasion of Whitehead. Christians and non-Christians find his vision inspiring, and many have worked from his panentheistic view of God, the cosmos, and the future of the global community. Among them are Gustavo Gutiérrez, Juan Luis Segundo, Leonardo Boff, Rosemary Ruether, Sallie McFague, and Matthew Fox, whom we consider in a later chapter on liberation and ecological theology.

82. Ibid., 250–51.

7

Process Theology

Whitehead, Hartshorne, Cobb, and Griffin

The most familiar type of panentheism in North American circles is process theology, an understanding of God based on the philosophy of Alfred North Whitehead (1861–1947). Whitehead was an English mathematician and philosopher who completed his academic career at Harvard University. Influenced by British idealism and the evolutionary philosophies of Lloyd Morgan and Samuel Alexander,[1] Whitehead's system proceeds from natural science and concludes that the universe as we know it requires a basic reality, God, that both grounds and participates in its development. Process theology is the philosophical elaboration of this view of God and the world. It considers itself the most rational of contemporary worldviews, much as Deism did in the eighteenth century. It is part of a family of panentheisms that grew from the marriage of post-Darwinian science and post-Schellingian theology. Sibling views include those of Fechner, Peirce, James, Bergson, and Teilhard.[2]

1. Alfred North Whitehead, *Science and the Modern World: The Lowell Lectures, 1925* (New York: Macmillan, 1950), xi.
2. See David Griffin et al., *Founders of Constructive Postmodern Philosophy: Peirce, James, Bergson, Whitehead, and Hartshorne* (Albany: State University of New York Press, 1993); also Charles Hartshorne, preface to *The Divine Relativity: A Social Conception of God* (New Haven: Yale University Press, 1948).

Whitehead's philosophy has been influential among scholars in various disciplines, not just philosophy and theology.[3] Some follow his system less closely than others, and so *school of thought* is too precise a term. Nevertheless, there is a recognizable movement called process theology strongly associated with Whitehead's philosophy.[4] Our survey focuses on the central figures, Whitehead and three of his direct theological descendants: Charles Hartshorne, John Cobb, and David Griffin. Hartshorne was Whitehead's assistant and developed his own philosophy by revising parts of Whitehead's system. Cobb was Hartshorne's student, and Griffin was Cobb's student and collaborator. Their views are close enough to regard them as a school.

They are, however, religiously diverse. Whitehead and Hartshorne believe in God and appreciate Christianity but do not regard themselves specifically as Christian. Both develop their theology entirely from science and philosophy. Even so, Hartshorne focuses much more on religion and theology than Whitehead. Cobb and Griffin are modern Christians who adopt a synthesis of Whitehead and Hartshorne's ideas to explain Christian doctrines and elaborate a contemporary worldview.

Thus our survey identifies the characteristics of process panentheism in its generic and Christian forms.[5] It concludes with a brief comparison of process theology and evangelical free-will or open theism, which is sometimes charged with being a version of process theology.

Alfred North Whitehead

Whitehead's "Philosophy of Organism"

In *Science and the Modern World*, Whitehead argues that genuine science and belief in God are not at odds but in fact reinforce each other.[6] Modern science is the fruit of medieval theology's belief in a personal, rational God who created an intelligible natural order and commissioned humans to master

3. John B. Cobb and David Griffin, "Appendix B: A Guide to the Literature," in *Process Theology: An Introductory Exposition* (Philadelphia: Westminster, 1976), surveys the influence of Whitehead in philosophy, theology, and other disciplines.

4. Ewert Cousins, ed., *Process Theology: Basic Writings* (New York: Newman, 1971), includes essays by a number of representatives and includes a section on Teilhard de Chardin. Schubert Ogden, Norman Pittenger, Daniel Day Williams, Lewis Ford, and Marjorie Suchocki are other prominent promoters of process theology.

5. David Griffin, *Reenchantment without Supernaturalism: A Process Philosophy of Religion* (Ithaca, NY: Cornell University Press, 2001), is the best statement currently available.

6. Whitehead, "Religion and Science," chap. 12 in *Science and the Modern World*.

it.[7] The contemporary scientific worldview still requires grounding in some notion of God. "In the place of Aristotle's God as Prime Mover, we require God as the Principle of Concretion."[8] But the natural alliance of science and religion has been broken by a false dualism in post-Cartesian thought, the dualism of mind and matter as separate substances. Conceived as Infinite Mind, God is wholly external to the physical universe. And human minds are wholly other than the material world they seek to know. These dualisms, Whitehead charges, have led to insoluble problems for philosophy and theology as well as for science, where Darwinian evolution and Einsteinian relativity have undermined the mechanistic-materialist model of explanation developed from mind-matter dualism.

Whitehead's counterproposal is "the philosophy of organism," elaborated most fully and systematically in *Process and Reality*, the Gifford Lectures of 1927–1928.[9] We begin with an overview and then look more closely at how he constructs the whole from its basic components.

In summary, reality—the whole vast God-universe complex—is "organic" rather than a dualism of "mind and mechanism." It is energized by a creative process in which individual entities, including God, are constituted of basic events that continuously actualize themselves.[10] These events, the irreducible elements of reality, are "bits of experience," called "actual occasions," that realize themselves or "concresce" for an instant, then pass away or "perish."[11] The enduring objects we know—atoms, molecules, material objects, living things, and human beings—are organized "societies of actual occasions" that result from continuous series of actual occasions processing according to stable patterns. An analogy may help. Entities are constituted of bits of experience like the objects on a television screen, which are constituted by billions of electrical impulses too minute and rapid for humans to perceive, or like objects on a movie screen, which are produced by the rapid succession

7. Ibid., "The Origins of Modern Science," chap. 1.

8. Ibid., "God," chap. 11, p. 250.

9. Alfred North Whitehead, *Process and Reality: An Essay in Cosmology*, Gifford Lectures, 1927–1928 (New York: Macmillan, 1929); ed. David Griffin and Donald Sherburne, corrected ed. (New York: Free Press, 1978), 46/36. (Page references are to both editions.) I summarize Whitehead's ideas from this work as well as from Alfred North Whitehead, *Adventures in Ideas* (New York: Macmillan, 1933). John B. Cobb, "Introduction to Whitehead's Philosophy," chap. 1 in *A Christian Natural Theology* (Philadelphia: Westminster, 1965), is a very accessible summary. So is Cobb and Griffin, "Basic Concepts of Process Philosophy," in *Process Theology*. Charles Hartshorne, *Whitehead's Philosophy: Selected Essays, 1935–1970* (Lincoln: University of Nebraska Press, 1972), is more technical.

10. A preliminary overview of his system is in Whitehead, "The Categorial Scheme," and "Some Derivative Notions," chaps. 2–3 in part 1 of *Process and Reality*.

11. Ibid., 27–28/18. Process thought claims that actual occasions are detectable by scientific instruments and careful human introspection. They are not just philosophical assumptions.

of individual frames of film. Each of the things we experience is an orderly procession of countless actual occasions.

This dynamic is even true of God. "God is not to be treated as an exception to all metaphysical principles, invoked to save their collapse. He is their chief exemplification."[12] Thus "process" rather than "substance" or "being" is Whitehead's basic metaphysical category. Reality—the God-world complex—is a vast "organic" network or "nexus" of innumerable strands and organizations of an infinity of momentary events. To understand process theology, it is important to follow Whitehead's explanation of the whole universe, beginning with the basic atomic events, "actual occasions." A summary follows.

We begin by noting several characteristics of "actual occasions." Most basic is that each occasion is self-actualizing or self-creative.[13] Although conditioned and limited, it is not caused to exist by anything outside itself, even God. Indeed God himself is not an exception to this ontology. Thus "creativity," not God, is Whitehead's ultimate category: "In the philosophy of organism this ultimate is termed 'creativity'; and God is its primordial, non-temporal accident."[14]

Of equal importance is Whitehead's assertion that each occasion is an "experience," not a bit of matter or mind. Like Fechner, James, Bergson, and Teilhard, Whitehead posits a basic "stuff" that is neither mind nor matter but functions as both. Because the basic elements are bits of "experience," Whitehead's metaphysics is another instance of panpsychism ("everything is psyche").[15] Like other panpsychisms, his notion of experience does not necessarily involve sensation or consciousness, although they are complex kinds of experience. "Consciousness presupposes experience, and not experience consciousness."[16] Experience is basically "prehension," that is, response to what is other than itself. As each occasion of experience concresces or actualizes itself, it "prehends" something of what is beyond itself and shapes itself accordingly. Although each occasion is a self-creating individual, it also essentially relates to other realities in its immediate environment. These other realities are past actualities and future possibilities.

We begin with the past. Each actual occasion prehends its immediate predecessors as they cease to be actual. In this way the past influences what

12. Ibid., 521/343.

13. Ibid., 130/85.

14. Ibid., 11/7.

15. Charles Hartshorne, "Panpsychism," in *A History of Philosophical Systems*, ed. Vergilius Ferm (New York: Philosophical Library, 1950), 442–53. Griffin, *Reenchantment*, 6, prefers "panexperientialism."

16. Whitehead, *Process and Reality*, 83/53.

an occasion becomes but does not causally determine it. On the contrary, the effect of past occasions is an actual occasion's prehension or active acquisition of their influence on it. Thus Whitehead reverses the commonsense notion of causality: present reality is not caused by the past, but the present actually appropriates the past as its effect on the present. This gives him an explanation of the reality of the past: past events are not entirely gone but continue to live on in the present; they are "objectively immortal." Although each occasion prehends only the occasions in its immediate past, all present occasions together preserve and pass on the entire history of the universe. Each occasion has a significant portion of the history of the universe in its ancestry. It stands at the apex of a horizontal time-cone whose sides broaden steeply into the past. The past is no longer actual, but it is still real—"objectively immortal"—in the present.

The past is only one dimension or "vector" of the present. Each occasion also prehends a possible future. As it concresces, an occasion takes account of its potential, what it can become; it forms a "subjective aim"—what it seeks to be, its goal or purpose. Like the past, the future is real but not actual. If it were not real, time would freeze in the present and nothing could ever change. But the future is possible, not actual. It is open, not determined. Although the realm of possibility as a whole has a definite structure (discussed below), particular possibilities are variable and contingent. A present occasion might be able to prehend more than one possibility for itself. It might become a little different from its past. Thus choice and "novelty"—attaining new modes of existence—are intrinsic features of the creative process.

In sum, Whitehead's doctrine of actual occasions asserts that as each occasion concresces, it incorporates the content of the past and aims at the future. It is therefore "dipolar." Its self-actualization is the "satisfaction" or "enjoyment" of its existence, its realization of a possible future relative to an appropriated past. As soon as it comes to be, it perishes and becomes immediately available to the next generation of occasions, which repeat the process, and so on endlessly.

This analysis of the basic process that constitutes reality provides Whitehead an approach to a number of other philosophical problems. Chief among them is the mind-matter problem. Modern philosophy either posited mind and matter as basic substances (dualism) or designated one the basic substance and attempted to explain the other in terms of it (materialism and idealism). In Whitehead's panpsychism, occasions of experience are neither mind nor matter but are implicitly both physical and mental. The "physical pole" of an actual occasion is its prehension of its past, by which it appropriates the stable content of the past.[17] This physical activity is the source of "matter" and "mechanism" on higher levels of complexity: when numerous actual occasions process continuously in particular organizational patterns, they constitute enduring material objects that behave according to the laws of nature. But "matter" is not a basic substance; it is a mode or dimension of process. The same is true of mind, which is the capacity for prehending the future. An actual occasion's sensitivity to its future possibilities is its "mental pole," and what it chooses to become is its "subjective aim." In appropriating the future, therefore, every occasion exhibits the rudimentary characteristics of knowledge, freedom, choice, and purpose, which are the powers of mind and spirit. More complex societies of occasions, such as animals, have increasingly sophisticated modes of awareness, sensation, and consciousness. Humans are self-conscious and can reflect on things. Mind is not a substance but the organized realization of the implicit "mental" capacity of each actual occasion. Whitehead concludes that mind and matter are not antithetical or incommensurate substances but integrated and cooperative aspects of a basic process.[18]

Whitehead's notion of prehension also addresses the epistemological subject-object problem, which is correlated with mind-matter dualism in modern philosophy. If mind and matter are essentially different substances, it is difficult to say how mind or subjectivity can apprehend material objects in the world through the brain and bodily sense organs, which are material. None of the various theories of perception, sensation, imagination, and concept formation fully bridges the chasm between mind and matter. But if human minds and the things of nature are complex organizations of actual occasions, then their microlevel physical and mental prehensions are rudimentary forms of the perception and cognition that take place on the macrolevel in humans. Indeed the objects we perceive were subjects themselves before becoming objects for us. Rather than an ontological gap between subject and object, process philosophy posits continuity and reciprocity.

Whitehead's process ontology addresses other metaphysical issues as well. He replaces the traditional ideas of *being* and *substance* with his account of *process*. He defines *causality* as the present's appropriation of the past, not the past's determination of the present. *Laws of nature* are the basic categories and regular patterns according to which individual occasions, societies of occasions, and nexuses of societies of occasions actualize themselves. *Time* is a by-product of actual occasions processing in sequence, not a basic

17. Ibid., 49/33.
18. Ibid., 165/108.

metaphysical dimension, such as eternity in motion, as Plato thought, or a category of human understanding, as Kant thought. There is no time within each occasion but only among them. *Space*, like time, is a function of the proximity and availability of actual occasions to prehend each other. It is neither a metaphysical "container" of things nor a category of human understanding. These examples illustrate how a philosophy of nature grows from Whitehead's analysis of individual occasions.

Whitehead's system explains the entire universe in terms of actual occasions. The things that we humans ordinarily experience are not actual occasions but "societies of occasions."[19] Even atoms and molecules are societies. An entity is a group of occasions that occur in an organized structure or "society" that endures through time, exhibits distinguishing properties, and stands in relation to other entities. Thus a hydrogen atom is a society of a particular structure with distinctive characteristics and capacities. A living cell is a complex of structures and substructures of molecules that is distinct from other entities. All the natural objects, living things, and human artifacts among which we live are different types of "societies." In "democratic" societies such as stones and trees, all members cooperate but no one takes a leading role. But in some societies a guiding or determining function is taken by one part called a "dominant" or "monarchial occasion." In higher animals this center is consciousness, and in humans it is the ego, mind, spirit, or personality.[20] Whatever their generic and specific differences, all entities are societies of actual occasions. The entire universe is a complex, dynamic "nexus" of such societies. Whitehead's philosophy is not just "organic" but also "communal."

Entities, like individual occasions, embody the past and anticipate the future, changing over time. Thus possibilities are as necessary for entities—societies of occasions—as they are for individual occasions. If there are beautiful round red objects, for example, then beauty, roundness, and redness must be possible modes of existence. And if entities change their identity, characteristics, or behavior, then these alternative possibilities are likewise necessary for their existence. Logically, something must be *possible* for it to be *actual*.

These possibilities are "universals." The question of universal Forms or Ideals has preoccupied philosophers since Plato. In Whitehead's philosophy, universals are possible kinds of existence that entities can actualize. He calls them "eternal objects."[21] They are "eternal" because universal possibilities

19. Ibid., "The Order of Nature," chap. 3 of part 2.
20. Ibid., 164–67/107–9.
21. Ibid., 69–73/43–46.

neither come into being nor pass away. As Plato knew, triangularity is a form of existence whether or not there are any triangular things. But Plato regarded the Forms as *actually existing* ideal entities whereas Whitehead thinks of them as *possible* ways of existing. Whitehead calls them "objects" because they constitute all the categories and forms actualized by the objects in the world: quantities, shapes, physical properties and relations, qualities of sensation, kinds of natural and living things, kinds of cultural artifacts, structures of logic and language, aesthetic and moral qualities, and so on. Whitehead's "eternal objects" are an intentional "footnote to Plato."

Indeed, Whitehead's whole ontology is a footnote to Plato. Like Plato, Whitehead posits two realms or dimensions of reality: the actual (the universe of "actual occasions") and the possible ("the realm of eternal objects"). Like Plato's, Whitehead's God holds them together. But Whitehead's God is not Plato's Mind or Craftsman, generating a Soul to exemplify the ideal Forms in the material world. For Whitehead, there is no actual eternal realm. His God is much more a World-Soul whose mind continually thinks of universal possibilities for the actual world.

Whitehead's Doctrine of God

This section surveys the development of Whitehead's doctrine of God from *Science and the Modern World* through *Religion in the Making* to its fullest form in *Process and Reality*.[22]

In *Science and the Modern World*, Whitehead posits God as "the Principle of Concretion" that relates the actual world to the realm of possibility. The realm of possibilities may be limitless in number, but it is a rationally coherent set of categories that limit what is possible. (Round squares are not possible.) Whitehead argues that if the logical structure of possibility and the activity of actualization were identical, "Spinoza's one infinite substance" would result. But Whitehead's process ontology rules out such a substance. So there must be "a ground for limitation which stands among the attributes of the substantial activity." This ground is God, and that is as far as reason can go. "God is the ultimate limitation, and His existence is the ultimate irrationality. . . . God is not concrete, but He is the ground for concrete actuality." And so in *Science and the Modern World*, Whitehead identifies God with the realm of possibility, but he does not state that God actualizes himself or relates possibility to other actualities. Whitehead also stresses that God cannot be

22. Hartshorne, "Whitehead's Idea of God," chap. 5 in *Whitehead's Philosophy;* Cobb, "Whitehead's Doctrine of God," chap. 4 in *Christian Natural Theology.*

the origin of evil, for "it stands in his very nature to divide the Good from the Evil, and to establish Reason 'within her dominion supreme.'"[23]

Whitehead develops the connection between actuality, possibility, and God in *Religion in the Making*. "The all-inclusive universe" is the most comprehensive metaphysical reality. It consists of "the temporal world and its formative elements." Whitehead identifies these elements as "creativity," "the realm of ideal entities, or forms," and God. "The actual but non-temporal entity whereby the indetermination of mere creativity is transmuted into a determinate freedom ... is what men call God."[24] In other words, he now affirms that God is the actual entity who makes possibility available to the creativity of all other entities.

God is an "actual but non-temporal entity." He is nontemporal in that he includes the realm of "eternal ideas," the Ground of the possibility of the world. He is an actual entity because ordering possibilities is an activity and only actual entities can act. "The definite determination which imposes ordered balance on the world requires an actual entity imposing its own unchanged consistency of character on every phase." God is the necessary entity who provides ordered possibilities. Furthermore, to provide possibilities relevant to the actual world, God must comprehend it. "He must include in himself a synthesis of the total universe." Thus the relation in God of the ideal and the actual world is bilateral. "There is, therefore, in God's nature the aspect of the realm of forms [possibilities] as qualified by the world, and the aspect of the world as qualified by the forms."[25] Thus there are two aspects in God's nature, the eternal-ideal and the actual, and these aspects affect each other.

God determines possibilities, but he is not all-determining. Whitehead continues to distinguish "creativity, with its shifting character ever determined afresh by its own creatures, and God, upon whose wisdom all forms of order depend." Entities in the world have the power of self-actualization independent of God, and what they choose to become has an effect on him. God's role is not to create entities but to offer them ideal possibilities. "In the actual world, he confronts what is actual in it with what is possible." God proposes, but creatures dispose. He then responds to how well they actualize his ideals. "Every act leaves the world with a deeper or fainter impress of God. He then passes into his next relation to the world with enlarged, or diminished, presentation of ideal values."[26]

23. Whitehead, *Science and the Modern World*, 255–58.

24. Alfred North Whitehead, *Religion in the Making* (New York: Macmillan, 1926; repr. with glossary, New York: Fordham University Press, 1996), 90.

25. Ibid., 94, 98.

26. Ibid., 160, 159 bis.

Because God's ideals are good, any deficiency or evil actualized in the world is not his doing. Yet God always aims to improve things by continually comprehending the world in terms of his ideal values. "This transmutation of evil into good enters into the actual world by reason of the inclusion of the nature of God, which includes the ideal vision of each actual evil so met with a novel consequent as to issue in the restoration of goodness." God does not cause or prevent instances of evil, but he tries to make the best of them by viewing them in his own vision of the greater good. Thus "evil becomes a stepping stone in the all-embracing ideals of God."[27]

Religion in the Making completes the outline of Whitehead's doctrine of God. It presents God as an actual entity with two aspects. One is the eternal and infinite Ground of all possibility, the other his actual comprehension of, and response to, the world.

Process and Reality works out more details of God's relation to the world and spells out Whitehead's whole philosophy. It climaxes in the chapter "God and the World." Notably, Whitehead observes at the outset of the book that "the philosophy of organism is closely allied to Spinoza's scheme of thought" but has a different view of the ultimate. "In the philosophy of organism this ultimate is termed 'creativity'; and God is its primordial, nontemporal accident. In monistic philosophies, Spinoza or absolute idealism, this ultimate is God, who is also equivalently termed 'The Absolute.'"[28] Whitehead's replacement for Spinoza's Absolute God is Creativity, not another notion of God. His God is the "primordial accident" or supreme instance of Creativity.

In "God and the World," Whitehead reaffirms that the same ontological categories that explain the world also explain God. "God is not to be treated as an exception to all metaphysical principles, invoked to save their collapse. He is their chief exemplification." Whitehead therefore applies his process metaphysics, presented above, straightforwardly to God.

Like all actual entities, God has two aspects, one prehending future possibility and the other prehending past actuality. Thus "the nature of God is dipolar. He has a primordial nature and a consequent nature." But unlike other entities, God is all-comprehensive. His primordial nature includes all ideal possibilities and is therefore "free, complete, primordial, eternal, actually deficient, and unconscious." His consequent nature prehends the entire universe of actual occasions and their entire past. Thus it is "determined, incomplete, consequent, 'everlasting,' fully actual, and conscious."[29]

27. Ibid., 155.
28. Whitehead, *Process and Reality*, 11/7.
29. Ibid., 521/343, 524/345.

Whitehead explains more fully how God relates possibility to actual creatures. God's primordial nature includes all possible modes of existence, "the unlimited conceptual realization of the absolute wealth of potentiality." But God "conceptually feels" which particular possibilities best fit each occasion in the nexus of its own past and makes them available to each occasion. This best possibility is God's "initial aim." In addition, God exerts a "pull," an attraction, a final causality on entities to actualize the best possibility. "He is the lure for feeling, the eternal urge of desire." Thus God attracts each occasion to appropriate his "initial aim" as its own "subjective aim." God encourages creatures to be their best but does not cause them to be.

To function as the source of possibility for each occasion, God must prehend each entity and its place in the world. This is God's consequent nature, "derived from the objectification of the world in God." Just as each individual occasion prehends perishing occasions as it actualizes itself, so God prehends all the entities that collectively constitute the universe as he actualizes himself. Thus God's actuality is significantly shaped and limited by what creatures decide to be.

At the same time, however, God prehends each individual and the whole universe relative to his primordial nature—the maximal goodness and harmony he intuits for each in relation to all. "This prehension into God of each creature is directed with the subjective aim, and clothed with the subjective form, wholly derivative from his all-inclusive primordial valuation." Thus God "prehends every actuality for what it can be in such a perfected system."[30]

In this way God's relation to the world constitutes the "providence," "judgment," and "salvation" valued by religion. God's primordial nature providentially sustains the natural and moral orders that preserve and enhance the world. His prehension of the actual in terms of the ideal results in both judgment and salvation. Judgment is that "the revolts of destructive evil, purely self-regarding, are dismissed into their triviality of merely individual facts." Salvation is that "the good they did achieve in individual joy, in individual sorrow, in the introduction of needed contrast, is yet saved by its relation to the completed whole." In all his ways—providence, judgment, and salvation—God nurtures, attracts, and persuades but never determines. "God does not create the world, he saves it; or, more accurately, he is the poet of the world, with tender patience leading it by his vision of truth, beauty, and goodness."[31]

30. Ibid., 523/345, 525/346.
31. Ibid., 525–26/346.

Whitehead does not accept traditional ideas of heaven and hell, but he does affirm a kind of "immortality" or "everlasting life." When actual occasions prehend their predecessors, which are just passing from existence, they preserve their content and make them "objectively immortal." God does the same on a cosmic scale. "The consequent nature of God is the fluent world become 'everlasting' by its objective immortality in God."[32] Although individuals do not continue to be actual, they "live on" in God, progressively perfected as their contributions to the world are appropriated by subsequent actualities in ways that increasingly exemplify the ideals of God's primordial nature.

Process and Reality culminates with a litany celebrating the correlativity of God and the world: "It is as true to say that God is permanent and the World fluent, as that the World is permanent and God is fluent. It is as true to say that God is one and the World many, as that the World is one and God many." Subsequent lines make the parallel point about eminent actuality, immanence, and transcendence. The finale is most striking: "It is as true to say that God creates the World, as that the World creates God."[33]

Whitehead's Panentheism

Although he does not use the term, there is no question of Whitehead's panentheism. He distinguishes God and the world: "God and the World stand over against each other." The difference is not merely conceptual, as it was for Spinoza. Things are not caused by God but have the real power of self-actualization.[34] Yet all things are in God, and he is in all things. "Each temporal occasion embodies God, and is embodied in God." This relationship is not contingent or voluntary on God's part; it is intrinsic to the divine nature. "In God's nature, permanence is primordial and flux is derivative from the World." God and the world are parts of a greater dynamic whole. "Neither God, nor the World, reaches static completion. Both are in the grip of the ultimate metaphysical ground, the creative advance into novelty." As a footnote to Plato, Whitehead's God is not Mind or the Demiurge but the World-Soul, cognizant of the ideal Forms as possibilities, inviting the world to make itself in their image. God is "the great companion—the fellow-sufferer who understands."[35]

32. Ibid., 527/347.
33. Ibid., 528/348.
34. Hartshorne classifies Whitehead as a panentheist precisely because genuine creaturely freedom is what distinguishes his view from pantheism and deterministic theism. See Charles Hartshorne and William Reese, *Philosophers Speak of God* (Chicago: University of Chicago Press, 1953), 273–77.
35. Whitehead, *Process and Reality*, 529/348–49, 532/351.

Charles Hartshorne

Charles Hartshorne (1897–2000) was Whitehead's assistant at Harvard and had a long and productive philosophical career at the University of Chicago, Emory University, and the University of Texas.[36] He studied Peirce, James, Bergson, Heidegger, and other philosophers who stress "becoming," but his own system is most heavily indebted to Whitehead. For the most part, he accepts the process ontology outlined above, but he makes two important modifications of Whitehead's thought: his view of God as a person and his elaboration of dipolar theism.[37]

God as a Living Person

Whitehead regarded God as a single actual entity with a primordial nature of eternal possibilities and a consequent nature that prehends the universe. But Hartshorne charges that Whitehead's view of God is problematic in some ways.[38] For one thing, Whitehead's God is an actual occasion, not a society of occasions like other entities. Thus Whitehead cannot use his own principles to explain fully how a Cosmic Actual Entity can interrelate with other entities in the world. Most important, a God subject to Creativity is not ultimate.

Hartshorne proposes instead that Whitehead's God be reconceived as a living person. Whitehead had analyzed higher animals and humans as complex societies of actual occasions, centered and guided by a "dominant" or "monarchial occasion." The human person consists of atoms and molecules in structures that constitute an organism whose brain enables personal, self-conscious, intelligent engagement with other beings in its natural, social, and transcendental environments. Humans are complex societies with a monarchial member. Whitehead said that "the real actual things that endure are all societies."[39] Hartshorne affirms Whitehead's claim and asserts that God too is a person, a monarchial society who includes the whole universe

---

36. Alan Gragg, *Charles Hartshorne* (Waco: Word, 1973), is a helpful introduction.

37. Charles Hartshorne, *Reality as Social Process* (Glencoe, IL: Free Press; Boston: Beacon, 1953), summarizes Hartshorne's whole philosophy, culminating in his view of God. His specifically theological books are *Man's Vision of God and the Logic of Theism* (Chicago: Willett, Clark, 1941); *Divine Relativity*; Hartshorne and Reese, *Philosophers Speak of God*; Charles Hartshorne, *The Logic of Perfection and Other Essays in Neo-classical Metaphysics* (La Salle, IL: Open Court, 1962); *Anselm's Discovery: A Re-examination of the Ontological Proof for God's Existence* (La Salle, IL: Open Court, 1965); *A Natural Theology for Our Time* (La Salle, IL: Open Court, 1967); and *Omnipotence and Other Theological Mistakes* (Albany: State University of New York Press, 1983).

38. These problems are discussed in Hartshorne, *Whitehead's Philosophy*, 71–90; Cobb, *Christian Natural Theology*, 176–214; and Griffin, *Reenchantment*, 150–56.

39. Alfred North Whitehead, *Adventures of Ideas* (New York: Simon and Schuster, 1953), 204.

in himself. "The conception of God which our argument leads to is that of a social being, dominant or ruling over the world society, yet not merely from outside, in a tyrannical or non-social way; but rather as that member of the society which exerts the supreme conserving and coordinating influence."[40] Hartshorne stands squarely in the tradition of *Timaeus*. "The world consists of individuals, but the totality of individuals as a physical or spatial whole is God's body, the Soul of which is God."[41]

This revision enables Hartshorne to affirm Whitehead's view of God-world interaction in a way that fully applies Whitehead's ontology. As an embodied person, God is genuinely dipolar; he has a primordial and a consequent nature. Like humans, God self-consciously envisions future possibilities and orders them for current actualities. Like humans, God is present in his body and guides or controls it in a variety of ways without compromising the relatively autonomous functioning of its many parts. Conversely, God's body is part of his identity and influences his mind. The experiences and actions of the individuals in the world collectively constitute God's consequent nature. They are the data for his responsive action, guided by his ideals for the entire cosmos. Thus Hartshorne also preserves Whitehead's views that the whole universe is "objectively immortal" in God and that God compassionately suffers the pain and evil that occur in the world. Hartshorne concurs that by incorporating the past in terms of the ideal future, God rejects what is evil while saving and enhancing the good.[42]

Hartshorne recognizes significant differences between divine and human embodiment.[43] God envisions all possibility and comprehends all actuality, whereas humans are limited. Humans are mortal, but God is not. Humans forget much of the past, but God remembers all. Humans relate to other beings externally, whereas all God's relations are internal to himself, since he is incarnate in the entire cosmos. Furthermore, God is immediately aware of, and responsive to, all individuals in his entire body, whereas humans consciously relate to some body parts and events but cannot access others. Humans tend to focus on particulars, whereas God sees all. Hartshorne's view of God's comprehensive intuition has an interesting wrinkle: "God is like other animals, rather than like us, in the following way: for the other animals, the field of perception is almost the whole."[44] Whitehead conceives

40. Hartshorne, *Reality as Social Process*, 40.
41. Hartshorne, *Omnipotence*, 94.
42. Hartshorne, *Reality as Social Process*, 41–43.
43. Hartshorne, "The Theological Analogies and the Cosmic Organism," chap. 5 in *Man's Vision of God*.
44. Hartshorne, *Omnipotence*, 93.

of God as a single actual occasion. Hartshorne understands him as a living person.

God as Supremely Relative

In addition to the modifications implied by his different model of God, Hartshorne worked out process theology much more fully. Whitehead's treatment of God largely sketched out what was required by his scientific-philosophical cosmology. He did not engage in extensive elaboration of the dipolar view of God or the arguments for it. Hartshorne does both.

Hartshorne's reflections on God's dipolar nature proceed from a critique of classical theism's "monopolar" view that God's nature is absolute, necessary, simple, eternal, immutable, and perfect. In brief, Hartshorne argues that such a God could not produce a world in which there is genuine contingency, change, and personal interaction, nor could he relate or respond to such a world.[45] The classical view of God in fact implies Spinoza's pantheism, he argues. It has been refuted by modern philosophy and science, leaving atheism as the only apparent option. In addition, such an eternal Being is not the engaged and responsive God of religion, especially Christianity.

In contrast, Hartshorne urges that a dipolar understanding of God is both religiously satisfying and philosophically tenable: God is both absolute and relative, necessary and contingent, simple and complex, and so forth. He appeals to what logician Morris Cohen calls "the Law of Polarity," which "may be traced back through Hegel to Heraclitus and Plato." This law stipulates that "ultimate contraries are correlatives, mutually interdependent. Thus "nothing real can be described by the wholly one-sided assertion of simplicity, being, actuality, and the like, each in 'pure' form, devoid and independent of complexity, becoming, potentiality, and related contraries."[46] Accordingly, classical theism and materialism are both ruled out. The principle of polarity does not violate the law of noncontradiction because it does not both assert and deny the same thing *in the same way*. It is not contradictory to claim that a cone is both round and pointed or that God is dipolar.

Hartshorne works out this doctrine of God most fully in *The Divine Relativity*. He labels his theology "Surrelativism" or "Panentheism" and acknowl-

---

45. Hartshorne, "Failure of the Historical Doctrines," chap. 3 in *Divine Relativity*; Hartshorne and Reese, introduction to *Philosophers Speak of God*; Hartshorne, "Three Ideas of God," in *Reality as Social Process*; "Philosophical and Religious Uses of 'God,'" chap. 1 in *A Natural Theology for Our Time*; Charles Hartshorne, *Aquinas to Whitehead: Seven Centuries of Metaphysics of Religion* (Milwaukee: Marquette University Publications, 1976).

46. Hartshorne and Reese, *Philosophers Speak of God*, 2.

edges that it was anticipated by Plato, Schelling, Fechner, and Whitehead. He argues that because God is a person—a social being—who is inclusive of all other actualities, he is supremely relative. He relates and is related to everything that is. "God, as supremely excellent and concrete, must be conceived not as wholly absolute or immutable, but rather as supremely-relative, 'surrelative.'" God is also absolute, however, "because of his superior relativity, containing an abstract character or essence in respect to which . . . he is indeed strictly absolute and immutable."[47] In sum, "God, and only God, is in one aspect of his being strictly or maximally absolute, and in another aspect no less strictly or maximally relative."[48] "Absolute" and "relative" are fundamental dipolar attributes of God.

Necessity and contingency are likewise correlative attributes. "God is the only unconditionally 'necessary' existent. What is unconditionally neces-sary in God, however, is not all of God, though it is unique to him. And in another aspect, God is not only possessed of accidents, but he is the sole being who possesses or could possibly possess all actual accidental being as his own actuality."[49] God's sheer existence and nature are necessary, but his actual existence is full of the contingency and unpredictability of the beings that constitute the world, because the world is his body.

Contingency does not detract from God's perfection. In classical theism perfection means absolute completeness, the actuality of all possibilities for God. If God were to increase in excellence, he would change, which involves time—which is impossible for an eternal, immutable Being. But if the Perfect Being is "the self-surpassing surpasser of all," then he is both "the most excellent being" and yet capable of endlessly including in himself greater and higher levels of beauty, goodness, knowledge, and other values actualized in the world.[50] God is perfect in that he exemplifies all maximal excellences abstractly. But he is always open to greater perfection in that he can include more actual excellence in his consequent nature. Whatever the quality of the actual world, however, God's primordial nature is always all-surpassing in excellence.

Hartshorne also argues that God's excellent character and power are not incompatible with the existence of evil. Divine omnipotence does not mean

---

47. Hartshorne, preface to *Divine Relativity*, ix. See also "Relative, Absolute, and Superrelative: The Concept of Deity," in *Reality as Social Process*, 122: "*What is super-relative (reflexively transcendent) can be absolute in one aspect of abstract element of its being, and can also contain a world of relative things as its concrete parts.*"

48. Hartshorne, *Divine Reality*, 32.

49. Ibid., 32.

50. Ibid., 20.

that God mysteriously causes all things to act in precise detail according to his eternal knowledge and will. It means that he does everything possible to enable creatures to exercise their power. "His power is absolutely maximal, the greatest possible, but even the greatest possible power is still one power among others, is not the only power. God can do everything that a God can do, everything that could be done by 'a being with no possible superior.'" God does everything possible so that creatures make the right choices. "Adequate cosmic power is power to set conditions which are maximally favorable to desirable decisions on the part of local agents."[51] But God's power leaves the autonomy of creatures intact, even if they choose to do evil.

Similarly, God's knowledge is both complete and limited. "There is in God something absolute or non-relative, his cognitive adequacy. Nevertheless, in knowing any actual thing, God himself is related and relativized with respect to that thing." God's knowledge is absolute and complete because he knows all things exactly as they actually are. But it is therefore relative to what they actually are. "Knowledge adequate to its objects must be knowledge of the actual as actual and of the possible as possible."[52] Therefore God knows the past and present completely by prehending them cognitively. But the future is merely possible. To know it truly is to know it as possible. Therefore God does not know what free creatures will do before they do it, as classical theism asserts.

Hartshorne's redefinition of absoluteness, necessity, perfection, omnipotence, and omniscience are typical of his treatment of all the divine attributes in his dipolar view of God as the supreme personal-social Being. God is both absolute and relative, being and becoming, potential and actual, abstract and concrete, necessary and contingent, eternal and temporal, immutable and changing, cause and effect, and maximally excellent yet always improving. Since process theology claims to modify rather than repudiate classical theology, Hartshorne often calls his perspective "neo-classical theism."

Hartshorne not only articulates neoclassical theism's view of God but also develops arguments for God's existence more extensively than Whitehead.[53] He argues polemically that the atheism of Marx, Freud, Dewey, and Russell is self-defeating because it undermines their humanism. True humanism must be grounded in God.[54] Positively, Hartshorne defends as sound a number of

51. Ibid., 138, 135.

52. Ibid., 122, 121.

53. Griffin, "Natural Theology Based on Naturalistic Theism," chap. 5 in *Reenchantment*, summarizes Whitehead's and Hartshorne's arguments for God's existence.

54. Charles Hartshorne, *Beyond Humanism: Essays in the New Philosophy of Nature* (Chicago: Willett, Clark, 1937; repr., Lincoln: University of Nebraska Press, 1968).

traditional arguments for God's existence, provided that classical theism's monopolar view of God is replaced by the dipolar view.

Hartshorne pays most attention to the ontological argument.[55] In *Proslogion* Anselm argued that the very idea of God entails his existence. By definition, God is the greatest conceivable being. Either such a being actually exists or it is merely an idea. If it is merely an idea, then a greater being is conceivable: one who exists. Thus the definition of God entails that God exists. The ontological argument has been debated, affirmed, and rejected for centuries.

One issue is the assumption that there is such a state as maximal, unsurpassable greatness, excellence, or perfection of being. Perhaps greatness is open-ended or can be realized in multiple ways. Hartshorne defends the ontological argument by claiming that the objection to greatness as maximal excellence applies to the classical definition of God embraced by Anselm but not to neoclassical theism. Dipolar theism understands maximal excellence both as God's abstract nature and his unsurpassed yet ever-increasing actual existence. "If God is surpassable, even though only by Himself, then He can include quantity in His quality, without the quantity being that presumably impossible thing, an unsurpassable quantity."[56] Thus Hartshorne claims that dipolar theism meets this objection to the ontological argument.

The other issue is the alleged fallacy of assuming that the necessity of an idea entails its existence—that because the concept of God is necessary, his existence is necessary. Here is an illustration of the problem. Although a triangle necessarily (by definition) has three sides and although a bachelor necessarily is an unmarried adult male, triangles and bachelors do not necessarily exist. It is a mistake to slide from the necessity of something's nature to the necessity of its existence. There is, however, a response. Hartshorne was among the first contemporary philosophers to recognize Anselm's point, that the metaphysical mode of God's existence is different from islands, triangles, and bachelors. God is by nature a necessary being. Islands, triangles, and bachelors are contingent beings. They might or might not exist. But if God exists, he exists *necessarily*. "Thus if God logically could be necessary He must be."[57] And if God does not exist, his nonexistence is necessary. Thus his existence is *impossible*, not just a contingent matter of fact. This response to the ontological argument's detractors is not obviously fallacious.

---

55. Hartshorne, "Ten Ontological or Modal Proofs for God's Existence," chap. 2 in *Logic of Perfection*; *Anselm's Discovery*; also *A Natural Theology for Our Time* (La Salle, IL: Open Court, 1967).

56. Hartshorne, *Anselm's Discovery*, 29.

57. Hartshorne, "The Irreducibly Modal Structure of the Argument," chap. 2, pt. 6 in *Logic of Perfection*, 53.

Hartshorne's version of the argument conjoins his definition of maximal perfection with divine necessity. "Conclusion: The concept of divinity or perfection is not contingent. Either its exemplification is impossible or it is necessary. . . . Either 'God' is without coherent meaning, or divinity exists necessarily."[58] He then defends his notion of perfection as intelligible and unavoidable. Thus God/Perfection exists necessarily. The ontological argument is sound.

But Hartshorne is cautious about his conclusion: "God merely qua 'necessarily-existing individual' is not God in His concrete actuality, but is merely the abstract necessity that there be some such actuality."[59] But Hartshorne does claim to strengthen the case for process theology. Whitehead merely inferred God from the order of the actual world, and thus the necessity of his existence is contingent on our world. Hartshorne's ontological argument is stronger: God is necessary whether this world exists or not. Since God is dipolar, he must have some world or other, but not necessarily this world.

Armed with a weightier notion of necessity, Hartshorne also reformulates cosmological and teleological arguments for a dipolar God. "Fully developed, each of the arguments points not simply to the theistic conclusion, but to the neo-classical form of this conclusion."[60] Taken together, these arguments provide a solid cumulative case for God's existence, he claims. Thus Hartshorne considers dipolar theism to be the most rational worldview there is.

Hartshorne's Panentheism

Hartshorne not only identifies himself as a panentheist; he is also the main source of the term's current popularity. All its characteristics are immediately evident in his thought.[61] He distinguishes God as the supreme, all-comprehensive person from all other entities. He locates all things actual and possible, concrete and abstract, in God ontologically. "The mere essence of God contains no universe. We are truly 'outside' the divine essence, though inside God."[62]

Hartshorne also identifies his theology with the great tradition of panentheism "from Plato's *Timaeus* through the obscurities of Schelling's *Ages of the World* and the clearer pages of Fechner's *Zend Avesta* to Whitehead's

58. Hartshorne, *Logic of Perfection*, 70.

59. Ibid., 94.

60. Charles Hartshorne, *Creative Synthesis and Philosophical Method* (La Salle, IL: Open Court, 1970), 296.

61. Griffin, *Reenchantment*, 140–43; Gragg, "Panentheism," in *Charles Hartshorne*, 91–97.

62. Hartshorne and Reese, *Philosophers Speak of God*, 22.

Process and Reality."[63] Plato's World-Soul is alive and well in his thought: "The world . . . is God's body, the Soul of which is God."[64] In addition, the dialectical logic that leads this tradition toward panentheism is encoded in the Law of Polarity, "which may be traced back through Hegel to Heraclitus and Plato."[65] Hartshorne is surely one of the twentieth century's most self-consciously faithful representatives of this tradition.

Hartshorne's classification of kinds of panentheism is worth noting. In *Philosophers Speak of God*, Hartshorne and Reese distinguish three kinds of panentheism from other kinds of theism and pantheism. All panentheism views God as "Eternal-Temporal Consciousness, Knowing and Including the World." "Modern panentheism," which Hartshorne endorses, further specifies that God includes the world "in His own Actuality [but not in His Essence]." It recognizes God's dipolar nature and locates the world in one part of God. "Ancient or quasi-panentheism," which he claims is present in the Judeo-Christian Scriptures and Plato, is not explicitly dipolar and does not clearly distinguish between God's essence and actuality. It simply places the world in God, leaving the issue of creaturely autonomy ambiguous. But if God is absolute and necessary, as this tradition affirms, then the world and whatever happens in it are inevitable extensions of the divine essence. Thus Hartshorne and Reese call ancient panentheism "quasi-panentheism." The issue for them, considered below, is creaturely freedom in relation to God. The third variety, "limited panentheism," is held by William James and others. It recognizes dipolarity but limits God's knowledge and inclusion of the world: "Knowing or Partially Knowing, and Partially Including the World." This God is finite.[66] This sort of finite theism is also a species of panentheism.

Hartshorne affirms that God's maximal greatness is consistent with creaturely freedom. Indeed, he regards freedom as the most crucial issue. If God is wholly absolute and necessary, he has no alternatives but wills what he wills absolutely. But then he cannot be personal: "What is 'personality' but an enduring individual character or essence in a flux of such responses? . . . What has made certain ideas of God impersonal has been the denial of alternativeness."[67] Even worse, God is the cause of evil in the world. Freedom is likewise essential for humans. Without it we cannot be persons with responsibility who can relate with love and knowledge.

63. Hartshorne, *Divine Relativity*, xi; also Hartshorne and Reese, table of contents and "Introduction: The Standpoint of Panentheism," in *Philosophers Speak of God*.

64. Hartshorne, *Omnipotence*, 94.

65. Hartshorne and Reese, *Philosophers Speak of God*, 2.

66. Ibid., xiii.

67. Ibid., 22.

Hartshorne makes self-creation or self-determination the litmus test for the crucial ontological distinction between God and creatures. If God is the All-Determining Will or Absolute Cause, then he is the only real being or substance, and Spinozan pantheism is true.[68] Panentheism is distinct from pantheism precisely because it affirms creaturely self-determination.[69] Process ontology insists that self-actualization, not merely individual "substance" or "being," is what distinguishes creatures ontologically from God.[70] Ambivalence on creaturely freedom even separates classical panentheism—ancient or quasi-panentheism—from modern panentheism, according to Hartshorne. By this standard, Schleiermacher's "absolute dependence" of creatures on the Creator is "ancient," but Schelling's notion of divine and human freedom is genuinely modern.[71]

John Cobb and David Griffin's Christian Process Theology

Whitehead and Hartshorne both frequently comment on Christ, Christianity, and specific Christian doctrines even though neither identifies himself as Christian.[72] In this, however, their work provided some direction to John Cobb and David Ray Griffin as they refined process thought and developed Christian process theology. Here follows a brief introduction to Cobb and Griffin individually and a summary of their collaborative presentation *Process Theology*.

Cobb was a student of Hartshorne's at Chicago and has taught many years at the Claremont School of Theology. He has developed a Christian process worldview well beyond the discipline of theology. He has written many books and articles and been active in promoting personal and social ethics, environmental ethics, politics, interreligious dialogue, and pastoral theology.[73] But he has also contributed to process theology itself.

68. Ibid., 189–91.
69. Hartshorne, "Pantheism and Panentheism," *EncRel* 11:165–71.
70. Griffin, *Reenchantment*, 142: "Panentheism is crucially different from pantheism because God transcends the universe in the sense that God has God's own creative power, distinct from that of the universe of finite actualities. Hence, each finite actual entity has its own creativity with which to exercise some degree of self-determination, so that it transcends the divine influence upon it."
71. Hartshorne and Reese, *Philosophers Speak of God*, 233–36.
72. E.g., Whitehead, "The New Reformation," in *Adventures of Ideas*; Hartshorne, "Tragic and Sublime Aspects of Christian Love," in *Reality as Social Process*.
73. Examples are John B. Cobb, *Christ in a Pluralistic Age* (Philadelphia: Westminster, 1975); *Process Philosophy as Political Theology* (Philadelphia: Westminster, 1982); *Beyond Dialogue: Toward a Mutual Transformation of Christianity and Buddhism* (Philadelphia: Fortress, 1982); *Sustaining the Common*

In his *Christian Natural Theology*, Cobb develops "A Whiteheadian Doctrine of God" that is highly appreciative of Whitehead but finally opts for Hartshorne's model of God as a person. "My conclusion, then, is that the chief reason for insisting that God is an actual entity can be satisfied by the view that he is a living person, that this view makes the doctrine of God more coherent, and that no serious new difficulties are raised."[74] Cobb also finds it necessary, however, to correct Hartshorne's theology with something from Whitehead. According to Griffin, Hartshorne's notion of God as a living person "did not retain the idea of a realm of eternal objects primordially envisaged by God."[75] Cobb reasserts that God "envisages all possibility eternally,"[76] thus synthesizing Whitehead's and Hartshorne's doctrine of God.

David Griffin, philosopher of religion at Claremont School of Theology, is currently the leading process thinker. He has written on theological, philosophical, religious, social, and cultural issues.[77] A recent work of his, *Reenchantment without Supernaturalism: A Process Philosophy of Religion*, is a philosophically clear elaboration and defense of process philosophy and its implications for religion and Christian theology, perhaps the best presentation of process thought to date. Most interesting for our purpose is the fact that Griffin adopts Cobb's synthetic model of God. "By combining elements of Whitehead's position with elements of Hartshorne's position, we can develop a coherent doctrine of God that does equal justice to the two kinds of divine dipolarity essential to process theism."[78] The views of Cobb and Griffin are very close on many issues.

Their *Process Theology* is an excellent summary of their position and its application to Christian doctrine, ethics, and worldview. The sections on God and the world are particularly interesting. Appealing to contemporary religious sensibilities, the preface identifies five traditional views of God that process theology rejects: "God as Cosmic Moralist" who is fixated on morality and punishes immoral behavior; "God as the Unchanging and Passionless Absolute" who cannot have feelings or respond to creatures; "God as Controlling Power"

Good: Christian Reflections on the Global Economy (Cleveland: Pilgrim, 1994); *Grace and Responsibility: A Wesleyan Theology for Today* (Nashville: Abingdon, 1995).

74. Cobb, *Christian Natural Theology*, 192.

75. Griffin, *Reenchantment*, 159.

76. Cobb, *Christian Natural Theology*, 187.

77. Examples are David Griffin, *A Process Christology* (Philadelphia: Westminster, 1973); *God, Power, and Evil: A Process Theodicy* (Philadelphia: Westminster, 1976); *God and Religion in the Postmodern World* (Albany: State University of New York Press, 1989); *Parapsychology, Philosophy, and Spirituality: A Postmodern Exploration* (Albany: State University of New York Press, 1997); *Religion and Scientific Naturalism: Overcoming the Conflicts* (Albany: State University of New York Press, 2000).

78. Cobb, *Christian Natural Theology*, 160.

who determines everything that happens in the world and even causes evil; "God as Sanctioner of the Status Quo" who is focused on preserving sameness; and "God as Male," which is "the archetype of the dominant, inflexible, unemotional, completely independent (read 'strong') male."[79]

The chapter "God as Creative-Responsive Love" is a clear and accessible introduction to the Whitehead-Hartshorne view of God. It also addresses what Cobb and Griffin regard as the negative implications of classical theism and the traditional misrepresentations of God mentioned above. Whereas the God of Anselm and Aquinas loves by doing good but not by feeling or responding, the dipolar God manifests genuinely "responsive love." In his supreme relatedness and consequent nature, "God enjoys our enjoyments and suffers with our sufferings." God is also "creative love."[80] His action in the world is neither all-determining nor split between natural and "miraculous" supernatural modes of operation. These traditional ideas have foundered on modern science and the problem of evil, according to Cobb and Griffin. Science has eliminated the need to appeal to special miraculous interventions in the natural order.[81] Cobb and Griffin find it unthinkable that an all-determining loving God would allow so much evil in the world. So they offer their alternative. "Process theology provides a way of recovering the conviction that God acts creatively in the world and of understanding this creative activity as the expression of divine love for the world."[82]

Process theology does so by regarding "divine creative love as persuasive." God presents good and attractive possibilities for creatures' self-realization, but he does not foreordain or even foreknow what they choose to do. "God as an actuality is essentially related to the world. Since actuality as such is partially self-creative, future events are not yet determinate, so that even perfect knowledge cannot know the future, and God does not wholly control the world. Any divine influence must be persuasive, not coercive." The reason is love: "If we truly love others we do not seek to control them." Cobb and Griffin recognize that "the divine creative activity involves risk," but they argue that because God is not controlling, "the occurrence of genuine evil is not incompatible with God's beneficence toward all his creatures."[83] God is loving and powerful but not responsible for evil.

The models of God as Cosmic Moralist and Controlling Power have been conjoined in traditional religion to give the impression that God wants

79. Cobb and Griffin, *Process Theology*, 8–10.
80. Ibid., 48.
81. This is a key point in Griffin, *Reenchantment*.
82. Cobb and Griffin, *Process Theology*, 51.
83. Ibid., 52–3.

people to fight against many things, such as sexual pleasure, that they find intrinsically good and enjoyable for themselves and others. In contrast, process theology presents "Divine Creative Love as Promoting Enjoyment." "Enjoyment" in Whitehead's thought is not primarily pleasure but the experience of maximal actualization of an occasion's positive possibilities. Pleasure is rightly found in such experience. "Process theology sees God's fundamental aim to be the promotion of the creatures' own enjoyment." Morality is what God wills, and God wills that his creatures flourish. Thus, "in process thought, morality stands in the service of enjoyment."[84] Process ethics does not justify individual hedonism or self-indulgence, however, because the enjoyment of each creature is relative to the good of all God's creatures within the close-knit community of the universe.

Because divine Creative Love is "Adventurous," God is not the Sanctioner of the Status Quo or the Cosmic Moralist. The primordial nature of God is the source of order, but self-actualization inevitably involves novelty. "In brief, although God is the source of order, the order is derivative from novelty, and both order and novelty are good only insofar as they contribute to the enjoyment of experience." Not all order is good. For example, "no type of social order is to be maintained if it no longer tends to maximize the enjoyment of the members of the society."[85] God is no exception to this rule. "God's own life is an adventure, for the novel enjoyments that are promoted among the creatures are then the experiences providing the material for God's own enjoyment."

Finally, God as creative-responsive love means that God cannot be represented as exclusively or stereotypically male: "active, unresponsive, impassive, inflexible, impatient, and moralistic." But neither is God antimasculine or exclusively feminine. He has both male and female characteristics. "The positive aspects of these 'masculine' attributes can be retained, without their destructive implications, if they are incorporated into a revolutionized concept of God into which the stereotypical traits are integrated." God should be represented by both masculine and feminine imagery. "The process dipolar notion of deity has some affinity with the Taoist notion of the Tao, in which the 'feminine' and 'masculine' (yin and yang) dimensions of reality are perfectly integrated."[86] A later chapter of this book notes the indebtedness of many feminist theologians to this gender-inclusive view of God.

Cobb and Griffin present explanations of the Christian doctrines of Christ, the Trinity, and salvation. Christ is the incarnation of God's creative-respon-

84. Ibid., 54–57, 56–57.
85. Ibid., 57–61, quote at 60.
86. Ibid., 61–62.

sive love. John 1 speaks of the Logos, or Word, who is God, who creates, and who "becomes flesh." The Logos is the primordial nature of God, which is the ideal structure of all possible worlds. "The *incarnate* Logos is Christ. In this broadest sense, Christ is present in all things." As the Ground of human existence, "Christ is the giver of both responsive and creative human love." Christ is broader than Jesus, but Jesus is unique. "Whereas Christ is incarnate in everyone, Jesus is Christ because the incarnation is constitutive of his very selfhood." For this reason, Jesus is "God's decisive revelation."[87] With respect to the content of revelation, "the vision of reality that is expressed through the sayings and actions of Jesus is one in which the primary reality with which we have to do is the creative-responsive love of God." Definitions of faith and conversion follow: "Accepting Jesus as the decisive revelation of what the divine reality is like opens us to being creatively transformed." Seeking God's kingdom means that Christians are to participate in the historical "force field" of creative-responsive love begun by Jesus. The resurrected Christ is still present in the world as the continuation of God's love in "the church as the Body of Christ and as the extension of that incarnation which was begun in Jesus."[88] These examples illustrate how Cobb and Griffin construe Christian doctrine in terms of process theology.

They approach the Trinity in the same way. Process theology as such affirms one God with two natures, not one God in three persons. Cobb and Griffin are frank about their difference with historic Christian trinitarian doctrine. "When 'person' is taken in its modern sense [as rational agent], God is one person. When 'person' is taken in its traditional sense [as relation], two persons can be distinguished, God as creative love and God as responsive love." The preincarnate Word is the primordial nature of God. The incarnate Christ is the primordial nature of God positively embodied in the world, excluding its evil. God's active immanence in the world is the Holy Spirit. Cobb and Griffin affirm "two persons" but cannot consistently correlate Christ with one divine nature and the Holy Spirit with the other. They do not even mention the Father, perhaps because they reject exclusively masculine language for God. They criticize the traditional doctrine of the Trinity as "a source of distortion, and an artificial game that has brought theology into justifiable disrepute."[89]

Their doctrines of salvation and eschatology, "the last things," likewise depend heavily on Whiteheadian thought. God saves the world by making the good "objectively immortal" and regretting evil as he prehends the world, ever

87. Ibid., 98, 101, 105.
88. Ibid., 102, 107.
89. Ibid., 109.

luring it toward a better future. They recommend Teilhard's "zest" for Omega, however, as a necessary supplement to Whitehead's "lure" toward the future. Zest for Omega recognizes greater motivation in creatures to cooperate in achieving a positive goal for history.[90] Even so, Cobb and Griffin have no certainty of attaining the kingdom of God: "The Whiteheadian, unlike Teilhard, must assert that . . . the future is open. There is no assurance that the human species will move forward." Process theology can foresee "no End at which the process would come to rest," and so it lacks an eschaton and consummation.[91]

Regarding the future of human individuals, Whitehead declares himself "entirely neutral on the question of immortality," allowing that "in some important sense the existence of the soul may be freed from its dependence on the body."[92] Hartshorne outright rejects the notion of a subjective after-life.[93] Cobb and Griffin leave this issue open in *Process Theology*. Later Cobb argues for the resurrection of the soul[94] as a new kind of existence without an earthly organism. Griffin has developed a similar case.[95]

Cobb and Griffin have contributed a great deal to articulating a Christian version of process theology. Traditional Christians understandably distance themselves both from this view of God and its implications for the core doctrines of the faith. Some traditional Christians have, however, attempted to appropriate aspects or affirmations of process theology in ways they judge compatible with orthodox evangelical Christianity.[96]

Process Theology and Free-Will (Open) Theism

The best-known current example is free-will theism, also called open theism,[97] which has generated a hot debate within evangelical Christian-

90. Ian Barbour, "Teilhard's Process Metaphysics," in *Process Theology*, ed. Cousins, 323–50, is a general comparison of Teilhard's and Whitehead's systems.

91. Cobb and Griffin, *Process Theology*, 117–18.

92. Whitehead, *Religion in the Making*, 111; *Adventures of Ideas*, 267. It is difficult, however, to see in Whitehead's ontology how a "monarchial occasion" could survive apart from the "organic society" of which it is a member. Even God does not have enough power to make it happen.

93. Hartshorne, *Omnipotence*, 117–18.

94. John B. Cobb, "The Resurrection of the Soul," *Harvard Theological Review* 80/2 (1987): 213–27.

95. Griffin, "The Plausibility of Life after Death," in *Reenchantment*, 241–46.

96. See, e.g., Ronald Nash, ed., *Process Theology* (Grand Rapids: Baker, 1987). Some authors, such as Arthur Holmes, Donald Bloesch, Carl Henry, William Craig, and Thomas Morris, are highly critical. Others, while mainly critical, validate some points of process theology: David Basinger, Norris Clark, and Clark Pinnock.

97. See Richard Rice, *The Openness of God: The Relationship between Divine Foreknowledge and Human Free Will* (Washington, DC: Review and Herald, 1980; rev. ed., Minneapolis: Bethany House, 1985); William Hasker, *God, Time, and Knowledge* (Ithaca, NY: Cornell University Press, 1989); Clark Pinnock

ity. Because it agrees with aspects of process theology, some critics have alleged that it is a process wolf in evangelical sheep's clothing.[98] A dialogue between process theists, including Cobb and Griffin, and free-will theists has clarified the similarities and differences between the two theologies.[99] It is instructive to consider the consensus they reached.

Evangelical theologian Clark Pinnock identifies the issues on which he can "appreciate the contributions of process theology." These include "a dynamic understanding of the world and God's interactive relations with it," as well as "bipolarity in God, human self-determination, and divine persuasion." Furthermore, he writes, "we both accept the need to critique classical substantive metaphysics and we both reject the notion that God is an absolute being, unaffected by the world." Both sides insist on God's love, compassion, and sensitivity. "We do not believe that God determines the course of events unilaterally. We believe that the future is open and that some kinds of change even belong to the divine perfection and are not alien to it. We believe that God not only affects creatures but that creatures affect God. We both think that God suffers when things go badly for creatures. We both hold to the reality of libertarian freedom and consequently we both recognize that genuine evils exist."[100] It is not surprising, given these agreements, that open theists are sometimes thought to be closet process theists.

But there are deep and significant differences. Pinnock identifies two basic ones. The first is the normative order of Scripture and philosophy. Open theism professes that Scripture is fundamental, whereas process theology proceeds from philosophy. This difference generates a second: "For openness theists the ultimate metaphysical fact is God, not God and the world. Insistence on the world's necessity for God seems to conflict with God's free and sovereign love." Pinnock elaborates: "In the openness model, God still reserves the power to control everything, whereas in process thought God cannot override the freedom of creatures." Open theists hold that "God, if not essentially related to the world, is only allowing Godself to be affected by the world and is not necessarily affected by it."[101] Free-will

---

et al., *The Openness of God: A Biblical Challenge to the Traditional Understanding of God* (Downers Grove, IL: InterVarsity, 1994); David Basinger, *The Case for Freewill Theism* (Downers Grove, IL: InterVarsity, 1996); John Sanders, *The God Who Risks* (Downers Grove, IL: InterVarsity, 1998); and Gregory Boyd, *God of the Possible* (Grand Rapids: Baker, 2000).

98. See, e.g., Royce Gruenler's charges in "God at Risk," *Christianity Today*, March 5, 2001, 56.

99. John B. Cobb and Clark Pinnock, eds., *Searching for an Adequate God: A Dialogue between Process and Free Will Theists* (Grand Rapids: Eerdmans, 2000).

100. Ibid., ix–x.

101. Ibid., x–xi.

theism's strong affirmation of God's essential independence cuts against process theology.[102]

Griffin confirms these differences.[103] He lists and rejects free-will theism's assertions that God can exist without a world; that God can exercise full power of determination over the actions of creatures if he so chooses; that he has created the world by choice from nothing; that he can and has intervened supernaturally in his normal providence of the universe; that he is not necessarily but voluntarily interactive with creatures (and thus dipolar); that God's love is necessary internally (within the Trinity) but only contingent externally (for the world that he has chosen to create); and that he will inevitably triumph over evil. Griffin finds these differences so significant that he classifies this theology as "classical free-will theism" because it is much closer to Augustine, Aquinas, and Calvin than to process thought. "Both are forms of classical theism, in that both hold that all power essentially belongs to God, so that God could, if God so chose, create a world in which all events are determined by God." He agrees that open theism departs from classical theism in holding that God has chosen to grant freedom to creatures.[104] It seems clear that open theism is not a species of process theology.

Open theism might nevertheless be "voluntary panentheism," where God has freely chosen to involve the world panentheistically. Whether it is panentheism depends on what "being in God" amounts to. Open theism denies that the world is essential to or part of God. But if being in God means that the effects of creatures on God are fully and sufficiently internalized by God and if God's existence and identity (not his essence), like creatures' existence and identity, is codetermined by all his relationships and the effects of his relationships, then creatures indeed become "part of God's life." By God's choice, creatures continuously determine God's existence ad hoc—what he can know and do, cannot know and do, must know and do, what he risks, and what he actually does choose to do in order to bring about his complete victory at the end. In other words, if open theism holds a relational ontology, its understanding of the God-world relation might very well turn out to be panentheistic. We return to this discussion in the last chapter.

102. It cuts against almost all panentheism. A few panentheists, however, such as Clayton, hold that the world is a free choice for God. Therefore affirming the essential independence of God from creation is not sufficient to avoid panentheism. We consider this in the final chapter.

103. Cobb and Pinnock, eds., *Searching for an Adequate God*, 10–14.

104. Ibid., 8.

Conclusion

Hartshorne might be correct that Whiteheadian process theology is the paradigmatic case of modern panentheism. Proud of its roots in the tradition of the Platonic World-Soul, it just as proudly affirms the modern theme of creaturely freedom in relation to God. Because God is the Soul and the world is his body, each influences the other. Creatures have a causal effect on God. Thus God is dipolar, possessing both an unchanging essence and a changing existence. Although God does not need *this* world, it is his nature to embody some world or other. Based on modern science and an elaborate system of philosophy, process theology sets a high intellectual standard for modern panentheism.

It is, however, just one of a number of panentheisms that share common nineteenth-century roots. Schelling's emphasis on divine and human freedom emerging from an organically modeled universe also inspired Fechner, Peirce, James, Alexander, Bergson, and Teilhard to develop science-based theologies in which God's personality develops through interaction with the world he embodies. Interestingly, this entire generation of thinkers proceed from a "neutral" panpsychic ontology: the basic "stuff" of which the universe consists is neither matter nor spirit but functions as both. The "organic" view of matter and spirit that results conduces to an "organic" view of God's relation with the world. Read in historical context, Whitehead presents a sophisticated variation on a common theme.

As an approach to Christian theology, process thought is likewise in the modernist tradition. Like Hegel and Schelling, it reinterprets Christianity in terms of a dynamic philosophy instead of generating a contemporary worldview in terms of traditional Christianity. The doctrines that it generates are typical of modernist Christianity rather than historic Roman Catholic or Protestant teaching.

8

Tillich's Existential Panentheism

Paul Tillich (1886–1965) embraced Christian Neoplatonism and German romanticism more self-consciously than any other twentieth-century panentheist. His *History of Christian Thought* highlights the importance of Neoplatonism in the formation of the classical Christian worldview. He concludes that both of the greatest influences on nineteenth-century theology represent Christian Neoplatonism: Schleiermacher, its mystical tendency; and Hegel, its philosophical framework.[1] But Tillich elsewhere makes clear that existential interests attracted him to the mature Schelling's philosophy of freedom more than Schleiermacher's pietism or Hegel's rationalism. "What I learned from Schelling became determinative of my own philosophical and theological development."[2] Revealing his genealogy more broadly, he

---

1. Paul Tillich, *A History of Christian Thought: From Its Judaic and Hellenistic Origins to Existentialism*, ed. Carl Braaten (New York: Simon and Schuster, 1968), 292–93.

2. Paul Tillich, "Schelling's Criticism of Hegel," in *Perspectives on 19th and 20th Century Protestant Theology*, ed. Carl Braaten (New York: Harper and Row, 1967), 141–52, quote at 142. In his foreword to Paul Tillich, *Gesammelte Werke*, 14 vols. (Stuttgart: Evangelisches Vertragswerk, 1959–1975), vol. 1, he writes, "The influence of my Schelling studies on the whole of my further development is very strong." Quoted from Victor Nuovo, introduction to Paul Tillich, *Mysticism and Guilt-Consciousness in Schelling's Philosophical Development*, trans. Victor Nuovo (Lewisburg, PA: Bucknell University Press, 1974), 9. Also Paul Tillich, *The Construction of the History of Religion in Schelling's Positive Philosophy: Its Presuppositions and Principles*, trans. Victor Nuovo (Lewisburg, PA: Bucknell University Press, 1974).

confides that "his spiritual father was Schleiermacher, his intellectual father was Schelling, and his grandfather on both sides was Jakob Böhme."[3] Tillich's theology, broadly summarized, is an adaptation of Schelling's philosophy of divine-human freedom, amplified by Heidegger's existential ontology and stated in Christian language. It is an *existential* panentheism, locating the human quest for authentic existence in God.

Born in Germany to a Lutheran pastor's family, Tillich studied philosophy and theology.[4] After serving as a chaplain in World War I, he became a professor at the University of Berlin. His political views brought him into trouble with Hitler, and so he moved to the United States in 1933 and taught at Union Seminary in New York until 1955. He then held positions at Harvard and Chicago Divinity School. Although he did not found a "school" of theology, he has been an important influence on movements such as the death-of-God theology and feminist theology and on theologians such as John Robinson and John Macquarrie. His thought is still discussed regularly at international conferences.[5]

This chapter highlights how Tillich's doctrine of God, stated popularly in *The Courage to Be* and academically in the first volume of his *Systematic Theology*,[6] is rooted in the tradition of Böhme, Hegel, and Schelling.[7] Sections focus on Tillich's correlation of philosophy and theology, his existential ontology, and his doctrine of God. The final section reflects on his panentheism.

---

3. John Newport, *Paul Tillich* (Waco: Word, 1984), 76. Newport quotes theologian Nels Ferre, to whom Tillich made this comment.

4. Paul Tillich, "Autobiographical Reflections," in *The Theology of Paul Tillich*, ed. C. Kegley and R. Bretall (New York: Macmillan, 1952), 3–21; Newport, "Paul Tillich: Life of an Identifying and Participating Philosophical Theologian," chap. 1 in *Paul Tillich*.

5. E.g., Gert Hummel, ed., *God and Being: Contributions Made to the II. International Paul Tillich Symposium, Held in Frankfurt, 1988* (New York: de Gruyter, 1989); Gert Hummel, ed., *History and Truth—a Dialogue with Paul Tillich: Proceedings of the VI. International Symposium, Held in Frankfurt/Main, 1996* (New York: de Gruyter, 1998).

6. Paul Tillich, *The Courage to Be* (London: Nisbet, 1952); *Systematic Theology*, 3 vols. (Chicago: University of Chicago Press, 1951–1963).

7. Adrian Thatcher, *The Ontology of Paul Tillich* (Oxford: Oxford University Press, 1978), details his debt to Schelling, Hegel, and Böhme as well as the broader tradition of Christian thought. Also Newport, "Historical Influences on Tillich's Basic Idea and Basic Method," chap. 4 in *Paul Tillich*; and Ian E. Thompson, "The Influence of Schelling, and Tillich's Distinctive Ideas," in *Being and Meaning: Paul Tillich's Theory of Meaning, Truth, and Logic* (Edinburgh: Edinburgh University Press, 1981), 30–32.

For his theology as whole, see Stanley J. Grenz and Roger E. Olson, "Paul Tillich," in *Twentieth-Century Theology: God and the World in a Transitional Age* (Downers Grove, IL: InterVarsity, 1992), 114–30; James Livingston, *Modern Christian Thought: From the Enlightenment to Vatican II* (New York: Macmillan, 1971), 356–70; David Kelsey, *The Fabric of Paul Tillich's Theology* (New Haven: Yale University Press, 1957); Newport, *Paul Tillich*; and John Heywood Thomas, *Tillich* (New York: Continuum, 2000).

Tillich's Correlation of Philosophy and Theology

Tillich's famous method of correlation developed from his study of Schelling's dialectic of reason and revelation.[8] The dialectical correlation of reason and revelation are crucial for Tillich's theology because they eventually entail dynamic panentheism. In brief, reason gives a philosophical analysis of human existence, and revelation provides religious symbols that express the meaning of human existence—participation in God. The dialectical correlation of reason and revelation generates theology, which is the existential-philosophical interpretation of religious symbols. Because Tillich's philosophy appropriates much from Schelling, his theology is a species of dynamic panentheism, an existential panentheism. So we begin with his method.

The Correlation of Philosophy and Theology

The motive of Tillich's theology is apologetical concern to demonstrate that the gospel is the answer to humanity's basic needs and questions. Thus he correlates the Christian faith with existential philosophy's diagnosis of our deepest concerns. "I use the method of correlation. I try to show that the Christian message is the answer to all the problems involved in self-criticizing humanism; today we call this existentialism."[9]

In each historical situation, philosophy articulates the human questions its own way, and theology specifies the revealed answer. In *Systematic Theology* Tillich explains that existentialism is the best philosophy for his era because it most pointedly raises "the question of a reality in which the self-estrangement of our existence is overcome, a reality of reconciliation and reunion, of creativity, meaning, and hope." The affirmation of this reality he calls "the 'New Being,'" which becomes a synonym for "salvation." Philosophy cannot tell us where to find New Being even though it raises the right question. But "theology answers this question by saying: 'In Jesus the Christ.'"[10] Scripture alone is not sufficient to define New Being, according to Tillich. The Christian message is "contained in the Bible, but it is not identical with the Bible."[11] It

8. "The method that Tillich follows in his second Schelling dissertation is a variation of this dialectical method; it reappears in his later work as the 'method of correlation'" (Nuovo, introduction to Tillich, *Construction of the History of Religion*, 14).

9. Tillich, *History of Christian Thought*, 293. He elaborates the method of correlation in the introduction to *Systematic Theology*, vol. 1. See Newport, "Tillich's Basic Purpose: Apologist to Intellectuals," and "The Method of Correlation," chaps. 2 and 5 in *Tillich*.

10. Tillich, *Systematic Theology*, 1:49.

11. Ibid., 1:4. The Bible is God's Word in that it is "the document of the final revelation" and "participates in the final revelation," but the Word is "New Being in Christ" (158–59).

requires interpretation. Theology must use current philosophy to state the unchanging truth of the biblical message for each historical situation.

Theology can correlate with philosophy because both are concerned with ultimate reality. "Philosophy necessarily asks the question of reality as a whole, the question of the structure of being. Theology necessarily asks the same question, for that which concerns us ultimately must belong to reality as a whole; it must belong to being."[12] More precisely, the focus of theology is "*what concerns us ultimately*," in other words, "*that which determines our being or not-being*."[13] Both disciplines address human existence in relation to ultimate reality, which religion calls "God."

Reason and revelation are distinct but correlative sources. Through reason philosophy engages the universal logos—the intelligibility of being in general. The source of theological knowledge is revelation, "the Logos 'who became flesh,' that is, the logos manifesting itself in a particular historical event."[14] Philosophy and theology both consider intelligible manifestations of the same ultimate reality, one universal and the other particular.

Tillich insists that reason needs revelation.[15] Modern rationalism's unsatisfiable demand for complete verification of claims about the ultimate has led to skepticism and left us with mere scientific and technical reason. This situation "must lead either to a desperate resignation of truth or to the quest for revelation."[16] Revelation is crucial because it discloses a mystery that reason cannot. "The mystery which is revealed is of ultimate concern to us because it is the ground of our being." Revelation occurs in any event in which a person existentially encounters the Ground of being.[17] Thus the "Word of God" speaks in anything that reveals the meaning of life. Revelation takes place in nature, history, communities, and especially in linguistic utterances.[18] In all its expressions, the meaning of God's Word is New Being, "the being of the Christ."[19]

Revelation never fully dispels the mystery of being, but what it does disclose is reasonable. "Revelation is the manifestation of the depth of reason and the ground of being."[20] Historically speaking, Tillich judges that mystery

12. Ibid., 1:20–21.
13. Ibid., 1:12, 14.
14. Ibid., 1:22–28, quote at 23.
15. Ibid., "Reason and the Quest for Revelation," chap. 1 in vol. 1, part 1. Newport, "Reason and the Quest for Revelation," chap. 6 in *Tillich*.
16. Tillich, *Systematic Theology*, 1:105.
17. Ibid., "The Reality of Revelation," chap. 2, 1:110–11.
18. Ibid., 1:118–26.
19. Ibid., 1:158–59.
20. Ibid., 1:117.

and rationality are properly balanced "in men like Plotinus, Eckhart, Nicholas of Cusa, Spinoza, and Böhme,"[21] not to mention Schelling. Tillich's theology strongly correlates reason and revelation.

Philosophy Is Conceptually Definitive for Theology

Although reason and revelation are correlative, Tillich gives philosophy conceptual priority. "A consequence of the method used in apologetic theology is that the concept of revelation is approached 'from below,' from man in the situation of revelation, and not from 'above,' from the divine ground of revelation." Because philosophy works "from below," it properly determines the conceptual framework for theological reflection on revelation. Tillich therefore approaches the doctrine of God through a philosophical analysis of being: "A doctrine of God as the ground of revelation presupposes the doctrine of Being and God."[22]

Philosophy defines the terms of theology for another reason. Its assertions about God are conceptual and nonsymbolic, whereas theology combines literal and symbolic. Tillich states that "religious assertions are symbolic," that "ontological assertions are literal," and that "theological assertions are literal descriptions of the correlation between the religious symbols and the ontological concepts."[23] In philosophy, "the statement that God is being-itself is a nonsymbolic statement. It does not point beyond itself. It means what it says directly and properly." The discipline of ontology can state the conceptual truth of God's nature clearly because God is both "the ground of the structure of beings" and "he *is* this structure."[24] Tillich's philosophy therefore determines the conceptual framework of his theology.

Theology is symbolic because it articulates the meaning of religious symbols. A symbol is not a mere sign that arbitrarily refers to something, for it "participates in the reality of that for which it stands." Participation is not intellectual reflection but existential engagement—living interaction. This

21. Ibid., 1:141.

22. Ibid., 1:155–56.

23. Thatcher, *Ontology*, 38, notes that Tillich "fully accepted" this formulation by R. P. Scharlemann, "Tillich's Method of Correlation: Two Proposed Revisions," *JR* 40 (1966): 95. Tillich's assent is in his "Rejoinder" in the same issue, 184. It is his late and definitive position. He was not always consistent and developed. In Tillich, *The Courage to Be*, 169 and 171, he denies any nonsymbolic reference to God: "Every assertion about being-itself is either metaphorical or symbolic"; "To speak unsymbolically about being-itself is untrue." In Tillich, introduction to *Systematic Theology*, 2:10, he seems to affirm both positions: "If we say that God is the infinite, or the unconditional, or being-itself, we speak rationally and ecstatically at the same time. . . . This dialectical situation is the conceptual expression of man's existential situation."

24. Tillich, *Systematic Theology*, 1:238–39.

is what Tillich means when he says that "the religious symbol, the symbol which points to the divine, can be a true symbol only if it participates in the power of the divine to which it points." Religious language does not enable us to "gain knowledge of God by drawing conclusions about the infinite from the finite." Instead it conveys the meaning of existential participation in God[25] (which, as we will see, amounts to existential panentheism). It is worth noting again that Tillich appropriates his view of religious symbols and his method of correlation mainly from Schelling's mature philosophy of religion.

Tillich's Existential Ontology

The philosophical discipline through which Tillich approaches theology is existential ontology, the study of human being and nonbeing, because "it is the finitude of being which drives us to the question of God." He develops his ontology from Heidegger's analysis of human existence as *Dasein* in *Being and Time*. Heidegger approaches Being through human being. He "calls 'Dasein' ('being-there') the place where the structure of being is manifest."[26] Tillich steers Heidegger's analysis toward theology along two parallel routes. In *Systematic Theology* he develops a theoretical account of the basic categories of human existence in relation to being, nonbeing, and being-itself, which he applies to God.[27] In *The Courage to Be*, he uses Heidegger's concepts of anxiety and resolve to argue that "the courage to be" in the face of nonbeing reveals the power of being-itself, "the God beyond God."[28] We summarize both routes.

"Being and the Question of God" is the existential-ontological section of the first volume of *Systematic Theology*.[29] The first part presents Heidegger's argument that self and world constitute a single ontological structure. The second section considers three sets of polar "ontological elements" that are constitutive of human being in the world: individualization and participation, dynamics and form, and freedom and destiny.[30] Tillich's third section,

25. Ibid., 1:238–40.

26. Ibid., 1:166, 168. In the next chapter we consider Heidegger, his debt to Schelling's philosophy of freedom, and his implicit panentheism.

27. Newport, "Tillich's Basic Idea (Ontology)," chap. 3 in *Tillich*.

28. Tillich, *The Courage to Be*, 140–43, discusses *Being and Time*.

29. Tillich, *Systematic Theology*, "Being and God," chap. 1 of vol. 1, part 2.

30. Tillich's account of freedom and destiny in particular is based on Schelling by way of Martin Heidegger, *Schelling's Treatise on the Essence of Human Freedom*, trans. Joan Stambaugh (Athens, OH: Ohio University Press, 1985), who also lectured on this subject.

"Being and Finitude," examines how these polarities—as well as the categories of time, space, substance, causality, essence, and existence—reflect the fundamental polarities of being/nonbeing and finitude/infinity. A final section treats the traditional arguments for God's existence not as proofs but as indications that the question of God is inherent in reason itself. The trajectory of Tillich's entire existential ontology—analysis of the constitutive structure of human existence—is captured in the summary of one section: All these categories "express the union of being and nonbeing in everything finite. They articulate the courage which accepts the anxiety of nonbeing. The question of God is the question of the possibility of this courage."[31] Thus Tillich's *Systematic Theology* charts the academic route through his ontology of human existence to God and relates it to courage.

The more existential journey is mapped in *The Courage to Be*. It surveys the phenomena of courage and anxiety as understood in the history of culture, society, religion, and philosophy and pays special attention to twentieth-century existentialism. Tillich concludes that Heidegger carried through "the Existential analysis of the courage to be as oneself more fully than anyone else." But Heidegger did so "more destructively" than anyone because, in Tillich's judgment, he makes the human individual ultimate.[32] Tillich counters that "the ultimate power of self-affirmation can only be the power of being-itself." He surveys the kinds of human encounter with being-itself that elicit the courage to face guilt and death—in particular, mysticism and the personal piety of Protestant Christianity. He concludes, *"The courage to be is rooted in the God who appears when God has disappeared in the anxiety of doubt."*[33] The final chapter is a sketch of this "God beyond God," being-itself that includes being and nonbeing, the same view that is fully elaborated in *Systematic Theology*. The parallel routes from ontology to theology arrive at the same point.

It is apparent even before Tillich begins the section on God in *Systematic Theology* that he is committed to the tradition of dialectical panentheism. His existential ontology is organized around the polarities generated by being and nonbeing in human life. Human being and nonbeing in turn participate in being-itself. Being and nonbeing in being-itself are exactly what Böhme and Schelling mean by the Ground and Abyss in the Divine—the

31. Tillich, *Systematic Theology*, 1:198. Newport, "Being and the Question of God," chap. 7 in *Tillich*.

32. Tillich, *The Courage to Be*, 141. We will see in a later chapter that although Heidegger strictly separated philosophy from theology, he was probably a panentheist of some sort. He does not deserve Tillich's charge of radical humanism.

33. Ibid., 158, 180.

positive, negative, and unitive potencies in God, manifest in the world.[34] Tillich makes explicit his connection with this tradition at a number of points in his ontology. Early in *The Courage to Be* he mentions Plotinus, Pseudo-Dionysius, Böhme, Hegel, Schelling, Heidegger, Whitehead, and others in connection with the relation of being, nonbeing, and God. He notes that Böhme "made the classical statement that all things are rooted in a Yes and a No."[35] In *Systematic Theology* he highlights "Böhme's *Ungrund*, Schelling's 'first potency,' Hegel's 'antithesis,' the 'contingent' and 'the given' in God in recent theism, [and] Berdyaev's 'meontic freedom'" as concepts that "relate nonbeing dialectically to being-itself and consequently to God."[36] Tillich's theological orientation is clear before he begins his doctrine of God.[37]

Tillich's Doctrine of God and the World

The Concept of God in Religion and Philosophy

Like Schleiermacher, Hegel, and Schelling, Tillich approaches the doctrine of God through the history of religions. "'God' is the answer to the question implied in man's finitude; he is the name for that which concerns man ultimately." But human beliefs about the ultimate are never adequate. They are caught in the "inescapable inner tension in the idea of God" between absolute transcendence and the belief that humans really do interact with God.[38] The history of religions has worked through this tension dialectically and has culminated in Christian trinitarianism.[39] Tillich summarizes: "The concreteness of man's ultimate concern drives him toward polytheistic structures; the reaction of the absolute element against these drives him toward monotheistic structures; . . . and the need for a balance between the concrete and the absolute drives him toward trinitarian structures."[40] Thus

34. According to Nuovo, "Tillich develops Schelling's doctrines of God, the world, and man in the light of his doctrine of the potencies." This doctrine is "the underlying structure of Tillich's thought" (introduction to Tillich, *Construction of the History of Religion*, 15).

35. Tillich, *Courage to Be*, 31.

36. Tillich, *Systematic Theology*, 1:189. The reference to recent theism is probably to process theology, which Tillich discusses on pp. 180–81 and elsewhere. Berdyaev is presented in our next chapter.

37. Thatcher, *Ontology*, is a masterful exposition in terms of the whole philosophical tradition since Plato and Neoplatonism. Also Newport, "Historical Influences on Tillich's Basic Idea and Basic Method," chap. 4 in *Tillich*; Thomas, "God, Being and Existence," chap. 4 in *Tillich*.

38. Tillich, *Systematic Theology*, 1:211.

39. Ibid., 1:215–35; also Tillich, *Construction of the History of Religion*.

40. Tillich, *Systematic Theology*, 1:221.

trinitarian monotheism "is an attempt to speak of the living God, the God in whom the ultimate and the concrete are united."[41]

In philosophy, "the tension in the idea of God is transformed into the fundamental philosophical question how being-itself, if taken in its absolute sense, can account for the relativities of reality." But because philosophy follows and reflects the history of religion, it likewise culminates in dialectical triunity. "In its philosophical transformation trinitarian monotheism appears . . . as dialectical realism," which "tries to unite the structural oneness of everything within the absolute with the undecided and unfinished manifoldness of the real."[42] Tillich regards Hegel as the prime example of "dialectical realism." This reading of the history of religion reinforces Tillich's philosophical commitment to dynamic panentheism as he approaches the doctrine of God.

Tillich's Doctrine of God

"The God beyond God" in *The Courage to Be* is a popular version of the same doctrine of God elaborated in *Systematic Theology*.[43] Courage discloses God: "Courage has revealing power, the courage to be is the key to being-itself." Several points are noteworthy in Tillich's brief account of what courage unveils about being-itself. First, courage manifests the dialectical relation of being and nonbeing: "Being embraces itself and that which is opposed to it, non-being. Non-being belongs to being, it cannot be separated from it." Second, the dialectic of being and nonbeing implies the power of being. "If we speak of the power of being-itself we indicate that being affirms itself against non-being." Third, the dialectic of being and nonbeing not only constitutes God's own existence but also powers him beyond himself in the world: "Non-being drives being out of its seclusion, it forces it to affirm itself dynamically." Because of nonbeing in God, there is revelation, world, and life. Fourth, the divine life includes the world and its suffering. "If we say that non-being belongs to being-itself, we say that finitude and anxiety belong to being-itself. . . . The infinite embraces itself and the finite, the Yes includes itself and the No which it takes into itself."

By asserting that "the infinite embraces itself and the finite," Tillich implicitly affirms panentheism. He clearly echoes Schelling and Böhme when he writes, "Non-being makes God a living God. Without the No he has to overcome in himself and in his creature, the divine Yes to himself would be

41. Ibid., 1:228–29.
42. Ibid., 1:231, 234–35.
43. The quotes in this and the next paragraph are from Tillich, *Courage to Be*, 169–72.

lifeless." Tillich also notes that Neoplatonism, Hegel, process philosophers, and trinitarian theology share this emphasis on the dialectical dynamic of being.

Being-itself, in which human being and nonbeing participate, is Tillich's "God beyond God."[44] Confidence in this God he calls "absolute faith." Absolute faith is expressed in mysticism, personal theism, and even in the courage of atheists. The God that Tillich wants to "move beyond" is the God of personal theism. He is willing to accept "theism" as a generic affirmation of God in religious symbolism and popular piety. But Tillich charges that when theologians confuse this symbol with ultimate reality by positing a personal being outside the world—an omnipotent Governor and omniscient Judge—they make God into "an object," "an invincible tyrant," "a being, not being-itself."[45] This theology is not just an intellectual mistake; it is also idolatry. Tillich affirms Nietzsche's atheism as a legitimate revolt against it. Even this atheism expresses the courage to be.

Tillich's doctrine of God in *Systematic Theology*, "The Actuality of God," has four sections: "God as Being," "God as Living," "God as Creating," and "God as Related." Each is implicitly panentheistic.

The first section, "God as Being," presents several closely associated philosophical definitions of God. Tillich asserts first that "the being of God is being-itself," or "being as being." God is also "the ground of being" and "the power of being." It follows that God is not a being, not even the Highest Being, for this would make him a finite being like a creature, with a gap between his real and ideal being. "As being-itself, God is beyond the contrast of essential and existential being."[46] In sum, God is being-itself, the Ground and power of being.

These definitions in turn imply concepts of transcendence and immanence. "As the power of being, God transcends every being and also the totality of beings—the world.... Being-itself infinitely transcends every finite being." At the same time, all things are immanent in God: "Everything finite participates in being-itself and in its infinity. Otherwise it would not have the power of being."[47] The immanence of the finite in infinite being-itself implies panentheism.

Immanence and transcendence, defined in this way, further imply a duality in the divine nature. "This double relation of all beings to being-itself gives being-itself a double characteristic."[48] Where process theologians speak of

44. Ibid., 172–80.
45. Ibid., 175.
46. Tillich, *Systematic Theology*, 1:235–36.
47. Ibid., 1:237.
48. Ibid.

dipolarity in God, Tillich refers to the creative and abysmal Ground, the positive and negative potencies identified by Böhme and Schelling.[49] The creative aspect means "that everything participates in the power of being." But in the abyss, "all beings are infinitely transcended by their creative ground."[50] In addition, Tillich agrees with process theology that genuine freedom is necessary for a sufficient ontological distinction between God and world: "Infinite divinity and finite human freedom make the world transcendent to God and God transcendent to the world."[51] Note again that creaturely freedom is what distinguishes panentheism from pantheism.

Tillich follows the correlation of philosophy and religion as he transitions from the concept of "God as being" to the symbol, God as living. He draws a dialectical conclusion for theology: "If we call God 'the living God,' we deny that he is a pure identity of being with being. . . . We assert that he is the eternal process in which separation is posited and is overcome by reunion."[52] In other words, the living God is eternally dialectical.

"God as living" is Tillich's most basic and comprehensive theological category. It focuses on God as Spirit and culminates in the Trinity.[53] His dialectical analysis of God as living applies the pairs of polar elements from his existential ontology (individualization and participation, dynamics and form, freedom and destiny). He argues that religion tends to separate these elements as it symbolizes aspects of our relationship with God. The correction is philosophical: "Within the divine life, every ontological element includes its polar element completely, without tension and without the threat of dissolution, for God is being-itself." Here Tillich affirms Nicholas of Cusa's view that in God is the coincidence of opposites, a theme deepened by Böhme, Hegel, and Schelling.[54]

Tillich argues that the idea of a "personal God" improperly separates the ontological polarity of individualization and participation. He recognizes that "person" is a legitimate religious symbol because "man cannot be ultimately concerned about anything that is less than personal." But he objects that "ordinary theism has made God a heavenly, completely perfect person who resides above the world and mankind. The protest of atheism against

49. Thatcher, *Ontology*, 52–58; Thomas, *Tillich*, 70–72.

50. Tillich, *Systematic Theology*, 1:237.

51. Ibid., 1:263.

52. Ibid., 1:242.

53. Recall that "Living God" is also the primary epithet for Herder, Schleiermacher, and Schelling. It is a biblical expression but is most prominent in the tradition of Plato's World-Soul.

54. Tillich, *Systematic Theology*, 1:241–44. "This transcendence [of the infinite over the finite] does not contradict but rather confirms the coincidence of the opposites" (263).

such a highest person is correct." Existential ontology again provides correction. God is "the principle of participation as well as the principle of individualization. The divine life participates in every life as its ground and aim."[55] Ultimately God is not a person or three persons but the Life that empowers human persons.

Tillich regards the second ontological polarity, dynamics and form, as "central for any present-day doctrine of God." He reasons that if "God is being-itself, this includes both rest and becoming, both the static and the dynamic elements." Classical theism is therefore inadequate: "The God who is *actus purus* is not the living God." Instead Tillich commends Böhme, Schelling, Berdyaev, Hartshorne, and others who have affirmed both dynamics and form in God.[56]

The polarity of freedom and destiny likewise applies to God symbolically. Divine freedom "means that that which is man's ultimate concern is in no way dependent on man or on any finite being or on any finite concern." Tillich does not consider divine freedom to involve choice between alternative possibilities. Ultimately freedom and destiny are one in God. "If we say that God is his own destiny, we point both to the infinite mystery of being and to the participation of God in becoming and in history."[57] Here Tillich reaffirms Schelling's correlation of divine and human freedom in history and destiny.

"The living God" culminates in "God as spirit *and* the trinitarian principles." Like Hegel and Schelling, Tillich asserts that the living God is Spirit because Life becomes Spirit. "Actualized as life, being-itself is fulfilled as *spirit*." "Spirit" is the most important theological category for Tillich, "the most embracing, direct, and unrestricted symbol for the divine life."[58] Because it contains all the ontological polarities of human life, Spirit has its clearest analogue in the spiritual-mental-physical existence of humans: "Life as spirit is the life of the soul, which includes mind and body, but not as realities alongside the soul. . . . It is the all-embracing function in which all elements of the structure of being participate."[59] As the macroanalogy of the human microcosm, Tillich's Spirit is a descendent of Plato's World-Soul through Schelling's divine-human personalism.

55. Ibid., 1:244–45.
56. Ibid., 1:245–47.
57. Ibid., 1:248–49.
58. Ibid., 1:249.
59. Ibid., 1:250, 277: "Certainly one cannot say that God is body. But if it is said that he is Spirit, the ontological elements of vitality and personality are included and, with them, the participation of bodily existence in the divine life."

The Trinity

Living Spirit is dialectical triunity: "God's life is life as spirit, and the trinitarian principles are moments within the process of the divine life." Tillich's debt to the gnostic triunity of Böhme, Schelling, and Hegel is explicit.[60] "The first principle is the basis of Godhead, that which makes God God." This is the creative ground, which is also "the abyss" (*Ungrund*) in which are *will* and infinite *power of being*: "the power of being infinitely resisting nonbeing, giving the power of being to everything that is." There is also a second principle, the *logos*, or reason, that particularizes, orders, and defines the first principle: "The *logos* opens the divine ground, its infinity and its darkness, and it makes its fulness distinguishable, definite, finite." These principles need each other. "Without the second principle the first principle would be chaos, burning fire, but it would not be the creative Ground. Without the second principle God is demonic." And the second without the first would be abstract, static, and sterile. Further, the second principle moves God beyond himself into the world. "In the *logos* God speaks his 'word,' both in himself and beyond himself."[61] Note Tillich's debt to Böhme's language.

The third principle, the Spirit, is "the actualization of the other two principles." It unifies God in himself: "Through the Spirit the divine fulness is posited in the divine life as something definite, and at the same time it is reunited in the divine ground." The Spirit also includes creatures in God: "The finite is posited as finite within the process of the divine life, but it is reunited with the infinite within the same process." Because it unifies the other two principles, *Spirit* refers both to God and to the Holy Spirit. "The third principle is in a way the whole (God *is* Spirit), and in a way it is a special principle (God has the Spirit as he has the *logos*)." Tillich's approach to the Trinity as the dialectical unity of potencies in the divine Life is a straightforward continuation of the legacy of Böhme, Hegel, and Schelling in German theology.[62]

Creation, Fall, and Evil

Tillich's implicit panentheism is evident in his view of God's creative relation to the world. The constitutive ontological categories of created being, such as time and space, are part of God. "If the finite is posited within

---

60. Thatcher, *Ontology*, 52–62, is a detailed demonstration.

61. Tillich, *Systematic Theology*, 1:250–51.

62. Ibid., 1:249–52. Tillich maintains this approach when he completes the doctrine of the trinity in relation to the doctrine of Christ in vol. 2. Thatcher, *Ontology*, 91, judges that "Tillich has fallen into the *error of confusing the triadic structure of dialectical thinking with triadic structure of Trinitarian thinking.*"

the process of the divine life, the forms of finitude (the categories) are also present in it." Thus "the divine life includes temporality, but is not subject to it." For the same reason, "God's omnipresence is his creative participation in the spatial existence of his creatures."[63]

God's creating is not a sovereign choice but an aspect of the divine nature. "The divine life and the divine creativity are not different. God is creative because he is God." The combination of being and nonbeing in God is what makes him creative.[64] Tillich's explanation of creation *ex nihilo* spells this out. Tillich notes the Greek distinction between *ouk on*, the complete absence of being, and *me on*, the nonbeing full of potential for being. He points out that classical Christianity rejects meontic nonbeing because it would be an ultimate principle outside God from which he creates. Tillich does not reject meontic nonbeing but places it in God. "If God is called the living God, if he is the ground of the creative processes of life, if history has significance for him, if there is no negative principle in addition to him which could account for evil and sin, how can one avoid positing a dialectical negativity in God himself?"[65] Creation *ex nihilo* means that God naturally creates the world from "the nothing" in himself.

Tillich follows Böhme and Schelling further in thinking of creation as an event in which free creatures rupture their oneness with God and thus "fall." In God there is unity deeper than the distinction between the ideal essence of things and their actual existence, which does not measure up to their ideal essence. "The creative process of the divine life precedes the differentiation between essences and existents." The exercise of human freedom breaks this unity, and thus humanity becomes distinct from its essence in God. "To be outside the divine life means to stand in actualized freedom, in an existence which is no longer united with essence." Because actual existence inevitably deviates from the ideal, human self-actualization is "the point at which creation and the fall coincide."[66] There is no chronological sequence. The same free human act both creates humans human and constitutes their fall. As we have seen, this doctrine predates Tillich by centuries.

This view of creation and fall also provides Tillich with a theodicy, a theological explanation of evil. The very nature of God makes evil a risk. "If God is creative in himself, . . . He must create . . . life, that which includes freedom

63. Tillich, *Systematic Theology*, 1:257, 277.

64. Ibid., 1:252–54.

65. Ibid., 1:188–89. See Thatcher, *Ontology*, chap. 3, "Non-Being."

66. Tillich, *Systematic Theology*, 1:254–56; "The Transition from Essence to Existence and the Symbol of 'the Fall,'" 2:29–42; Thatcher, "The Transition from Essence to Existence," chap. 6 in *Ontology*; Thomas, "Existence and Estrangement," chap. 5 in *Tillich*.

and with it the dangers of freedom."[67] God makes evil possible; we humans inevitably make it actual. "The goodness of man's created nature is that he is given the possibility and necessity of actualizing himself and of becoming independent by his self-actualization, in spite of the estrangement unavoidably connected with it."[68] God does not cause evil, but the reality of God makes the existence of evil inevitable, as it does the ultimate divine-human triumph over evil. Tillich's theodicy is virtually identical to Schelling's.

Providence, Salvation, and Eschatology

Schelling likewise shapes Tillich's understanding of salvation, which is the reconciliation and reunion of humanity and God through mutual participation in history. The purpose of creation is to actualize all creaturely potential, including good and evil, so that evil is transcended and the goodness of creation is fulfilled in God when existing humanity finally coincides with its own essence. Tillich summarizes the whole process at the end of the third volume of *Systematic Theology*: "Creation into time produces the possibility of self-realization, estrangement, and reconciliation of the creature, which, in eschatological terminology, is the way from essence through existence to essentialization."[69] Human freedom is the way God moves creation toward its goal. "God's directing creativity always creates through the freedom of man and through the spontaneity and structural wholeness of all creatures." Because God works entirely through creatures, there are no supernatural miracles. Tillich denies "special divine activity [that] will alter the conditions of finitude and estrangement."[70] Further, because God works through the world, the fulfillment of the world also fulfills God. "The world process means something for God.... The eternal act of creation is driven by a love which finds fulfilment only through the other who has the freedom to accept or reject. God, so to speak, drives toward the actualization and essentialization of everything that has being." Divine-cosmic fulfillment is not arrival at a temporal point of completion but an ever greater approximation of existence to essence through participation in God's eternity: "The eternal dimension of what happens in the universe is the Divine Life itself."[71]

67. Tillich, *Systematic Theology*, 1:269.
68. Ibid., 1:259.
69. Ibid., 3:422. Newport, "History and the Quest for the Kingdom of God," chap. 10 in *Tillich*; Thomas, "History and the Kingdom of God," chap. 9 in *Tillich*. Essentialization is explained below.
70. Tillich, *Systematic Theology*, 1:266–67.
71. Ibid., 3:422.

Salvation, philosophically stated, is "the way from essence through existence to essentialization." Essentialization is complete conformity of actual existence to essence. It occurs through authentic participation in the power of being, which progressively closes the gap between one's essence in God and one's existential estrangement from it.

The religious language of the Christian gospel and core Christian doctrines is made intelligible by the philosophical understanding of being and the New Being. Religiously stated, the gospel is the good news that humans are not on their own to overcome nonbeing. God, the power of being-itself, ensures that nonbeing will not prevail. Therefore humans need not despair. They can affirm life with absolute faith, hope, and courage in spite of the suffering and meaninglessness of life. Tillich calls this positive way of living New Being. It is a new mode of human existence that overcomes "the Fall." Jesus is the Christ, the human being in whom the divine power of New Being is fully manifest. In Christ, God is fully present. And thereby Christ both realizes divine New Being in himself and mediates it to others. The gospel is the good news of New Being in Jesus Christ. The Holy Spirit is the power that awakens (regenerates) and sustains "absolute faith," the courage of New Being. Sanctification is progress toward New Being. And so forth.[72] Tillich regards himself as a Christian, but he holds that New Being is possible for humans whether or not Jesus actually lived and whether or not humans know of him.[73] For Tillich, Jesus is not the sole means of salvation but the greatest symbol of it.

Tillich's Panentheism

Its Unique Character

If panentheism means that God includes all things in himself ontologically while also transcending them, there is no question that Tillich qualifies. He states the position plainly: "God as being-itself transcends nonbeing absolutely. On the other hand, God as creative life includes the finite and, with it, nonbeing, although nonbeing is eternally conquered and the finite is

---

72. Ibid., "The Reality of the Christ," part 2 of vol. 2, states all these interpretations of doctrine, especially the sections titled "The Expressions of the New Being in Jesus as the Christ," 2:121–25, and "The New Being in Jesus as the Christ as the Power of Salvation," 2:165–80. Thatcher, "New Being," chap. 7 in *Ontology*; Newport, "Existence and the Quest for the New Being," chap. 8 in *Tillich*; Thomas, "The New Being: Incarnation and Resurrection," chap. 6 in *Tillich*. "New Being" is a positive theological version of Heidegger's notion of "authentic existence."

73. See Newport, "Non-Judeo-Christian Religions," chap. 11 in *Tillich*.

eternally reunited within the infinity of the divine life."[74] Grenz and Olson concur: "That this is a form of panentheism is beyond dispute."[75] Even Hartshorne embraces him: "I therefore (joyfully) acclaim him as one of the rapidly growing company of 'dipolar' theists or 'panentheists' to which some of us are proud to belong."[76]

Tillich's panentheism is an inheritance from the ancient theological family he proudly embraces. From Plato's World-Soul through Plotinus's dialectically emanating One, Nicholas of Cusa's "coincidence of opposites," Böhme's "eternal unity of the Yes and No," Hegel's dialectical trinitarianism, and Schelling's divine-human self-actualization in history, the theological ancestry of Tillich's theology is the most vital branch of the panentheist tradition. His appeals to Heidegger, Berdyaev, and the process theologians confirm the connection.

Following Schelling, Tillich's panentheism is clearly modern in emphasizing the mutual participation of God and creatures. God himself is actualized and enriched in nature but culminates in the progressive exercise of human freedom in history. Tillich updates Schelling's ideas by his use of Heidegger's ontology of human existence. Instead of Schelling's dialectic of nature and history, Tillich speaks of *existential* participation in God. This term includes the whole ontology of humanness—the natural and historical dimensions as well as the subjective dynamics of faith, courage, hope, and understanding. This existential panentheism is Tillich's unique contribution.[77] Existential panentheism is real when humans live in God authentically. Only on this existential basis can religion symbolize the truth and can theology conceptualize it.

Its Philosophical Flaw

But there is a flaw, a tension in Tillich's doctrine of God that cannot be explained by the gap he posits between existence and thought, religion and philosophy, or symbols and concepts. When Tillich repeatedly asserts propositions such as "God as being-itself transcends nonbeing absolutely, but God as creative life includes the finite and nonbeing," he is asserting a contradiction, not a theological mix of concepts and symbols. If it is true *ontologically* that being-itself is absolutely beyond being and nonbeing, then

74. Tillich, *Systematic Theology*, 1:270.
75. Grenz and Olson, *Twentieth-Century Theology*, 126, also 130.
76. Charles Hartshorne, "Tillich's Doctrine of God," in *The Theology of Paul Tillich*, ed. Kegley and Bretall, 166.
77. Tillich, "Existentialism and Christian Theology," in *Systematic Theology*, 2:27–29.

it cannot be true *existentially* and *theologically* that being-itself includes being and nonbeing, because Tillich's ontology is existential. He cannot have it both ways: either transcendence is absolute or it is not. He seems to fall back toward the position of young Schelling, who asserted both the utter oneness and transcendence of the Absolute and also the participation of creatures in God. Hegel ridiculed this incoherence, and Schelling later abandoned it. Tillich seems to stand by it:[78] "The God above God and the God to whom we can pray are the same God."[79]

The problem of reconciling the "God beyond God" with the God of existential participation has not gone unnoticed by Tillich's peers. Although Hartshorne welcomes him into the circle of panentheists, he complains that his view of God "is not without difficulties. . . . In Tillich's case there is either somewhat less coherence or I have not been able to find the key."[80] In a masterful analysis, Adrian Thatcher demonstrates that Tillich's "fundamental ambiguity . . . seems to have been inherent in the tradition in which he stands, going right back as far as Plato."[81] The tension is between Plotinus's One, relocated in the Abyss by Böhme,[82] and the World-Soul, the God involved in the world. Thatcher judges that Schelling's way of combining the Absolute One and the World-Soul "becomes incompatible. Tillich deliberately places himself in the Schellingian tradition and is open to the same accusation."[83]

This incoherence in Tillich's view is relieved if the term "absolute" is transferred from God's unity and transcendence to God as such. In that case being-itself would be absolute, but it would also contain, unify, and transcend the difference between being and nonbeing. Like the God of Böhme, and later Schelling, Hegel, and Hartshorne, Tillich's God would be both absolute and dipolar. But it cannot also be the Absolute One of Neoplatonism or young Schelling.

Most of those who appropriate Tillich's theology overlook its inner tension and simply work from his panentheistic synthesis: the God beyond God is the

78. Thompson, *Being and Meaning*, 39–42, argues that Tillich attempted to modify Schelling's principle of identity. Tillich discusses the tension in Schelling's combination of ideas in *Perspectives on 19th and 20th Century Protestant Theology*, 142–45, without recognizing a contradiction.

79. Paul Tillich, "The God above God" (1961), in Tillich, *Theological Writings/Theologische Schriften*, ed. Gert Hummel (New York: de Gruyter, 1992), 417–21.

80. Hartshorne, "Tillich's Doctrine of God," 166.

81. Thatcher, *Ontology*, 83–88, quote at 87.

82. John Herman Randall, "The Ontology of Paul Tillich," in *The Theology of Paul Tillich*, ed. Kegley and Bretall, 143: "For the Platonic tradition [the One] stands one step 'above' intellect and *Noûs*; following Böhme and Schelling, Tillich locates it one step 'below,' in the 'depths.'"

83. Thatcher, *Ontology*, 88. He credits Arthur O. Lovejoy, *The Great Chain of Being: The History of an Idea* (Cambridge, MA: Harvard University Press, 1936; repr., 1964), for spelling out the tension in the theology of this tradition.

one in whom we participate existentially. Feminist theologians, for example, base foundational arguments that God is both "masculine" and "feminine" on his affirmation that God is both transcendent and immanent.[84] The significant influence of Tillich on feminist theologians and others as diverse as John Robinson and James Cone is noted in subsequent chapters.

84. Mary Ann Stenger, "The Limits and Possibilities of Tillich's Ontology for Cross-Cultural and Feminist Theology," in *God and Being*, ed. Gert Hummel, 250–68, esp. 263–64.

9

Diversity in Twentieth-Century Philosophy, Theology, and Religion

Teilhard, Whitehead, and Tillich are the most famous panentheists of the mid-twentieth century but surely not the only ones. The proliferation that began with Schelling and Hegel in the nineteenth century continued apace in the twentieth century as panentheism offered an alternative worldview to traditional theism, idealism, naturalism, and humanism. As a general way of understanding the divine and the world, it is not limited to the tradition of Christian Neoplatonism but is found in non-Christian and non-Western religious thinkers as well.

This chapter is an illustration of this diversity, not a catalog. It highlights a few well-known philosophers and theologians from the Protestant, Roman Catholic, and Orthodox traditions of Christianity together with prominent thinkers from non-Christian religions who are implicit panentheists. The philosophers from the Christian tradition are Martin Heidegger, Hans-Georg Gadamer, and Nicolai Berdyaev. The theologians are William Temple, John Robinson, John Macquarrie, Karl Rahner, and Hans Küng. From the non-Christian religions, Martin Buber represents Judaism; Muhammed Iqbal, Islam; Sarvepalli Radhakrishnan, Hinduism; Alan Watts and Masao Abe, Zen Buddhism; and Miriam Starhawk, Wiccan neopaganism.

The greatest significance of this diversity is that panentheism has become the common framework amid the pluralism of world religions. In mainline intellectual circles, panentheism has gained the position held by Deism in the Enlightenment. It is widely regarded as the universal "natural religion" or "rational theology" implicit in the various positive religions. Like English in international affairs, panentheism has become the common language in the mainstream dialogue of world religions.

Philosophers in the Christian Tradition

Martin Heidegger

Martin Heidegger (1889–1976), the most famous German philosopher of the century, wrote too little about God to be classified conclusively. But his occasional theological statements strongly suggest panentheism, and his philosophy is highly conducive to it. Prominent panentheists such as Tillich, Rahner, and Macquarrie express deep indebtedness.

Heidegger is sometimes thought to be an existentialist preoccupied with the vicissitudes of human life. But his perennial philosophical interest is Being, *Sein*. His famous early work, *Being and Time* (1927), does focus on human existence, but only because that is the "place" where Being is encountered and questioned.[1]

Heidegger's term for the ontological structure of human existence, *Dasein*, is, literally, "being there," that is, "being-in-the-world." To be human is to find oneself situated in the world with a particular history, personality, and view of the world. Human life is "ek-sistence," "standing out" toward the future from one's present situation. Ironically, life is essentially "being-toward-death" because existence culminates in nonexistence. The threat of nonbeing elicits existential anxiety, a state of mind in which this truth about human nature is disclosed. In response, one can live "authentically" or "inauthentically," courageously realizing one's unique potential or avoiding the challenge. Heidegger's basic point is that, whatever its level of authenticity, human existence is essentially temporal—unavoidably engaged in the present, toward the future, shaped by the past. *Being and Time* therefore concludes that temporality is the basic ontological infrastructure and meaning of *Dasein*.

Because Being is encountered by time-bound humans, Heidegger denies that absolute, unchanging knowledge of it is possible. Because it is revealed

---

1. Martin Heidegger, *Sein und Zeit* (Tübingen: Max Niemeyer, 1953). There are two English translations: *Being and Time*, trans. John Macquarrie and Edward Robinson (New York: Harper and Row, 1962); and *Being and Time*, trans. Joan Stambaugh (Albany: State University Press of New York, 1996). Tillich bases his existential ontology on Heidegger's *Being and Time*.

in the being of humans, he wonders whether Being itself is temporal: "Does *time* itself reveal itself as the horizon of *being*?" In a famous footnote he explicitly affirms the temporality of God. "If the eternity of *God* could be philosophically 'constructed,' it could be understood only as more primordial and 'infinite' temporality."[2] On this issue he sides with modern panentheism against classical theism.

Being and Time has stimulated significant theological reflection, much of it panentheistic. For example, Schubert Ogden, a process theologian, uses Heidegger's anthropology and his theological footnote to propose that God is the maximal *Dasein*—being-in-the-world—and therefore that God is essentially temporal, although without the temporal limitations of human *Dasein*. Ogden recommends the theology of Whitehead and Hartshorne to flesh out the implications of Heidegger's comment about God.[3]

After *Being and Time* Heidegger ponders Being more directly. His "Letter on Humanism" (1947) emphasizes that Being is not a mere human abstraction but a reality that reveals itself in and to humans, making them responsible for its truth.[4] Ironically, the pervasive immanence of Being makes it most difficult to grasp and understand: "Being is the nearest. Yet the near remains farthest from man." Heidegger rejects the traditional identification of Being with God: "'Being'... is not God and not a cosmic ground."[5] Yet God can be encountered in the experience of Being as the numinous or holy: "The holy, which alone is the essential sphere of divinity, which in turn alone affords a dimension for the gods and for God, comes to radiate only when Being itself beforehand and after extensive preparation has been illuminated and is experienced in its truth."[6] Here Heidegger clearly affirms "the holy" as the

---

2. Heidegger, *Being and Time*, 437, 427 n. 13. I quote Stambaugh but use the original pagination, found in both translations.

3. Schubert Ogden, "The Temporality of God," chap. 5 in *The Reality of God* (San Francisco: Harper and Row, 1966). This essay includes a clear summary of *Being and Time*.

Charles Hartshorne, *A Natural Theology for Our Time* (La Salle, IL: Open Court, 1967), 135, agrees with Ogden: "Heidegger's hint that not mere eternity but infinite temporality may be the key to the idea of God I take, with Ogden, to point toward panentheism." Also Eugene Long, "God and Temporality: A Heideggerian View," in *God and Temporality*, ed. B. Clark and E. Long (New York: Paragon House, 1984), 121–31, quote from 129. God's temporality "in some sense transcends and presumably includes within itself the temporality of finite persons." God's inclusion of humanity entails panentheism.

4. Martin Heidegger, "Letter on Humanism," in *Basic Writings*, ed. David Krell (New York: Harper and Row, 1977), 210: "Man is rather 'thrown' from Being itself into the truth of Being, so that ek-sisting in this fashion he might guard the truth of Being."

5. Ibid. Heidegger is in line with Plotinus, not Augustine and Aquinas. He rejects the traditional concept of Being as God and cosmic Ground but is open to a dynamic notion of Being. Nevertheless, both Tillich and Macquarrie apply Heidegger's view of Being to God.

6. Ibid., 218. Heidegger is indebted to Rudolf Otto's *Idea of the Holy* (1917), which grounds religion in the experience of the numinous, the holy or sacred.

sphere of religion and the possibility of encountering God. But he says little more because he believes that the task of philosophy is to ponder Being, not to judge the claims of religion or the reality of God.[7]

In spite of his theological reticence, evidence suggests that Heidegger affirmed the reality of God. He studied for the priesthood as a young man, regularly reflected on God and religion, affirmed openness to God in a significant interview late in life,[8] and requested a Catholic burial.[9] But there is insufficient evidence to reconstruct his theology beyond some basic themes.

In any case, Heidegger's mature thought has stimulated much theological analysis and discussion.[10] Taken together, his comments about God seem to imply a panentheism of some sort. He criticizes the "onto-theology" of classical theism and declares God to be "dead."[11] He states that God must be thought of as infinitely temporal. Heidegger distinguishes God and creatures, emphasizing the "facticity" of worldly beings, which are ontologically different from both Being and "the Divine." He asserts that the God of religion actively and dynamically reveals himself in "the gift" of being and time.[12] John Williams summarizes a key feature of Heidegger's theology: "God's supremacy must have some limitations. If there is to be any genuine interaction between God and man, then God must in some sense be relative to man, rather than absolute in all respects."[13] Like Ogden, Williams finds that Heidegger's views are in harmony with the "panentheistic American

7. John Caputo, *The Mystical Element in Heidegger's Thought* (New York: Fordham University Press, 1986); Robert Gall, *Beyond Theism and Atheism: Heidegger's Significance for Religious Thinking* (Boston: Martinus Nijhoff, 1987); Jeff Owen Prudhomme, *God and Being: Heidegger's Relation to Theology* (Atlantic Highlands, NJ: Humanities, 1997); Laurence Hemming, *Heidegger's Atheism: The Refusal of a Theological Voice* (Notre Dame, IN: Notre Dame University Press, 2002).

8. "Only a God Can Save Us," an interview with Heidegger in 1966, published in *Der Spiegel*, May 31, 1976, 193–219, after his death. John Macquarrie, *Heidegger and Christianity* (New York: Continuum, 1994), 104–5.

9. See John Macquarrie, "Being and Giving: Heidegger and the Concept of God," in *God: The Contemporary Discussion*, ed. F. Sontag and H. D. Bryant (New York: Rose of Sharon, 1982), 154; and John Caputo, "Heidegger and Theology," in *The Cambridge Companion to Heidegger*, ed. Charles Guignon (New York: Cambridge University Press, 1993). Hans-Georg Gadamer gave a memorial lecture, "An Invocation to the Vanished God," after Heidegger's death.

10. James Robinson and John B. Cobb, eds., *The Later Heidegger and Theology* (New York: Harper and Row, 1963); Prudhomme, "The Theological Reception of Heidegger's Thought," in *God and Being*, 30–37.

11. Martin Heidegger, "The Last God," in *Contributions to Philosophy*, trans. P. Emad and K. Maly (Bloomington: Indiana University Press, 1999), 288–93; Otto Pöggeler, "The Departure of the Last God," part 4, chap. 3 in *The Paths of Heidegger's Life and Thought*, trans. J. Bailiff (Amherst, NY: Humanity, 1997).

12. Macquarrie, "Being and Giving"; John Caputo, "Heidegger's Gods," chap. 9 in *Demythologizing Heidegger* (Bloomington: Indiana University Press, 1993).

13. John Williams, *Martin Heidegger's Philosophy of Religion* ([Toronto?]: Canadian Corporation for Studies in Religion, 1977), 148.

theology" of James, Whitehead, and Hartshorne. John Macquarrie likewise concludes that Heidegger's idea of God is panentheistic.[14]

Circumstantial evidence of Heidegger's panentheism is his significant debt to Schelling and indirectly to Böhme.[15] Much of his basic terminology comes directly from Schelling: for example, Being and human being (*Sein und Dasein*), nothingness (*das Nichtige*), the groundless (*Ungrund*), as well as the "thrownness" (*Geworfenheit*), fallenness (*Verfallenheit*), authenticity (*Eigentlichkeit*), historicity (*Geschichtlichkeit*), and destiny (*Geschick*) of human existence. This legacy is so strong that Heidegger's philosophy can be read as a twentieth-century adaptation of Schelling's personal-historical panentheism without Schelling's explicitly religious language.

Following Böhme and Schelling, Heidegger stands in the Neoplatonic tradition.[16] He insists that God transcends Being. With Eriugena he asserts that the human world is God's essential self-revelation. His notion of *Gelassenheit*—openness to Being—comes directly from his study of Meister Eckhart.[17] In historical perspective, he is a contemporary Neoplatonist with a dynamic anthropocentric view of time and being similar to Bergson's.[18] All things considered, he is implicitly a dynamic panentheist.

Hans-Georg Gadamer

Hans-Georg Gadamer (1900–2003), a nonpracticing Lutheran, gave a memorial address for Heidegger titled "An Invocation to the Vanished God."[19] It indicates Gadamer's interest in philosophical theology. In the tradition of Hegel and Heidegger, Gadamer's hermeneutics is based on the principle that the ontological structure of reality is linguistic: "Being that can be understood is language."[20] The linguistic nature of human existence

14. Macquarrie, *Heidegger and Christianity*, 99–100.

15. Martin Heidegger, *Schelling's Treatise on the Essence of Human Freedom*, trans. Joan Stambaugh (Athens, OH: Ohio University Press, 1985). Caputo, *The Mystical Element in Heidegger's Thought*, 98.

16. Macquarrie, *Heidegger and Christianity*, 98–99; John Macquarrie, *In Search of Deity: An Essay in Dialectical Theism*, Gifford Lectures, 1983 (New York: Crossroad, 1985), 153–55.

17. George Pattison, "Mysticism," in *The Routledge Philosophy Guide Book to the Later Heidegger* (New York: Routledge, 2000), 201.

18. William Blattner, "Heidegger and the Plotinian Tradition," in *Heidegger's Temporal Idealism* (Cambridge: Cambridge University Press, 1999), 261–71.

19. Gadamer emphasizes Heidegger's implicit spirituality and theology; see also Hans-Georg Gadamer, *Heidegger's Ways*, trans. John Stanley (Albany: State University of New York Press, 1994), esp. "Being Spirit God," chap. 15.

20. Hans-Georg Gadamer, *Truth and Method*, trans. J. Weinsheimer and D. Marshall, 2nd rev. ed. (New York: Crossroad, 1989), 427. See Patricia A. Johnson, "Gadamer: Incarnation, Finitude, and the Experience of Divine Infinitude," *Faith and Philosophy* 10/4 (1993): 539–52.

is not merely finite. It is constituted by participation in what the Christian tradition symbolizes as the divine Word that creates the world and is incarnate in Jesus Christ.[21] The world is a natural expression of divine Being, which is essentially Word, because it is the nature of the eternal Word to express itself. A word is not an unexpressed thought. A word "has its being in its revealing. Exactly the same is true in the mystery of the Trinity."[22] It is the essence of the divine Word to reveal the depths of God within the Trinity and also in the world. It is apparent that Gadamer's hermeneutical ontology is grounded in the panentheistic tradition of Eriugena, Nicholas of Cusa, Böhme, and Schelling.

Gadamer's implicit panentheism is further evident in his view that the history of God's being involves the history of human verbalizing its being-in-the-world in relation to its Ground. The history of authentic speaking of the divine is the progressive self-revelation of the eternal Word. Thus the being of God is temporal and progressive as well as linguistic. Gadamer adapts Schelling's view that God actualizes and thereby manifests himself through religious language and symbols. Gadamer's Word-based philosophy has stimulated the theology of the "new hermeneutics," developed by Ernst Fuchs, Gerhard Ebeling, and John Dominic Crossan.[23]

Nicolai Berdyaev

Nicolai Berdyaev (1874–1948) was born to a noble family, studied philosophy, embraced Marxism, became a Russian Orthodox Christian, was expelled from the USSR in 1922, and finally settled in Paris. His philosophy, aimed against both Communism and Enlightenment individualism, is a Christian existentialism that emphasizes interpersonal communion and solidarity between humans and God.

Berdyaev was deeply influenced by Sergei Bulgakov (1870–1944), an economist turned Orthodox priest and theologian. Bulgakov, a trinitarian panentheist, is the immediate inspiration for many of Berdyaev's ideas about the inner community of the Trinity and its expression in the creation

21. Gadamer, *Truth and Method*, 420: "The greater miracle of language lies not in the fact that the Word becomes flesh and emerges in external being, but that that which emerges and externalizes itself in utterance is always already a word. . . . The Word is with God from eternity."

22. Ibid., 421. See Jens Zimmermann, "Gadamer's Philosophical Hermeneutics," chap. 5 in *Recovering Theological Hermeneutics* (Grand Rapids: Baker, 2004), 169–73, who points out that Gadamer's correlation of language and Trinity follows Nicholas of Cusa.

23. Anthony Thiselton, "The Later Heidegger, Gadamer, and the New Hermeneutics," part 12 in *The Two Horizons* (Grand Rapids: Eerdmans, 1980).

and redemption of the world.[24] In addition to Russian Orthodox theology, Berdyaev draws from the broad tradition of Christian Neoplatonism and German idealism. He makes significant appeals to Eckhart, Nicholas of Cusa, Hegel, Schelling, Bergson, and Buber, and he published studies of Böhme.[25] He sets out a panentheism in which the eternal Trinity, which includes divine humanity, expresses itself in the cosmos and humanity, climaxes in the incarnation of Christ, and culminates in humanity's eschatological deiformity in God.[26]

Berdyaev holds that God is both absolute and personal. As absolute, he is not static but is the eternal dynamic union of freedom and determination, of being and nonbeing (*Urgrund* and *Ungrund*).[27] As personal, God must be three persons because an I requires both a Thou and a He to be a community. In the perichoretic (mutually inherent) love of the Trinity, God is the identity in which all oppositions coincide.[28] The eternal Son, however, is not simply divine. He is "the divine, absolute, Man, the God-Man and that, not only on earth in our natural historic world, but also in heaven in the divine reality of the Trinity."[29] The Man in God is why humanity is the icon of God, why the incarnation of Christ as God-Man is not a metaphysical conundrum, and why the final deiformity of humanity compromises neither divine nor human nature.

Berdyaev believes that creation is "the realization of the Divine Trinity within the inner life of the Absolute, as a mystery of freedom and love." God expresses his love and fulfills his longing through human freedom. Berdyaev agrees with Böhme and Schelling that freedom is an eternal element of Deity beyond even God's control (*Ungrund*). "God the Creator has absolute power over being, but not over freedom. . . . This is why there is tragedy and evil in the world." The human exercise of freedom is both the actualization of creation and the "fall" from God that inevitably causes evil.

---

24. Michael Aksionov Meerson, "Sergius Bulgakov's Trinitarian Synthesis," in *The Trinity of Love in Modern Russian Theology* (Quincy, IL: Franciscan, 1998), 158–87. Bulgakov is the source of Berdyaev's idea that the Trinity must be a We of three: I, Thou, He.

25. See, e.g., Nicolai Berdyaev, "God, Man, and the God-Man," chap. 6 in *Freedom and the Spirit*, trans. O. F. Clarke (London: Centenary, 1935); "The Origin of Good and Evil," in *The Destiny of Man*, trans. Natalie Duddington (London: Geoffrey Bles, 1937), 29, refers to his work on Böhme. See also Michel Vallon, "The Divine Mystery: From No-thing to All Things," part 2, chap. 1 in *An Apostle of Freedom: Life and Teachings of Nicolas Berdyaev* (New York: Philosophical Library, 1960); and Meerson, "Berdiaev: Christian Mysticism Grounds the Doctrine of God's Humanity," chap. 5 in *Trinity of Love*.

26. In Orthodox theology, redeemed humans are ultimately made "deiform": their human nature is enhanced to conform as fully as possible to the divine nature without becoming divine.

27. Berdyaev, "The Origin of Good and Evil," 28–30; see Vallon, "The Divine Mystery," 149–53.

28. Meerson, "Berdiaev," 104–8. Florensky and Bulgakov had already developed this idea.

29. Berdyaev, "God, Man, and the God-Man," 198.

Since the world is the realization of God, there is "the presence of tragic conflict in God. It is what Jacob Böhme calls the theogonic process . . . the perpetual birth of God out of the *Ungrund*." Berdyaev, following Böhme and Schelling, believes that this view of freedom and the fall "is the only way to understand evil without making God responsible for it."[30]

But God takes the lead in overcoming evil. We humans can bear evil "because God suffers in it too. God shares his creatures' destiny. He sacrifices himself for the world and for man whom he loves and yearns for." Like Böhme and Schelling, Berdyaev affirms that divine-human cooperation will ultimately bring the kingdom.[31] The effect of divine-human effort is reciprocal: "The interior life of God is realized by man and by the world. The interior life of man and of the world is realized by God." What culminates eschatologically is the full actuality of what is eternally essential: that Man is in God and God in Man. "The Kingdom of God is that of God-humanity, in which God is finally in man and man in God, and this is realized in the Spirit."[32] Berdyaev's theology is clearly a dynamic trinitarian panentheism.

Theologians in the Christian Tradition

William Temple

William Temple (1881–1944) was an academic theologian who became archbishop of Canterbury. In order to advocate Christian orthodoxy, he expresses his views in terms of the science and philosophy of his time.[33] This synthesis is clearest in his Gifford Lectures, *Nature, Man, and God*, where he engages Whitehead's process theology.[34] Temple agrees that God is involved in the world process and thus that he has a "primordial" and a "consequent nature." But he argues that Whitehead should have moved "beyond Organ-

30. Berdyaev, "Origin of Good and Evil," 29–30.

31. Ibid. "God, Man, and the God-Man," 197: "Because of the very nature of God Himself who is infinite love and the cause of the divine plan of creation itself, the Kingdom of God can be realized only through man's cooperation and the participation of creation itself." Moltmann adopts Berdyaev's theology virtually intact.

32. Berdyaev, "God, Man, and the God-Man," 200, 197.

33. Joseph Fletcher, "William Temple," in *Handbook of Christian Theologians*, ed. M. Marty and D. Peerman, enlarged ed. (Nashville: Abingdon, 1984), 247: "His world view was akin to Whitehead's and L. S. Thornton's theistic process-doctrine, and was suggested to him by the creative or emergent evolution of Samuel Alexander and Lloyd Morgan."

34. William Temple, *Nature, Man, and God*, Gifford Lectures, 1932–1933, 1933–1934 (London: Macmillan, 1934).

ism to Personality" to acknowledge that God, not Creativity, is the ultimate source of novelty in the world.[35]

Temple emphasizes the transcendence of God as a person in relation to his immanence in the cosmic process. "God is active in the world, and its process is His activity. Yet He is more than this; He is creator and therefore transcendent." It is God's nature to create the world. "Because He is, and is creative, He must create; therefore the universe is necessary to Him in the sense that He can only be Himself by creating it." Thus God is both immanent and transcendent. "God as immanent is correlative with the world; but that is not the whole nature of God."[36]

The necessity of creation is an expression not only of divine creativity but also of love, culminating in the suffering love of Christ. "It is not incidental to God's eternity that (if the Christian Gospel be true) He lived and suffered and triumphed in the process of time. . . . His eternal being is such as to necessitate its happening." Thus Temple rejects as un-Christian the view that "the eternal is unaffected by the historical." With Whitehead, he insists on a dipolar theology. God is by nature both eternal and temporal, absolute and relative, necessary and contingent. *The eternal is the ground of the historical,* and not vice versa; *but the relation is necessary, not contingent—essential, not incidental.* [37]

Temple's theology is a significant attempt to appropriate science-based process panentheism for orthodox Christianity.

John A. T. Robinson

John Robinson (1919–1983), Anglican bishop of Woolwich, caused a stir during the 1960s with *Honest to God.*[38] His aim is to "make Christianity meaningful" to modern people, to educate Christians theologically, and to dispel childish views of God as "an old man in the sky." The strategy of *Honest to God* is to discard "traditional orthodox supernaturalism" and to reinterpret Jesus Christ and Christianity according to a popularized version of Tillich's panentheism.[39] A subsequent book, *Exploration into God,* shifts toward Teilhard de Chardin's.[40]

---

35. Ibid., 259–60, 436, 448. Hartshorne later made the same point.

36. Ibid., 269–70. Lectures 10 and 11 treat immanence and transcendence.

37. Ibid., 448.

38. David Edwards, ed., *The Honest to God Debate* (Philadelphia: Westminster, 1963); Stanley J. Grenz and Roger E. Olson, *Twentieth-Century Theology: God and the World in a Transitional Age* (Downers Grove, IL: InterVarsity, 1992), 161–64.

39. John A. T. Robinson, *Honest to God* (Philadelphia: Westminster, 1962), 17, 13, 8.

40. John A. T. Robinson, *Exploration into God* (Stanford, CA: Stanford University Press, 1967).

In *Honest to God* Robinson credits Tillich's sermon "The Depth of Existence" for his own "awakening." Quoting Tillich's *Systematic Theology* and *The Courage to Be*, Robinson declares the end of theism and replaces theism with the ground of our being.[41] He claims not to reject divine transcendence but to redefine it in terms of "depth." His elaboration is straight from Tillich: God is "not . . . another Being *at all*," but "the inexhaustible depth and ground of all being, of our ultimate concern," "the creative ground and meaning of all our existence." God's Spirit and love connect our individual existence to "the unfathomable abyss of all being in God."[42] Robinson does not use the term *panentheism* in *Honest to God*, but he does place himself where it is located, "between naturalism and supernaturalism" and "between theism and pantheism."[43]

Exploration into God explicitly affirms "'panentheism'. . . the view that God is in everything and everything is in God."[44] Robinson aims to preserve "God as personal" while affirming Tillich's theology and the 1960s emphasis on the "worldliness" of religion.[45] He finds the solution "in the worldly mysticism of Teilhard de Chardin," which provides an alternative between "pantheistic monism" and "theistic dualism."[46] To model panentheism, Robinson introduces the idea of a force field, "the divine field as a physicist might talk of a magnetic field."[47] He blends this idea with Martin Buber's view of God and world as an "*I-Thou* nexus." God is thus the divine force field within which all finite persons can relate in love: "The whole of reality too must ultimately be seen in terms, not of a God, a monarchical Being supreme among individual entities, but of a divine 'field' in which the finite *Thous* are constituted what they are in the freedom of a wholly personalizing love." The "most daring vision," Robinson contends, is Teilhard's "eschatological panentheism," where God is the "Center of centers."[48] In fairness to Teilhard, however, we should note that Robinson's "divine field" is not itself personal. Rather, it is the grounding power context that makes interpersonal relations possible for humans. Teilhard's God is triunely personal in a more traditional sense.[49]

41. Robinson, *Honest to God*, 21–22. "The End of Theism" and "The Ground of Our Being" are chapter titles.

    42. Ibid., 46–47, 60.

    43. Ibid., 127–33.

    44. Robinson, *Exploration into God*, 86–87; also 92 and 160–61.

    45. Ibid., "Prologue: Quest for the Personal."

    46. Ibid., 88.

    47. Ibid., chap. 5, "The Divine Field."

    48. Ibid., 159–60.

    49. See the discussion of Teilhard in chap. 6, above.

John Macquarrie

John Macquarrie (b. 1919) is an Anglican theologian and retired professor of divinity at Christ Church College, Oxford.[50] His early theology is existentialist, and he remains significantly indebted to Heidegger.[51] His *Principles of Christian Theology* is explicitly panentheistic. In *Search of Deity*, his Gifford Lectures, presents a "dialectical theism," which is a more elaborate panentheism. We briefly consider each book.

In *Principles of Christian Theology*, Macquarrie's definitive epithet for God is "Holy Being."[52] Following Heidegger, he denies that Holy Being is a being, the Supreme Being. God is certainly not the self-sufficient, transcendent Monarch of classical theism. Instead, "Being always includes becoming, and the essence of Being is the dynamic act of letting-be." Being is the dynamic power of existence, the power that enables beings to be. God is transcendent in that this power is of a different nature from the world, it precedes the world, and the world depends on it. But God is also essentially immanent. As the power of being, God in himself does not "exist:" "There 'is' no being apart from beings." It is God's nature to empower beings: "It is of his very essence (letting-be) to create." So a world must exist. In fact, "God cannot be conceived apart from the world." Furthermore, the relationship between God and world is in some respects "symmetrical and reciprocal." "God is affected by the world as well as affecting it, for creation entails risk and vulnerability; God is in time and history, as well as above them." Reflecting on his theology, Macquarrie observes, "Perhaps the view I have been putting forward can be described as panentheistic, but the word is not important, for panentheism is itself really a variety of theism."

Accordingly, *In Search of Deity* identifies with panentheism but prefers the term "dialectical theism."[53] Dialectical theism is the implicitly trinitarian tradition of Plotinus, Dionysius, Eriugena, Nicholas of Cusa, Leibniz, Hegel, Whitehead, and Heidegger. Macquarrie presents each of their views

50. Eugene Long, *Existence, Being, and God: An Introduction to the Philosophical Theology of John Macquarrie* (New York: Paragon House, 1985); Georgina Morley, *The Grace of Being: John Macquarrie's Natural Theology* (Bristol, IN: Wyndham Hall, 2001); Owen Cummings, *John Macquarrie, a Master of Theology* (New York and Mahwah, NJ: Paulist, 2002).

51. Among other works, John Macquarrie translated Heidegger's *Being and Time* and wrote *An Existentialist Theology: A Comparison of Heidegger and Bultmann* (London: SCM, 1955) and *Heidegger and Christianity: Hensley Henson Lectures, 1993–1994* (New York: Continuum, 1994).

52. John Macquarrie, *Principles of Christian Theology*, 2nd ed. (New York: Charles Scribner's Sons, 1977). All references in this paragraph are from pp. 118–22.

53. Macquarrie, *In Search of Deity*, 54: "I am not intending to make much use of the term 'panentheism,' although it must already be apparent that I have a good deal of sympathy with the position for which it stands. . . . I prefer the term 'dialectical theism.'"

of God in part 2. Part 3 is his contribution to this tradition. He identifies six dialectical oppositions that are intrinsic to the divine nature and that theology must affirm. First is being and nonbeing. God is the One who is no-thing but the source of all being. Second is one and many. This opposition pertains both to the triunity of God himself and its expression in the one God/many beings polarity. Third is the knowability and incomprehensibility of God. Fourth is transcendence and immanence, the main issue in his previous theology. Fifth is impassibility and passibility. Here Macquarrie reaffirms his view that God is affected by creatures and therefore suffers. The sixth polarity follows: God is both eternal and temporal. God is dipolar because he is the unity of all these oppositions.

In sum, Macquarrie's theology is a contemporary expression of the tradition of Christian Neoplatonism using a Heideggerian ontology. As such, it is a panentheism that is very similar to those of Tillich and Robinson.[54]

Karl Rahner

Karl Rahner (1904–1984) is probably the most influential Catholic theologian of the twentieth century, a status apparent already at Vatican II.[55] His writings are numerous and difficult, and so we rely mainly on *Foundations of Christian Faith*, his final summary.[56] Basic tenets of his theology are implicitly panentheistic, but he does not explicitly endorse this position. We consider this implication in his anthropology, his doctrine of the Trinity, and their conjunction in his theology of the incarnation.

Rahner studied with Heidegger and uses his analysis of human existence as the starting point for his own theological anthropology. Heidegger identified the ontological structures, called "existentials," of human being-in-the-world. Rahner adds a "supernatural existential" that bridges being-in-the-world with God. Although ontologically constitutive of human existence, the supernatural existential is not part of human nature but is supernaturally added to it. It is God's presence as the infinite Ground in the existence of all humans. Thus it affords "a capacity of dynamic self-movement of the spirit, given a priori with human nature directed toward all possible objects." With the supernatural existential, all people have implicit awareness of God

---

54. Ibid., 163, implies as much. He suggests that Heidegger "had a doctrine of God very similar to the one taught by Tillich, who probably derived his concept of being from Heidegger in the first place." Macquarrie is even more dependent on Heidegger.

55. Grenz and Olson, *Twentieth-Century Theology*, 238–54, here 239; Anne Carr, "Karl Rahner," in *Handbook of Christian Theologians*, ed. Marty and Peerman, 519–42.

56. Karl Rahner, *Foundations of Christian Faith: An Introduction to the Idea of Christianity*, trans. William Dych (New York: Seabury, 1978).

as the transcendental Ground of all things, and they also have an openness to specific divine revelation and genuine freedom to respond.[57] Rahner's supernatural existential suggests panentheism because it implies that the real presence of God is a constitutive part of the ontological structure of human existence and thus that all humans participate in God ontologically. This theme returns in his Christology, considered below.

A second panentheistic implication follows from an axiom in Rahner's doctrine of the Trinity, the famous "Rahner's Rule": "The 'economic' Trinity is the 'immanent' Trinity and the 'immanent' Trinity is the 'economic' Trinity."[58] The rule as stated is ambiguous. It might simply mean that the eternal Triune God himself is active in creating and redeeming the world. Another reading of the rule, however, identifies the immanent Trinity and economic Trinity so closely that one cannot be without the other—no Father and Son without the incarnation, no God without the world. In that case, the rule implies what Hegel taught—that it is essential for the immanent Trinity to actualize itself in history as the economic Trinity.[59] The latter reading of strong identity is confirmed by Rahner's doctrine of the incarnation, as follows.

Rahner's explanation of the incarnation brings his views of humanity and the Trinity together. Jesus Christ is the "climax" of God's supernatural-existential self-communication in all humans.[60] He is the God-Man, the dialectical unity and fulfillment both of human nature and of the self-communication of God to humanity. Rahner elaborates the incarnation in terms of a theology of cosmic evolution highly reminiscent of Teilhard de Chardin. "The God-Man is the initial beginning and definitive triumph of the movement of the world's self-transcendence into absolute closeness to the mystery of God." Using Teilhardian terminology, Rahner describes the history of the cosmos, aimed at the consummation of humanity, as the evolutionary process through which God "becomes its innermost life." The Spirit of God is the animating force (soul) of the world. God as the absolute Ground "becomes immediately interior to what is grounded by it [the cosmos]."[61] Rahner's cosmic-incarnational panentheism is very similar to Teilhard's.

57. Karl Rahner, *Hearers of the Word*, trans. Michael Richards (New York: Herder and Herder, 1969), 59. Its content is summarized in Rahner, "The Hearers of the Message," part 1 in *Foundations*.

58. Karl Rahner, *The Trinity*, trans. Joseph Donceel (New York: Herder and Herder, 1970), 21–22, and elaborated thereafter. "Economic Trinity" refers to the acts of the Trinity toward the world. "Immanent Trinity" is the Triune God in himself.

59. Moltmann, Pannenberg, and others take Rahner's Rule in this strong sense.

60. Rahner, *Foundations*, 176.

61. Ibid., "Christology within an Evolutionary View of the World," 178–202; quotes at 181, 191.

Rahner affirms a duality in God's nature and attributes. The finite and the infinite, for example, are dialectically unified in God: "The finite is no longer in opposition to the infinite, but is that which the infinite himself has become." Similarly, God's immutability is a "dialectical assertion" in relation to the incarnation: "In and in spite of his immutability he can truly become something: he himself, he in time."[62] Thus God is both immutable and changing.

Similarly, the divine will is both free and (self-)determined. Rahner frequently emphasizes God's freedom and grace in creation. God's becoming something is not "a sign that he is in need of something, but rather the height of his perfection." But he also emphasizes that God's self-expression in humanity is in his eternal nature, which implies its necessity: "God himself is man and remains so for all eternity. . . . Man is for all eternity the expression of the mystery of God which participates for all eternity in the mystery of its ground."[63] God could not refrain from the incarnation because it is an eternal expression of his nature. In sum, the existence of the cosmos, humanity, and the incarnation are natural and inevitable for God, and they participate in God. This result confirms the strong reading of Rahner's Rule: the immanent and economic Trinity are essentially and necessarily identical.

Rahner's doctrines of God, the Trinity, the incarnation, and humanity together imply dynamic panentheism.[64]

Hans Küng

Hans Küng (1928–) is a well-known progressive Roman Catholic theologian who has been disciplined by the church for his outspoken views on its authority and some of its teachings.[65] An able scholar and prolific writer, Küng has addressed a wide range of issues in theology, ethics, and interreligious dialogue from a Christian panentheism shaped by Hegel and Teilhard.

Küng's debt to Hegel is evident already in his massive work *The Incarnation of God* (1970). Although he retains a more personal view of God, Küng adapts Hegel's view of divine self-negation in the incarnation of Christ, as

---

62. Ibid., 226, 221.

63. Ibid., 221–22, 225.

64. Grenz and Olson, *Twentieth-Century Theology*, 254, conclude that "a panentheistic interdependence of God and creation lurks in the background" as "the ghost of Hegel."

65. Ibid., 254–70; John Kiwiet, "Emerging Leadership," chap. 1 in *Hans Küng* (Waco: Word, 1985).

well as his dialectical view of God's relation to the world as identity-in-difference. This, he thinks, preserves both immanence and transcendence while moving beyond the "static" God of classical theism: "There is 'no going back on Hegel' regarding the historicity of God."[66]

On Being a Christian, Küng's 1974 bestseller, urges that theology be done "in a genuinely dialectical way: the 'God of the philosophers' is—in the best Hegelian sense of the term—'cancelled and preserved' (*aufgehoben*) positively, negatively and supereminently in the 'God of Israel and of Jesus.'"[67]

Does God Exist? is a powerful apologetic dialogue with modern thought that defends faith in God as the only possible foundation for human certainty and security. Tracing the development "from Deism to Panentheism," Küng appropriates themes from Hegel, Teilhard, and Whitehead. He concludes, "God is in this world, and this world is in God. . . . God is not only a (supreme) finite—as a part of reality—alongside finite things. He is in fact the infinite in the finite . . . the absolute-relative, here-hereafter, transcendent-immanent, all-embracing and all-permeating most real reality in the heart of things, in man, in the history of mankind, in the world."[68] God thereby internalizes and redeems the suffering of the world.

In *Theology for the Third Millennium*, the foundation for his positive engagement with the non-Christian religions, he appeals to Hegel, Heidegger, and Whitehead, among others, to reaffirm "the historicity and worldliness of God" as "permanent findings" for any future theology.[69] Küng acknowledges that he is a panentheist.

Non-Christian Panentheists

Martin Buber and Judaism

Martin Buber (1878–1965) practiced Hasidic Judaism all his life. He studied philosophy in Berlin and eventually became a professor at the He-

66. Hans Küng, *The Incarnation of God: An Introduction to Hegel's Theological Thought as Prolegomena to a Future Christology*, trans. J. R. Stephenson (New York: Crossroad, 1987), 479. Alrah Pitchers, "Hegel as a Point of Departure for Küng's Christology," chap. 1, and "The Historicity of God," chap. 5.2 in *The Christology of Hans Küng: A Critical Examination* (Bern: Peter Lang, 1997); the latter chapter includes "The Dialectic in God."

67. Hans Küng, *On Being a Christian*, trans. Edward Quinn (Garden City, NY: Doubleday, 1976), 309.

68. Hans Küng, *Does God Exist? An Answer for Today*, trans. Edward Quinn (Garden City, NY: Doubleday, 1980), 127–88, quote at 185.

69. Hans Küng, *Theology for the Third Millennium: An Ecumenical View*, trans. Peter Heinegg (New York: Doubleday, 1988), 162–63.

brew University in Jerusalem. He enjoyed an international reputation as a religious thinker, and his most famous book, *I and Thou* (1923), has been widely influential among philosophers and theologians, including Tillich and Berdyaev.[70]

I and Thou outlines a relational-dialogical ontology that finally includes nature and humans in God.[71] Buber begins with the human capacity for two basic kinds of relationship: I-It and I-Thou or I-You. The former addresses others as objects of knowledge and use. The latter allows intimate personal mutuality. "The world as experience belongs to the basic word I-It. The basic word I-You establishes the world of relation." Even though nature is ordinarily an It, it can be a You, the first of the "three spheres in which the world of relation arises." The second sphere is life with humans, where language is basic to community, especially the language of personal address: you and I. The third kind of You relation is with spiritual beings. Here we encounter God, the eternal You: "In every You we address the eternal You, in every sphere according to its manner."[72] We can encounter God within all three spheres.

Buber explores a variety of It and You relations with nature, technology, language, social and economic life, art, and religion. Each discloses the all-comprehensive primordial I-You relation with God. In various ways Buber asserts that all things are in God: "In the relation to God, . . . everything is included." Thus "to comprehend all—all the world—in comprehending the You . . . to have nothing besides God, but to grasp everything in him, that is the perfect relationship."[73] This relationship of all things in God is primordial and ontological because God creates by his word of address. Thus Buber can paraphrase Genesis 1 (and John 1): "In the beginning is the relation—as category of being . . . the *a priori* of relation; *the innate You*."[74] It is "the absolute relationship that includes all relative relationships."[75]

God is transcendent as well as immanent: "God is the 'wholly other'; but he is also the wholly same; the wholly present." Thus "God embraces but is

70. Donald Moore, "Martin Buber: A Biographical Portrait," in *Martin Buber: Prophet of Religious Secularism*, 2nd ed. (New York: Fordham University Press, 1996), xviii–xxviii.

71. Martin Buber, *I and Thou*, trans. Walter Kaufmann (New York: Scribner's, 1970); Pedro Sevilla, *God as Person in the Writings of Martin Buber* (Manila: Loyola House of Studies, 1970); Maurice Friedman, *Martin Buber and the Eternal* (New York: Human Sciences, 1986); Pamela Vermes, *Buber* (New York: Grove, 1988); Moore, *Martin Buber*.

72. Buber, *I and Thou*, 53–57.

73. Ibid., 127.

74. Ibid., 78.

75. Ibid., 129.

not the universe; just so, God embraces but is not my self."[76] In all respects God includes yet transcends the world, which implies panentheism.

Buber further affirms that God needs the world: "Don't you know also that God needs you—in the fullness of his eternity, you? . . . You need God in order to be, and God needs you."[77] The reason for God's need of creation is implied but not stated: since God is "absolute person," he must have a You. Perhaps because Judaism does not have the Trinity to provide an I-You relation in God without creation, Buber concludes that God's I-You relation must be with creatures.

The mutuality of the I-You relationship implies that God is affected by his creatures. This dynamic is most explicit in prayer. "In prayer man . . . acts on God, albeit without exacting anything from God." Through spiritual contemplation "we eternally form God's form."[78] Divine-human cooperation and mutuality are so pervasive, he writes, that we humans "participate" in divine creation as God's "helpers and companions." Because God develops in relation to creatures, Buber speaks of "the emergence of the living God." So closely is God's history tied to ours that Buber can echo Schelling: "The world is not divine play, it is divine fate."[79] Involvement in the world is not inconsequential for God. It commits him to a destiny not entirely of his own making.

Buber's *I and Thou* presents a panentheism in which God transcends and includes humanity and the world by addressing us as "You," an eternal word that constitutes the very being of God and creatures in a relationship where humans can respond with "You."[80] Buber's theology primarily expresses a life of dialogue with God, not a system of ideas about God. He desires a living relationship with the personal-covenantal God of the Hebrew Scriptures.

Muhammed Iqbal: Islam

Sir Muhammed Iqbal (1877–1938) was born in a part of India that is now Pakistan; he studied in Germany and England and was politically and intellectually active in developing a modern Islamic worldview.[81] His

76. Ibid., 127, 143.

77. Ibid., 130.

78. Ibid., 130–31, 167.

79. Ibid., 130–31.

80. Buber is included as a modern panentheist by Charles Hartshorne and William Reese, *Philosophers Speak of God* (Chicago: University of Chicago Press, 1953), 302–6.

81. B. A. Dar, "Iqbal, Muhammed," *EncPhil* 4:212–13. I owe my awareness of Iqbal's panentheism to Hartshorne and Reese, *Philosophers Speak of God*, 294–97, who excerpt Muhammed Iqbal, *The Reconstruction of Religious Thought in Islam* (London: Oxford University Press, 1934).

roots are in the Sufi tradition, where mysticism has often been construed as pantheism: Allah is One; there is nothing besides Allah.[82] But Iqbal also dialogues with Western science and philosophy, in particular with Hegel, Whitehead, and Bergson. What results is a modern form of panentheism that fits between Sufism and standard Islamic theism.[83]

Iqbal conceives of Allah as the Ultimate Self or Absolute Ego, who, according to the Qur'an, "can afford to dispense with all the worlds." Yet nature is an aspect of God; it is "organic to the ultimate Self . . . as character is to the human self." Nature is "the creative activity of the Absolute Ego," "a living, ever-growing organism whose growth has no final external limits." Nature's only limit is "the immanent self which animates and sustains the whole." Thus Iqbal portrays God and the world as infinite soul and finite body.[84] He also embraces a kind of panpsychism in which all is ego: "Every atom of Divine Energy . . . is an ego."[85] The world and everything in it, from atoms to humans, are "ego-unities."

The free actions of created egos limit God: "The emergence of egos endowed with the power of spontaneous and hence unforeseeable action is, in a sense, a limitation of the freedom of the all-inclusive Ego." This is not a metaphysical limitation but God's choice, "born out of his own creative freedom." "He has chosen finite egos to be participators of His life, power, and freedom."[86] Thus creatures contribute to the becoming of God, the "realization of the infinite creative possibilities of His being."[87]

Although Iqbal sometimes refers to himself as a pantheist,[88] his view is panentheistic.[89] Absolute Ego includes the world of finite egos but is ontologically distinct from them. Their ontological distinctness is evident in their

82. William Stoddart, *Sufism* (New York: Paragon House, 1986); Martin Lings, *What Is Sufism?* (Cambridge, UK: Islamic Texts Society, 1993). Titus Burckhardt, *An Introduction to Sufism*, trans. D. M. Matheson (London, San Francisco: Thorsons, 1995), argues that traditional Sufism is not pantheism but what we are calling panentheism, that creatures are real in God.

83. M. S. Raschid, *Iqbal's Concept of God* (Boston: Kegan Paul International, 1981).

84. Iqbal, *Reconstruction*, 53–54, quoted from Hartshorne and Reese, *Philosophers Speak of God*, 294.

85. Iqbal, *Reconstruction*, 68 (Hartshorne and Reese, 296): "from the Ultimate Ego only egos proceed."

86. Iqbal, *Reconstruction*, 75–76 (Hartshorne and Reese, 296).

87. Iqbal, *Reconstruction*, 61 (Hartshorne and Reese, 295).

88. Raschid, *Iqbal's Concept of God*, 59.

89. Ibid., chap. 8, "Muslim Panentheism: The Modernist 'Reconstruction' of the Quranic Doctrine by Muhammed Iqbal"; Hartshorne and Reese, *Philosophers Speak of God*, 294–97. Raschid agrees with Hartshorne and Reese that Iqbal is a modern panentheist, but he disagrees that this is compatible with orthodox Islam.

spontaneous freedom, which limits God. Their inclusion is participation in the unfolding of the divine life.

Sarvepalli Radhakrishnan: Hinduism

Sarvepalli Radhakrishnan (1888–1975) was a philosopher who taught in India and at Oxford and a statesman who served as the president of India (1962–1967). Steeped in the Hindu tradition, he developed a panentheism that seeks common ground with Western philosophy and non-Hindu religions.

More precisely, he is a panentheist about current reality and a pantheistic monist about ultimate reality. The Hindu tradition includes both views. The great philosopher Śankara (788–820) was an absolute monist and strict pantheist who taught that God is absolutely one and that all distinctions and differences are merely temporary illusions. Rāmānuja (d. 1137), however, held that the world is the body of Brahman (God), that individual souls are real, and that souls do not disappear into God. Radhakrishnan holds with Rāmānuja that in temporal existence God is personal and souls are real. But ultimately all things become indistinguishable in Brahman, as Śankara held.[90] This synthesis is clear in *An Idealist View of Life*: "God, though immanent, is not identical with the world until the very end. Throughout the process there is an unrealised residuum in God, but it vanishes when we reach the end. ... God who is organic with it recedes into the background of the Absolute."[91] Radhakrishnan is a penultimate panentheist and an ultimate pantheist. We consider each phase in turn.

Concerning the present world, Radhakrishnan is a panentheist. *The Hindu View of Life* states this plainly: "Hindu thought takes care to emphasise the transcendent character of the Supreme.... The world is in God and not God in the universe. In the world we have the separate existence of the individuals."[92] *An Idealist View of Life* elaborates the details of his thought in dialogue with the Western tradition from Plato through Hegel. Radhakrishnan finds most in common with the recent evolutionary philosophies of Alexander, Bergson, and Whitehead, but he makes the point that his Rāmānujan position can stand on its own without Western thought.

90. Ninian Smart, "Radhakrishnan, Sarvepalli," *EncPhil* 7:62–63.

91. Sarvepalli Radhakrishnan, *An Idealist View of Life*, Hibbert Lectures, 1929, 2nd ed. (London: Allen and Unwin, 1947), 340.

92. Sarvepalli Radhakrishnan, *The Hindu View of Life* (London: Allen and Unwin; New York: Macmillan, 1927, repr. 1957), 70–71. Citation is from the reprinted edition. He even attributes this view to Śankara: "Sankara does not assert an identity between God and the world but only denies the independence of the world" (66).

An Idealist View of Life affirms all the characteristics of panentheism. God and the world are distinct: "Till the completion of the cosmic process, the individual retains his center as individual, and the completion is always transcendent to him, and so God is an 'other' over against him." He describes God's relation to the world as "organic," "as soul to body." The Divine Soul of the cosmos is involved in time, effort, and development: "Struggle and growth are real in the life of God. . . . God is essentially bound up with life in time." God is not all-determining but cooperates with free creatures: "God works as a creative genius does. . . . There is thus an element of indetermination throughout the process."[93] Radhakrishnan is a panentheist, stating the dual Hinduism of Rāmānuja in terms of Western thought.

But ultimately he is a monist. Absolute Reality is beyond the distinction of God and the world, which are finally transcended. "We call the supreme the Absolute, when we view it apart from the cosmos, [and we call it] God in relation to the cosmos. The absolute is the pre-cosmic nature of God, and God is the Absolute from the cosmic point of view."[94] God, self, and world are genuine manifestations of the Absolute. But the reason for their distinct existence remains a mystery. And so is their ultimate unity beyond all difference in the Absolute. In sum, Radhakrishnan is a penultimate panentheist and an ultimate pantheist.[95]

Masao Abe and Alan Watts: Zen Buddhism

Zen scholars also find common ground in Western panentheism. Masao Abe (1915–), a Japanese Zen master, observes, "In German mysticism, the Godhead or *Gottheit* is grasped as *Nichts* by Meister Eckhart and as *Ungrund* by Jakob Böhme. Furthermore, in Eckhart and Böhme the essence of God is not the Supreme Good but lies beyond good and evil. This is strikingly similar to the Buddhist understanding of ultimate Reality." Given this similarity, panentheism is obvious in Abe's summary of Zen: "The Buddhist idea of Nothingness is a positive and dynamic idea. . . . There is nothing outside Nothingness. You and I and everything else are included without losing our

93. Radhakrishnan, *Idealist View of Life*, 342, 338, 340.

94. Ibid., 345.

95. Hartshorne and Reese, *Philosophers Speak of God*, 306–10, overlook his pantheistic monism; M. N. Roy, "Indian Philosophy and Radhakrishnan," in *The Philosophy of Sarvepalli Radhakrishnan*, ed. Paul Schilpp (New York: Tudor, 1952), 548, stresses his monism and misses his panentheism: "His Absolute Idealism is the pantheistic monism of the scholastic theology of Samkaracharya, expounded in the language of modern academic philosophy."

particularity in the dynamic structure of this *positive* Nothingness."[96] Unlike the Western tradition, according to Abe, Zen does not favor the triumph of being over nonbeing but accepts both in perfect balance.

Alan Watts (1915–1973) was an Anglican priest who turned to Zen Buddhism and became a popular guru in the 1960s.[97] Like John Cobb and Hans Küng after him, he is a Western panentheist who found spiritual kinship in Zen Buddhism. In his early work, *Behold the Spirit*, Watts develops an all-inclusive view of God: "If the unity of God is truly all-inclusive and non-dual, it must include diversity and distinctions as well as one-ness; otherwise the principle of diversity must stand over against God as something opposite to and outside him." Although he emphasizes oneness, he distances himself from pantheism. "This inclusion of diversity is impossible for the God of pantheism, who cannot comprehend *real* diversity. The universe of the pantheist is *unreal*."[98] *Behold the Spirit* implies panentheism but does not mention it.

Beyond Theology explicitly endorses panentheism, appealing to scientific concepts of force fields and feedback systems.[99] "These unitary, relational, and 'fieldish' ways of thinking in the sciences give immense plausibility to non-dualist or pantheist (to be frightfully exact, 'panentheist') types of metaphysic." God is not a Being but an ineffable power, "a unified field—immensely complex and comprising the whole universe." God is "an invisible and intangible Ground underlying and producing everything that we sense . . . some kind of unifying and intelligent continuum."[100] By his own designation, Watts's Zen Buddhism is panentheistic.[101]

Starhawk: Wiccan Neopaganism

Varieties of panentheism are implicit in much of the so-called new spirituality, which is in part a return to ancient religions that predate Judeo-Christian

96. Masao Abe, *Zen and Western Thought* (Honolulu: University of Hawaii Press, 1985), 133, 199.

97. Michael Brannigan, *Everywhere and Nowhere: The Path of Alan Watts* (New York: Peter Lang, 1988); David Stuart, *Alan Watts* (Radnor, PA: Chilton, 1976).

98. Alan Watts, *Behold the Spirit: A Study in the Necessity of Mystical Religion* (New York: Pantheon, 1947), 141.

99. See Toshihiko Izutsu, "The Field Structure of Ultimate Reality," in *Toward a Philosophy of Zen Buddhism* (Teheran: Imperial Iranian Academy of Philosophy, 1977), 45–49.

100. Alan Watts, *Beyond Theology: The Art of Godmanship* (New York: Pantheon, 1964), 228, 222–23. Robinson and Pannenberg also use field theory.

101. David Clark seems unaware of panentheism as a distinct category in *The Pantheism of Alan Watts* (Downers Grove, IL: InterVarsity, 1978), 15: "What we have is not absolute monism, but a pantheism where the principles of One and many are opposed but related, like polar opposites in a single field." This sort of pantheism is commonly called panentheism.

monotheism. Examples are the New Age movement, Western adaptations of Hinduism and Buddhism, new forms of ancient animism and paganism that worship the all-inclusive Life Force, and even some pseudoscientific spiritualities such as Scientology.[102]

Wicca is a form of neopaganism, and Starhawk (Miriam Simos) is one of its best-known proponents. She is aware of its roots: "The Old Religion—call it Witchcraft, Wicca, the Craft, or with a slightly broader definition, Paganism or New Paganism—is both old and newly invented." She also recognizes its kinship with other "religions of immanence, whether we call them Witchcraft or Paganism or polytheism or spirituality . . . from Celtic, Greek, Native American, Eastern, or African mythology."[103]

Starhawk emphasizes that Wicca is a diverse set of practices, not a system of doctrine. Most Wiccans nevertheless share a general view of the divine and the world. The Council of American Witches has produced a document, "Principles of Wiccan Belief." They affirm a single cosmic Power that transcends gender yet manifests itself primarily in the correlation of genders. "We conceive of the Creative Power in the Universe as manifesting through polarity—as masculine and feminine—and that this same Creative Power lives in all people, and functions through the interaction of the masculine and feminine."[104] Starhawk shares this belief. She identifies the cosmic power as the Life Force, "the all, the interwoven fabric of being . . . the web of connection." The Life Force is primordially "God/dess," transcending and including sexual differentiation. But although she acknowledges gender balance in the Divine, Starhawk emphasizes its feminine side, addressing God/dess as "She" and promoting Wicca as Goddess worship. "Beneath all, it is a religion of connection with the Goddess, who is immanent in nature, in human beings, in relationships."[105] The Goddess has many names, including Isis, Astarte, Ishtar, Sophia, and Gaea, who is "Mother Nature" in Greek mythology. She has many roles: maiden, mother, healer, and crone. The God is "her male

102. Marilyn Ferguson, "Spiritual Adventure: Connection to the Source," chap. 11 in *The Aquarian Conspiracy: Personal and Social Transformation in the 1980s* (Los Angeles: Tarcher, 1980, repr. 1987); George Chryssides, "New Age, Witchcraft, and Paganism," chap. 9 in *Exploring New Religions* (New York: Cassell, 1999); Ann Moura, *Origins of Modern Witchcraft: The Evolution of a World Religion* (St. Paul, MN: Llewellyn, 2000).

103. Starhawk, *Dreaming the Dark: Magic, Sex, and Politics* (Boston: Beacon, 1982), xii, 72.

104. "Principles of Wiccan Belief," *Green Egg* 8/64 (1974): 32; it was adopted by the council April 11–14, 1974. Quoted from Margot Adler, *Drawing Down the Moon: Witches, Goddess-Worshippers, and Other Pagans in America Today*, rev. and expanded ed. (Boston: Beacon, 1986), 102.

Not all Wiccans agree. Adler, a well-known voice on National Public Radio, is a pluralist: She espouses "radical polytheism . . . the view that reality is multiple and diverse" (*Drawing Down the Moon*, viii).

105. Starhawk, *Dreaming the Dark*, 72, xii; see Aida Besançon Spencer, *The Goddess Revival* (Grand Rapids: Baker, 1995).

aspect, or . . . the other pole of that once-unbroken unity."[106] He too has many names and roles in the cycle of life and death.

Starhawk's presentation is more poetic than philosophical, and so her panentheism requires explication. First, both the world and the Divine are real. "To a Witch the world itself is what is real. The Goddess, the Gods, are not merely psychological entities . . . they too are real. . . . The immanent Goddess is not abstract."[107] Second, there is mutual immanence. The Goddess lives in all creatures. Creatures originate and emerge from the primordial Mother as humans do from our mothers' wombs. We live within the Goddess just as "we share an energy-field with our mothers" in the womb. We emerge from immanence as "we develop the awareness of an I-ness that separates out from the engulfing field."[108] The third aspect of panentheism is divine transcendence. Starhawk does not affirm a supernatural realm beyond the world but, like Giordano Bruno, locates transcendence in the depths of immanence in the world. Transcendence in her theology is the primordial unity, the "unbroken circle," the Life Force beyond sexual differentiation. This basic reality is ontologically deeper than the polarity of forces that generate all the creatures in the world. It is their source and the context within which they exist. God/dess is transcendent. Thus Starhawk affirms all the essential ingredients of panentheism.

Wicca has obvious affinities with other panentheisms that emphasize the gender polarity of the Life Force. In the Western tradition, the Gnostics, Böhme, Schelling, Tillich, Moltmann, the process theologians, and feminist theologians regard the masculine and the feminine as a basic manifestation of the dipolar nature of God. In the East, the yin-yang of Taoism and similar male-female imagery in Hinduism and Buddhism also play that role.

Conclusion

Panentheism has become widely embraced in the twentieth century. In the Christian West, it is mainly the diversification of the long-established tradition of Neoplatonism. But panentheism has also been implicit in non-Christian and non-Western traditions as well and has been discovered through interreligious dialogue.[109] Western panentheists, such as Watts, have

---

106. Starhawk, *Dreaming the Dark*, 73.

107. Ibid., 73.

108. Ibid., 74–75.

109. Keith Ward, "The World as the Body of God: A Panentheistic Metaphor," in *In Whom We Live and Move and Have Our Being: Panentheistic Reflections on God's Presence in a Scientific World*, ed. Philip

not mistakenly imposed their categories on other religions. Most of those we surveyed—Iqbal, Radhakrishnan, and Abe—are not from the Western Christian tradition, and yet they have articulated their own implicitly panentheistic beliefs in categories from the Western tradition.

The main difference among world panentheisms is whether the Divine is thought of as ultimately personal or impersonal. In the Jewish, Christian, and Muslim traditions, personal theism predominates and panentheists retain personal categories. Examples are Berdyaev's trinitarianism, Buber's I-Thou relation, and Iqbal's Ego-ego distinction. In primal and Asian religions, the prepersonal Force predominates, as evident in Radhakrishnan's Absolute, Watt's force field, and Starhawk's Life Force.

Personal or impersonal, panentheism is a broadly held, cross-cultural, interreligious way of affirming the value and freedom of the world while emphasizing the world's dynamic integration within a real transcendent divinity. It has come to be widely regarded as the common framework and basis for dialogue among the diverse world religions.

Clayton and Arthur Peacocke (Grand Rapids: Eerdmans, 2003), 62–72, argues that panentheism has a history in non-Western as well as Western thought.

IO

~~~~~~

Moltmann's Perichoretic Panentheism

Overview

Jürgen Moltmann is probably the most widely known and popular contemporary Protestant theologian. His many books have been translated into several languages, and he has lectured all over the world. Moltmann has developed the most extensive explicitly panentheistic Christian theology of the late twentieth century. He embraces panentheism because he is convinced that it is the most faithful contemporary model of the God of the Bible and explanation of the Christian faith. The contours of his theology reflect the dialectical trinitarian tradition of Böhme, Hegel, and Schelling. Moltmann's panentheism is *perichoretic*: he eventually makes perichoresis, the traditional doctrinal term for the mutual indwelling of the persons of the Trinity, his ontology. He applies it not only to the Trinity but to everything—the relation of creatures with each other and of all creation with God.

Moltmann is first and foremost a Christian. Born in 1926 in Germany to a nonreligious family, he was converted during the firebombing of Hamburg in World War II and was discipled in an English prisoner-of-war camp. He earned his doctorate in 1952 at the University of Göttingen, where he was impressed by the Reformed theology of Karl Barth, Otto Weber, and others. He pastored a small Reformed church and then taught in a seminary.

From 1963 to his retirement, he was a professor of systematic theology at the University of Tübingen.[1]

Moltmann's lifelong project has been to relate all aspects of theology to the coming kingdom of God.[2] Addressing the gospel to secularists and Marxists, he has intended to counter the supernaturalism of Barth and the religious existentialism of Bultmann, which separate God's activity from ordinary world history. Moltmann emphasizes God's constant involvement in the world order, bringing his final kingdom—the redemption and full communion of all creation within the life of the Trinity.

The development of this project is evident from the titles of his major books. *Theology of Hope* (1964) represents God as "the power of the future" at work in the present world, eliciting the promised kingdom and justifying human hope in spite of injustice, suffering, and evil. Moltmann's work first implies panentheism in *The Crucified God* (1973). This book finds God at the heart of world history—in the interaction of love and abandonment between the Father and the Son in Jesus's crucifixion and resurrection. Through the Son, the suffering and renewal of all humanity are taken into the life of the Triune God. *The Church in the Power of the Spirit* (1975) explains how the Spirit that unites Father and Son imparts the new life of the kingdom to God's people. *The Trinity and the Kingdom* (1980) is pivotal because, as the title suggests, it elaborates Moltmann's whole theological project in terms of its two main foci. *God in Creation*, the Gifford Lectures of 1984–1985, explores the role of God's Spirit in creation and providence, advancing the world toward its fulfillment. It fully deploys his perichoretic ontology. *The Way of Jesus Christ* (1989), Moltmann's Christology, considers Jesus as Messiah, Suffering Servant, resurrected Lord, Cosmic Christ, and the One to Come. *The Spirit of Life* (1991) explores the ways that humans experience life and new life in the person of the Holy Spirit. *The Coming of God* (1995) is Moltmann's eschatology—the final consummation of individual human lives, the whole creation, and the Trinity itself. In these

---

1. On his life and career, see Jürgen Moltmann, "My Theological Career," in *History and the Triune God: Contributions to Trinitarian Theology* (New York: Crossroad, 1992), 165–82; Geiko Müller-Fahrenholz, "In the Prison Camp: Liberation," chap. 1 in *The Kingdom and the Power: The Theology of Jürgen Moltmann*, trans. John Bowdon (London: SCM, 2000); Stanley J. Grenz and Roger E. Olson, "Jürgen Moltmann," in *Twentieth-Century Theology: God and the World in a Transitional Age* (Downers Grove, IL: InterVarsity, 1992), 172–74.

2. Fine studies of his whole theology are Richard Bauckham, *The Theology of Jürgen Moltmann* (Edinburgh: T&T Clark, 1995), with a very good summary in chap. 1, "Moltmann's Theology: An Overview"; Müller-Fahrenholz, *Kingdom and the Power*; and Tae Wha Yoo, *The Spirit of Liberation: Jürgen Moltmann's Trinitarian Pneumatology* (Zoetermeer, Neth.: Uitgeverij Meinema, 2003). Another very good summary is Grenz and Olson, "Jürgen Moltmann."

and many other works, Moltmann unfolds and applies his vision of the creation, liberation, reconciliation, and consummation of the world as the history of the trinitarian God, culminating in his kingdom.

Throughout this project, Moltmann progressively articulates an "eschatological, trinitarian panentheism"[3] based on the concept of perichoresis. Although he began as a Reformed theologian, he sides with Christian panentheism on virtually every issue over which it differs from Augustinian-Reformed theology. The sources and characteristics of Moltmann's panentheism are our focus, not an overview of his rich and complex theology as a whole.

The sections that follow trace the development of Moltmann's perichoretic panentheism. The first section deals with its seeds in his prepanentheistic theology of hope. The next points out the emerging features of his panentheism in *The Crucified God*. The third and main section surveys his entire system as presented in *The Trinity and the Kingdom*. The section on *God in Creation* focuses on his application of perichoresis throughout his whole system. The section on *The Coming of God* notes the full actuality of divine-world perichoresis in the consummation of the kingdom. A final section reflects on Moltmann's panentheism as a Christian theology.

Dialectical Ontology and the Theology of Hope

Moltmann has been familiar with the dialectical tradition from the outset. His first book treats the origins of dialectical theology.[4] He has also appropriated Hegelian thought from his lifelong engagement with Ernst Bloch, a Marxist philosopher, and from the Marxist social theory of the Frankfurt school.[5] Bloch's influential *Principle of Hope* argues in Hegelian fashion that being and nonbeing dialectically entail becoming, which in turn implies "not-yet-being." Applied to history, this means that the "not yet"—the utopian, eschatological future of humanity—is implicit in the present, empowering its development and grounding human hope. Bloch asserts that Commu-

---

3. Grenz and Olson, *Twentieth-Century Theology*, 179. These are Moltmann's own terms.

4. Jürgen Moltmann, *Anfänge der dialektischen Theologie* (Munich: Kaiser, 1962).

5. See Leszek Kolakowski, "The Frankfort School and 'Critical Theory,'" chap. 10, including Jürgen Habermas, and "Ernst Bloch: Marxism as Future Gnosis," chap. 12 in *Main Currents of Marxism*, trans. P. S. Falla, 3 vols. (New York: Oxford University Press, 1981), vol. 3. On Moltmann's dialogue with Bloch, see Richard Bauckham, "The Emergence of the Theology of Hope: In Dialogue with Ernst Bloch," chap. 1 in *Moltmann: Messianic Theology in the Making* (London: Marshall Pickering, 1987); M. Douglas Meeks, *Origins of the Theology of Hope* (Philadelphia: Fortress, 1974); Grenz and Olson, *Twentieth-Century Theology*, 174–76.

nism will finally realize the Perfect Being—fully mature humanity—that the religions have mistakenly postulated as "God."[6]

Moltmann's *Theology of Hope* counters that hope for utopia is groundless unless there is a God who is the power of the future and moves the present toward human fulfillment. Bloch's thesis fails, he claims, because the future is not fully determined or empowered by the past and present and cannot be extrapolated from them. Moltmann concedes that the reality of God cannot be proven by traditional natural theology or Hegelian philosophy of history. But he points to traces of God in the world, "the promise of the future." "God reveals himself in the form of promise and in the history that is marked by promise."[7] The reality of this promise is proclaimed in the Christian gospel: the God who kept his promise to Israel in Jesus Christ will surely bring his promised kingdom. This kingdom is not otherworldly but will transform this world, including "the realization of the eschatological *hope of justice*, the *humanizing* of man, the *socializing* of humanity, *peace* for all creation."[8] Moltmann claims that God's promised future guarantees what Bloch hoped for but could not ensure with his dialectical-historical ontology.

Although Moltmann's critique of Bloch is valid, his counterproposal depends on a puzzling "eschatological ontology." It posits that the reality of God is entirely in the future, yet he affects the present. "God is not 'beyond us' or 'in us,' but ahead of us in the horizons of the future opened to us in his promises. . . . The 'future' must be considered as the mode of God's being."[9] Grenz and Olson explain: "In his ontology, then, the future is not determined by the present but itself determines the present. The future is 'ontologically prior' to the present and the past. It is not *becoming* from the present, but *coming* to it, drawing it forward into totally new forms of reality."[10] Moltmann's *Theology of Hope* is richly biblical, but philosophically it presents a counterintuitive view of God's transcendence as the future, and it does not explain how a future reality can be immanent and effective in the present. This gap between God's transcendence and immanence indicates that Moltmann's theology is not yet panentheistic.

6. Ernst Bloch, *The Principle of Hope*, trans. N. Plaice, S. Plaice, and P. Knight (Cambridge, MA: MIT Press, 1986), translation of *Das Prinzip der Hoffnung* (1954); Kolakowski, *Marxism*, 3:438.

7. Jürgen Moltmann, *Theology of Hope: On the Ground and the Implications of a Christian Eschatology*, trans. James Leitch (New York: Harper and Row, 1967), 42.

8. Ibid., 329.

9. Jürgen Moltmann, "Theology as Eschatology," in *The Future of Hope*, ed. Frederick Herzog (New York: Herder and Herder, 1970), 9, quoted from Grenz and Olson, *Twentieth-Century Theology*, 176, 179. This essay expands on *Theology of Hope*.

10. Grenz and Olson, *Twentieth-Century Theology*, 176.

The Crucified God

Theology of Hope does not account for God's presence, especially in the depths of injustice, suffering, and death. *The Crucified God* compensates by centering the Triune God in the crucifixion of Jesus. Moltmann proposes to derive all topics of theology, including the Trinity and the future of God's kingdom, from his theology of the cross. To make his case, he embraces dialectical thought. He quotes "Schelling's words: 'Every being can be revealed only in its opposite. Love only in hatred, unity only in conflict.' Applied to Christian theology, this means that God is only revealed as 'God' in his opposite: godlessness and abandonment by God. In concrete terms, God is revealed in the cross of Christ who was abandoned by God."[11] In this way Moltmann makes dialectical negation the formal principle of this theology. In addition, to connect the cross with the Trinity, he adopts Rahner's Rule, that "the economic Trinity is the immanent Trinity and the immanent Trinity *is* the economic Trinity."[12] In sum, Moltmann argues that the Triune God is immanent in history in the love, suffering, and death of the cross.

His dialectical exposition of the crucifixion is complex. The relation between God and Jesus on the cross is not between the immutable, transcendent God and the human nature of Jesus but *within* God. "What happened on the cross is an event between God and God. It was a deep division in God himself, in so far as God abandoned God and contradicted himself, and at the same time a unity in God, in so far as God was at one with God and corresponded to himself." This dialectical division and reconciliation within God is how the persons of the Trinity become who they are. "These persons constitute themselves in their relationship with each other." The Father and Son constitute one another in their mutual suffering love. "The Son suffers in his love being forsaken by the Father as he dies. The Father suffers in his love the grief of the death of the Son." The Spirit is the spirit of love between the Father and Son.[13] Thus the Trinity is actualized at the cross. Without the cross there would be no Trinity.

11. Jürgen Moltmann, *The Crucified God: The Cross of Christ as the Foundation and Criticism of Christian Theology*, trans. R. A. Wilson and John Bowdon (New York: Harper and Row, 1974), 27. Also Bauckham, "The Crucified God and Auschwitz," chap. 3 in *Moltmann*; "Divine Suffering," chap. 3 in *Theology of Jürgen Moltmann*; Müller-Fahrenholz, "Everything Is Decided by the Cross," chap. 4 in *Kingdom and the Power*.

12. Moltmann, *Crucified God*, 240. Rahner is discussed in chap. 9, above.

13. Moltmann, *Crucified God*, 244–45.

Moltmann proceeds from the analysis of the crucifixion in Hegel's account of Christianity in *Lectures on the Philosophy of Religion.*[14] He follows Hegel (and Böhme) in viewing the existence of God as a dialectical unity that actualizes itself in history. The actualization of the Trinity is not limited to the cross but incorporates all of cosmic history, including evil and death. "If one describes the life of God within the Trinity as the 'history of God' (Hegel), this history of God contains within itself the whole abyss of godforsakenness, absolute death and non-God." Moltmann's inclusion of everything in God enables him to bring together his doctrines of the Trinity, salvation, and the future kingdom. "All human history, however much it may be determined by guilt and death, is taken up into this 'history of God,' i.e. into the Trinity, and integrated into the future of the 'history of God.'"[15] The pieces of his entire theological project are now in place.

Moltmann, however, reverses Hegel in a crucial way. Hegel posits the negation of the Father in the incarnation of the Son and then the negation of the Son in the crucifixion. Both Father and Son are dialectically transformed or "sublated" into the Spirit that lives in the church and Christendom. The three persons do not coexist in communion but are successive modes of Absolute Spirit's relation to the world. Moltmann, in contrast, affirms the ongoing community of three distinct persons, making them the primary reality of God. The one God is an abstraction if distinguished from the event on Golgotha: "'God' is not another nature or a heavenly person or a moral authority, but in fact an 'event.'" He draws an implication for the Christian life from this startling thesis: "One does not simply pray to God as a heavenly Thou, but prays *in* God . . . *in* this event . . . through the Son to the Father in the Spirit."[16] We participate in the "event" of God.

Moltmann does not yet identify his position as panentheism, but the requisite hallmarks are present. First, he positions his theology where panentheism stands, "beyond Theism and Atheism."[17] Traditional theism "thinks of God at man's expense as an all-powerful, perfect and infinite being." Atheism rightly defends human freedom by denying that such a Being exists, but it wrongly deifies humanity. Moltmann affirms God and human freedom but rejects the traditional view of God. Second, Moltmann's alternative, for which he appeals to Hegel, posits that God has two natures: "God is not only other-worldly but also this-worldly; he is not only God,

---

14. See the section on Hegel in chap. 4, above, with its references to the *Lectures on the Philosophy of Religion.*
15. Moltmann, *Crucified God,* 246.
16. Ibid., 247.
17. Ibid., 249–52.

but also man; he is not only rule, authority and law, but the event of suffering, liberating love." He credits process theology with recognizing two
divine natures: "God both transcends the world and is immanent in history,
as process theology says in the bipolar concept of God without trinitarian
thought." Third, God and humans participate in a common history. If we
"think of the Trinity as a dialectical event, indeed as the event of the cross
and then as eschatologically open history," he writes, we can also affirm that
"we participate in the trinitarian process of God's history."[18] Finally, invok-
ing process theology again, Moltmann explores divine *pathos*, God's feeling
our feelings and suffering our pain.[19] In sum, *The Crucified God* develops
central biblical themes using an implicit panentheism adapted mainly from
the dialectical tradition of Hegel.[20]

The Trinity and the Kingdom

The Trinity and the Kingdom is Moltmann's most important work because
it presents an overview of his theological project as a whole. He develops
a full account of the Trinity in relation to God's coming Kingdom—the
creation, liberation, reconciliation, and final consummation of the universe.
He also explicitly adopts the term *panentheism*. Subsequent books amplify
aspects of this comprehensive perspective but change it very little.

Moltmann's doctrine of God does not begin with the one God as classical
theism and philosophical idealism do. Instead "we are beginning with the
trinity of the Persons and shall then go on to ask about the unity." He treats
the three persons, Father, Son, and Holy Spirit, in their mutual relations
and interaction within the world. Thus he proposes "a social doctrine of the
Trinity" based on "the history of the Trinity's relations of fellowship, which
are open to men and women, open to the world." Moltmann's book is rich
with biblical material and Christian theological insight. He intentionally
adopts "panentheistic ideas from the Jewish and the Christian traditions"
as the main source for framing his relational doctrine of the Trinity.[21] His
debt to kabbalism, Böhme, Hegel, Schelling, and Berdyaev is extensive.

    18. Ibid., 255–56. On the relation between Moltmann and process theology, see John O'Donnell,
*Trinity and Temporality: The Christian Doctrine of God in the Light of Process Theology and the Theology of
Hope* (New York: Oxford University Press, 1983).
    19. Moltmann, *Crucified God*, 267–78. Bauckham, "Divine Suffering," chap. 3 in *Theology of Jürgen
Moltmann.*
    20. Bauckham, *Moltmann*, 107; Grenz and Olson, *Twentieth-Century Theology*, 179–82.
    21. Jürgen Moltmann, *The Trinity and the Kingdom: The Doctrine of God*, trans. Margaret Kohl
(San Francisco: Harper and Row, 1981), 19. Bauckham, "The Trinitarian History of God," chap. 4 in

Divine Suffering and the Problem of Evil

Moltmann begins with the theme of *The Crucified God*, encountering the Trinity in divine suffering. "God suffers with us—God suffers from us—God suffers for us: it is this experience of God that reveals the triune God."[22] He draws from several panentheistic sources to articulate a doctrine of *theopathy*, "The Passion of God." In kabbalistic thought, he notes, God is "bipolar." God self-differentiates in going out of himself into the life and suffering of Israel's people to redeem them. The Jewish theologian Abraham Heschel expresses a bipolar view of God in his doctrine of divine pathos.[23] The Anglican theologian C. E. Rolt proposes a view of the Trinity in which divine self-love must be fulfilled by suffering, which entails involvement in evil and posits an "'opposition' within God himself." "We are reminded here of Jakob Böhme," Moltmann observes.[24] The Spanish Christian philosopher Miguel de Unamuno draws from Böhme, Hegel, and Kierkegaard to develop a theology of the infinite sorrow of God. In *The Tragic Sense of Life*, Unamuno argues that tragedy is intrinsic to God's life as well as to creatures. Divine sorrow is inevitable, but so is its culmination in eschatological joy.[25]

Moltmann's main inspiration is Berdyaev's idea of the "tragedy in God,"[26] including his appropriation of Böhme's "dark nature in God" and Schelling's idea that world history is a painful theogonic (God-generating) process. Berdyaev argues that God's eternal love "thirsts" to share itself with its Other, not only the Father for the Son in the Spirit but also with creation. For Berdyaev, Moltmann observes, "the creation of the world is nothing other than 'a history of the divine love between God and his Other self.'" But to love the Other means to allow its freedom, which includes the fallibility and evil of finite creatures. Berdyaev concludes that the existence of God inevitably involves tragic suffering and evil as well as love, goodness, and ultimate triumph.[27] Moltmann's doctrine of divine suffering incorporates Berdyaev's view and the other panentheistic sources mentioned.

Moltmann; "The Holy Spirit in the Trinity," and "The Trinity and Human Freedom," chaps. 7 and 8 in *Theology of Jürgen Moltmann*; Müller-Fahrenholz, "On Unification—The Theology of the Trinity as a Retelling of God's History of Love," chap. 8 in *Kingdom and the Power*.

22. Moltmann, *Trinity and the Kingdom*, 4.

23. Ibid., 27–30.

24. Ibid., 34. C. E. Rolt, *The World's Redemption* (New York: Longmans, Green, 1913).

25. Moltmann, *Trinity and the Kingdom*, 36–42. Miguel de Unamuno, *The Tragic Sense of Life in Men and in Peoples*, trans. J. E. Crawford Flitch (London: Macmillan, 1921).

26. Moltmann, *Trinity and the Kingdom*, 42–47. Berdyaev was presented in chap. 9, above.

27. This theodicy was worked out in Schelling's *Philosophical Inquiries into the Nature of Human Freedom*. See chap. 4, above.

Moltmann connects divine suffering to the problem of evil. He dismisses traditional theism as incapable of a theodicy—an adequate explanation of evil. He asserts that belief in an omnipotent, omniscient, "kindly," transcendent Being is completely incompatible with the suffering of a single child. "A God who lets the innocent suffer and who permits senseless death is not worthy to be called God at all." Instead Moltmann proposes that God and evil must go together and that the problem of evil is only resolved eschatologically in the kingdom. He also rejects the Augustinian notion that evil and suffering are primarily consequences of sin. Instead he chooses the (Neoplatonic) view that finite existence is naturally conflictual: "Initial creation is also a creation capable of suffering, and capable of producing suffering."[28] This natural capacity for suffering, evil, and death is inevitably realized in order that it be transformed by God in Christ. Moltmann does affirm that Christ's death on the cross deals with human sin and guilt, but more basically it expresses the suffering love intrinsic to the divine life.[29]

Divine Freedom, Love, and Need of the World

God's suffering and the problem of evil immediately raise the question of God's freedom. "Is the suffering God free or is he a prisoner of his own history?"[30] Moltmann rejects the Augustinian-Scotist-Reformed view that God is the all-powerful sovereign Lord who is free whether to create a world. He dismisses that notion of freedom as empty. "The person who is truly free no longer has to choose." The position he takes is compatibilism—freedom and necessity are compatible and correlative—which is standard fare in the panentheist tradition: "If we lift the concept of necessity out of the context of compulsive necessity and determination by something external, then in God *necessity* and *freedom* coincide; they are what is for him axiomatic, self-evident." In other words, God is free in creating because creation is the uncoerced expression of his own nature. "It is God's free self-determination, and at the same time the overflowing of his goodness, which belongs to his essential nature."[31] Moltmann even defends divine emanation: "It is

28. Moltmann, *Trinity and the Kingdom*, 47, 51.

29. See also Jürgen Moltmann, "The Apocalyptic Sufferings of Christ," chap. 4 in *The Way of Jesus Christ: Christology in Messianic Terms*, trans. Margaret Kohl (San Francisco: Harper, 1990). Also Bauckham, "Theodicy," chap. 4 in *Theology of Jürgen Moltmann*.

30. Moltmann, *Trinity and the Kingdom*, 52–56, quote at 52.

31. Ibid., 55, 107, 54. Moltmann reiterates this position in several subsequent books without alteration. Thus Jürgen Moltmann, *God in Creation: A New Theology of Creation and the Spirit of God*, trans. Margaret Kohl (San Francisco: Harper and Row, 1985), 75: "There is no external necessity which occasions his creativity, and no inner compulsion which could determine it."

therefore wrong to polemicize continually against the neo-Platonic doctrine of emanation in considering the Christian doctrine of creation."[32]

At issue is not just God's freedom but his love. "Love is a self-evident, unquestionable 'overflowing of goodness' which is therefore never open to choice at any time." The fact that God must love is no limitation of his freedom. Moltmann's section titled "God Is Love" reveals the extent of his solidarity with the tradition of dialectical panentheism. Following Böhme, Hegel, Schelling, and Berdyaev, he interprets God's love dialectically, so that the divine Being includes negativity (Nonbeing) and pain. "When we say 'God *is* love,' then we mean that he is in eternity this process of self-differentiation and self-identification; a process which contains the whole pain of the negative in itself." The dialectical love in God inevitably overflows. Quoting Dionysius and Berdyaev, Moltmann concludes that "God 'needs' the world and man. If God is love, then he neither will nor can be without the one who is his beloved."[33]

Moltmann expands Berdyaev's position by explaining more precisely why God's love requires the world. Perfect love must affirm the Other, which is not possible within the Trinity. "The inner-trinitarian love is the *love of like for like*, not the love for one who is essentially different. It is necessary love, not free love." But God's perfect love is both necessary and free. Thus "he communicates himself to his like *and* to his Other." This is why the immanent Trinity must overflow into creation. "Creation is a part of the eternal love affair between the Father and the Son. . . . Creation exists because the eternal love communicates himself creatively to his Other."[34] Because God is love, the world must exist.

Self-Limitation in God: Creation, Space, and Time

Love affirms the being and freedom of the Other, and God therefore limits himself in relation to the world. Self-limitation is internal to God because

32. Moltmann, *Trinity and the Kingdom*, 113, also 54. *God in Creation*, 75–83, distances itself somewhat from Neoplatonic emanation but still affirms truth in it. God inevitably creates the world but does so by love, not by an act of will or by natural emanation. On this topic, Colin Gunton, "The End of Causality? The Reformers and Their Predecessors," in *The Doctrine of Creation: Essays in Dogmatics, History, and Philosophy* (Edinburgh: T&T Clark, 1997), 63, observes that Moltmann is "a recent heir" of the tradition of Plotinus and Hegel.

33. Moltmann, *Trinity and the Kingdom*, 57–58. *God in Creation*, 75: "God's freedom is not the almighty power for which everything is possible. It is love, which means the self-communication of the good." Grenz and Olson, *Twentieth-Century Theology*, 186, observe that "the deity of God is made ontologically dependent on world history."

34. Moltmann, *Trinity and the Kingdom*, 58–59.

the world is implicit in the divine nature. Moltmann rejects Augustine's classification of creation as an exclusively external act, involving no self-limitation. Creation "is at the same time 'an act of God inwardly,' which means that it is something that God suffers and endures. For God, creation means self-limitation, the withdrawal of himself, that is to say self-humiliation."[35] For Moltmann, humiliation and self-emptying (*kenōsis*) not only pertain to the incarnation of Christ but also inhere originally in God's creating. "The divine kenosis which begins with the creation of the world reaches its perfected and completed form in the incarnation of the Son."[36] For this concept of *kenōsis*, Moltmann appeals to Isaak Dorner, the nineteenth-century theologian who championed Schelling's philosophy and used it to revise the doctrines of divine immutability and the *kenōsis* of Christ.[37]

Moltmann adopts the Jewish kabbalist concept of *zimsum*—divine contraction—to explain divine self-limitation in creation. If God is truly infinite and omnipresent, the argument goes, there can be no "outside" of God. Instead we must "assume a *self-limitation* of the infinite, omnipresent God, preceding his creation. . . . God must have made room for this finitude beforehand, 'in himself.'" The "nothing" or nonbeing that the term *creatio ex nihilo* refers to is the primordial result of divine contraction. "It is only God's withdrawal into himself which gives that *nihil* the space in which God then becomes creatively active." This dialectic of nothingness and creativity, of contraction and expansion in God is very similar to the interaction of the "divine potencies" in the theologies of Böhme and Schelling, whom Moltmann references.[38] The synthesis of God's self-negation and creativity in turn constitutes the time, space, existence, and freedom of finite creatures within God. "Has God not therefore created the world 'in himself,' giving it time *in* his eternity, finitude *in* his infinity, space *in* his omnipresence and freedom *in* his selfless love?" The finite world, with time, space, and all its other transcendental dimensions—they are loving expressions of the divine nature.[39] All these implications of divine self-limitation are worked out more fully in *God in Creation* and considered in the next section.

35. Ibid., 59.

36. Ibid., 118. Moltmann, *God in Creation*, asserts the *kenōsis* of the Spirit.

37. Moltmann, *Trinity and the Kingdom*, 236–39, notes. Dorner is presented in chap. 5, above.

38. Moltmann, *Trinity and the Kingdom*, 109 and 237, notes. The idea of divine contraction is found in Pseudo-Dionysius, Eriugena, Eckhart, and Nicholas of Cusa before their modern heirs.

39. Ibid., 109. Like Böhme, Schelling, Tillich, and Macquarrie, Moltmann observes the aptness of maternal imagery for God's loving generation of creation. "Creation as God's act in and out of God must rather be called a feminine concept, a bringing forth." Moltmann, *God in Creation*, 300, identifies "the panentheistic understanding of the world as the sheltering and nurturing divine environment for everything living" as the common meaning of the symbol of World Mother and the Cosmic Christ.

God-World Mutuality and "Christian Panentheism"

For Moltmann, divine love entails the mutuality of God and world—reciprocal giving and receiving, need and satisfaction. "If God is love, then he does not merely emanate, flow out of himself; he also expects and needs love: his world is intended to be his home." Indeed, Moltmann states that his entire project in *The Trinity and the Kingdom* proceeds "from the assumption that the relationship between God and the world has a *reciprocal* character." Thus the world affects God. "His world puts its impress on God too, through its reactions, its aberrations and its own initiatives."[40] The mutuality of the divine persons among themselves and in their relation with the world is completed in the eschaton. "Everything ends with God's being 'all in all' (1 Cor. 15:28). *God in the world and the world in God. . . . That is the home of the Trinity.*"[41]

Moltmann realizes that these are "panentheistic visions." And so he advocates "Christian panentheism" as the best alternative to "Christian theism" and "Christian pantheism." Christian theism affirms the Creator-creature difference but views creation as an arbitrary act of God's free will. Christian pantheism rightly views creation as natural for God, he concedes, but it loses the independence of creatures. Moltmann concludes that Christian panentheism preserves the best of both theism and pantheism: the Creator-creature distinction, the freedom of creatures, and the necessity of the world for God. "*Christian panentheism*, on the other hand, started from the divine essence: Creation is a fruit for 'his Other' and for the Other's free response to the divine love. That is why the idea of the world is inherent in the nature of God himself from eternity." Panentheism is the correct position because it avoids both the arbitrariness of classical theism and the determinism of pantheism. "One way of reconciling the elements of truth in Christian theism and Christian pantheism emerges when we cease to interpret God's liberty as arbitrariness, and the nature of God as a divine natural law. . . . In God *necessity* and *freedom* coincide."[42] Thus Moltmann champions what he himself labels Christian panentheism.

The very concept of God entails panentheism, according to Moltmann. "For it is impossible to conceive of a God who is not a creative God. A non-creative God would be imperfect compared with the God who is eternally creative. And if God's eternal being is love, then the divine love is also more

---

See also Moltmann, "The Motherly Father and the Power of His Mercy," in *History and the Triune God*, 19–25.

40. Moltmann, *Trinity and the Kingdom*, 99, 98.
41. Ibid., 105.
42. Ibid., 105–7.

blessed in giving than in receiving. God cannot find bliss in eternal self-love if selflessness is part of love's very nature."[43] Creator-creature mutuality is the key reason Moltmann gives for embracing Christian panentheism.

The Trinity

The complexity of Creator-creature mutuality is detailed in Moltmann's extensive account of the economic Trinity—each of the divine persons in correlation with the others as they cooperate in the creation, liberation, and consummation of the world. Because all three persons are involved in all phases of history, Moltmann speaks of "Trinitarian Creation," "Trinitarian Incarnation," and "Trinitarian Glorification."[44]

But his approach makes the unity of God a challenge. If Deity is constituted of three different persons,[45] how is God One? The only alternative Moltmann sees is to begin with divine oneness and then account for the three persons. He thinks that this approach reflects "the philosophical postulate of absolute unity" instead of Scripture. "If the biblical testimony is chosen as point of departure, then we shall have to start from the three Persons of the history of Christ. If philosophical logic is made the starting point, then the enquirer proceeds from the One God." Here Moltmann apparently overlooks the fact that the One God is also prior in the Old Testament Scriptures. In any case, he chooses to make divine unity the problem.[46] His proposed solution has two components: one eschatological, the other perichoretic.

To begin, Moltmann argues that the unity of God is eschatological. God is completely One only in the fulfillment of the kingdom. "The unity of the Father, the Son and the Spirit is then the eschatological question about the consummation of the trinitarian history of God."[47] This means that God is three but not yet fully One. The more history progresses, the more God becomes One. Since divine unification involves not only the three persons but also creation, Moltmann's trinitarianism is panentheistic as well as eschatological. God's full self-unity depends upon his complete communion with creation.

Eschatological triunity has implications for the relation of the economic and the immanent Trinity. Moltmann still identifies them, following Rahner's Rule, but he distinguishes them as well. The immanent Trinity is God's

---

43. Ibid., 106.
44. Titles of summary sections, ibid., chap. 4, "The World of the Trinity."
45. Ibid., 189: "The 'three Persons' are different, not merely in their relations to one another, but also in respect of their character as Persons."
46. Ibid., 149.
47. Ibid.

perfect triunity in eternity. The economic Trinity is the actualization of that essence in world history. "The economic Trinity completes and perfects itself to immanent Trinity when the history and experience of salvation are completed and perfected. When everything is 'in God' and 'God is all in all,' then the economic Trinity is raised into and transcended in the immanent Trinity." The economic Trinity is not merely the temporal expression of the eternal immanent Trinity, as in classical theism, but actually shapes it. "The economic Trinity not only reveals the immanent Trinity; it also has a retroactive effect on it."[48] The dual aspects of the triune nature are mutually effective: God's triune essence shapes his trinitarian existence and his trinitarian existence actualizes his triune essence. Like most dynamic panentheism, Moltmann's God has two interactive natures.

Perichoresis—mutual indwelling or communion—is the second aspect of Moltmann's account of divine unity. God is not one Substance, Being, or Absolute Subject. God's oneness consists in the perfect communion of the persons: "The concept of God's unity cannot in the trinitarian sense be fitted into the homogeneity of the one divine substance, or into the identity of the absolute subject either; and least of all into one of the three Persons of the Trinity. It must be perceived in the *perichoresis* of the divine Persons."[49] The three persons are in such complete and intimate communion that they constitute one divine reality.

Moltmann acknowledges the danger of tritheism—affirming three divine beings without ontological unity. To avoid this heresy, he adopts an ontology of persons that is social: personal existence is essentially communal and developmental. Surveying the concepts of the divine person in the history of trinitarian theology, he discovers in Hegel the view he seeks. "The substantial understanding of person (Boethius) and the relational understanding of person (Augustine) was now expanded by the historical understanding of person (Hegel). The Persons do not merely 'exist' in their relations; they also realize themselves in one another by virtue of self-surrendering love." As persons in this sense, Father, Son, and Holy Spirit constitute One God. "By virtue of their eternal love they live in one another to such an extent, and dwell in one another to such an extent, that they are one. . . . The unity of the triunity lies in the eternal perichoresis of the trinitarian persons."[50] Notice that this is Moltmann's explanation of the unity of God's eternal essence, which, as noted above, is not yet identical with his existence. Divine

---

48. Ibid., 160–61.
49. Ibid., 149–50.
50. Ibid., 174–75. Also Yoo, "Perichoresis and Unity," in *Spirit of Liberation*, 55–64.

existence in history is alienated from the divine essence. Divine perichoresis is not yet complete, and so God is not yet actually One.

This account of divine unity does not settle the issue of tritheism. Although he adopts Hegel's ontology of persons, Moltmann rejects his dialectical theory of divine unity. He substitutes perichoresis for dialectic. This enables him to avoid Hegel's trinitarian modalism (i.e., the persons are three ways in which the one God relates). But it does not provide a strong ontological account of essential divine unity. Hegel's social ontology implies that persons are essentially interdependent and that communities are ontological units that are more than aggregates of individuals. But his analysis does not make social units anything other than communities of persons. To illustrate, a family is ontologically real, but even a perfect family unit is not an analogy for the oneness of God. In the Christian tradition, perichoresis does not constitute divine unity but expresses it. It is doubtful whether Moltmann's idea of essential triunity is an adequate account of God's oneness.

In sum, *The Trinity and the Kingdom* elaborates Moltmann's trinitarian panentheism. The entire history and destiny of the world are included in the life of the Trinity. "To throw open the circulatory movement of the divine light and the divine relationships, and to take men and women, with the whole of creation, into the life-stream of the triune God: that is the meaning of creation, reconciliation and glorification."[51]

God in Creation: Perichoresis Universalized

God in Creation is Moltmann's doctrine of the Spirit's role in creating and sustaining the world toward its consummation. It elaborates the perspective set out in *The Trinity and the Kingdom*.[52] Several aspects of his panentheism are expanded, especially the role and scope of perichoresis.

The Universality of Perichoresis

The mutuality of God and the cosmos is axiomatic for Moltmann already in *The Crucified God*. In *The Trinity and the Kingdom* he introduces the classical term *perichoresis* to speak of the mutual relations among the divine persons in God. In *God in Creation* Moltmann develops this theme further by extending

51. Moltmann, *Trinity and the Kingdom*, 178.
52. Moltmann, *God in Creation*, xii. Bauckham, "Creation and Evolution," chap. 9 in *Theology of Jürgen Moltmann*; Müller-Fahrenholz, "Creation: The Wonder of Existence," chap. 9 in *The Kingdom and the Power*.

the concept of perichoresis to all relations, including mutual interpenetration among beings in the world and their mutual interpenetration with God. "All relationships which are analogous to God reflect the primal, reciprocal indwelling and mutual interpenetration of the trinitarian perichoresis: God *in* the world and the world *in* God; heaven and earth *in* the kingdom of God pervaded by his glory; soul and body united *in* the life-giving Spirit to a human whole; woman and man *in* the kingdom of unconditional and unconditioned love, freed to be true and complete human beings."[53] For Moltmann, all things consist in a vast perichoretic network. Perichoresis is the structural dynamic of all reality. It functions as Moltmann's implicit ontology: to be is to be perichoretically involved. Since the God-world relation is perichoretic, Moltmann's mature theology can be labeled *perichoretic panentheism*.

Zimsum *and the Nothingness of God*

Moltmann continues to posit an oppositional dynamic in God that issues in creation. "The trinitarian doctrine of creation therefore does not start from an antithesis between God and the world. . . . It proceeds differently, starting from an immanent *tension* in God himself. . . . So in God's creation of the world we can perceive a self-differentiation and a self-identification on God's part."[54] Moltmann again appeals to the kabbalist notion of *zimsum* and ideas of Nicholas of Cusa, Schelling, and others to derive finite space, time, existence, and power from the essential tension he locates in God.

For Moltmann, the "nothing" of creation *ex nihilo* is the primal consequence of God's self-limitation or self-negation. "God makes room for his creation by withdrawing his presence . . . a partial negation of the divine Being." "Nothingness" is therefore "the non-being of the Creator." Moltmann develops this idea in the vein of Böhme and Schelling as a potentially destructive, demonic force. "The *nihil* in which God creates his creation is God-forsakenness, hell, absolute death; and it is against the threat of this that he maintains his creation in life." A threat to creation lurks in God himself. "Creation is therefore threatened, not merely by its own non-being, but also by the non-being of God its Creator—that is to say, by Nothingness itself." So God must restrain his own negativity to maintain the creation in existence. God deals with it by turning it into something positive. It is God's own self-negation that both separates and binds Father and Son on the cross so that reconciliation and redemption result. In the end, the negative dynamic in God's creativity is transformed into

53. Moltmann, *God in Creation*, 17.
54. Ibid., 14–15.

his eternal kingdom. "*Creatio ex nihilo* in the beginning is the preparation and promise of the redeeming *annihilatio nihil* [annihilation of nonbeing], from which the eternal being of creation proceeds."[55] Given the inevitable triumph of God's goodness, however, "there is no 'dark side' to God—no side where he could also be conceived of as the destroyer of his own creation and of his own being as Creator."[56] Eternal death and hell would result only if creatures could isolate themselves from God's redemptive transformation of nothingness. Like Böhme, Schelling, Berdyaev, and the modern Neoplatonic tradition, Moltmann views history as the means by which God actualizes and finally transcends the primordial nonbeing inherent in himself.

Zimsum, *Time, and Space*

God in Creation devotes an entire chapter each to time and space as aspects of God's self-limitation. In response to Augustine's notion that God is eternal and creation is temporal, Moltmann counters that time originates in God's self-limitation. God "withdraws his eternity into himself in order to give his creation its time. Between his essential eternity on the one hand and creaturely temporality on the other, there is therefore *God's own time* which he designated for his creation through his creative resolve, and the temporal era of creation which is thereby inaugurated."[57] Although eternal in essence, God as Creator makes himself temporal and is involved in time.

Regarding space, Moltmann agrees with the "pan-entheistic" idea of the seventeenth-century Neoplatonists Henry More and Isaac Newton that space is an attribute of God. But he rejects their notion of absolute space, which implies that space is an aspect of God's eternal essence. Instead Moltmann argues it is an aspect of God's creative self-limitation: "The created world does not exist in 'the absolute space' of the divine Being; it exists in the space God yielded up for it through his creative resolve."[58] Time and space are parallel dimensions of divine contraction.

Zimsum, *Heaven, and Earth*

Moltmann also uses the concept of *zimsum*, self-contraction, to explain heaven and earth as modes of divine power. If God is all-powerful, creaturely power requires the limitation of divine power. Moltmann defines heaven as

55. Ibid., 87–90.
56. Ibid., 168.
57. Ibid., 116–17.
58. Ibid., 156.

the creative power of God, and earth as the self-limiting way God actualizes his power. Just as time and space result from divine contraction, "so the
divine potentialities and potencies described in the term 'heaven' are qualified
through God's designation of himself to be Creator: and they are unfolded
and disclosed by the Creator in the time and in the space of creation." Thus
creation is "an *ec-static* reality" and an "open system" whose foundation and
unity is God's creative, self-limited power. "We call the determined side of
this system 'earth,' the undetermined side 'heaven.'"[59] Details of Moltmann's
panentheism are now clearer. Time, space, heaven, and earth are "in God"
because they are self-modifications of God but are not part of his eternal
nature. Moltmann's account of contracted divine potentialities and potencies
echoes the dialectical "divine potencies" of Böhme and Schelling.

Cosmic Evolution and "Trinitarian Panentheism"

Moltmann focuses on the role of the Spirit in cosmic evolution much
more than on Christ, who is Teilhard's emphasis. In the Spirit, God-cosmos
immanence and transcendence are mutual.

> All individual systems of matter and life, and all their complexes of com-
> munication as a whole, "ex-ist" into a transcendence and subsist out of that
> transcendence. If we call this transcendence of the world "God," we can then
> tentatively say: The world in its different parts and as a whole is a system open
> to God. God is its extra-worldly encompassing *milieu*, from which, and in
> which, it lives. God is its extra-worldly *forecourt*, into which it is evolving. . . .
> We then have to understand God for his part as a Being open to the world.
> He encompasses the world with the possibilities of his Being, and interpen-
> etrates it with the powers of his Spirit. Through the energies of his Spirit, he
> is present in the world and immanent in each individual system.[60]

This mutual immanence and transcendence of God and the world fits
our definition of modern dynamic panentheism perfectly.

In *God in Creation* Moltmann continues to identify his position as "trinitarian panentheism" in distinction from monotheism, pantheism, and even the
"differentiated panentheism" of the Spinozan-romantic World-Soul. "The
trinitarian concept of creation integrates the elements of truth in monotheism and pantheism. In the panentheistic view, God having created the
world, also dwells in it, and conversely the world which he has created exists

59. Ibid., 166, 163.
60. Ibid., 205–6.

in him. This is a concept which can really only be thought and described in trinitarian terms."[61]

The Coming of God

God in Creation looks forward to the complete consummation of all things in God. *The Coming of God* is Moltmann's eschatology—his account of the final fulfillment of human individuals, the cosmos, and the Triune God in the eternal kingdom.[62]

Consummation: Universal Salvation

Moltmann is emphatically universalistic: all creatures will be saved. God will, however, condemn all sin. "In that Judgment all sins, every wickedness and every act of violence, the whole injustice of this murderous and suffering world, will be condemned and annihilated." But God will save all creatures, even the devil. "In the divine Judgment all sinners, the wicked and the violent, the murderers and the children of Satan, the Devil and the fallen angels will be liberated and saved from their deadly perdition through transformation into their true, created being." The reason for universal salvation is God's love—the same love that motivates creation: "God remains true to himself, and does not give up what he has once created and affirmed, or allow it to be lost."[63] Moltmann explicitly ties the salvation and fulfillment of all things to the cross of Christ, highlighting a basic theme of his theology since *The Crucified God*: "*The true Christian foundation for the hope of universal salvation is the theology of the cross, and the realistic consequence of the theology of the cross can only be the restoration of all things.*"[64]

Consummation: Zimsum Reversed

God accomplishes the consummation of creation by a positive reversal of his creative self-limitation. In the beginning he restricted or "negated"

---

61. Ibid., 98; also 102–3, 206–12, 300.

62. Jürgen Moltmann, *The Coming of God: Christian Eschatology*, trans. Margaret Kohl (Minneapolis: Fortress, 1996). Also Richard Bauckham, ed., *God Will Be All in All: The Eschatology of Jürgen Moltmann* (Edinburgh: T&T Clark, 1999), which contains several articles by Moltmann responding to analyses of his eschatology. Also Müller-Fahrenholz, "What Remains Is Expectation: *The Coming of God*," chap. 12 in *Kingdom and the Power*.

63. Moltmann, *The Coming of God*, 255. It is not clear how God can both guarantee this outcome and continue to allow genuine creaturely freedom.

64. Ibid., 251.

himself in order to have time, space, being, and power for creation. In the end he negates this self-negation. God "re-expands" to include within himself the creation that was born and matured in the ontological place he had provided by contracting himself. *Zimsum* is reversed. Just as the primordial moment sprang from God's creative self-restriction, "so the eschatological moment will spring from the resolve to redeem and the 'derestriction' of God determined upon in that." God does not simply de-create or absorb creation. He takes it into himself fully actualized. "God does not de-restrict himself in order to annihilate his creation, and to put himself in its place and its time; his purpose is to dwell in his creation and in it to be 'all in all.'" Time and space are taken into God's eternity and omnipresence, losing their limitations. The same un-restriction that fulfills creation completes God as well. "God completes in himself his eschatological de-restriction of himself: he appears in his creation in the splendour of his unveiled glory."[65] In dialectical language, the action by which God fulfills himself in all things involves a negation of the self-negation by which he originally created.

Consummation: Perichoretic Panentheism Perfected

What results is "the completion of history and creation, its perfecting into the kingdom of glory in which God himself 'indwells' his creation." There is to be "a new divine presence" in creation reminiscent of the rabbinic-kabbalistic doctrine of Shechinah, the indwelling glory of God. "The Creator no longer remains over against his creation. He dwells in it, and finds in it his rest. . . . It is interpenetrated by divine presence, and participates in the inexhaustible fulness of God's life."[66] The relationship is mutual because the world also dwells in God: "A mutual indwelling of the world in God and God in the world will come into being." This mutuality is so complete that God shares creaturely attributes and creatures share divine attributes, "a kind of cosmic *perichoresis* of divine and cosmic attributes." More precisely, "created beings participate in the divine attributes of eternity and omnipresence, just as the indwelling God has participated in their limited time and their restricted space."[67]

Moltmann distinguishes his position from pantheism by maintaining the difference between God and world. "God remains God, and the world remains creation. Through their mutual indwellings, they remain unmingled and undivided." Perichoresis is the guarantee. It entails the continued exis-

---

65. Ibid., 294–95.
66. Ibid., 280, 295.
67. Ibid., 295, 307.

tence of God's creatures and precludes pantheistic homogeneity. "The concept of mutual interpenetration makes it possible to preserve both the unity and the difference of what is diverse in kind: God and human being, heaven and earth, person and nature, the spiritual and the sensuous." Human autonomy coincides with divine sovereignty. "God's rule over them is simultaneously their participation in that rule. That can be regarded as the reconciliation of the sovereignty of God and human freedom."[68]

The perfected perichoresis of God and the world exemplifies panentheism perfectly.[69] God and the world remain ontologically distinct and transcend each other. But they are also mutually immanent and cooperative. This final outcome is implicit in the eternal nature of God.

Moltmann's Panentheism as Christian Theology

Jürgen Moltmann offers the most fully articulated, explicitly panentheistic Christian theology in history. It is panentheistic because the perichoretic mutuality of God and world is ontologically constitutive for both. It is trinitarian because Father, Son, and Holy Spirit develop in identity and unity through their involvement in the world. It is eschatological because the fullness and unity of the Trinity coincide with the complete perichoresis of God and creation in the consummation of the kingdom.[70]

The topics and content of Moltmann's work are based in Scripture and the Christian theological tradition. The philosophical framework of his theology is the legacy of Neoplatonic dialectical ontology, projected into God by Böhme and historicized by Hegel and Schelling.[71] Moltmann maintains the primacy of the Christian faith and uses philosophy to systematize its

68. Ibid., 307, 278, 318–19. Yoo, *Spirit of Liberation,* 207–9, however, argues that the reversal of *zimsum* leaves Moltmann's panentheism "dangerously close to the brink of pantheism." His "panentheism can hardly be distinguished from pantheism."

69. In spite of Moltmann's tendency to speak of God's indwelling the world rather than the world's being in God, he finally emphasizes both in terms of "reciprocal perichoresis." See Moltmann, "The World in God or God in the World? Response to Richard Bauckham," in *God Will Be All in All,* ed. Bauckham, 35–41.

70. Moltmann's panentheism is most fully addressed by Grenz and Olson, *Twentieth-Century Theology,* 179–86; and Yoo, *Spirit of Liberation,* 37, 207–9.

71. Consider two recent examples of his appropriation of this tradition. Moltmann defends Giordano Bruno's view of God and world in Jürgen Moltmann, "From the Closed World to the Infinite Universe," in *Science and Wisdom,* trans. Margaret Kohl (Minneapolis: Fortress, 2003), 158–71. In "Tao—the Chinese Mystery of the World," ibid., 172–93, he relates the Neoplatonic idea that "everything comes from God—everything goes to God" to the Christian tradition, Hegel, and then to Taoism: "We interpret the triad oneness–twoness–threeness . . . as the 'self-evolving process' of the Tao" (189). See chap. 9, above, for other attempts to relate Western and non-Western panentheism.

doctrines. He does not, like Hegel, assimilate Christianity into philosophy or, like Schelling, into religion.

But this philosophical tradition gives distinctive shape to Moltmann's theological project as a whole. The dialectical or creative-oppositional dynamic it posits in God entails a duality and tension in the divine nature itself; it entails that God requires a world, that he actualizes his implicitly triune nature in world history, that creating the world inevitably actualizes evil, that divine self-actualization inevitably involves the suffering and redemption of the world, and that the fulfillment of God requires and includes the fulfillment of the whole world.

This overall theological perspective is clearly Neoplatonic when compared, for example, with the Augustinian-Reformed tradition of Christianity. In that tradition God is perfectly and eternally triune, good, loving, omniscient, omnipotent, and sovereignly free whether or not he creates a world; he is free whether to permit a fall; and he is therefore fully gracious and agapic in the love by which he creates, sustains, redeems, and perfects the world. Although they affirm many of the same basic doctrines, these are two quite different understandings of the Christian faith as a whole. Moltmann was educated as a Reformed theologian, but he abandoned that tradition early in his career and has not returned.

II

Pannenberg's Panentheistic Force Field

Is Pannenberg a Panentheist?

It is easy to assume that Wolfhart Pannenberg is a panentheist because his theology is similar to Moltmann's in many ways.[1] Both men begin by affirming that the God of the Bible is actively involved in history as the power of the future. Both develop theological systems focusing on the Trinity and its inclusion of all things in the kingdom of God. And both employ post-Hegelian philosophy to articulate Christian theologies that challenge Ernst Bloch, Marxist humanism, and scientific naturalism.[2] One might expect Pannenberg to champion panentheism as enthusiastically as Moltmann.

But he explicitly rejects it: "The trinitarian theism of traditional Christian theology is therefore still superior to the vagueness and misleading implications of the notion of panentheism."[3] Scholarly literature is consistent with

---

1. For comparison, see Roger Olson, "Trinity and Eschatology: The Historical Being of God in Jürgen Moltmann and Wolfhart Pannenberg," *Scottish Journal of Theology* 36 (1983): 213–27.

2. Wolfhart Pannenberg, "The God of Hope," in *Basic Questions in Theology*, trans. George Kehm and R. A. Wilson, 3 vols. (vols. 1–2, Philadelphia: Fortress, 1970–1971; vol. 3, London: SCM, 1973), 2:234–49, exemplifies the similarities. His eschatological ontology of God as "the power of the future" (242–43) and his critique of Bloch are very similar to Moltmann's. Pannenberg also asserts that "the being of God and that of the kingdom are identical, since the being of God is his lordship" (240) and that "*the doctrine of the Trinity* is the seal of the pure futurity of God" (249). The ontological correlation of the triune God and the history of the world is a lifelong emphasis of both thinkers.

3. Wolfhart Pannenberg, comments posted January 2005, www.metanexus.net/metanexus_online/printer_friendly.asp?8798, on the Metanexus Institute website, as one of the reviews and commendations in the book announcement of Philip Clayton and Arthur Peacocke, eds., *In Whom We Live and Move and Have Our Being: Panentheistic Reflections on God's Presence in a Scientific World* (Grand Rapids: Eerdmans, 2003). He also denies being a panentheist in Wolfhart Pannenberg, *Introduction to Systematic Theology* (Grand Rapids: Eerdmans, 1991), 45.

this assertion. He is rarely identified as a panentheist, and some commentators deny that he is.[4]

Nevertheless, this chapter argues that Pannenberg is implicitly panentheistic in spite of his rejection of the "vague and misleading" kinds. The following overview of his lifelong theological project notes the symptoms of panentheism in his work. The subsequent study of his mature *Systematic Theology* confirms the diagnosis. Specifically, Pannenberg locates the existence of the world within the triune life of God, which he thinks of as an infinite, all-inclusive force field.

An Overview of His Life and Theology

Pannenberg was born in 1928 in a part of Germany that is now in Poland. He survived World War II and lived for a time under Communism.[5] He became a Christian as a young man through an unexpected mystical experience, a Christian teacher, and a growing conviction that Christianity provides the most satisfying answers to the perennial human questions. He studied philosophy at university, then theology with Karl Barth, and earned a doctorate in theology at Heidelberg. He taught at a Lutheran seminary and the University of Mainz and was professor of theology at the University of Munich from 1968 until his retirement in 1994. Pannenberg developed his theology over four decades in numerous articles[6] and books,[7] culminating in his three-volume *Systematic Theology*.[8] This chapter first provides an

4. Pannenberg is never mentioned as a panentheist in Clayton and Peacocke, eds., *In Whom We Live*, although it is the most diverse and comprehensive anthology on panentheism to date. Stanley J. Grenz and Roger E. Olson, *Twentieth-Century Theology: God and the World in a Transitional Age* (Downers Grove, IL: InterVarsity, 1992), identify a number of theologians as panentheists, but not Pannenberg. Elsewhere Grenz denies that he is a panentheist: Stanley J. Grenz, *Reason for Hope: The Systematic Theology of Wolfhart Pannenberg* (New York: Oxford University Press, 1990), 211.

5. Wolfhart Pannenberg, "An Autobiographical Sketch," in *The Theology of Wolfhart Pannenberg: Twelve American Critiques, with an Autobiographical Essay and Response*, ed. Carl Braaten and Philip Clayton (Minneapolis: Augsburg, 1988), 11–18.

6. Collections of earlier essays are found in Pannenberg, *Basic Questions*. For a bibliography complete to 1988, see Philip Clayton, "A Pannenberg Bibliography," in *Theology of Wolfhart Pannenberg*, ed. Braaten and Clayton, 337–42.

7. Important are Wolfhart Pannenberg, *Jesus—God and Man* (1964), trans. Lewis Wilkins and Duane Priebe (Philadelphia: Westminster, 1968); *The Idea of God and Human Freedom* (1971), trans. R. A. Wilson (Philadelphia: Westminster, 1973); *Theology and the Philosophy of Science* (1973), trans. Francis McDonagh (Philadelphia: Westminster, 1976); *Anthropology in Theological Perspective* (1983), trans. Matthew O'Connell (Philadelphia: Westminster, 1985); and *Metaphysics and the Idea of God* (1988), trans. Philip Clayton (Grand Rapids: Eerdmans, 1990).

8. Wolfhart Pannenberg, *Systematic Theology*, ed. Geoffrey Bromiley, 3 vols. (Grand Rapids: Eerdmans, 1991–1998), a translation of *Systematische Theologie* (1988–1993).

overview of his project as a whole. Then it highlights the elements of panentheism implicit in his theology as it developed, including the key concept
of his complete system, the divine force field.[9]

The Goal, Epistemology, and Methodology of His Theology

Like Moltmann, the young Pannenberg envisioned a Christian theology
that could challenge the scientific materialism, Marxist humanism, and
religious relativism of the mid-twentieth century. Much more than Moltmann, he has emphasized that philosophical reflection on science and history
provides a rational foundation for the truth that is proclaimed in Scripture,
celebrated in the church's worship, and articulated in Christian theology—
that the God manifest in the historical Jesus Christ is the Lord of all reality
and ought to be worshiped by all humans. The main themes of this lifelong
project are evident in his earliest publications.

Pannenberg's 1961 essay "What Is Truth?" outlines the epistemology
he uses to make his case. Truth is not eternal and changeless, as in Greek
philosophy, but dynamic and historical, as in Hebrew religion. Absolute
truth is the ultimate synthesis of all particular truths, a coherent totality
that develops through time. Particular truths, in turn, have their meaning
and truth value only within the emerging whole, whose final content lies
in the unrealized future. But if the final truth is future, then how is true
knowledge possible in the present? Pannenberg regards Hegel's system as
"the most significant attempt at a solution to this problem." Hegel rightly
sees that absolute truth, which he attributes to God, can be attained only
at the end of history. But Pannenberg raises an "earthshaking objection" to
Hegel: his absolute rationalism implicitly closes the future, thus distorting
the truth and misrepresenting God. Pannenberg points out that subsequent philosophy has emphasized Hegel's failure, but it has not solved the
problem he posed. Facing this situation, Pannenberg makes the startling
assertion that Christianity provides the solution to "the impasses of the
Hegelian conception of truth." It does so by proclaiming that although
absolute truth will be revealed fully only at the end of history, God has
already revealed ultimate reality *proleptically*—in a partial and anticipatory
way—in the resurrection of Jesus Christ.[10] His resurrection is the beginning

---

9. Christiaan Mostert, *God and the Future: Wolfhart Pannenberg's Eschatological Doctrine of God* (New
York: T&T Clark, 2002); Grenz, *Reason for Hope*; and David Polk, *On the Way to God: An Exploration into
the Theology of Wolfhart Pannenberg* (Lanham, MD: University Press of America, 1989), are studies of his
mature system. Grenz and Olson, *Twentieth-Century Theology*, 186–99, is a good short introduction.

10. Pannenberg, "What Is Truth?" in *Basic Questions*, 2:1–27, quotes at 21–22, 24.

of the end of all things—their fulfillment in God. Thus it is the basis for true knowledge in the present.

Pannenberg does not regard his appeal to Christianity as arbitrary or irrational. In fact, he continues Hegel's quest for knowledge of universal truth. But he develops a less rationalistic method than Hegel's.[11] In dialogue with the hermeneutics (theories of interpretation) of Wilhelm Dilthey, Heidegger, Gadamer, and Jürgen Habermas, Pannenberg sketches a more open method of understanding history. By construing the data of the past and present as integral parts of a developing whole that is intelligible but not yet complete, it is possible to draw tentative but justified conclusions that anticipate the future trajectory of the whole. In other words, Pannenberg replaces Hegel's dialectical logic with a dialogical historical hermeneutics that correlates knowledge of parts within the developing whole. Applying this method, he asserts that the resurrection of Jesus Christ offers the key to universal knowledge because it has already revealed the final future of history. "Hegel was unable to see this because the eschatological character of the message of Jesus was hidden to him."[12] In this way Pannenberg uses his philosophical method to prepare the way for the Christian faith.

Philosophical Theology Supports the Christian Faith

But what if the gospel, and thus the resurrection, is just a brilliant fiction? Pannenberg is willing to test the faith on the field of rationality. Christian proclamation is not "mere assertion" but "derived from an experience of God" that is "capable of verification."[13] He supports his historical-critical defense of the Judeo-Christian proclamation with an extensive foundation in philosophical theology, which we therefore briefly summarize.

Pannenberg's philosophical theology as a whole is broadly Hegelian in scope and structure. It considers how God manifests himself implicitly in nature. It traces how nature culminates in humanity. It then follows how human culture and history peak in religion, where God reveals himself explicitly. We now turn to a brief summary of his philosophy of nature, philosophical anthropology, and philosophy of religion to show how Pannenberg argues that all things point to God.

11. Philip Clayton, "Anticipation and Theological Method," in *Theology of Wolfhart Pannenberg*, ed. Braaten and Clayton, 122–50, is an insightful exposition and critique.

12. Pannenberg, "Hermeneutic and Universal History" (1963) and "On Historical and Theological Hermeneutic" (1964), in *Basic Questions*, 1:96–136, 137–81, quote at 135.

13. Pannenberg, "The Question of God," ibid., 2:201–33, quote at 206–7.

Pannenberg's philosophy of nature and God is set forth in two books: *Theology and the Philosophy of Science* and *Toward a Theology of Nature*.[14] Most noteworthy is his concept of a *force field*, which is basic to his theology of nature and eventually to his whole systematic theology. "The field concept could be used in theology to make the effective presence of God in every single phenomenon intelligible."[15] Applying his part-whole hermeneutics, he points out that the special sciences raise philosophical questions about nature and human knowledge of it. Addressing these questions, philosophy in turn points toward theology because scientific knowledge of nature eventually raises the question of an ultimate Ground, God. Thus science is not epistemologically self-sufficient and cannot be used to defend atheism.

Pannenberg's philosophy of humanity and God is worked out in two books, *What Is Man?* and *Anthropology in Theological Perspective*.[16] The latter work is a comprehensive reflection on "the phenomena of human existence as investigated in human biology, psychology, cultural anthropology, or sociology and examines the findings of these disciplines with an eye to implications that may be relevant to religion and theology."[17] Using his part-whole method, Pannenberg argues that the contribution of the special disciplines toward an integral understanding of human existence inevitably poses questions about the human spirit that are uniquely addressed by the world religions and especially by the Christian proclamation.

His philosophical analysis of religion clears a reasonable path to God's revelation in Jesus Christ. He begins from the human intuition of infinity: "Human subjectivity in its infinite self-transcendence . . . always presupposes an infinity transcending itself."[18] Although modern atheists, such as Ludwig Feuerbach, Sigmund Freud, and Bloch, allege that the idea of transcendent infinity is a mere anthropomorphic projection, Pannenberg counters that the phenomenology of religion suggests that the Infinite, which the religions call God, is real. In addition, religion offers widely attested evidence of a *personal* God because humans genuinely seem to encounter a free, nonmanipulable, intentional power that transcends them. Religions reasonably interpret this power as personal because freedom and intentionality are key characteristics

14. Wolfhart Pannenberg, *Toward a Theology of Nature: Essays on Science and Faith*, ed. Ted Peters (Louisville: Westminster/John Knox, 1993).

15. Pannenberg, "The Doctrine of Creation and Modern Science" (1988), ibid., 39.

16. Wolfhart Pannenberg, *What Is Man? Contemporary Anthropology in Theological Perspective* (1964), trans. Duane Priebe (Philadelphia: Fortress, 1970).

17. Pannenberg, *Anthropology in Theological Perspective*, 21.

18. Pannenberg, "Types of Atheism and Their Theological Significance" (1960), in *Basic Questions*, 2:184–200, 191.

of personhood.[19] Thus the phenomenology of religion suggests that "man participates in the personal reality of the divine," not that the concept of God is mere anthropomorphism.[20] For this reason, Pannenberg concludes, *dogmatic* atheism is uncritical and philosophically untenable. He argues extensively that the history of religions is an implicit quest for the God of Jesus Christ.[21]

In sum, Pannenberg has articulated a post-Hegelian philosophical theology of nature, humanity, and religion to prepare a way for proclamation of Jesus Christ.

The Historical Truth of Christian Revelation

But Pannenberg has not waited to proclaim the gospel until the rational way is complete. He asserts the presence of the Christian God in universal history already in "Dogmatic Theses on the Doctrine of Revelation" (1961).[22] Countering Barth's supernatural view of revelation and all those who iso-late redemptive history (*Heilsgeschichte*) from universal history, Pannenberg explicitly aligns himself with Lessing, Herder, Schleiermacher, Hegel, and Schelling, for whom "the totality of reality in its temporal development" is "the self-communication of God."[23] Following them, he affirms that God is actually present in nature and history. He insists, however, that redemptive history—God's particular activity in Israel and in Jesus Christ—is not only embedded in world history but is also its central focus, meaning, and goal. Christianity cannot be supplanted by religion or philosophy. He further as-serts that God has manifested himself empirically, universally, and sufficiently in the historical event of Jesus's resurrection. "It is through the resurrection that the God of Israel has substantiated his deity in an ultimate way and is now manifest as the God of all men."[24] Although absolute proof awaits the eschaton, Pannenberg claims that the witness of Scripture, the church's

---

19. Pannenberg, "The Question of God," 231. Pannenberg agrees with Fichte, Feuerbach, Nietz-sche, and Heidegger that traditional theism's view of God as a transcendent, self-conscious, personal Being is dead. But he defends a more current notion of a personal God.

20. Pannenberg, "God of Hope," 2:244–46.

21. Pannenberg, "Toward a Theology of the History of Religions," in *Basic Questions*, 2:65–118. Schleiermacher, Hegel, and Schelling also took this line. See Carl Braaten, "The Place of Christianity among the World Religions: Wolfhart Pannenberg's Theology of Religion and the History of Religions," in *Theology of Wolfhart Pannenberg*, ed. Braaten and Clayton, 287–312.

22. Wolfhart Pannenberg, "Dogmatic Theses on the Doctrine of Revelation" and the introduction in *Revelation as History*, ed. Wolfhart Pannenberg, trans. David Granskou (New York: Macmillan, 1968). This book includes like-minded articles by several young colleagues.

23. Pannenberg, introduction, ibid., 16.

24. Pannenberg, "Dogmatic Theses," 142.

proclamation and worship, and theology's explanation of God's activity in history are sufficient evidence for humans to recognize that the truth of Christianity is the answer to their ultimate questions.[25]

Pannenberg argues that Christ's resurrection is supported by reason and is not a blind leap of faith. He makes this case at length in *Jesus—God and Man* (1964). Using his hermeneutical-historical method, he dialogues with historical-critical scholarship and modern skepticism about the biblical accounts of the empty tomb, the postresurrection appearances of Jesus, and his postascension appearance to Paul en route to Damascus. He concludes that Jesus's resurrection is a real but extraordinary historical event. Understood in its context in Second Temple Judaism, the resurrection vindicates Jesus's claim to have divine authority and inaugurates the eschatological reign of God.[26] Based on the historicity of the resurrection, Pannenberg erects his Christology from Scripture. He offers sustained treatments of Jesus's divinity, humanity, roles as the mediator of creation and the Savior who atones for the sins of the world, and his lordship over all things. Extrapolating from Jesus's relation to God, he outlines the doctrine of the Trinity that is finally completed in his *Systematic Theology*.

This completes the overview of Pannenberg's theological project. He has developed a Christian theology with the same historical-hermeneutical method that he uses in philosophy. In this way he has made a case that even the core doctrines of the Christian faith satisfy contemporary standards of rationality.

Symptoms of Panentheism

Several aspects of Pannenberg's project suggest panentheism. First, he explicitly identifies with the panentheistic tradition of Herder, Schleiermacher, Hegel, and Schelling regarding "the totality of reality in its temporal development" as "the self-communication of God."[27] God is in world history. Second, he also affirms that the world is in God. His theology of science proposes that the cosmos exists within God's Spirit as its primordial force field.[28] His philosophy of religion concludes that "man participates in the personal reality

---

25. Ibid., 144: "While it is only the whole of history that demonstrates the deity of the one God, and this result can only be given at the end of all history, there is still one particular event that has absolute meaning as the revelation of God, namely, the Christ event insofar as it anticipates the end of history." On the evidential importance of the church's theological witness, see 149: "Thesis 6: In the formulation of the non-Jewish conceptions of revelation in the Gentile Christian church, the universality of the eschatological self-vindication of God in the fate of Jesus Christ comes to actual expression."

26. Pannenberg, *Jesus—God and Man*, chap. 3.

27. Pannenberg, introduction to *Revelation as History*, 16.

28. Pannenberg, "The Doctrine of Creation and Modern Science," 37–41.

of the divine."[29] These two points together yield the mutual "in-ness" of God and the world that is typical of generic panentheism.

Third, Pannenberg holds that the God-world relation is ontological, involving God's very being. This implies that God has two natures because the divine essence is both changeless and changing with the world: "Although the essence of God is from everlasting to everlasting the same, it does have a history in time."[30] Fourth, the historicity of God is further necessitated by the kingdom and the Trinity, two fundamental themes throughout Pannenberg's theology. The consummation of the world as God's kingdom is essential to God's very being: "the being of God and that of the kingdom are identical, since the being of God is his lordship."[31] The Trinity in history is the being—the triune essence—of God. "In the fate of Jesus, the God of Israel is revealed as the triune God. The event of revelation should not be separated from the being of God himself."[32] By implication, the economic Trinity is the actualization of the ontological Trinity.

To summarize all four points, the actualization of the Trinity and the kingdom in history involves God's essential being, which entails that the mutual "in-ness" of God and the world is ontological. All the symptoms of panentheism are present.

Pannenberg's Panentheism: The Divine Force Field

The following survey of Pannenberg's *Systematic Theology* focuses on the fundamental concept of the divine force field and the comprehensive role it plays throughout his theology. The analysis confirms that he is a trinitarian panentheist.

The Divine Force Field: Pannenberg's Basic Idea

The unifying concept of Pannenberg's entire theology is the idea that the divine essence, which he identifies with the Spirit, is an infinite, all-inclusive "force field" in which the ontological Trinity exists necessarily and the cosmos exists contingently.[33] Constituting this force field, the ontological Trin-

---

29. Pannenberg, "God of Hope," 2:244–46.

30. Ibid., 240.

31. Ibid.

32. Pannenberg, "Dogmatic Theses," 143.

33. "The persons of the trinitarian Godhead and the independent creation are singularities arising from the dynamic field of the Spirit's activity" (Ted Peters, "Editor's Introduction: Pannenberg on Theology and Science," in Pannenberg, *Toward a Theology of Nature*, 14).

ity actualizes itself as the economic Trinity in the cosmos until the cosmos is fully included within the Trinity as the kingdom of God. All aspects of Pannenberg's theology—his doctrine of God and God's activity in creation, redemption, and consummation—radiate from the central notion that God is an infinite triune force field of creative love. It is the key to his panentheism, "the incorporation of creatures . . . into the unity of the trinitarian life."[34]

The following sections elaborate Pannenberg's concept of a force field in relation to the divine essence, the Trinity, the true Infinite, creation, and the consummation of the kingdom.

The Divine Essence: Spirit as Force Field

Pannenberg contends that God's nature—the divine essence—is Spirit, a force field. "The essence of the Godhead is indeed Spirit. It is Spirit as a dynamic field."[35] The image of the divine force field is suggested by the biblical notions of *ruach* and *pneuma*, which suggest to him that Spirit is not a person or mind but a "creative and life-giving dynamic. The Spirit is the force field of God's mighty presence (Ps. 139:7)."[36] But the concept of a force field originates in Stoic philosophy. Following the church fathers, Pannenberg adopts the idea but rejects Stoic naturalism. For theology he prefers a modern scientific version of the concept: "The biblical statements about the Spirit of God are much closer than the classical idea of God as nous [mind] to Michael Faraday's idea of a universal force field in relation to which all material, corpuscular constructs are to be regarded as secondary manifestations."[37] A force field is an enduring, orderly power within whose range entities are generated, sustained, and empowered to act and interact according to their own natures. Science has identified cosmic, atomic, magnetic, gravitational, organic, ecological, and other kinds of physical force fields. Pannenberg likens the Spirit of God to a force field except that Spirit is infinite, ultimate, and nonphysical. "The field theories of science, then, can be considered as approximations to the metaphysical reality of the all-pervading spiritual field of God's creative presence in the universe."[38] In this

---

34. Pannenberg, *Systematic Theology*, 3:646. Pannenberg, "A Response to My American Friends," in *Theology of Wolfhart Pannenberg*, 324, affirms that field theory "is of central importance in my metaphysical and theological vision."

35. Pannenberg, *Systematic Theology*, 1:429.

36. Ibid., 1:381, 383: "The life-giving Spirit is the deity of God, his essence."

37. Ibid., 1:383. Faraday (1791–1864) was an English scientist.

38. Pannenberg, "The Doctrine of Creation in an Age of Scientific Cosmology," in *Introduction to Systematic Theology*, 37–52, 47.

dimension, God is neither a person nor a mind. "As a field ... the Spirit would be impersonal."[39]

The Divine Force Field as Immanent Trinity

But God is not merely undifferentiated, impersonal Spirit. He is the unity of three persons. Pannenberg now uses the notion of a force field to explain the Trinity. "The deity as field can find equal manifestation in all three persons." The three persons are "eternal forms," "concretions," and "individual aspects of the dynamic field of the eternal Godhead." More fully stated: "The idea of the divine life as a dynamic field sees the divine Spirit who unites the three persons as proceeding from the Father, received by the Son, and common to both, ... the force-field of their fellowship that is distinct from them both."[40] Thus Spirit is both the nonpersonal divine essence and the third person of the Trinity. "The Spirit comes forth as a separate hypostasis as he comes over against the Son and the Father as the divine essence, common to both, and actually unites them."[41] In this way Pannenberg explains the immanent (ontological) Trinity as the essential infrastructure of the basic force field. The one divine nature or force field is manifest in and unifies three persons.

Pannenberg is not a modalist (i.e., one who holds that the persons are merely modes of God's existence). He is usually considered to be a social trinitarian, although his version is different from Moltmann's.[42] The three persons are not merely modes of one, more ultimate reality, the divine force field. They are the essential infrastructure of the force field. They co-constitute their own identity and unity. With respect to their identity, "the persons simply are what they are in their relations to one another, which both distinguish them from one another and bring them into communion with one another."[43] Pannenberg even asserts that "the relations between the persons are constitutive not merely for their distinctions but also for their deity."[44] The activity

39. Pannenberg, *Systematic Theology*, 1:383–84: "The living essence of God as Spirit ... [is] force, not subject."

40. Ibid., 1:383: "As a field ... the Spirit would be impersonal. ... But he stands over against the Father and the Son as his own center of action"; and 1:429: "The essence of the Godhead is indeed Spirit. It is Spirit as a dynamic field, and as its manifestation in the coming forth of the Son shows itself to be the work of the Father, the dynamic of the Spirit radiates from the Father, but in such a way that the Son receives it as gift, and it fills him and radiates back from him to the Father."

41. Ibid., 1:429.

42. Olson, "Trinity and Eschatology."

43. Pannenberg, *Systematic Theology*, 1:320.

44. Ibid., 1:323.

of the three persons must be constitutive of the unity of God as well: "The self-actualization of the one God is one of reciprocity in the relations of the persons and the result of their mutual self-giving to one another."[45] Thus threeness and oneness are correlative essential characteristics of the divine force field.

The Identity of Immanent and Economic Trinity

Pannenberg endorses Rahner's Rule, that "the immanent Trinity is identical with the economic Trinity."[46] This means that "the immanent Trinity is to be found in the Trinity of salvation history. God is the same in his eternal essence as he reveals himself to be historically."[47] The economic Trinity is therefore the actualization of the essential (immanent, ontological) Trinity itself, not a mere temporal reflection of it: "The relation of the immanent to the economic Trinity, of God's inner trinitarian life to his acts in salvation history inasmuch as these are not external to his deity but express his presence in the world, may very well be described as self-actualization."[48] He even asserts that "the events of history in some way bear on the identity of [God's] eternal essence."[49] Pannenberg, however, denies that self-actualization entails "a divine becoming in history, as though the trinitarian God were the result of history and achieved reality only at its eschatological consummation." God's becoming is only half the story for Pannenberg. The other half is that the ontological Trinity is eternally real: "The eschatological consummation is only the locus of the decision that the trinitarian God is always the true God from eternity to eternity."[50] Behind this assertion is Pannenberg's proleptic ontology of the future: the full, transcendent, eternal reality of God is future and "retroactively" affects the present.

The self-actualization of the immanent Trinity necessarily involves the activity of the triune persons in world history, the economic Trinity. He explains why this is so: "Relations among the three persons that are defined as mutual self-distinction cannot be reduced to relations of origin in the traditional sense. The Father does not merely beget the Son. He also hands over his kingdom to him and receives it back from him. The Son is not merely begotten of the Father. He is also obedient to him and he thereby

---

45. Ibid., 2:394.

46. Ibid., 1:328, 405.

47. Ibid., 2:391.

48. Ibid., 2:393. Further, "the reality that is achieved in the eternal fellowship of the Trinity and by the economy of its action in the world is one and the same."

49. Ibid., 1:334.

50. Ibid., 1:331.

glorifies him as the one God. The Spirit is not just breathed. He also fills the Son and glorifies him in his obedience to the Father, thereby glorifying the Father himself."[51] The actions of all three persons in history progressively instantiate the very being of the Triune God. The triune essence of God is becoming increasingly actual as history approaches the eschaton. In this way, God's being, which is immutable, is becoming.

God's existence—the actuality of his essence—is immanent in the world. "We must not think of God's existence as simply transcendent, as an existence outside this world. We must think of it as an active presence in the reality of the world."[52] Conversely, all of creation is actually immanent in the eternity of God. "In virtue of trinitarian differentiation God's eternity includes the time of creatures in its full range, from the beginning of creation to its eschatological consummation."[53]

But if the ontological and economic Trinity are identical, is not the world a necessity for God? Could God be God without the world? In the end, Pannenberg's position is not entirely clear or is not clearly coherent. On the one hand, he concedes that "materially the deity of God is inconceivable without the consummation of his kingdom, and that it is thus dependent upon the eschatological coming of his kingdom."[54] And so the world is necessary for God in some sense. On the other hand, Pannenberg repeatedly denies that the creation and the incarnation are necessary in God's essence.[55] The eternal God is ontologically free not to create. Creation and incarnation are voluntary acts of divine love. Love is God's motive for creation, but this does not make creation necessary.[56] "The creation of the world does not rest on any inner necessity of the divine nature that compelled God to make his creation; rather, the creation is a free act of God on the part of the Son as well as the Father." Pannenberg likewise denies that God's involvement in history implies a deficiency or need in God: "His eternal existence in the fellowship of Father, Son, and Holy Spirit is presupposed and his eternal essence needs no completion by his

51. Ibid., 1:320.
52. Ibid., 1:357.
53. Ibid., 1:405–6. This genuine mutual immanence amounts to panentheism.
54. Ibid., 1:331.
55. Ibid., 2:1: "If the world has its origin in a free act of God, it does not emanate by necessity from the divine essence or belong by necessity to the deity of God. It might not have existed. Its existence is therefore contingent."
56. Ibid., 2:19: "The freedom of the divine origin of the world on the one hand and God's holding fast to his creation on the other belong together. The nature of the link may be deduced from the concept of divine love as the world's origin. God's love and freedom are inseparably related, but we must not misconstrue love as caprice" or "an emotional force that overpowers all personal freedom."

coming into the world." In short, the ontological Trinity "did not need the existence of a world."[57]

So is the world necessary or not? Pannenberg holds that the world is not absolutely necessary, but necessary given God's choice to create. "Without his lordship over creation, God would not be God. The act of creation is certainly a product of the freedom of God, but once the world of creation came into existence, lordship over it became the condition and proof of deity." Pannenberg insists that God is ontologically triune whether or not he eternally wills to actualize the economic Trinity in the world. With respect to Rahner's Rule, then, his affirmation of the essential identity of the economic and the ontological Trinity means that God's triune essence is genuinely present in the world but not that being in the world is intrinsic to the triune essence.

Pannenberg's explanation, however, still leaves questions of adequacy and coherence. Just what is this "eternal decision," and what if God had chosen not to actualize the Trinity in creation?[58] The final section of this chapter links these issues to his panentheism.

The Divine Force Field as the True Infinite

Pannenberg argues that the divine force field is the true Infinite. He selects infinity as the basic attribute of the divine reality, the attribute of all attributes, because "the Infinite is the antithesis to the finite as such." He has a precise definition in mind, the one we have encountered in Nicholas of Cusa, Hegel, and Moltmann. "The Infinite that is merely a negation of the finite is not yet truly seen as the Infinite (as Hegel showed), for it is defined by delimitation from something else, i.e., the finite. . . . The Infinite is truly infinite only when it transcends its own antithesis to the finite."[59] This

---

57. Ibid., 2:389–90; further, "the manifestation of his lordship over the world does not make good a lack in his eternal being but incorporates his creatures into the eternal fellowship of the Son with the Father through the Spirit."

58. Pannenberg's position makes sense only if his ontology of the future does. God's free decision whether to create the world is *eternal*; that is, it is a future reality that has been retroactively effective in the past and present since creation. On the second point, what if God's eternal decision had been not to create the world? In that case the ontological Trinity would be "real" but not actual, in the sense that the future is real but not actual. But then the ontological Trinity would be different. It would be pure possibility, not actuality. And it would not be the Father, Son, and Spirit because their self-differentiation and unity involve the creation of the world and the incarnation of Christ. So, if not creating the world makes a difference to the very essence of God, then perhaps the world is essentially necessary in spite of Pannenberg's denial.

59. Pannenberg, *Systematic Theology*, 1:399–400. See "The Infinity of God: His Holiness, Eternity, Omnipotence, and Omnipresence," 397–421; also "The Problem of the Absolute," chap. 2 in *Metaphysics and the Idea of God*.

dialectical concept of the Infinite entails panentheism because the infinite God must include the finite ontologically.

Pannenberg claims not to impose a philosophical concept of infinity on theology but to find it in Scripture: "The biblical idea of the divine Spirit implies the thought of God as infinite."[60] He sees it in "the dynamic that marks the Spirit in the biblical sense. . . . It tells us that we have to think of the Infinite as negation, as the opposite of the finite, but also that it comprehends this antithesis in itself." As a result, "the distinction [between finite and infinite] is both grounded in the work of God's Spirit and removed by it."[61] Pannenberg claims that the concept of infinity in dialectical philosophy captures the biblical presentation of the unlimited reality of God. He analyzes all of God's attributes as aspects of his Infinity.

Eternity is the first aspect of infinity that Pannenberg considers. It clarifies his relation to the panentheist tradition. He follows Plato, Plotinus, and Boethius in defining eternity as infinite fullness and duration without succession, "the presence of the totality of life . . . the whole simultaneously as undivided perfection . . . authentic duration and not just a negation of time." Eternity is neither the absolute antithesis of time nor infinite, everlasting time. Time is the partial and sequential manifestation of eternity and therefore presupposes it.[62]

But Pannenberg argues that Plotinus's account of eternity and time is coherent only if God is "not undifferentiated identity but intrinsically differentiated unity," a characteristic that "demands the doctrine of the Trinity." Pannenberg's identification of the true Infinite with the Trinity implies that God's eternity includes actual time, not just potential time: "In virtue of trinitarian differentiation God's eternity includes the time of creatures in its full range, from the beginning of creation to its eschatological consummation."[63] The true Infinite will be fully actual—completely containing the finite—only when the Trinity is fulfilled in the kingdom. The claim that God includes actual time and history in his eternal being is another indicator of panentheism.

---

60. Pannenberg, *Systematic Theology*, 1:396.

61. Ibid., 1:400–401.

62. Ibid., 1:403–4.

63. Ibid., 1:405–6; 409: "This takes place when it [Plotinus's view of time] is given a trinitarian interpretation which in distinction from Plotinus sees that creation and the historical march of cosmic time are embraced by the economy of God for which world history is the path that leads to the future of God's glory."

Pannenberg's discussion of eternity illustrates that he appropriates the philosophical theology of Plotinus—with two major modifications. The first modification is the Christian affirmation that the Eternal One is triune. The second is the post-Hegelian perspective on the Eternal One, according to which the full, transcendent actuality of God is not "above" world history but is in the future.[64] "God is eternal because he has no future outside himself. His future is that of himself and all that is distinct from him."[65] "The God of the future" brings us full circle, back to the post-Hegelian, post-Marxist ontological priority of the future, posited in Pannenberg's and Moltmann's early "God of Hope" and never relinquished. In sum, the Neoplatonic Great Chain of Being emanates from and returns to the *future* triune One.

Pannenberg derives other attributes from infinity as well. As infinity implies eternity, so eternity implies freedom. "The eternal God as the absolute future, in the fellowship of Father, Son, and Spirit, is the free origin of himself and his creatures." God's omnipresence likewise follows from his infinity. "As in the case of his eternity, then, there are combined in his omnipresence elements of both immanence and transcendence in keeping with the criterion of the true Infinite."[66] The true Infinite must utterly transcend and yet be inclusively present in all finite entities and polarities, even the finite-infinite distinctions of number, time, and space. Because God is omnipresent, he is also omnipotent. His power is everywhere, encompassing all creatures. But it is not absolute, monarchial, all-determining power. It "can be thought of only as the power of divine love and not as the assertion of a particular authority against all opposition." God's power gives each creature freedom within limits and thus "the opportunity by accepting its own limits to transcend them and in this way itself to participate in infinity."[67] In sum, for Pannenberg, all the attributes of infinity eventually lead to God's love.

Love is the greatest of God's attributes, that which most fully expresses the divine nature as the infinite force field. Love enables Pannenberg to resolve the ultimate philosophical challenge: accounting for the unity of God by showing "that the Infinite is truly infinite." As true Infinite, God is not merely an individual distinct from others but the Absolute One who includes all distinct individuals. "As the one who is not one among others, God must be absolute. As one, the Absolute is also all." The Absolute must be all because, as true Infinite, it cannot be other than the many or it would

64. Pannenberg explains the reality of the future in relation to Plotinus and Hegel in "Concept and Anticipation," chap. 8 in *Metaphysics and the Idea of God*.

65. Pannenberg, *Systematic Theology*, 1:410.

66. Ibid., 1:411, 412.

67. Ibid., 1:422.

be limited and finite. On the contrary, it cannot be identical with the many, for then either there would be no real One or no real many. Thus the Absolute "is not all in one (pantheism) but transcends the difference of one and all. It is thus the One that also embraces all."[68] This Absolute is the one true Infinite that includes the finite many.[69] In making his case, Pannenberg references Plotinus, Pseudo-Dionysius, Nicholas of Cusa, Hegel, and Isaak Dorner. It is a classic case of panentheism.

True to his historical-hermeneutical methodology, he does not claim rational closure and certainty. Philosophical theology is merely an abstraction from the dynamic reality of God. "Only with the consummation of the world in the kingdom of God does God's love reach its goal and the doctrine of God reach its conclusion. Only then do we fully know God as the true Infinite who is not merely opposed by the world of the finite, and thus himself finite." God's love makes him manifest as the true Infinite and will ultimately make his complete Deity self-evident to all.[70]

In sum, Pannenberg's doctrine of God asserts that God is the absolute, infinite, triune force field of love whose essence both eternally transcends the world and is immanently present in it, revealing and actualizing himself as the Triune God by fully including the world as his kingdom. This seems to be a clear case of historical-eschatological trinitarian panentheism.

The Divine Force Field and Creation

Pannenberg affirms the doctrine of creation from nothing and also rejects the notion of nothingness as the indeterminate potency in God—the tradition of Böhme through Moltmann.[71] Instead he uses his idea of the divine force field to explain God's act of creation. Appealing to shared philosophical roots, he develops a theology of the creative Spirit from Michael Faraday's notion of a single, all-embracing force field within which physical entities are forms of forces that become independent realities.[72] "The Spirit of God can be understood as the supreme field of power that pervades all of creation. Each finite event or being is to be considered as a special manifestation of

68. Ibid., 1:443–44.

69. John O'Donnell, "Pannenberg's Doctrine of God," *Gregorianum*, 72/1 (1991): 91: "The infinite embraces within itself even the opposition between finite and infinite. For the relation between God and the world, this means that God lets the world be world, hence be autonomous, but God embraces the world within his own infinite life. God is distinct from the world but not separate from it."

70. Pannenberg, *Systematic Theology*, 1:447–48.

71. Ibid., 2:12–17.

72. Ibid., 2:79–84. The Stoic notion was adapted by Christian theology, from which it was modified for modern science by Newton and others.

that field, and their movements are responsive to its forces."[73] Creatures are manifestations or individuations of the ordering-empowering divine field that interact with it.

Within the triune force field, the Logos orders all creation in cooperation with the Spirit: "Whereas the creative dynamic in the events of creation relates to the Spirit, the Logos is the origin of the distinguishing form of the creature in the totality of its existence and in the ensemble of distinctions and relation of creatures in the order of nature."[74] In other words, the Spirit is the energy that makes creatures possible and empowers them; the preincarnate Son, self-distinguished and reciprocally related to Father and Spirit, constitutes the order of nature with the kinds of creatures that develop within it. Creation occurs continuously as God's Spirit, "a field of creative presence, a comprehensive field of force . . . releases event after event into finite existence." Because God is ontologically prior, "every single event as well as the sequence of such events springs contingently from the future of God."[75] God sustains creatures the same way he creates them: "Continued creaturely existence is possible only by participation in God. . . . The life of creatures as participation in God that transcends their own finitude is the special work of the Spirit in creation."[76]

Surprisingly, Pannenberg claims that his notion of participation in God "does not carry pantheistic *or panentheistic* connotations."[77] He does not state what he means by panentheism. But the panentheistic implication of his position seems undeniable. The divine force field is literally the immediate context from which and within which the cosmos of finite entities exists.

Pannenberg's treatment of time, space, and energy further confirms his panentheism.[78] He traces the concepts of time, space, and energy through modern philosophy and science, noting their correlation in the field theories of physics since Einstein. He then draws a theological conclusion: "the spatialization of time in physics—already . . . in the model of space-time

73. Pannenberg, *Introduction to Systematic Theology*, 46.

74. Pannenberg, *Systematic Theology*, 2:110.

75. Pannenberg, *Introduction to Systematic Theology*, 49.

76. Pannenberg, *Systematic Theology*, 2:33.

77. Pannenberg, *Introduction to Systematic Theology*, 45, emphasis mine. Here is a longer excerpt: "The Spirit animates the creatures in raising them beyond themselves to participate in some measure in the life of the eternal God, who is Spirit. Such a statement does not carry pantheistic or panentheistic connotations, because the Spirit is always transcendent, and only by transcending themselves do the creatures participate in the spiritual dynamics." But divine transcendence and participation in God by relatively autonomous creatures are key characteristics of panentheism, and so it is puzzling why Pannenberg thinks they distance him from panentheism.

78. Pannenberg, "Space and Time as Aspects of the Spirit's Working," in *Systematic Theology*, 2:84–102.

or a universal field comprising space, time, and energy—may be described as an extrapolation of all limited participation in the eternal presence of God."[79] In other words, Pannenberg holds that *physics and theology deal with the very same force field from different points of view.* This implies that space, time, and energy are not wholly nondivine artifacts made by God; they are differentiated aspects of the divine force field itself.[80] Creatures are distinct from God but exist in God as individuations of divine energy. It is hard to see how this avoids being panentheism.

The Divine Force Field and the Eschaton

Pannenberg envisions the entire history of the universe from creation to the eschaton as continuous divine action that draws creatures into ever more complete participation in God. "The developed structure of God's outward action embraces not only the creation of the world but also the themes of reconciliation, redemption, and consummation."[81] God endows creatures with independent existence and redeems them by overcoming their destructive uses of freedom in order to include them in himself. The Spirit and creation share a common goal. "The goal of the Spirit's dynamic is to give creaturely forms duration by a share in eternity and to protect them against the tendency to disintegrate that follows from their independence."[82] From its side, "the goal of all creation, not just humanity, is to share in the life of God."[83] Following this historical trajectory, Pannenberg's *Systematic Theology* articulates his rich and erudite doctrines of humanity, sin, Christ, salvation and reconciliation, and the Spirit's work in the church and history. Limitations of focus and space move us directly to his eschatology.[84]

His apocalyptic vision is unmistakably panentheistic. "The eschatological salvation at which Christian hope is directed fulfills the deepest longing of humans and all creation . . . because it means participation in the eternal life of God"[85] or, more specifically, "participation in the eternal

---

79. Pannenberg, "The Doctrine of Creation and Modern Science," 43–44. As Peters observes, "Editor's Introduction," 14: "He does not say that spirit is *like* a force field. He says spirit *is* a force field." See also Philip Hefner, "The Role of Science in Pannenberg's Theological Thinking," in *Theology of Wolfhart Pannenberg,* ed. Braaten and Clayton, esp. 271–81 on the concept of field.

80. Pannenberg, *Systematic Theology,* 2:89 n. 229, rejects Moltmann's adoption of *zimsum*—time and space as precosmic divine contractions.

81. Ibid., 2:7.

82. Ibid., 2:102. He generally affirms Teilhard, Rahner, Moltmann, and others on this point.

83. Ibid., 2:136. See also "Creation and Eschatology, Sec. 1," 1:136–46.

84. See esp. ibid., vol. 3, chap. 15, "The Consummation of Creation in the Kingdom of God."

85. Ibid., 3:527.

life of the trinitarian God in the fellowship of the Son and the Father by the Spirit."[86]

Pannenberg emphasizes that in eternity each creature, certainly each human being, must retain its identity and independent existence because existence and freedom are necessary for the mutuality of love and glory between creatures and God. This mutuality requires the inclusion of time in eternity because time is essential for individual existence and freedom. Individual identity is not, however, determined in time but only in relation to eternity. "On the path of their history in time objects and people exist only in anticipation of that which they will be in the light of their final future, the advent of God."[87] We are what we will become. The identity of creatures therefore requires a "view of temporality in the simultaneity of the eternal present," a notion of eternity that does not exclude time but includes "the difference between time and eternity." This inclusive notion is found in the eternity of God, the true Infinite. Time flows from the force field of divine love, "the emergence of the eschatological future of the eternal God in the time of the creature. Even though itself eternal, the love of God brings forth time, works in time, and is thus present in time." Divine love simultaneously draws all things into its eternity: "Only in the eschatological future will God consummate . . . creation for participation in God's own eternal life."[88] In a manner not entirely clear to our time-bound minds, Pannenberg assures us, eternal life already includes and preserves the individuality and temporality of creatures, who will be eternally preserved, fulfilled, and perfected in eschatological participation in God.[89]

We conclude by quoting the finale to Pannenberg's *Systematic Theology*, which summarizes the activity of the triune Spirit of love—the comprehensive scope of the divine force field:

> On the whole path from the beginning of creation by way of reconciliation to the eschatological future of salvation, the march of the divine economy of salvation is an expression of the incursion of the eternal future of God to the salvation of creatures and thus a manifestation of the divine love. Here is the eternal basis of God's coming forth from the immanence of the divine life as the economic Trinity and of the incorporation of creatures, mediated thereby, into the unity of the trinitarian life. The distinction and unity of the

86. Ibid., 3:626.
87. Ibid., 3:531.
88. Ibid., 3:643–45.
89. This position is quite different from one that affirms the continuity of time, activity, and relationships. See John Polkinghorne's criticism and alternative to Pannenberg in "New Creation," chap. 10 in *The God of Hope and the End of the World* (New Haven: Yale University Press, 2002), esp. 117–19.

immanent and economic trinity constitute the heartbeat of the divine love, and with a single such heartbeat this love encompasses the whole world of creatures.[90]

Everything in Pannenberg's theology is explained in terms of the divine force field.

Pannenberg's Historical-Trinitarian Panentheism

A Panentheist After All

I have argued that Pannenberg's theology is a case of trinitarian panentheism because of his concept of the divine force field. It is Spirit—the eternal, infinite, Triune God. But it is also the field of energy, time, and space from which creatures are individuated and within which they exist. They literally subsist from and in the Spirit. Thus all creatures participate ontologically in God, yet God infinitely transcends them. This position readily fits the classical definition of panentheism.[91]

In fact, the main contours of Pannenberg's system look like Neoplatonism horizontalized. All things come from God, are within God, and return to God. But the Transcendent One is in the eternal future before us, not the eternal present above us. Not surprisingly, Pannenberg frequently expresses appreciation for thinkers in the panentheist tradition: Plotinus, Dionysius, Nicholas of Cusa, the German romantics, Hegel, Alexander, Bergson, Teilhard, Whitehead, and Moltmann prominent among them.

Nevertheless, Pannenberg criticizes panentheism and denies holding it. He does not discuss it extensively as such. But he implies that he thinks of panentheism as a sub-Christian philosophy with two major flaws: it lacks a doctrine of the Trinity, and it affirms that the world is natural and inevitable for God.

The importance of the Trinity for Pannenberg is both religious and philosophical. First, it is a truth implicit in God's historical self-revelation in Jesus Christ and therefore taught by Scripture and the church. He regards any view of God that lacks it to be religiously incomplete and—if taken as definitive—distorted. Second, without a Triune God, philosophy cannot

90. Pannenberg, *Systematic Theology*, 3:646. Grenz and Olson, *Twentieth-Century Theology*, 193, point out that the force field "is the same concept that describes the divine essence functions as the principle of the relation of God to creation and as the principle of the participation of creation in the divine life."

91. Grenz and Olson, *Twentieth-Century Theology*, 194, observe that "God is the 'field' in which creation and history arise" but do not mention panentheism in relation to Pannenberg.

account for the diversity of creation in relation to the Absolute One. Recall his judgment that Plotinus's view of eternity is incoherent without a doctrine of the Trinity. Lack of an adequate account of the Trinity is one of his major criticisms of Whitehead's process theology and also of Hegel, whom he admires in many ways. It is worth noting that Pannenberg's doctrine of the Trinity does not draw on the legacy of Jakob Böhme, which conflates the Trinity with dialectical ontology in an attempt to make it intelligible. Pannenberg draws much more from patristic theology and much less from modern "suffering God" theology than Moltmann does.

A second likely reason Pannenberg rejects panentheism is its common affirmation that the world is somehow necessary for God.[92] Typical panentheism either holds that the world is an inevitable emanation, as in Neoplatonism, or espouses the Christian view that the world is an expression of God's love, which needs a beloved. These views often claim that God is free and that creation is not necessary. But that claim is true only if freedom and determinism are compatible: God is neither compelled nor coerced to create the world, but it is his nature inevitably to do so. Pannenberg does not wish to speculate: "The thought that God might not have made the world rests on an abstraction from God's actual self-determination." But he strongly affirms that God would be fully God without the world, that creation is a free act, and that the world is contingent.[93] Nevertheless, it is not clear that his own identification of the ontological and the economic Trinity is consistent with the possible nonexistence of the world.[94]

In any case, if the Trinity and God's freedom are Pannenberg's reasons for rejecting panentheism, affirming both doctrines is not sufficient to avoid panentheism. There are many panentheists who affirm the Trinity in the tradition from Böhme to Moltmann, and others who do so outside that tradition, such as Teilhard and Temple. It is simply false that all panentheism is nontrinitarian. Moltmann even argues that the only tenable kind of panentheism is trinitarian.

Furthermore, it is not true that panentheism must regard the world as "natural" for God, although almost all versions do. Philip Clayton, a leading

92. This is Grenz's reason for denying that Pannenberg is a panentheist (*Reason for Hope*, 73–74, 211).

93. Pannenberg, *Systematic Theology*, 2:9. Ibid., 2:15–35, surveys the history of this debate from Plato, Neoplatonism, Nicholas of Cusa, Spinoza, Leibniz, Hegel, and Whitehead. He thinks Proclus makes emanation dialectically necessary whereas Plotinus holds that the world resulted from a contingent "fall" of the Soul.

94. See "The Identity of Immanent and Economic Trinity" and its final footnote, above.

contemporary panentheist and former student of Pannenberg's, affirms the libertarian freedom of God in creating the world.[95] But the point stands simply as a matter of definition. It is sufficient for *pan-en-theism* that "all creatures exist in God" ontologically. Whether this "in-ness" is due to God's nature or God's choice is a debate among panentheists, and so this issue does not distinguish between panentheists and nonpanentheists. Even if Pannenberg can coherently affirm that creation is a free act of God chosen from equally possible alternatives, he would still be a panentheist.[96]

Not a Typical Contemporary Panentheist

Pannenberg is not, however, a typical contemporary panentheist in at least one significant way. He does not stress that creatures affect God or codetermine the course of history. This sets him apart from process theologians, Moltmann, and even from open theists. He does affirm the freedom of creatures and the "risk" God takes.[97] He even speaks of mutual love and glorification.[98] But he does not develop the idea that God is affected by, changed by, or responsive to the individual feelings and actions of creatures.[99] He stresses the "all-determining" nature of divine action from creation to the eschaton so strongly that some have wondered whether implicitly he is a determinist.[100] Although the divine force field does allow creatures freedom within itself, God's lordship in creation, redemption, and consummation is eternally decided and so temporally powerful that nothing can stop it or even change it.[101] In this respect Pannenberg's panentheism is more classical than contemporary. He is more like Plotinus than like Moltmann, the process theologians, and others who insist on mutually effective interaction between God and the world.

95. Philip Clayton, "Panentheism Today: A Constructive Systematic Evaluation," in *In Whom We Live*, ed. Clayton and Peacocke, 254. He argues his position from Christianity and from the later Schelling, for whom the existence of God and world are ultimately contingent.

96. Roger Olson, "Wolfhart Pannenberg's Doctrine of the Trinity," 175–206, makes the same point although he does not discuss panentheism: "God's relation to the world must be thought of as a moment in God's own life—even if a freely chosen one" (204 in *Scottish Journal of Theology* 43/2 [1990]: 175–206).

97. Pannenberg, *Systematic Theology*, 3:643.

98. Ibid., 3:625–26.

99. Grenz, *Reason for Hope*, 211: "God is affected by the world but not in the sense that this adds to the divine reality. Rather, the effect lies in the demonstration of the rulership of God over all creation, without which God would not be God and cannot be 'all in all.'"

100. Polk, "God, Power, and Freedom," in *On the Way to God*, 270–80; also David McKenzie, *Wolfhart Pannenberg and Religious Philosophy* (Lanham, MD: University Press of America, 1980), 123–33.

101. Mostert, "An All-Determining or Determinist God," in *God and the Future*, 175–82, concludes that, for Pannenberg, the general course of history is determined but individual events are not.

Conclusion

Pannenberg is perhaps the most thoughtful and learned of contemporary theologians and, among world-class panentheists, one who is most concerned with preserving the continuity of his views with the historic Christian tradition.

Nevertheless, two of his most basic ideas remain problematic. First, identifying the cosmic force field with the Spirit of God instead of viewing it as a creation of God seems to undermine or breach the God-world difference at a basic level. Second, his ontology of the future remains puzzling.

It is difficult to understand how the future, which is the realm of possibility and not actual existence, can be the locus of an essence with "retroactive" power that elicits and determines the present. How can anything not yet actual have positive power? What is actually present is the God who will be fully actual at the eschaton. One therefore wonders whether the Eternal One, the true Infinite, the Perfect Being, and the ontological Trinity can do all the work Pannenberg assigns them if they are presently no more than the partially actualized essence of God's own potential future. In my view, the ontology of the future is counterintuitive and philosophically unconvincing.[102]

Without these two foundational ideas—the ontology of the future and God as the force field of the cosmos—the magnificent edifice of Pannenberg's system cannot remain standing.

---

102. Pannenberg defends the reality of the future in "Concept and Anticipation," chap. 8 in *Metaphysics and the Idea of God*. Mostert, "The Ontological Priority of the Future," chap. 4 in *God and the Future*, is very illuminating. See also Lewis Ford, "The Nature of the Power of the Future," 140–42; Philip Clayton, "Anticipation and Theological Method," 140–42; Pannenberg, "Response to My American Friends," 323–24, in *Theology of Wolfhart Pannenberg*, ed. Braaten and Clayton; and Grenz and Olson, *Twentieth-Century Theology*, 198–99.

An illustration may help explain the issue. An acorn contains the essence of an oak tree and thus the power to become an oak tree. But the acorn is actual and the oak tree is not. The mature tree is not an actual being whose essence exercises "retroactive power" that brings the acorn into being and structures its growth. It is simply what the acorn will become, a potential in the acorn. Analogously, the present God-world nexus may contain the essential power to become the eschatological consummation of the kingdom in the Trinity—the actual ontological Trinity, the true Infinite, the Perfect Being, the One. But in that case, the present contains and actualizes God's future potential, not the reverse. How can what is only possible, not actual, exercise any positive power at all? Arguing that God as true Infinite must somehow be both seems more question-begging than compelling. In the end, it is not clear that Pannenberg's view is coherent.

It seems that viewing God as the power of the future is a purely hypothetical postulation that is necessary to ground a comprehensive theology without a traditional, pre-Hegelian notion of divine eternity and transcendence. The force of the argument is transcendental: we must suppose that God is the power of the future because otherwise we have no way of doing theology adequately without recourse to the old ideas of classical theism. To be exact: classical theism is an alternative.

12

~~~~~~

Panentheistic Liberation
and Ecological Theologies

The 1960s were a time of youthful idealism, radical critique, and social upheaval. The young at heart were sure that life would improve when people were liberated from the dysfunctional and oppressive "establishment." If traditional religion, morality, and the social-economic-political order were revolutionized, they believed, then love, peace, and justice would flourish. The baby boomers were bursting with zeal to change things. A variety of liberation movements took shape during this time—ethnic, racial, and cultural liberation, sexual and gender liberation, national liberation from colonialism, even animal and environmental liberation.

Christians who participated in these liberation movements viewed their critique of the status quo as God's Word prophetically denouncing sin. They saw their revolutionary activities as God's redemptive work. Liberation theology is the result of reflection on the Christian rationale for participation in these liberation movements. Specific liberation theologies represent the perspectives of particular groups, such as women, African Americans, Latin Americans, and Native Americans. Most of these theologies also share a vision of universal liberation that extends beyond particular interest groups to include the entire human community and the earth.

Although not all liberation theologians embrace panentheism, many have found its alternative view of God and the world attractive for several reasons. First, liberationists are suspicious of classical theism because its sovereign, transcendent God looks like an absolute monarch and often has been used to sanction oppressive and unjust social orders. Panentheism views God as more immanent, sympathetic, and cooperative with humans. Second, like panentheism since Hegel and Schelling, liberation theology insists that salvation begins in this world, transforming social structures. Both theologies emphasize the coincidence of world history and redemptive history. Finally, there are themes in panentheism that appeal to particular kinds of liberation theology. For example, social-political liberationists appeal to Teilhard and Moltmann for social models of the Trinity and the God-world relation. Feminists appreciate allusions to the feminine aspect of the divine in the writings of Böhme, Schelling, Tillich, Hartshorne, and Moltmann. Ecological theologians resonate with the ancient tradition that the world is God's body. For a variety of reasons, panentheism is attractive to liberation theology.

Much liberation panentheism is implicit simply because its focus is on practical theology and social ethics rather than the ontology of the God-world relation. When explicated, however, these theologies exhibit the characteristic features of modern dynamic panentheism.[1]

Like other chapters, this is a sampling, not a complete catalog. It considers selected panentheists who represent major branches of liberation theology: James Cone for black theology; Gustavo Gutiérrez, Juan Luis Segundo, and Leonardo Boff for Latin American liberation theology; Rosemary Ruether and Sallie McFague for feminist-ecological theology; and Matthew Fox for cosmic-creation spirituality.[2]

James Cone's Black Theology

James Cone, professor of systematic theology at Union Seminary in New York, is the most influential representative of black theology in the United

1. Stanley J. Grenz and Roger E. Olson, *Twentieth-Century Theology: God and the World in a Transitional Age* (Downers Grove, IL: InterVarsity, 1992), 201, generalize that liberation theologies move "too far in the opposite direction of the divine immanence, thereby failing to create the biblical balance between God as transcendent and as immanent." This places them close to panentheism.

2. The appeal of panentheism for liberation theologians is very broad. To illustrate, David A. Pailin, *A Gentle Touch: From a Theology of Handicap to a Theology of Human Being* (London: SPCK, 1992), is a theology of liberation for the impaired based mainly on process theology. I thank Heidi De Jonge, a former student at Calvin Seminary, for this reference.

States. Energized by the struggle for civil rights in the 1960s, Cone expresses the righteous anger of Malcolm X and the Black Power movement more than the pacifism of Dr. Martin Luther King Jr. His major work, *A Black Theology of Liberation*, implies panentheism in two ways: he uses Tillich's theology extensively, and he explicitly rejects the alternatives to panentheism.[3] Although Cone's influence on black theology is profound, the movement as a whole is not typically or characteristically panentheistic.[4]

A Black Theology of Liberation makes very clear that Cone is not interested in traditional theological categories or "white" academic theology. Given that all theology is written from the perspectives and interests of particular groups of people, he aims to articulate what the Christian faith means for the liberation of oppressed African Americans. But he does universalize the meaning of "Black" to include all suffering people. Thus Cone claims that "God is Black" because God identifies with all the oppressed and strives for their liberation.[5] "The blackness of God means that God has made the oppressed condition God's own condition."[6]

Although he repudiates "white" theology, Cone's black theology, in large measure, is Tillich's theology applied to the African American situation. "Though Tillich was not speaking of the black situation, his words are applicable to it. . . . God's word is our word; God's existence, our existence. This is the meaning of black culture and its relationship to divine revelation." He also invokes Tillich when calling for black liberation: "This is what Paul Tillich calls the courage to be—that is, the courage to affirm one's being in spite of those elements of existence which threaten being. It is the courage to be black in spite of white racists."[7]

Cone's doctrine of God explicitly adopts Tillich's notion of God as being-itself.[8] "Tillich describes God as being-itself, which provides the only answer to human estrangement," he writes. This concept of God is the basis for the struggle against oppression. "Because being-itself is free from the threat of nonbeing or nothingness, it is the source of human courage—the ability to

3. James H. Cone, *A Black Theology of Liberation*, 20th anniversary ed. (New York: Orbis, 1990). In the new preface, xviii, Cone takes distance from his original reliance on Karl Barth but does not reconsider his reliance on Tillich.

4. Rufus Burrow, *James H. Cone and Black Liberation Theology* (Jefferson, NC: MacFarland, 1994); Dwight Hopkins, *Introducing Black Theology of Liberation* (New York: Orbis, 1999); J. Deotis Roberts, *Black Religion, Black Theology* (Harrisburg, PA: Trinity Press International, 2003); Grenz and Olson, "Black Liberation Theology," in *Twentieth-Century Theology*, 201–9.

5. Cone, "The Content of Theology," chap. 1 in *Black Theology*.

6. Ibid., 63.

7. Ibid., 28, 54.

8. Ibid., chap. 4, "God in Black Theology."

affirm being in spite of the presence of non-being." Cone also uses Tillich's concept of divine-human participation in being/nonbeing to identify God ontologically with the oppressed. "God is identified with the oppressed to the point that their experience becomes God's experience."[9]

Accordingly, Cone's account of divine immanence and transcendence applies Tillich's infinite/finite correlation to black liberation. "To speak of God is to speak, on the one hand, of the presence of the infinite in the finite concrete world. On the other hand, the infinite can never be reduced to the finite." God's immanence is his presence in the struggle for liberation. "The immanence of God is the infinite expressing itself in the finite. It is God becoming concrete in finite human existence.... For blacks this means that God has taken on blackness, has moved into the black liberation struggle." God's transcendence is his limitless liberating power in the world, not his existence beyond it. "God is not 'above' or 'beyond' the world. Rather transcendence refers to human purpose as defined by the infinite in the struggle for liberation."[10]

Cone's theology is implicitly panentheistic because it follows Tillich so closely. He adopts Tillich's doctrine of God, his view of human participation in the being of God, and his understanding of salvation as New Being. Cone applies these ideas to the oppression and liberation of black people. The implication of his theology is that participation in black liberation is participation in God. Tillich's existential panentheism becomes black-liberation panentheism.

Cone also implies approval of panentheism by rejecting all the other options. In discussing God's providence, the freedom of creatures, and evil, he explicitly repudiates Deism, pantheism, and "traditional Christian theology" as represented by Emil Brunner. Instead he adopts the position of Tillich and Macquarrie,[11] both of whom are dynamic panentheists in the line of Schelling. So, although he does not name panentheism, Cone's rejection of the other options and his endorsement of panentheists imply a commitment to panentheism.

Latin American Liberation Theology

Most Latin American liberation theologians are faithful Roman Catholics who base their work on Scripture, church tradition, and the declarations of

9. Ibid., 60–63.

10. Ibid., 76–78. On p. 66 he gives another view of transcendence: "The Wholly Otherness of God means . . . God's blackness, which is wholly unlike whiteness."

11. Ibid., 78–81. He also rejects pantheism on pp. 14 and 28.

Vatican II.[12] Their panentheism derives mainly from the deep and pervasive influence of Teilhard de Chardin and Karl Rahner.[13]

Gustavo Gutiérrez

Gustavo Gutiérrez, widely regarded as the father of Latin American liberation theology, was born in Lima, Peru, in 1928. He became a priest, studied in Rome and France, and taught at the Catholic University in Lima. He lived among the poor.[14]

A Theology of Liberation (1971) is the movement's first scholarly elaboration.[15] Gutiérrez uses Catholic teaching, especially documents of Vatican II, to articulate a view of salvation that includes social, economic, political, and cultural liberation as well as reconciliation with God. He argues that the church has often failed to live up to its own teaching and that its praxis should mirror God's "preferential option for the poor." It is not possible to identify him definitively as a panentheist because he does not develop an ontology of the God-world relation. But key ideas he adopts from Teilhard de Chardin and Rahner are panentheistic.

Gutiérrez appeals to Teilhard in order to embrace the modern struggle for human freedom, which is "liberation from all that limits or keeps man from self-fulfillment."[16] He expresses particular appreciation for the socialist strand of liberation philosophy: Hegel's view that history is the drive for freedom, Marx's economics and social critique, and Herbert Marcuse's Marxist-Freudian theory of personal-social dynamics. But Gutiérrez asserts that socialist philosophy by itself is insufficient. The full meaning of liberation can be understood only as an integral part of God's redemption of the world in Christ. Appealing to Vatican II, Gutiérrez endorses Teilhard's correlation of human development and divine salvation, the culmination of the humanized cosmos in Christ. "The writings of Teilhard de Chardin, among others, have greatly influenced the trend toward reaffirmation of Christ as Lord of history and the cosmos."[17]

---

12. David Tombs, *Latin American Liberation Theology* (Boston: Brill Academic, 2002); Alfred Hennelly, ed., *Liberation Theology: A Documentary History* (New York: Orbis, 1990).

13. John Cooper, "Teilhard, Marx, and the World-view of Prominent Latin American Liberation Theologians," *Calvin Theological Journal* 24/2 (1989): 241–62.

14. Alfred Hennelly, "Gustavo Gutiérrez," in *Liberation Theologies* (Mystic, CT: Twenty-Third, 1995), 10–25.

15. Gustavo Gutiérrez, *A Theology of Liberation: History, Politics, and Salvation*, trans. Sister Caridad Inda and John Eagleson (Maryknoll, NY: Orbis, 1973).

16. Ibid., "Man the Master of His Own Destiny," 27–33, quote at 27.

17. Ibid., 76 n. 35. This note also comments on the influence of Teilhard on key documents of Vatican II, esp. *Gaudium et spes* [Joy and Hope], to which Gutiérrez repeatedly appeals. Gutiérrez, 173, 175, identifies deficiencies in Teilhard's socioeconomic perspective that socialism corrects.

The vision of the new humanity that Gutiérrez synthesizes with Teilhard's cosmic Christology is, however, more politically socialist than Teilhard's account. Indeed, for Gutiérrez, liberation and salvation are synonymous: "The fullness of liberation—a free gift from Christ—is communion with God and with other men."[18]

Teilhard's panentheism consists in his view that the history of the universe is God's self-incarnation culminating in Jesus Christ. In Christ, the world is God's body. Gutiérrez implicitly adopts panentheism by appropriating Teilhard's cosmic Christology to support his own assimilation of socioeconomic liberation into the Christian understanding of salvation.

His appropriation of Rahner's supernatural existential is more evidence of a commitment to panentheism. Gutiérrez clearly affirms Rahner's definition of this term: God's universal salvific presence in humanity, "a gratuitous ontologico-real determinant of his nature." This concept implies panentheism because it entails that all humans participate ontologically in the existence of God, who is present in all humanity.[19]

Gutiérrez conjoins Rahner's supernatural existential with Teilhard's cosmic Christology as he links God's immanence with social justice and liberation. The cosmic incarnation involves two dynamics, universalization and internalization. "Christ is the point of convergence of both processes." In Christ, God is really present in each human and in the entire world. "The God made flesh, the God present in each and every man, is no more 'spiritual' than the God present on the mountain and in the temple. He is even more 'material.'" Since God in Christ is really present in all humans, acts of justice and injustice done to humans are literally done to God. "We find the Lord in our encounters with men, especially the poor, marginated, and exploited ones. An act of love towards them is an act of love towards God."[20] Gutiérrez's implicit panentheism enables him to link justice and liberation with God ontologically, not just morally and spiritually.

Juan Luis Segundo

If Gutiérrez is the father of Latin American liberation theology, Juan Luis Segundo (1925–1996) is its dean.[21] Born in Uruguay, he became a Jesuit,

---

18. Gutiérrez, *Theology of Liberation*, 36.

19. Ibid., 70–71. Rahner is presented in chap. 8, above.

20. Ibid., "Encountering God in History," 193, 201. Grenz and Olson, *Twentieth-Century Theology*, 224, conclude that Gutiérrez's "almost total neglect of transcendence . . . makes his a form of secular theology." But his panentheism also affirms God and salvation beyond this world.

21. Alfred Hennelly, *Theologies in Conflict: The Challenge of Juan Luis Segundo* (Maryknoll, NY: Orbis, 1979), 26.

studied at Louvain and the Sorbonne, and taught at a number of universities in South and North America. He became familiar with panentheism by studying Nicolai Berdyaev and especially Teilhard, whose theology is foundational to his thought.

Segundo's *Liberation of Theology* (1975) focuses on liberation hermeneutics and the interrelation of faith and political ideology.[22] Since all perspectives are implicitly political, he argues, commitment to the liberation of the oppressed is necessary for understanding Scripture and doing theology correctly. He applies "ideological suspicion" to all exegesis and theology not devoted to liberation praxis, looking for ways that they support oppression. In addition, his two five-volume works of liberation theology, *A Theology for Artisans of a New Humanity* and *Jesus of Nazareth Yesterday and Today*, synthesize socialist philosophy with a modified Teilhardian theology, a perspective very similar to Gutiérrez's.

Our Idea of God contains clear evidence of panentheism. Segundo quotes Buber, Berdyaev, and Teilhard to promote the interpersonal nature of God against the impersonal Ground of being popularized by Tillich and Robinson. But he makes clear that God's otherness is not "some extramundane transcendence." "The Father, Son, and Holy Spirit are not 'out there' or 'up there.' But neither are they my own depth."[23] His personalism is explicitly Teilhardian: "Teilhard de Chardin is quite right in saying that the process of hominization, founded on love and directed by it, consists in fashioning ever more complex 'systems' of love in which each individual person is a center." Unlike Teilhard, he emphasizes that God uses violence as well as love to bring liberation to communal fulfillment. "Jesus was God *incarnate*. And total, exclusive opposition between love and violence is not historical."[24] By implication, violence promoting liberation helps incarnate God. This is liberation panentheism.

Teilhard's cosmic Christology is pervasive in Segundo's *Evolutionary Approach to Jesus of Nazareth*.[25] But he modifies some aspects. He finds Teilhard's evolutionary projection of the Omega point too optimistic and too spiritual. It underestimates the power of death and negative entropy, and it ultimately leaves the physical cosmos behind. Segundo embraces entropy, violence, and death. But he also stresses resurrection and the new earth as truths of super-

22. Juan Luis Segundo, *Liberation of Theology*, trans. John Drury (Maryknoll, NY: Orbis, 1976).

23. Juan Luis Segundo, *A Theology for Artisans of a New Humanity*, vol. 3, *Our Idea of God* (1968), trans. John Drury (New York: Orbis, 1973), 86–93, quotes at 93.

24. Ibid., 164–65.

25. Juan Luis Segundo, *Jesus of Nazareth*, vol. 5, *An Evolutionary Approach to Jesus of Nazareth* (1982), trans. John Drury (New York: Orbis, 1988).

natural revelation.[26] To supplement Teilhard, he adopts Gregory Bateson's science-based panentheistic model of God as the mind ordering the chaotic universe. This model is neither "an infinite being apart from the world" nor "pantheism."[27] Yet Segundo sees God concentrated in the human quest for liberation. God is not "a spectator of the human struggle for meaning. Instead God is identified with its culmination. . . . God coincides with the meaning of human work."[28] Segundo's writings clearly imply a dynamic panentheism of liberating action.

Leonardo Boff

Leonardo Boff was born in Brazil in 1938, did graduate study in Germany, and taught theology in Rio de Janeiro. He left the priesthood in 1993 after a period of silence imposed by the Vatican. A prolific writer, Boff has vigorously promoted the cause of liberation and criticized the church for not doing so. He shares the same general political-theological perspective as Gutiérrez and Segundo, and he intentionally adopts the term *panentheism*.

His well-known book *Trinity and Society* (1986) proceeds from Scripture, the ecumenical creeds, and Catholic theology to elaborate a doctrine of the Trinity that reinforces human liberation and social justice. Strongly influenced by Moltmann, Boff emphasizes the social aspect of the Trinity, the perichoretic union (mutual indwelling) of Father, Son, and Spirit, and God's perichoretic relationship with all of creation.[29] The most explicit evidence of panentheism is the section "Creation as the Body of the Trinity." Here Boff summarizes the entire history of the universe as the progressive embodiment of the Trinity. It begins with creation: "The Trinity in creation seeks to insert creation in the Trinity." Impelled by the transforming power of the Spirit and the liberating action of the Son, the process culminates in the eschaton. "The universe in the triune God will be the body of the Trinity, showing forth, in the limited form of creation, the full possibility of the communion of the divine Three."[30] The history of the world is the Trinity's self-actualization. Boff's view of the union of the world with God is ontological because his ontology is perichoretic: to be is to be in communion.

---

26. Ibid., 97–100.

27. Ibid., 101–2. See Gregory Bateson, *Mind and Nature: A Necessary Unity* (New York: E. P. Dutton, 1979).

28. Segundo, *Evolutionary Approach*, 104–5.

29. Leonardo Boff, "A New Starting Point: The Community and Social Aspect of the Trinity" and "Another New Starting Point: The Trans-sexist Theology of the Maternal Father and Paternal Mother," 118–22, in *Trinity and Society*, trans. Paul Burns (New York: Orbis, 1988).

30. Ibid., 230–31.

Indeed, the oneness of God himself is constituted by the "perichoresis and eternal communion" of the three distinct persons.[31] Boff is a panentheist in *Trinity and Society* but does not yet use the term.

Ecology and Liberation explicitly promotes "Christian panentheism."[32] This book extends Boff's concern for human liberation to include nature. "The ecclesial community must feel part of the human community, and the human community has to feel that it is part of the cosmic community. They all form part of the trinitarian community of Father, Son, and Holy Spirit." He even states that creation is a reproduction of divine triunity. The three divine persons are one through "the links of life, the loving correlations, the eternal interplay of relations among them.... They are one God-communion, the one God-relation, the one God-love. The universe is a reproduction of this diversity and of this union."[33] Boff employs Moltmann's perichoretic ontology throughout the book.

Although Boff affirms Teilhard's Cosmic Christ, he follows Moltmann in emphasizing the immanence of the Spirit in all living things. "Everything is a manifestation of life ... self-interactive energy at the highest level of complexity." The Christian category or image for the universal power of life is the Holy Spirit, he states. By implication, creation is the Spirit's body, since the Spirit is incarnate in it. "The Spirit dwells in creation in the same way as the Son, who is incarnate in the humanity of Jesus."[34] Here again perichoresis is the model for the Spirit's relation with creation.

At this point Boff introduces panentheism, "a particularly appropriate idea for the cosmic ubiquity of the Spirit." Panentheism is "a very old and noble Christian concept." He distinguishes it from pantheism, which mistakenly views creatures as manifestations of the divine substance and denies their autonomy. Instead Boff recommends panentheism because it affirms the distinction between God and creature and acknowledges that each has "relative autonomy." It also insists on their essential interrelatedness. "Not everything is God, but God is in everything. ... And then, vice versa, everything is in God." Boff promotes Christian panentheism because it "gives rise to a new integrative and holistic spirituality that can unite heaven and earth" and because it demands environmental stewardship.[35]

31. Ibid., 235. He acknowledges that this view risks "tri-theism."

32. Leonardo Boff, "Ecology and Theology: Christian Panentheism," in *Ecology and Liberation: A New Paradigm*, trans. John Cumming (New York: Orbis, 1995), 43–51.

33. Ibid., 48.

34. Ibid., 49. He summarizes and endorses Teilhard's views of cosmogenesis, anthropogenesis, Christogenesis, and theogenesis (p. 152).

35. Ibid., 50–51.

Boff's perspective readily supports the extension of liberation beyond humans to our earthly home. This cosmic understanding of liberation is also common among feminist theologians.

Feminist-Ecological Theology

Panentheism is attractive to feminist theologians not only because it promotes universal liberation but also because its view of God is more gender-balanced, at least implicitly. Thus transcendence is the "masculine" aspect of the Divine, and immanence is its "feminine" side. We consider Rosemary Ruether and Sallie McFague. But others could have been included. Virginia Mollenkott implies panentheism when she designates nature as "The Divine Milieu."[36] Elizabeth Johnson's feminist doctrine of God, *She Who Is*, explicitly endorses panentheism.[37]

Rosemary Ruether

Rosemary Ruether is the senior and most influential of Christian feminist theologians. She teaches at Garrett-Evangelical Seminary and Northwestern University. Although her starting point is feminist, her vision of liberation includes all humans and the earth.[38] The influences on her panentheism are eclectic and include Whitehead, Teilhard, and Tillich. Her own position stresses divine immanence in nature and is not distinctly Christian.

Ruether considers *Sexism and God-Talk* to be her "systematic theology" because it covers the whole range of theological topics.[39] She begins by taking women's experience of oppression and liberation as revelatory of the divine: "What does promote the full humanity of women is of the Holy, it does reflect true relation to the divine."[40] She then surveys many religions and worldviews, including Christianity, to glean insights useful for ecological-feminist theology. She rejects the Western theological tradition as a "hierarchical chain of being and chain of command" that "starts with non-

36. Virginia Ramey Mollenkott, *The Divine Feminine: The Biblical Imagery of God as Female* (New York: Crossroad, 1983), esp. chap. 18, "The Divine Milieu."

37. Elizabeth Johnson, *She Who Is: The Mystery of God in Feminist Theological Discourse* (New York: Crossroad, 1992), esp. "The World in God," 230–32.

38. Hennelly, "Rosemary Ruether," in *Liberation Theologies*, 55–69.

39. Rosemary Ruether, "New Introduction," in *Sexism and God-Talk: Toward a Feminist Theology, with a New Introduction* (Boston: Beacon, 1993), xv. She adopts Macquarrie's term for theology, *God-talk*, and his view of God as Holy Being.

40. Ibid., 12–20, quote at 19.

material spirit (God) as the source of the chain of being and continues down to nonspiritual 'matter' as the bottom." This hierarchy justifies structures of domination, "male over female, owner over worker," and "human over non-human nature."[41] Her own notion of divinity is prima facie gender-inclusive: "I use the term God/ess, a written symbol intended to combine both the masculine and feminine forms of the word for the divine while preserving the Judeo-Christian affirmation that divinity is one."[42]

But Ruether's underlying view weights the feminine-maternal aspect in favor of an immanent, naturalistic view of the divine. For Ruether, God/ess is "the primal Matrix."[43] *Matrix* comes from *mater*, Latin for "mother" and the root of "matter." The primacy of the maternal is signaled already in Ruether's opening "feminist midrash," "The Kenosis of the Father," in which the Father-God turns out to be the Son of his Mother, the Queen of Heaven and "Creatrix of all things."[44] Ruether eventually renders this symbol of the primordial divine Mother more ontologically precise as the primal cosmic Matrix from which all things emerge.

Ruether is not a materialist, however. She adopts Teilhard's notion of primordial and tangential energy. "Spirit and matter are not dichotomized but are the inside and outside of the same thing. . . . Energy, organized in patterns and relationships, is the basis for what we experience as visible things." This primordial Energy is "the spirit, the life energy that lies in every being."[45]

Primordial Energy emanates from the divine Matrix, the primal source of personhood. "That great matrix that supports the energy-matter of our individuated beings is itself the ground of all personhood as well."[46] Fully actualized, the Divine includes the entire cosmic community: "That great collective personhood is the Holy Being."[47] Paraphrasing Martin Buber, she writes, "We respond not just as 'I to it,' but as 'I to thou,' to the spirit, the life energy that lies in every being in its own form of existence." In the end, Ruether's God-talk is fundamentally feminine: God/ess is "Divine Wisdom [*Sophia*]; the empowering Matrix; She, in whom we live and move and have our being."[48] Ultimate reality is the great Mother whose energy generates,

41. Ibid., 85.
42. Ibid., 46.
43. Ibid., 85.
44. Ibid., 2.
45. Ibid., 85–87.
46. Ibid., 258.
47. Ibid.
48. Ibid., 266. Notice Ruether's use of Buber's terminology.

surrounds, and nurtures male and female humans and the whole cosmos in the nonhierarchical community that she embodies.

Ruether's divine Matrix combines Teilhard's community-evolving energy and Tillich's Ground of being/New Being without their distinctively Christian interpretation. This theology is the foundation of her view that liberation must include the earth. "The 'brotherhood of man' needs to be widened to embrace not only women but also the whole community of life."[49]

Ruether's ecological theology is developed in *Gaia and God*, which explores whether "Gaia, the living and sacred earth, and God, the monotheistic deity of the biblical traditions, [are] on speaking terms."[50] Ruether pursues her answer through the history of cosmology in the religions, theology, philosophy, and science. She is well aware of the panentheistic tradition, referring to Plato, Neoplatonism, Eckhart, Nicholas of Cusa, Bruno, Spinoza, Böhme, the Cambridge Platonists, Fichte, Hegel, Schelling, and Coleridge, among others. In stating her own view, she critically engages three contemporary ecological theologians: Teilhard, Whitehead, and Fox.[51] Ruether concludes that "both of these voices, Gaia and God, are our own voices. We need to claim them."[52] But her theology turns out to be much more the voice of Gaia than God because she continues to invoke the Divine as the "creative Matrix of the whole," and "the matrix of all interconnections of the whole universe."[53]

Ruether's view is close to naturalistic pantheism because the Divine is the community-producing power of cosmic energy. A case can be made that she is a panentheist because she adopts key theological ideas from panentheists. Accordingly she affirms an ontological distinction between the Divine and the nondivine, mind and matter, the One and the many. Their unity is "coincidence," not union or identity. "What we have traditionally called 'God,' 'the mind,' or rational pattern holding all things together, and what we have called 'matter,' the 'ground' of physical objects, come together. The disintegration of the many into infinitely small 'bits,' and the One, or unifying whole that connects all things together, coincide."[54] Her distinction

---

49. Ibid., 87.

50. Rosemary Ruether, *Gaia and God: An Ecofeminist Theology of Earth Healing* (San Francisco: Harper, 1994), 1. Gaia is the name of Mother Nature in Greek mythology.

51. Ibid., "Healing the World: The Sacramental Tradition," chap. 9. In a letter to Sallie McFague, she points out "the strong current in neo-Platonism which cultivates a 'cosmos piety' of the visible world as an embodied God, found in the Hermetic theology and even in Plotinus and Plato's *Timaeus*, . . . a view very similar to yours" (Sallie McFague, *Models of God: Theology for an Ecological, Nuclear Age* [Philadelphia: Fortress, 1987], 200 n. 9).

52. Ruether, *Gaia and God*, 254.

53. Ibid., 253, 248.

54. Ibid., 248–49.

here between the one divine Matrix and many finite things is ontological. Furthermore, the activity of finite beings is actually cocreative of the world, which entails some actual independence from as well as participation in the whole. "The small selves and the Great Self are finally one, for as She bodies forth in us, all the beings respond in the bodying forth of their diverse creative work that makes the world."[55] Ruether is just on the panentheistic side of the border with naturalistic pantheism.

Her naturalism is likewise evident in her treatment of personal language for God. Unlike Teilhard, Buber, and Hartshorne, Ruether's personal language for the divine Self as Thou is purely figurative and anthropomorphic. She raises the issue herself: "Is it a universe with which we can commune, as heart to heart, thought to thought, as I and Thou?" Her answer does not affirm an ontological Thou, a real Mind other than humanity. Instead she writes, "We are . . . the 'mind,' of the universe, the place where the universe becomes conscious of itself." What is more, human consciousness is only temporary. At death "the light of consciousness goes out, and with it our 'self.'"[56] By implication, when the human race dies out, cosmic personhood will go with it. There is no everlasting I or Thou. The enduring, all-pervading divine Matrix is person-generating Energy, the Ground of being, not a person.

Sallie McFague

Sallie McFague is a professor of theology at Vanderbilt University. Like Ruether, her feminist starting point readily expands to include the liberation of the whole earth.[57] Her first book, *Metaphorical Theology*, argues that there are many legitimate metaphors and models of God. *Models of God* then explores four models—"mother," "lover," "friend," and "the World as God's body." *The Body of God* develops that model at length.[58] McFague endorses panentheism.

Models of God elaborates an alternative to the monarchial model of God as almighty Father-King, which McFague claims "implies the wrong kind of divine activity" and "encourages passivity on the part of human beings." "Body,""mother,""lover," and "friend" are a cluster of theological models that, taken together, rightly suggest partnership with God: "We alone can—like

55. Ibid., 253.

56. Ibid., 249, 251.

57. Hennelly, "Sallie McFague," in *Liberation Theologies*, 279–87.

58. Sallie McFague, *Metaphorical Theology: Models of God in Religious Language* (Philadelphia: Fortress); *The Body of God: An Ecological Theology* (Minneapolis: Fortress, 1993).

God—mother, love, and befriend the world, the body of God." These three personal-agent models cannot be separated from the "body" model because the God-world relation must express the "holistic sensibility there can be no spirit/body split."[59] Neither humans nor God can exist without a body.

McFague recognizes her distance from the traditional view of the sovereign God, especially his power and control. With divine embodiment "the notions of vulnerability, shared responsibility, and risk are inevitable." The creatures in God's body are free to do evil that God cannot prevent. "The God who suffers with the world cannot wipe out evil: evil is not only part of the process but its power depends also on us." McFague even recognizes that evil must originate in God, a position "not unlike that of Boehme, Schelling, and Tillich."[60] But she finds the gain to be worth the loss of divine sovereignty: a God who can empathize and partner with us in seeking wholeness. "The model of the world as God's body encourages holistic attitudes of responsibility for and care of the vulnerable and oppressed; it is nonhierarchical and acts through persuasion and attraction; it has a great deal to say about the body and nature."[61] Her terms "persuasion and attraction" intentionally echo process theology.

McFague labels her model "monist" and "panentheistic; that is, a view of the God-world relationship in which all things have their origins in God and nothing exists outside God, though this does not mean that God is reduced to these things."[62] Taking distance from pantheism, she emphasizes genuine human individuality, agency, and community: "We are not mere submerged parts of the body of God but relate to God as to another Thou."[63]

The Body of God elaborates this image at length. Beginning with the ecological crisis, McFague outlines an organic, postmodern, scientific model of the cosmos that concludes that all beings are essentially embodied and ecologically interdependent. This model becomes the basis for her ecological theology. She expands on *Models of God* by developing the combined "agential" and "organic" models to replace the "deistic, dialogical, and monarchial" models. "Combining the organic [the world as the body of God] and the agential [God as the spirit of the body] results in a personal and ecological way of reimagining the tradition's Lord of creation in terms compatible with contemporary science."[64] She works out her view in critical dialogue

59. McFague, *Models of God*, 68, 76, 74.
60. Ibid., 72, 75, 201 n. 18.
61. Ibid., 78.
62. Ibid., 72; she appeals to Tillich and Rahner, 201 n. 15.
63. Ibid., 76.
64. McFague, *Body of God*, 135.

with Teilhard and Whitehead, whom she identifies as "panentheistic, not pantheistic."[65]

McFague believes that science has explained the organic nature of God's body, so she turns to the remaining question: "What of the agential or personal aspect, the spirit?" Her answer rejects the idea that "God is Mind or Will." "Spirit theology suggests another possibility: that God is not primarily the orderer and controller of the universe but its source and empowerment, the breath that enlivens and energizes it." She reads the Hebrew term *ruach*, spirit, as "breath of life" but not as mind or will. Thus she locates God's activity in biological and biocultural evolution, "the breath of life that gives all bodies, all forms of matter, the energy or power to become themselves." Humans are special, however, because we are where God becomes a conscious spirit. Divine energy "works *through* human beings: we become the mind and heart as well as the hands and feet of the body of God on our planet."[66] In the end, McFague's model of God as World-Spirit seems to undercut her agent model because agents such as mothers and friends are persons with their own minds and wills as well as bodies.

Her view of the Divine is much the same as Ruether's, an ultimately nonpersonal cosmic life and person-generating power. Both thinkers appropriate the long panentheistic tradition. Ruether points this out in a letter to McFague: "The strong current in neo-Platonism which cultivates a 'cosmos piety' of the visible world as an embodied God, found in the Hermetic theology and even in Plotinus and Plato's *Timaeus*, . . . [is] a view very similar to yours."[67]

McFague identifies herself as a panentheist, not a pantheist: "A panentheistic view of the relation of God and the world is compatible with our model of God as the spirit that is the source, the life, the breath of all reality. Everything that is is *in* God and God is *in* all things and yet God is not identical with the universe, for the universe is dependent on God in a way that God is not dependent on the universe."[68] The distinctness of God and cosmos consists in this asymmetry of their relationship. But one wonders whether God would still exist if the universe ceased to exist.

Three other topics McFague addresses also entail panentheism: creation, transcendence, and the Trinity. For God's act of creation, McFague rejects the "production model" of Genesis 1 in favor of "a combination of the pro-creative and emanationist models: God bodies forth the universe, which is

65. Ibid., 141.
66. Ibid., 142, 144–45, 148.
67. McFague, *Models of God*, 200 n. 9.
68. McFague, *Body of God*, 149.

enlivened and empowered by its source."The Divine generates and sustains its own body. With respect to transcendence, she writes, "We look for divine transcendence not apart from the material universe, but in those aspects of the material universe that are 'surpassing, excelling or extraordinary.'" In other words, she affirms "transcendent immanence, or an immanental transcendence" reminiscent of Giordano Bruno.[69] Regarding the Trinity, McFague suggests replacing Father, Son, and Holy Spirit with "the mystery of God (the invisible face or first person), the physicality of God (the visible body or second person), and the mediation of the invisible and visible (the spirit or third person)."[70] This account confirms that her panentheism is nontrinitarian according to the definition used by Teilhard, Moltmann, and Pannenberg.

In sum, McFague's feminist starting point culminates in an ecological panentheism of the world as God's body. Like Boff and Ruether, she claims that "the good news is not only for individual human beings and not even only for oppressed groups of human beings, but for the entire creation."[71]

Matthew Fox's Creation Spirituality

Matthew Fox became a Roman Catholic priest in 1967 but was disciplined by the Vatican during the 1980s in part because of his ongoing collaboration with Miriam Starhawk, a Wiccan. He left the Catholic Church in 1993 and became an Episcopal priest in 1994. He is founder and president of the University of Creation Spirituality in Oakland, California. Not associated primarily with liberation theology, his vision nevertheless includes the liberation of humanity in its emphasis on the divine presence in all creatures and the whole creation. Fox's overall perspective has much in common with Boff, Ruether, and McFague.[72]

Fox's commitment to panentheism is stated in his sixth thesis of creation spirituality: "Theism (the idea that God is 'out there' or above and beyond the universe) is false. All things are in God and God is in all things (panentheism)."[73]

He endorses panentheism throughout *The Coming of the Cosmic Christ*, perhaps his best-known work. The book begins with a bad dream, "Your

69. Ibid., 153–54.

70. Ibid., 193.

71. Ibid., 201.

72. Ruether discusses Fox in *Gaia and God*, 240–42.

73. Matthew Fox, "95 Theses or Articles of Faith for a Christianity for a Third Millennium," chap. 5 in *A New Reformation: Creation Spirituality and the Transformation of Christianity* (Rochester, VT: Inner Traditions, 2006).

Mother Is Dying," in which our Mother includes nature, culture, social
bonds, traditional religions, the church, and human solidarity. But Fox sees
hope in the growing renewal of world-affirming mysticism, a spirituality he
labels panentheistic. "Healthy mysticism is panentheistic. This means that
it is not theistic, which envisions divinity 'out there' or even 'in here' in a
dualistic manner that separates creation from divinity. Panentheism means
'all things in God and God in all things.'"[74]

To explain panentheistic mysticism, Fox introduces Teilhard's concept of
the Cosmic Christ. "Teilhard de Chardin calls the Cosmic Christ the 'third
nature' of Christ ... 'neither human nor divine but cosmic.'"[75] He traces
the Cosmic Christ from Scripture and Christian tradition, especially the
incarnation theology of the Greek fathers, the Eastern church, and some
Western mystics. He judges that the Western Augustinian tradition has been
too preoccupied with the personal salvation of individuals from sin and guilt,
which has had terribly negative consequences for Western Christianity and
culture. He notes positive exceptions in Western Christianity. Hildegaard
of Bingen, Thomas Aquinas, and Dante affirmed the Cosmic Christ. He
identifies Francis of Assisi, Meister Eckhart, Julian of Norwich, and Nicholas
of Cusa as panentheists.[76]

Following Teilhard, Fox's Cosmic Christ does not intend to negate the
significance of Jesus's incarnation, life, death, and resurrection but expands
them to include all people and the entire cosmos. Christ is the life and coherence of the whole creation, the connection of all things. The life, death,
and resurrection of Jesus symbolize and include the suffering and rebirth of
Mother Earth and all her children. The whole creation is being reborn.

Fox calls for conversion to a new vision. "Embracing the Cosmic Christ
will demand a paradigm shift.... A shift from anthropocentrism to a living
cosmology, from Newton to Einstein, from parts-mentality to wholeness,
from rationalism to mysticism, from obedience as a prime moral virtue
to creativity as a prime moral virtue, from personal salvation to communal healing, i.e., compassion as salvation, from theism (God outside us) to
panentheism (God in us and us in God), from fall-redemption religion to
creation-centered spirituality, from the ascetic to the aesthetic."[77] Panentheism is integral to his entire world-and-life view.

74. Matthew Fox, *The Coming of the Cosmic Christ: The Healing of Mother Earth and the Birth of
a Global Renaissance* (San Francisco: Harper and Row, 1988), 57.

75. Ibid., 83.

76. Ibid., 113, 122–23, 126. Eckhart is his favorite. See Matthew Fox, *Breakthrough: Meister
Eckhart's Creation Spirituality* (Garden City, NY: Doubleday, 1980).

77. Fox, *Cosmic Christ*, 134–35.

The major applications of Fox's paradigm seem pitched more toward the secure and affluent than the poor and oppressed, as can be seen in chapter titles in *The Cosmic Christ*: "A Renaissance of Sexual Mysticism," "Honoring the Child Within," and "The Return of the Personal Arts." But he also urges environmental stewardship, social justice, global peace, and what he calls "deep ecumenism," which affirms the presence of the Cosmic Christ in all religions and spiritualities.[78]

Panentheism is integral to Fox's cosmic Christology and creation spirituality. But his interests are spirituality and practice, not philosophy. Consequently, he reiterates a basic definition of panentheism but does not develop it: "all things in God and God in all things."[79]

Conclusion

The theologians in this chapter find panentheism highly conducive to their interest in the liberation of particular groups of people as part of the renewal of the whole creation. If all things are in God or the world is God's body, then humans of both genders from all ethnic groups and social classes are included in cosmic salvation. God shares all human oppression and suffering, and all humans share in the life of God, which is liberating and enhancing the universe. Thus the interests of liberation theology and the emphases of panentheism coincide. Because they are primarily interested in ethical and practical issues, most liberation and ecological theologians have not contributed much to the philosophical refinement of panentheism.

The diversity of liberation theologies concerns more than their interest in different kinds of liberation. They are diverse in attitude toward historic Christianity. Although critical of oppressive traditions, most Latin Americans strive to remain consistent with post–Vatican II orthodoxy. Cone and Fox use primarily Christian terminology but understand it as symbolic of more generic kinds of liberation. Ruether and McFague relativize Christian language to a more broadly naturalistic view of cosmic liberation.

Liberation theologians are also diverse in their intellectual sources. Teilhard's cosmic Christology, Moltmann's trinitarian cosmology, Tillich's existential theology, and Whitehead's process theology, in different proportions and combinations, are important to most of them. Most are aware of their roots in the Neoplatonic and Christian dialectical traditions as well.

78. Ibid., part 5. Fox certainly decries social, economic, and political oppression, but they are not his primary focus.
79. Ibid., 57.

Finally, they are diverse with respect to the fundamental nature of the Divine. Most emphasize the irreducibly personal or tripersonal nature of God. It is surprising that the feminist theologians Ruether and McFague, for whom one might expect personhood to be of highest value, view the Divine as a personalizing power or Ground rather than as a person or triunity of persons. Their basic theological model is more organic than social.

13

Panentheism in Theological Cosmology

The most vital and interesting discussions of panentheism are currently taking place among scientifically informed theologians and theologically informed scientists.[1] Many such scholars affirm panentheism because they find it to be the most reasonable way of combining state-of-the-art science with belief in God—for many, the Christian God. This chapter considers some major contributors to this dialogue: Ian Barbour, Paul Davies, Arthur Peacocke, and Philip Clayton. It concludes with John Polkinghorne, who claims to reject panentheism for this world but affirms it for the world to come. As with the previous survey chapters, this selection is representative rather than exhaustive.

Considering these thinkers together is natural because they are part of an identifiable group who have sustained a long-running dialogue.[2] In the big picture they are continuing the project that has been under way since Plato's *Timaeus*—constructing a theological-scientific cosmology that correlates divine immanence and transcendence. They self-consciously build on the

1. Philip Clayton and Arthur Peacocke, eds., *In Whom We Live and Move and Have Our Being: Panentheistic Reflections on God's Presence in a Scientific World* (Grand Rapids: Eerdmans, 2003), is a fine example.

2. John Polkinghorne, *Scientists as Theologians: A Comparison of the Writings of Ian Barbour, Arthur Peacocke, and John Polkinghorne* (London: SPCK, 1996), is an example. Most of them are involved with and/or have been awarded prizes by the Templeton Foundation, a philanthropic organization that promotes positive dialogue between science and religion.

science-based theologies developed since Hegel and Schelling by Fechner, Lotze, Peirce, James, Alexander, Bergson, Teilhard, and Whitehead. Everyone in the chapter accepts the idea that the universe is a system of emergent levels of complexity that points to God. Some understand God's relation to the world as analogous to the mind-body relation. Others propose more general theories of divine interaction with the world. But each develops a version of panentheism. Most of these thinkers are Christian and readily draw from the theological ideas of Teilhard, Temple, Moltmann, Pannenberg, and other panentheistic Christian theologians who have engaged science.

Barbour's Qualified Process Panentheism

For decades, Ian Barbour, emeritus professor of science and religion at Carlton College in Minnesota, has promoted process thought as the most promising framework for relating science and religion. Already in the 1960s his comprehensive book *Issues in Science and Religion* recommended Whitehead's process metaphysics, qualified by Christian emphases, as the best route to pursue in this endeavor.[3] He has steered that course his entire career.[4]

Process Theology

Barbour's fullest elaboration of his theology is in his Gifford Lectures, *Religion in an Age of Science*. Chapter 8 of that volume presents an engaging summary of process thought—both its philosophy and its theology.[5] He explains and defends the conditioned self-creativity of entities, their prehension in the consequent nature of God, and the persuasive influence of God's primordial nature on the world. He also summarizes the theologies of Whitehead, Hartshorne, Cobb, and Griffin. Barbour concludes that process thought is a viable synthesis of science and theology. But he refrains from endorsing it until "God and Nature," chapter 9 of *Religion in an Age of Science*.

In that chapter, Barbour identifies process thought not simply as a viable framework for a synthesis of science and theology but as the best one.[6]

3. Ian Barbour, *Issues in Science and Religion* (New York: Prentice-Hall, 1966).

4. See Ian Barbour, *Religion in an Age of Science*, Gifford Lectures, 1989–1991 (San Francisco: Harper and Row, 1990); also *When Science Meets Religion* (San Francisco: HarperCollins, 2000); and *Nature, Human Nature, and God* (Minneapolis: Augsburg Fortress, 2002).

5. See chap. 7, above, for a summary of process theology.

6. The other theological models he considers are God's self-limitation, Bultmann's existentialist theology, God as agent, and the world as God's body. All make points that Barbour endorses, but he finds none as coherent and comprehensive as process theology.

Process theology's greatest strength, he says, is its model of God as creative participant in the world. God is "the leader of a cosmic community" that is both social and ecological. Because the world as a whole is more like a community than an organism, Barbour prefers Whitehead's pluralistic model to Hartshorne's mind-body analogy for God's relation to the world.[7]

Barbour identifies six key reasons God as creative participant is the best alternative to classical theism. First, process theology affirms human freedom, recognizes our limitations, and "strongly endorses our responsibility to work creatively to further God's purposes." Next is the problem of evil and suffering. "By accepting the limitations of divine power we avoid blaming God for particular forms of evil and suffering. . . . Instead of God the judge . . . we have God the friend, with us in our suffering and working with us to redeem it." Third, process thought promotes gender justice by modeling God inclusively. "The goal in picturing both divine and human virtues is to integrate masculine/feminine attributes within a new wholeness." The fourth advantage is interreligious dialogue because "process thought allows us to acknowledge that God's creative presence is at work at all points in nature and history." We can both affirm our own religious community and be open to others. Fifth, the process view of God is especially compatible with evolutionary biology, respect for all of nature, and a view of humanity that does not dichotomize body and mind. Finally, process theology affirms both law and chance in nature and its development. On all of these issues, Barbour concludes that process theology is superior both to classical theism and to other modern theologies.[8]

Barbour's Qualifications

Barbour acknowledges some legitimate criticisms of process theology but thinks that they can be addressed. First, process philosophy can be used as a rigid system that undercuts religion. He counters that "Christianity cannot be identified with any metaphysical system," although it does present a view of reality that philosophy can attempt to state. A second issue is God's transcendence and power. "Transcendence is indeed less emphasized in process theology than in classical Christianity, but it is still strongly represented." With respect to power, "the process God does have power, but it is the evocative power of love and inspiration, not controlling, unilateral power." Barbour argues that the process notion of power is con-

7. Barbour, *Religion in an Age of Science*, 260–61.
8. Ibid., 261–62.

sistent with the Christian view that God is love. He does admit, however, two significant differences between the power of the process God and the Christian God. First, whereas Christians think that "the qualifications of divine omnipotence are voluntary and temporary, for Whiteheadians the limitations are metaphysical and necessary." Second, "process theology does call into question the traditional expectation of an absolute victory over evil," although it is reasonably confident in God's persuasive power. In the end, Barbour endorses the essential ideas of process theology with some Christian qualifications. This is perfectly legitimate, he observes: "Many process insights may be accepted without accepting the total Whiteheadian scheme."[9]

His final conclusion is that "the reformulations of the classical tradition proposed in process theology are indeed justified" and that "they have fewer weaknesses than the other models considered." But his endorsement of process theology is tentative for both epistemological and spiritual reasons. Epistemologically, "all models are limited and partial," even process theology. Spiritually, "only in worship can we acknowledge the mystery of God and the pretensions of any system of thought claiming to have mapped out God's ways."[10]

Barbour's theology is a nondogmatic Christian modification of process thought. But none of his adaptations alter its thoroughly panentheistic character. Asserting that self-limitation in creation is voluntary for God does not negate the correlative relationship of God and creation or the existence of creation in the consequent nature of God, as explained by process theology and endorsed by Barbour.

The Uniformitarian Panentheism of Davies

Paul Davies is an astrophysicist and philosopher who taught at the English universities of London and Cambridge and is now at Macquarie University in Australia. A self-professed "deist" for most of his career, he has recently asserted that "panentheism is the theology that most closely matches my understanding of the relationship between God and the physical universe."[11]

9. Ibid., 263–67.

10. Ibid., 267–70.

11. Paul Davies, "Teleology without Teleology: Purpose through Emergent Complexity," in *In Whom We Live*, ed. Clayton and Peacocke, 96; also 99, 100, 108. Ibid., 99, he identifies his position in *The Cosmic Blueprint: New Discoveries in Nature's Creative Ability to Order the Universe* (New York: Simon and Schuster, 1988) as "deism." This is also his position in *The Mind of God: The Scientific Basis for a Rational World* (New York: Simon and Schuster, 1992).

Models of Divine Action

Davies explains his position by contrasting three models of divine action in the world: interventionism, noninterventionism, and uniformitarianism. He rejects the first, considers the second, and modifies the third to define his own panentheism, a "teleology without teleology."

Interventionism is the view that "God's special actions break the ordinary flow of physical processes and entail a violation of the laws of nature." Although it is favored by conservative Christians and other traditional religious believers, Davies rejects interventionism as "decidedly unappealing" to most scientists because it suggests that God is a nonnatural force in nature alongside and competing with natural forces. He thinks that most theologians would object to interventionism because "it reduces God to an aspect of nature in competition with other aspects."[12]

Noninterventionist views propose ways that God can "act effectively in nature through specific events—making a real difference in what actually comes to pass—but in ways that do not interrupt these processes or violate the laws of nature." One current model—"bottom-up causality"—suggests that God can act on the level of subatomic indeterminacy to produce a variety of significantly different results in higher levels of nature. According to another model, "top-down causality," the universe is not a closed system. The whole universe as well as particular parts are open to being affected in ways analogous to the human mind's causal influence on the body. We know that minds exercise "top-down" influence on our brains even though science cannot explain how this occurs. This kind of causation is noninterventionist because it does not impose on bodily existence from the outside or violate the laws that govern it. Thus "there is no logical impediment to God acting in a somewhat similar manner. Indeed, panentheists frequently appeal to the analogy between our minds acting on our bodies and God acting on the universe as a whole."[13] But Davies does not endorse this model either.

A third view is uniformitarianism, which holds that God created the universe with a carefully chosen set of laws that combine uniformity and randomness to produce "the emergence of genuinely novel complexity in nature." Thus "the intrinsic creativity of nature results from the inherently self-organizing potentialities of the laws of nature" without God's influence on particular events. Davies states that this was his position when he was a "deist."[14]

12. Davies, "Teleology," 97.
13. Ibid., 97–99.
14. Ibid., 99–100.

Uniformitarian Panentheism

To arrive at his panentheism, which he calls modified uniformitarianism, Davies goes beyond deism by emphasizing "God's continuing role of creating the universe afresh at each moment." God does not create the universe and then leave it on its own but remains continuously involved. This view is still uniformitarian, however, because God is present "without in any way bringing about particular events which nature 'on its own' would not have produced."[15]

In this model the universe is like a chess game. God sets the rules, never changes them, and allows creatures freedom to play within them. Like increasingly skillful players, creatures eventually realize the sophisticated possibilities that the rules allow. "God selects very special laws that guarantee a trend toward greater richness, diversity, and complexity through spontaneous self-organization, but the final outcome in all its details is open and left to chance."[16] God's creation of a self-creating universe is "a teleology without teleology." He has designed and sustains the world so that genuinely new and more complex levels of existence emerge. The human race is its most spectacular advance. Because God is continuously creating this creative process, nature and humanity are "the product of an ingenious—even loving—designer."[17]

Davies endorses panentheism because it acknowledges God's ongoing nondeterministic involvement in the cosmos. "My point in appealing to panentheism is to propose that in choosing these particular laws God also chose not to determine the universe in detail but instead to give a vital, co-creative role to nature itself."[18] God is immanent in the universe by way of continuous lawful creation. All creatures are in God because his continuous creation is the context within which they exist and develop. They are really distinct from God because they have the power of self-development.

Davies affirms God's transcendence in two ways. First, God is free in creating. Davies notes that almost all scientists, even atheists, concede that "the universe as it exists is not necessary—that it could have been otherwise." Second, the basic laws that are conditions for time and space are outside time

15. Ibid., 100.

16. Ibid., 106. He calls his model "God as Chess Player." But as he explains it, God defines the rules and creatures play the game.

17. Ibid., 100–103. Davies argues that the only challenge to real design as opposed to merely apparent design is the existence of multiple universes. If there were multiple universes, we might just happen to be in the one that was conducive to our existence. It would appear designed but not really be designed. But we have no evidence of any other actual universe. So we are justified in believing in a real designer.

18. Ibid., 104.

and space. "God acts to create all that is, including space, time, and the laws of nature, and thus these laws are in this sense eternal, too." God himself is eternal. "Thus the selector God is, in this function at least, outside of time altogether." In sum, God is transcendent in that his act of creation is contingent and originates beyond creation and its dynamic remains changeless.

Davies's God is dipolar, both immanent and transcendent. He is also both temporal and eternal: "If God sustains the continually creative universe through time, then in this sense God possesses a temporal as well as an atemporal aspect."[19] Other dipolar attributes follow.

Davies concludes that "panentheism best expresses the concept, 'teleology without teleology.'" His theology is uniformitarian panentheism.

He recognizes that his model "will be regarded by many as too impoverished and remote a concept of God." He therefore raises the possibility of combining noninterventionist divine action with uniform divine action. This would enable those who regard evolution as statistically improbable to acknowledge God's direct involvement in bringing it about. "God may be more immediately involved in the process of evolutionary change when the laws of nature themselves are an expression of non-interventionist divine agency."[20] But Davies does not endorse this modification of his modified uniformitarian panentheism.

Peacocke's Naturalistic Sacramental Panentheism

Arthur Peacocke is a biochemist and a priest in the Church of England. He has taught at Oxford and Cambridge and has published widely on science and religion. For decades he has promoted "sacramental panentheism" as the best framework for integrating Christianity and contemporary science.[21] In a recently published summary of his thought, Peacocke reviews the developments in modern science that have motivated theologians to replace classical theism and deism with panentheism.[22]

19. Ibid., 102–3.
20. Ibid., 106.
21. Arthur Peacocke, *Creation and the World of Science*, Bampton Lectures, 1978 (Oxford: Clarendon, 1979), 207, introduces "the world within God (pan-en-theism)" and, 289–91, characterizes God's presence in the world as "sacramental." See also *God and the New Biology* (San Francisco: Harper and Row, 1986), 99, 122–27, for "a sacramental view of the cosmos." An extensive note in *Theology for a Scientific Age: Being and Becoming—Natural and Divine* (Oxford: Basil Blackwell, 1990), 207–8, endorses panentheism but expresses reservations about the use of the term because of its association with process theology and the idea that the world is "part of God," which Peacocke rejects.
22. Arthur Peacocke, "God's Presence in and to the World Unveiled by the Sciences," in *In Whom We Live*, ed. Clayton and Peacocke, 137–54.

Emergent Monism

Peacocke begins by noting that science shows the world to be structured as a dynamic system of complex hierarchies, "a series of levels of organization of matter in which each successive member is a whole constituted of parts preceding it in the hierarchy." On the one hand, the entire world is material. "All entities, all concrete particulars in the world, including human beings, are constituted of fundamental physical entities." On the other hand, genuinely new levels of existence emerge in the higher levels of complexity—especially the psychological, intellectual, social, moral, and spiritual capacities of the human mind and spirit. Thus Peacocke argues that body-mind dualism is no longer tenable. The higher levels, however, are not conceptually reducible to lower levels. Psychology does not factor down to physics. Peacocke calls this ontology "emergent monism."[23]

Science also understands that the world is dynamic and evolving. Material systems are not entirely static and homogeneous but acquire new levels of complexity and qualitatively new modes of existence over time. "The processes of the world by their inherent properties manifest a spontaneous creativity in which new properties emerge." As a result of these dynamics, human life in all its sophistication has evolved from the primitive universe. This is the scientific world picture that theology must engage.

The Panentheistic Model

So Peacocke turns to theology. He rejects classical theism because it places God entirely outside created reality and time and cannot explain how God can act within the world. He endorses panentheism because he thinks it fits better with science and with Scripture's teaching that God is engaged in the world. He rejects the notion, held by some panentheists, that the world is part of God. Instead, "in God" means "an ontological relation so that the world is conceived as within the Being of God but, nevertheless, with its own distinct ontology." Peacocke does not present a detailed theology of God's relation to the world, but he repeatedly endorses Moltmann's notion of *zimsum*, the ontological space constituted by divine self-limitation.[24] The panentheism he approves is "perichoretic," or interrelational.

23. Ibid., 138–40.
24. Ibid., 145–47: "All that is not God has its existence within God's operation and Being. The infinity of God includes all other finite entities, structures, and processes; God's infinity comprehends and incorporates all"; "God creates all-that-is *within* Godself."

Peacocke conjoins this relational panentheism with his ontology of nature, a physical monism with emergent levels of complexity and novelty. God is the creative force immanent in nature that generates the system of systems: "In a very strong sense, God is the immanent creator creating through the processes of the natural order. The processes are not themselves God, but the *action* of God as creator."[25] All God's interactions are within the world, and so Peacocke's view avoids supernatural interventionism. The world is likewise entirely within God. "If God incorporates both the individual systems and the total system of systems within Godself, as in the panentheistic model, then it is more conceivable that God could interact with all the complex systems at their own holistic levels."[26] Interactive panentheism provides a full account of God's involvement in the world as a whole and in all its parts.

With many in the panentheist tradition, Peacocke adopts the mind-body relation as an analogy of the God-world relation. "God is *internally* present to all the world's entities, structures, and processes in a way analogous to the way we as persons are present and act in our bodies."[27] The theological mind-body analogy has, however, three qualifications. First, God creates the world whereas we humans do not create our bodies. Second, God knows every being and event in the world whereas we are unaware of most of our bodies. Third, God is not "a person" but "suprapersonal" or "transpersonal" because he has many essential attributes that human persons do not.[28]

Peacocke admits that, according to his view, God is involved in natural and moral evil. "Creation is costly *to God*. Now, when the natural world, with all its suffering, is panentheistically conceived of as 'in God,' it follows that the evils of pain, suffering, and death in the world are internal to God's own self," including "the moral evil of human society." He also endorses maternal images for God, both the womb of God and the pain of childbirth,[29] because they express the ideas that God nurtures the world and experiences its pain.

From Christian sources Peacocke adopts "the feminine figure of Wisdom (*Sophia*)" as a personification of the action of the Triune God in the world: "This important concept of Wisdom (*Sophia*) unites intimately the divine activity of creation, human experience, and the processes of the natural world. It therefore constitutes a biblical resource for imaging the panentheism we

25. Ibid., 144.

26. Ibid., 147–50.

27. Ibid., 150.

28. Ibid., 150–51. This is a philosophical conclusion. He affirms the Christian doctrine of the Trinity.

29. Ibid., 151–52.

have been urging." Correlative with Wisdom is "the Word (*Logos*) of God," made flesh in the person of Jesus the Christ. The Word is the rationality of God's own creative action evident in nature and in human reason. "Again we have a panentheistic notion that unites, intimately, as three facets of one integrated and interlocked activity, the divine, the human, and the (nonhuman) natural."[30] Thus Peacocke synthesizes his panentheism and Christian theology.

Sacramental Panentheism

Following William Temple, Peacocke views the universe as "sacramental." The panentheist "sees God working in, with, and under natural processes. ... But in the Christian tradition, this is precisely what its sacraments do." Peacocke's final summary links the sacraments with the incarnation, both of which are believed to be the real presence of God in the world. Echoing Teilhard, he sees the incarnation as the fulfillment of the God who already exists in the world and is manifest most explicitly in the trajectory of human evolution, which culminates in Jesus Christ. For these reasons, Peacocke considers his "theological naturalism and panentheism" to be a "sacramental panentheism."[31]

Clayton's Emergent Personal Panentheism

Philip Clayton is professor of theology at Claremont School of Theology and professor of philosophy and religion at Claremont Graduate School. He has contributed to the science-theology dialogue in a number of books and articles, of which *God and Contemporary Science* is perhaps the best known. *The Problem of God in Modern Thought* is a significant account of the rise of panentheism in philosophical theology since Descartes.[32] Broadly speaking, Clayton forges his panentheism by using key themes in Peacocke's theological cosmology and Pannenberg's and Moltmann's cosmic theologies.[33] The following summary of his position focuses on how he argues that science

30. Ibid., 152–53.
31. Ibid., 153–54. The phrase "Theological Naturalism and Panentheism" is in the subtitle of the last section, 152–54.
32. Philip Clayton, *God and Contemporary Science* (Grand Rapids: Eerdmans, 1997); *The Problem of God in Modern Thought* (Grand Rapids: Eerdmans, 2000).
33. Clayton, preface to *God and Contemporary Science.* Philip Clayton, "Panentheism in Metaphysical and Scientific Perspective," in *In Whom We Live,* ed. Clayton and Peacocke, 73–91, summarizes this project.

points to something "personal" beyond the universe, on how the person-body analogy models the relation between God and the world, and, finally, on his appeal to Schelling's theology.

Emergentism and the Panentheistic Analogy

Peacocke's monistic emergentism provides Clayton a nonreductionistic, nondualistic view of the evolving, complex universe, a view that is highly conducive to panentheism. "Arthur Peacocke has already nicely described the way emergent systems represent a sort of nested hierarchy: parts are contained within wholes, which themselves become parts within greater wholes, and so forth." But the universe is not self-generating, and so this world picture points beyond itself. "Emergence propels one to metaphysics, and metaphysical reflection in turn suggests a theological postulate above and beyond the logic of emergence."[34] The part-whole structure of the universe provides a model for the relationship between the universe and its Ground. "If the same structure could be applied to God's relation to the world, it would comprehend the world as internal to God."[35] Thus the emergent universe suggests panentheism.

But is the grounding power personal or impersonal? Emergentism itself suggests that it is personal because human personhood is the highest product of evolution, "the emergence of mind (or mental properties) from the most complicated biological structure yet discovered, the human body and brain." Therefore Clayton affirms the personalist answer, what he calls "the panentheistic analogy," the body-mind relation taken as the model for the God-world relation. "The world is in some sense analogous to the body of God; God is analogous to the mind which indwells the body, though God is also more than the natural world taken as a whole."[36]

The Panentheistic Analogy Elaborated

Part of Clayton's case for this model is historical and philosophical. In *God and Contemporary Science* he surveys the development of theology "from classical theism to panentheism."[37] He notes the background of modern panentheism in Neoplatonism, Eriugena, Eckhart, Nicholas of Cusa, Bruno,

34. Clayton, "Panentheism in Metaphysical and Scientific Perspective," 89–91.
35. Ibid., 87–88.
36. Ibid., 83–84. Clayton, "Understanding Human and Divine Agency," chap. 8 in *God and Contemporary Science*, elaborates.
37. Ibid., the title of a section, 88–96.

and others who assert that "finite things are *in* God." He illustrates its modern development with the notion, stated by Newton and updated by Moltmann, that space (like time) is a divine attribute. "In short: finite space is contained within absolute space, the world is contained within God; yet the world is not identical to God. Precisely this is the core thesis of panentheism."

Clayton is aware that including nondivine beings in God is "a dialectical way of thinking that has not always been embraced within the Christian tradition."[38] But he insists that the concept of the true Infinite logically requires panentheism. "The infinite may without contradiction include within itself things that are by nature finite, but it may not stand *outside* of the finite. . . . Hence an infinite God must encompass the finite world that he created, making it in some sense 'within' himself. This is the conclusion that we call panentheism."[39] To show its plausibility, Clayton offers an ecological illustration. "Now imagine an ecosystem of 'all that is'; it too must be more than the sum total of its parts. If you also imagine that its identity is living and conscious, and (for this is the claim of theism) that its existence also preceded its being filled with living things, then you will have some sense of the dialectic between God and world envisioned by panentheism."[40] Clayton's model is strongly reminiscent of Plato's doctrine that the universe is a living being contained within the World-Soul. He views God as a personal agent and the universe as his body.

Clayton's person-body analogy models the world's effect on God, God's agency in the world, and God's transcendence of the world. We consider each in turn.

First, it is essential to panentheism that "God genuinely responds to and is affected by what his creatures do,"[41] as Hegel, Whitehead, Hartshorne, and Moltmann have affirmed. Creatures affect God because he "is present in each physical interaction and at each point in space, each interaction is a part of his being in the broadest sense, for it is 'in him [that] we live and move and have our being' (Acts 17:28)."[42] Thus God depends on being affected by the world. "God depends on the world because the nature of God's actual experience depends on interactions with finite creatures like ourselves."[43]

---

38. Ibid., 89–90.
39. Ibid., 99; also Clayton, "Panentheism in Metaphysical and Scientific Perspective," 81. He is aware of the antiquity of this argument as well as its modern use by Hegel, Schelling, Moltmann, and Pannenberg.
40. Ibid., 91.
41. Ibid., 94–95.
42. Ibid., 101.
43. Clayton, "Panentheism in Metaphysical and Scientific Perspective," 83.

But God also affects the world. As noted above, Clayton models divine agency on an emergent-developmental explanation of human personal agency. The human person is a complex reality that emerges from and is influenced by the human organism but that in turn exercises genuine causality in its organism: "Mental properties can also be the direct cause of other mental properties as well as the cause of changes in the physical world (e.g., one's own brain)." In an analogous way, God exercises genuine agency in the world without supernatural intervention.[44] Clayton's position is very similar to Peacocke's notion of God's "top-down" causality in the world.

Clayton's Christian belief moves him to emphasize God's transcendence and the disanalogies between God and humans. First, God is a distinct being and "not merely an emergent set of divine properties."[45] More basically, "God is not dependent on the world for existence but preceded the world and created it." Finally, God's eternity, omnipotence, and moral perfection are attributes that humans lack.[46]

Clayton emphasizes that his panentheism does not make the world necessary for God. God's initial decision to create the world is "a divine free choice." It is not necessary or inevitable in any sense. "A free creation remains free; any effect the world subsequently has on God is a consequence of the initial free decision rather than a sign of eternal necessity." God's choice to involve himself in history does shape his own history. But this does not change God's essential nature.[47] Clayton's panentheism is unusual in that it does not entail, even implicitly, the inevitability of the world or a compatibilist view of divine freedom.

Clayton's Affirmation of Schelling

Clayton's emphasis on divine freedom is reflected in his preference for Schelling's personalistic panentheism. *The Problem of God in Modern Thought* traces the development of panentheism since Descartes and Spinoza. Chapter 9, the climax, is devoted to Schelling's theology of freedom.[48] In brief, Clayton recounts the development of Schelling's philosophy from his youthful

44. Clayton, *God and Contemporary Science*, 259; see 247–58.

45. Clayton rejects as theologically inadequate Samuel Alexander's radical emergent theism, the view that "'God' or 'the divine' is an emergent property of the physical universe" ("Panentheism in Metaphysical and Scientific Perspective," 90).

46. Clayton, *God and Contemporary Science*, 260.

47. Ibid., 93; see 93–96.

48. Clayton, "Beyond the 'God beyond God'": Schelling's Theology of Freedom," chap. 9 in *The Problem of God*. Clayton prefers Schelling to Tillich's attempted modification of Schelling. See chap. 8, above, on Tillich's "philosophical flaw."

system of absolute identity, through his Böhmian personalism, to his final positive philosophy of revelation.[49] He prefers Schelling's emphasis on God's freedom to Hegel's rational determinism. He is not, however, uncritical of Schelling. He rejects his Böhmian speculation about the inner being of God and the necessity of the world. He likewise denies that God has a "dark side" and that creation is a spiritually negative "fall" from God.

But Clayton does follow Schelling in positing a duality in God's nature. God eternally has the potential freely to create or not to create a world and to manifest himself in a variety of ways consistent with, but not determined by, his eternal nature. Such eternal power entails self-knowledge and will. Therefore God is personal, independent of all worlds; the Ground of being in itself is personal. But if the truly infinite God freely chooses to create, he must have a history and destiny that include the world within himself. Thus his personhood will grow, develop, and become something other than it would have been if creatures had behaved differently or if he had not created anything at all. If he creates, "God-as-personal emerges from the infinite divine ground; as a being involved in actual relations with the world, God undergoes real change and development through those relations."[50] Clayton endorses Schelling's theology of divine freedom.[51]

The moral for theology and philosophy is that finite human minds cannot rationally determine God's nature from creation or read creation as a necessary consequence of God's nature. God's revelation is not irrational, but neither is it rationally necessary. This is why Schelling opted for a positive philosophy of revelation. Clayton follows him.

Clayton's theology is neo-Schellingian emergent personalist panentheism. Like Schelling, he holds that God is freely developing himself as a person in his body, the universe. His body and personality emerge and grow because of his action and creatures' effects on him, but his core personhood is transcendent and essentially independent of creation. As a Christian, Clayton construes God's personhood in terms of the Trinity and the incarnation of Jesus Christ.

49. See chap. 4, above.

50. Clayton, *The Problem of God*, 488.

51. Clayton abstracts this theme from Schelling's mature philosophy. Schelling holds that God's eternal option is to exist or not to exist. If he exists, he must generate a world. If the world does not exist, it is because God has chosen not to exist. Because God is good and wills to actualize all good, he freely chooses to exist in spite of the evil that inevitably comes with the existence of the world. See chap. 4, above, on Schelling's personalism.

When Clayton affirms the personal reality of God in himself independent of creation, and creation as a free choice among options, he is close to the voluntarism of the Scotist-Calvinist tradition of classical theism that I embrace. This is an issue for the final chapter.

Polkinghorne's Eschatological Panentheism

John Polkinghorne, Cambridge scientist and ordained Anglican theologian, is included in this chapter with qualification because his panentheism is provisional. "I do not accept panentheism (the idea that the creation is in God, though God exceeds creation) as a theological reality for the present world, but I do believe in it as the form of eschatological destiny for the world to come."[52] We briefly note his reservations about panentheism, his dipolar view of God, and his panentheistic vision of the eschaton.

Dipolar Theism, Not Panentheism

Polkinghorne rejects panentheism even though he shares its goal. "While I am sympathetic to what panentheism set out to achieve by way of balance between divine transcendence and divine immanence, I cannot myself see that it succeeds in doing so in an acceptable way."[53] His objection is clear: "Panentheism's defect is its denial of the true otherness of the world from God."[54] A key problem is that panentheism makes the world inevitable for God, a defect inherited from its Neoplatonic predecessor. "In the earlier centuries the threat came from neo-Platonism's alternative view, which depicted the world as being an emanation from the divine. . . . Panentheism represents a kind of modern version of emanationism, in its strong emphasis on the need for an absolute divine inclusivity."[55]

His own position seeks to correct classical theism's overemphasis on transcendence but without endorsing panentheism. "All that is necessary is to reaffirm that creatures live in the divine presence and in the context of the activity of the living God." He begins by adopting an Eastern Orthodox distinction between God's essential being and his energies, the "immanently active divine operations *ad extra*."[56] He then sketches a trinitarian theology of divine self-limitation or *kenōsis* that invokes Rahner's Rule and several key ideas of Moltmann, including *zimsum*—space and time as divine contractions.

52. John Polkinghorne, *The God of Hope and the End of the World* (New Haven: Yale University Press, 2002), 114–15.

53. John Polkinghorne, *Faith of a Physicist* (Princeton, NJ: Princeton University Press, 1994), 64.

54. Polkinghorne, *Science and the Trinity*, 95–97. He charges that panentheism does not leave enough room for creaturely freedom and self-determination. But most contemporary panentheists would argue that this is precisely what they affirm. Peacocke, *Theology for a Scientific Age*, 207, thinks that Polkinghorne misreads him.

55. Polkinghorne, *Science and the Trinity*, 97.

56. Ibid., 98.

Polkinghorne rejects the classical notion that God is purely eternal. His knowledge of the world is temporal. "If God's creation is intrinsically temporal, surely the Creator must know it in its temporality." Here he endorses Whitehead and Hartshorne's notion that God is dipolar—both eternal and temporal—without adopting their metaphysics. Since God's knowledge of the world is temporal, he knows only the present and past because the future is not actual. "In the kind of dipolar theism that I am seeking to espouse, God is understood to have *chosen* to possess only a current omniscience, temporally indexed. . . . God does not yet know all that will eventually become knowable."

Not knowing the future acts of free creatures does not, however, diminish God's power to redeem the world. Polkinghorne illustrates how God will succeed: "Think of William James's picture of the Grandmaster of cosmic chess, who will win the game whatever moves the creaturely opponent may make." He also affirms that "God's appropriate relationship with creation includes divine suffering in compassionate solidarity with the travail of creatures." Divine suffering implies God's openness to be changed by creatures, which entails God's involvement in time, which requires a dipolar doctrine of divine attributes.[57]

Divine dipolarity is clearest in the incarnation. "Christ is to be recognized precisely as the One who, in the two natures, human and divine, constitutes the bridge between the infinite life of the Creator and the finite lives of creatures." But the whole Trinity is dipolar in relation to creation. "The intimate complementarity of temporal and eternal within the unity of God also enables one rightly to speak of the Lamb slain from the foundation of the world (Rev. 13:8) and to speak of continuing divine participation in the travail of creation."[58]

One might wonder whether Polkinghorne's dipolar alternative to classical theism avoids panentheism. His views are similar to Peacocke's, Clayton's, and Moltmann's in many ways. His criticisms of panentheism do not always seem to apply to their views of the God-world relation. On a number of points, the difference appears to be more terminological than substantive. In any case, Polkinghorne claims to reject panentheism as a theology of the current world.

Eschatological Sacramental Panentheism

Polkinghorne explicitly affirms, however, eschatological panentheism. "Panentheism is true as an eschatological fulfillment, not a present reality."[59]

57. Ibid., 108–9.
58. Ibid., 114, 116.
59. Polkinghorne, *Faith of a Physicist*, 168.

When the kingdom comes, we will participate in God ontologically. "This destiny will indeed be a *theosis*, a sharing in the life of God." Even then Polkinghorne maintains divine transcendence by reiterating the difference between the eternal and temporal natures of God: "It will not be human participation in the ineffable life of the eternal divine pole. Rather, it will be an unending exploration of the riches of the temporal pole of deity, made accessible to us in Christ."[60] Polkinghorne emphasizes that God's kingdom will include the self-identical creatures of this world in forms of time, space, matter, and embodiment that are appropriate for the world to come. "God's final purpose is that creatures should enjoy fully the experience of the unveiled divine presence, and so share in the divine energies." Envisioning the real reciprocal presence of God in all things, Polkinghorne names his eschatology sacramental panentheism,[61] the same term that Peacocke applies to the present.

Conclusion

The scientist-theologians considered in this chapter all share a common picture of the universe as an evolving system of increasingly complex and diverse kinds of beings. All endorse panentheism, and all but one do so as the best synthesis of science and theology. All argue from science for a personal view of the God with whom the universe interacts. And all point out that God has both masculine and feminine characteristics.

But there are interesting differences among them. Barbour and Davies do not endorse the mind-body analogy for God's relation to the world whereas Peacocke and Clayton do. On the balance of power between Creator and creatures, Barbour endorses process thought, but he questions whether God is limited to persuasion and whether creatures are self-creative to the extent that process theology claims. Davies asserts that God has chosen to limit himself to empowering creatures for self-generation. Polkinghorne joins Peacocke and Clayton in combining divine self-limitation and creaturely freedom with an equally strong emphasis on God's active involvement in all things. All those considered in this chapter assert that God's act of creation is voluntary.

Concerning Christian theology, Davies does not say much, and Barbour makes some very general connections. Peacocke, Clayton, and Polkinghorne

---

60. Polkinghorne, *Science and the Trinity*, 115–16.

61. Ibid., 166. See ibid., all of chap. 6, "Eschatological Exploration." He does not fully agree with how Moltmann and Pannenberg explain the kingdom. Pannenberg especially seems to assimilate temporal existence into eternity in a way that supersedes the ongoing existence of individuals.

relate their panentheisms more frequently and extensively to the Christian doctrines of the Trinity, the incarnation, the image of God in humanity, redemption, the sacraments, and the eschatological kingdom of God.

None of these thinkers, however, has gone very far in articulating Christian theology. In comparison, Pannenberg, as a theologian, has written much more extensively about nature, science, and the philosophy of science than any of these scientist-theologians has written about Christian doctrine.

In the end, therefore, the whole panorama of contemporary Christian panentheism—its common affirmations, diverse expressions, and internal debates—comes into view only when the scientific theologies of this chapter are juxtaposed to the philosophical theology of Cobb and Griffin and the systematic theologies of such thinkers as Rahner, Macquarrie, Moltmann, and Pannenberg.[62]

62. Much of this panorama is covered in Clayton and Peacocke, eds., *In Whom We Live.*

14

Why I Am Not a Panentheist

The Nature of the Response

Plurality of Perspectives

This chapter is a critical and apologetic response to panentheism. No more than a brief address of some key biblical, theological, philosophical, and worldview issues is possible in these few pages.[1] But I outline a clear position that is more fully elaborated and defended by other classical Christian theists, a few of whom I reference. Before presenting its content, I wish to state the nature of my response.

The debate between panentheism and classical Christian theism concerns a number of factors that generate a plurality of perspectives. Beliefs about the Bible are one crucial factor: what is the nature of Scripture, what does it teach, and how should contemporary Christians be informed by its teaching? A traditional Protestant view of the Bible differs from Pannenberg's view, but not nearly as much as it does from Tillich's or David Griffin's. A second crucial factor is doctrinal orientation. Theologians committed to the historic ecumenical confessions, such as the Nicene Creed, and to more

---

1. Most of these issues were noted in chap. 1. In this chapter I refer to material in previous chapters, such as Hegel's dialectic and Teilhard's Christology, without providing page references. I assert my own positions without many references to sources or full justifications.

recent doctrinal standards, such as the Belgic Confession, the Westminster Confession, or the *Catechism of the Roman Catholic Church*, may have different views from those of theologians who are not committed to such standards. A third factor is one's philosophical-theological perspective. The Reformed tradition is distinctly Augustinian and Scotist in emphasizing God's sovereign freedom, and so it is strongly inclined against panentheism. Eastern Orthodox theology is more heavily indebted to Neoplatonism, and so a number of Orthodox theologians are willing to endorse carefully formulated versions of panentheism. Christians in Germany, such as Pannenberg and Moltmann, because their philosophical tradition is so strongly imprinted by Hegel and Schelling, are much more likely to understand the historic Christian faith panentheistically than, for example, the heirs of Dutch Calvinism, English Puritanism, or Scottish Presbyterianism. People may even have different intuitions about whether Aristotle's logic or Plato's dialectic better conforms to ultimate reality.

All these factors in various combinations make a simple debate, culminating in a consensus conclusion about the relation among biblical Christianity, classical theism, and panentheism, a practical impossibility. What is possible and fruitful is a dialogue among theologians who clearly state their views of Scripture, Christian doctrine, philosophical preferences, the arguments for their positions, and their criticisms of other positions with an attitude of respect and willingness to learn. This study has attempted to survey the history of panentheism in this spirit, and that is how I now present my own position. I hope that all readers can recognize the integrity of my views and that those who share a perspective like mine will conclude, as I have, that they should avoid panentheism.

Here then are my commitments. I affirm a traditional Christian view of Scripture as divinely inspired, infallibly true, and authoritative in all that it teaches; a Reformed interpretation of Scripture; the ecumenical Christian creeds, such as the Nicene Creed; and a theological perspective based on the Reformed confessions and historic Reformed theology. Thus I hold a robust notion of God's supernatural transcendence and freedom in relation to the world, as well as a strong view of God's acts in creation, providence, special revelation, miracles, and his saving acts in history, especially through the person and work of Jesus Christ and the Holy Spirit. I am predisposed toward classical theism because it has been the philosophical theology of the Augustinian-Calvinian tradition in which I stand.

I am also open-minded in several ways. First, I acknowledge that neither classical theism nor panentheism is intrinsically Christian or un-Christian. Both can represent "gods of the philosophers." Both have been used for historic Christian theology, and non-Christians have embraced both. Second, I acknowledge the challenges to classical theism raised by panentheists and other relational theologians regarding God's relation to time, change, and being affected by creatures. Third, I am prepared to consider revisions and alternatives to classical theism that are consistent with biblical and confessional teaching. I am open to regarding properly nuanced trinitarian panentheism as authentic Christian theology even though I cannot endorse it.

Various Theological Positions

Let me refine my response by identifying several distinct theological positions on the God-world relation: classical Christian theism, modified classical Christian theism, revised classical Christian theism, Christian panentheism, and non-Christian panentheism.

All classical Christian theism maintains an unqualified Creator–creature distinction. The traditional version affirms God's eternity. The modified version asserts that God is involved in time. It nuances his attributes accordingly but continues to affirm God's complete omniscience and omnipotence over all creatures, times, and places. If God responds to creatures temporally, it is by acting according to his sovereign knowledge and will. Revised classical theism goes further: it limits God's knowledge by time and limits his power relative to the choices and actions of creatures. Creatures affect God, who thus depends on them for some of his knowledge and possible actions.[2]

The difference between Christian and non-Christian panentheists is that Christians emphasize the Trinity and incarnation of Jesus Christ as the essential core of God's saving presence in the world whereas non-Christians present a more generic account. Other differences among panentheists, both Christian and non-Christian, leave some closer than others to various kinds of classical theism. The distinctions noted throughout this book are personal and nonpersonal, part-whole and relational, natural and/or voluntary, and classical (divine determinist) and modern (cooperative) panentheism.[3]

2. To illustrate: Charles Hodge, Benjamin Warfield, Herman Bavinck, and Louis Berkhof are traditional Reformed classical theists. Paul Helm, Eleonore Stump, and Norman Kretzmann are contemporary philosophers who are traditional classical theists. Richard Swinburne, Nicholas Wolterstorff, Alvin Plantinga, and William Lane Craig are modified classical theists. Open/free-will theists are revised classical theists.

3. Chapter 1 introduced these distinctions: God is either personal or the nonpersonal Ground; creatures are "in God" either as parts of God or as ontologically interrelated with God; God creates by choice, by nature, or both; and either creatures are not free to interact causally with God (classical) or they are (modern).

In opposition to panentheism, I present a fairly traditional version of classical theism, but I am open to minimal modifications concerning God's relation to time. It is important to note that traditional classical theism is not a single, monolithic position. It has variations and nuances on many issues, just as panentheism does. Broad generalizations risk being caricatures.[4] Many traditional theologians do not fit the stereotype that classical theism represents the God of the philosophers instead of the God of Abraham, Isaac, Jacob, and Jesus. I affirm them.

Here follow the main biblical, theological, philosophical, and worldview reasons I am not a panentheist. The chapter's conclusion comments briefly on the various kinds of classical theism and panentheism identified in this section.

The God of the Bible

Christian theology must faithfully articulate what Scripture reveals about God. There are at least four key biblical themes relevant to the differences between classical theism and panentheism: being "in God," God's activity in the world, God's ontological relation to the world, and the one God who is Father, Son, and Holy Spirit.

Being in God

First, Scripture itself speaks of being "in" God. In Acts 17:28 Paul borrows a line from a Greek poet, "For in him we live and move and have our being." Jesus prays in John 17:21, "Father, just as you are in me and I am in you. May they also be in us." Thus the mere assertion that creatures are "in God" cannot be dismissed as unbiblical. There is a prima facie "biblical panentheism." But this fact does not settle the issue because classical theism readily explains these texts with its own account of being in God. The real issue, discussed below, is the significant difference in how classical theism and panentheism understand divine immanence.

The God Who Responds

Second, modern panentheists and other relational theists are surely correct in claiming that Scripture presents God as acting and responding in ways

---

4. E.g., Reformed theologian Louis Berkhof's treatment of God's incommunicable attributes first notes the philosophical definitions of the absolute and infinity and then nuances or redefines them for use in Christian theology ("The Incommunicable Attributes," part 1, chap. 6 in *Systematic Theology* [Grand Rapids: Eerdmans, 1939, 1976]).

that are analogous to humans. This fact does not particularly favor panentheism, however, because most contemporary versions of classical theism also affirm that God relates and responds. Admittedly, it is more complicated for traditional classical theism to treat this presentation as completely anthropomorphic and explain how a wholly eternal, immutable God acts sequentially in history and interacts with creatures. Classical panentheism has a similar problem because, like classical theism, it affirms that God is the all-determining cause and is not affected by creatures.

The God-World Relation

Third, many panentheists propose that, analogically, the world is part of God, or that God is the World-Soul and the universe is his body, or that the best way to model the God-world relation is the mind-body relation. But such claims have no basis in Scripture. No biblical text suggests or implies that the world is part of God, either of his eternal nature or of his actual existence. It is true that Scripture, mainly the Old Testament, sometimes refers to God in bodily terms—his mouth, eyes, face, heart, breath, his right hand, and holy arm. But no such text represents the world as God's body or any creature as a divine body part. In fact, these anthropomorphisms accentuate the otherness of God and the world by representing him as one bodily being relating to other beings, not parts of himself. His mighty arm makes, upholds, governs, punishes, and saves the things he has made—artifacts other than himself. Even Scripture's rare birth metaphors for creation imply that the offspring is distinct from its parent, not part of its body. References to God's body metaphorically represent his powers to act in the world, not the world as his body. Thus the part-whole and soul/mind–person–body models do not represent this otherness as Scripture does. Their canonical source is Plato's *Timaeus*.

Scripture does speak of Christ as "the head over everything for the church, which is his body" (Eph. 1:22–23 and elsewhere). Here we have head-body language that Teilhard and others construe panentheistically: the world is in Christ, who is God, and so the world is God's body and Christ is its head. But this reading mixes biblical metaphors. In this text "head" means "ruler,"[5] not head of the cosmic divine body. It clearly says that God places all things "under his feet," which figuratively implies that all things are *not* part of Christ's body. For Paul, the church is Christ's body. Being in the body

5. W. W. Bauer, W. F. Arndt, and F. W. Gingrich, *Greek-English Lexicon of the New Testament and Other Early Christian Literature* (Chicago: University of Chicago Press, 1957), 431.

of Christ follows from being "in Christ," which is of ultimate importance for Paul as it is for John. But being in Christ is a communal redemptive relationship—belonging to the new people of God, the church—that is regenerated and sustained by the Holy Spirit. It is not a metaphor for the sort of *ontological* "in-ness" claimed by panentheism. In sum, standard exegesis of biblical language about being in Christ and being the body of Christ provides no foothold for World-Soul panentheism.

The Triune God

Finally, the Bible presents one God in three persons. The New Testament revelation of Father, Son, and Holy Spirit (e.g., Matt. 28:19) explicates the Old Testament proclamation "Hear, O Israel, the Lord our God, the Lord is one" (Deut. 6:4). I therefore agree with theologians, including panentheists such as Moltmann and Pannenberg, who judge that any Christian doctrine of God must be fully trinitarian. Process theology does not meet this test.

I have two major concerns, however, about post-Hegelian trinitarian panentheists. First, explaining divine triunity in terms of the dialectical unity of potencies in the tradition of Böhme, Hegel, and Schelling is philosophical speculation that goes far beyond biblical revelation. Worse, it distorts the biblical doctrine of God by imposing gnostic and Neoplatonic categories on it. There is no eternal antithesis-synthesis, conflict-resolution dynamic in the heart of the biblical God. This is the same kind of philosophical distortion that is alleged against classical theism. Second, modern panentheists who temporalize God have difficulty accounting for God's actual ontological triunity. For Pannenberg and Moltmann, God's actual existence is becoming more distinctly three and more completely one as history approaches the eschaton. The essential-ontological Trinity is eternally real but not yet completely actual. Teilhard's view of the Trinity has its own issues, but it is more adequate than the post-Hegelians'.

On these four general characteristics of the God of Scripture, panentheism is clearly not superior to classical Christian theism, and most versions are less than adequate.

Doctrinal and Theological Issues

This section theologically elaborates the issues raised in the previous section and highlights the differences between classical Christian theism and various kinds of panentheism regarding God's essence, existence, transcendence, and immanence. It outlines a version of classical theism taught by other Christian theologians as well, not the philosophical caricature of the biblical God.[6]

God's Self-Sufficiency and Freedom to Create

Classical theism strongly affirms God's aseity or self-sufficiency: God does not need or depend on anything other than himself. He exists absolutely, eternally, and necessarily, whether or not he creates the world. His creation of the world is thus a genuinely free choice from a number of possibilities, all of which are consistent with and dependent on his nature and existence: creating the actual world and/or creating another possible world, or creating nothing at all.[7] His choice includes whether and how to sustain the existence of the world he has created. The full extent of God's sovereignty over creation includes this choice. God is the Lord not only because he rules the world but also because he even decides whether and which world exists. He knows all possible creatures in all possible worlds from all eternity because he has complete knowledge of his own power to create and sustain them. In this ideal sense, our world and all possible worlds are "in God" from all eternity. But they are not part of him, and his nature does not entail that any be created. An important implication of God's ontological independence is that his act of creating is truly agapic—entirely loving and gracious in giving creatures existence.

Panentheists hold various positions on God and creation. Some, such as Neoplatonists and process theologians, readily affirm that God naturally and inevitably creates. Others, mainly Christians, assert that God's creative activity is loving and free. But they almost always affirm or imply a compatibilist (i.e., freedom and determinism are compatible) view of God's will, which implies that God inevitably creates and also that his love of creation is to

6. Stephen Charnock (1628–1680), *Discourses upon the Existence and Attributes of God* (New York: Robert Graves, 1873); François Turrettini (1623–1687), *Institutes of Elenctic Theology*, ed. James Dennison Jr., trans. G. M. Giger, 3 vols. (Phillipsburg, NJ: P&R, 1992–1997); Herman Bavinck (1854–1921), *Reformed Dogmatics*, vol. 2, *God and Creation*, ed. John Bolt, trans. John Vriend (Grand Rapids: Baker, 2004); and Berkhof, *Systematic Theology*, are the works of traditional Reformed theologians from different centuries whose views of God are philosophically aware and nuanced and avoid the negative caricature of classical theism as "the god of the philosophers, not the God of the Bible." A contemporary statement is by Laura Smit, "Who Is God?" in *Conversations with the Confessions: Dialogue in the Reformed Tradition*, ed. Joseph Small (Louisville: Geneva, 2005), 93–100.

7. Some classical theists may affirm the inevitability of the world for God or may be compatibilists, as some say Aquinas is. But Duns Scotus, the Reformed tradition, and many classical theists affirm that God's sovereignty extends over whether he actualizes any possible world. God's libertarian choice to create is logically possible but rare among panentheists.

some extent need-satisfying. Clayton's assertion of God's libertarian freedom is unusual and requires him to depart from the compatibilism of Schelling, whom he otherwise affirms. In sum, the panentheist tradition is inadequate on God's aseity and sovereignty in comparison with classical theism, especially the tradition of Scotus and the Reformed theologians, who emphasize the freedom of God's will, consistent with the rest of his nature.

Ironically, the notion of divine freedom that is embraced by most pan-entheisms actually deprives God of choice about creation. Neoplatonic and gnostic panentheisms locate divine freedom and contingency in the nonbeing or nothingness in God, an eternal urge to become something. The Christian doctrine of creation from nothing, construed in this way, likewise defines "nothing" as creative potential, the impulse to create, so that God is creative by nature. For example, Eriugena asserts that God must create in order to exist and know himself. Böhme speculates that the unity of the three divine potencies is eternally creative. Schelling gives God the option of existence or nonexistence but not of existing without the world. Tillich likewise affirms being and nonbeing in God. These notions of contingency or freedom in God do not affirm his choice to create but only what to create. Modern panentheism further limits God to creating creatures with the libertarian power of self-determination, as is evident, for example, in the process doctrine of divine prehension and Moltmann's notion of *zimsum*. Divine freedom is an oxymoron in almost all panentheism.

Divine Simplicity

Classical theism strongly affirms God's simplicity and immutability. Modern theologians challenge both attributes. I defend a traditional version of each.

Classical theists define simplicity in two ways. The strong version affirms that the divine nature in itself is absolutely without distinctions. In God, everything is logically identical. All theological distinctions are limited human concepts that do not truly apply to God. This position implicitly denies any genuine distinctions among the persons of the Trinity, the divine attributes, God's essence and existence, and God's nature and freedom. It therefore contradicts much that Christian theology affirms. But the strong version is not required by classical theism. Its source is Neoplatonism, where the One is beyond all differentiation and distinction. This definition of simplicity is affirmed by Plotinus, Dionysius, and young Schelling in addition to some important classical Christian theologians. I cannot defend it.

Most classical Christian theists in the tradition of Augustine and Aquinas identify the one God with being, mind, and goodness. Consequently, they are able to define simplicity not from absolute identity but from God's self-sufficiency. Because God is not created or dependent on anything outside himself, he is not composed of principles, properties, or constituents more basic than himself. Thus he is ontologically (not logically) simple.[8] This definition of simplicity rules out composition but not complexity in God—genuine distinctions among the persons of the Trinity, God's attributes, his essence and existence, and his nature and freedom.

Immutability

Classical theists have also differed regarding immutability. The strong version, which follows from logical simplicity, completely identifies God's essence and existence and thus makes everything that God is and does absolutely necessary and unalterable. There is no freedom or contingency in God. Absolutely nothing could have been otherwise. This "god of the philosophers" is in fact Spinoza's view.

But most classical Christian theists who affirm God's sovereignty over creation endorse a slightly different concept of immutability. God's nature is unchangeable, but sovereign freedom is part of his nature. God is eternally free to create or not to create and free to create what he chooses according to his infinite wisdom and goodness. God's will is immutable because he remains faithful to his eternal choice but not because he has no choice.

God's freedom to create also entails a distinction between his essence/nature and existence. If God had chosen not to create the world or not to become incarnate in Jesus Christ, then the full actuality of God's existence, including the life of the Trinity, would be different than it is. Thus classical Christian theism must affirm an element of contingency in God's life quite apart from the issue of his involvement in temporal change. But it does so consistent with a strong notion of the immutability of God's nature and his unchanging will.

Classical panentheists hold as strong a notion of immutability as classical theists: the emanation and return of all things to the One is inexorable. Böhmian speculations about nothingness and the Abyss attempt to acknowledge freedom and contingency in God's nature. But they go far beyond what is necessary to account for the sovereignty of God's will for creation, locating

---

8. Aquinas, *ST* Ia, q. 3. Aquinas is ambiguous, however, between these two senses of simplicity, sometimes seeming to assert absolute identity.

primordial chaos in the heart of God. Modern panentheists who integrate God's existence into the world have a thinner view of immutability: God's essence, including the pattern and goal of his existence, does not change, but God's actual existence constantly changes.

God's Actual Supernatural Transcendence

Given its view of aseity, classical theism has a much more robust view of actual divine transcendence than panentheism, especially the modern panentheisms that integrate God's existence with the world. Classical theism acknowledges that God has a full life above and beyond creation. It strongly correlates (but does not identify) God's essence and his actual existence, affirming that his entire life, which manifests all his essential attributes and free choices, is eternally and fully actual. The concept of God's infinity supports the classical affirmation of his actual transcendence. Because God infinitely transcends not only our world but also all possible worlds, whatever difference his eternal choice about creation makes to his existence is ontologically inconsequential relative to the infinite actuality of the divine life. That such a great God chooses to create, love, and save the world, especially a fallen world, is amazing grace because ontologically it makes virtually no difference to him. God's actual supernatural existence infinitely transcends his immanence in the world, no matter how genuine, immediate, and enduring it is. In classical Christian theism, it ultimately makes no sense to speak of ontological proportion or "balance" between transcendence and immanence.[9]

Classical Neoplatonism also has a notion of the actual infinite transcendence of the One, but unlike classical theism, it entails actual immanence. Thus transcendence and actual immanence are essentially correlative. Because God is the true Infinite, he must include all finite existence within himself. Modern panentheism lists heavily toward immanence even though it claims to "balance" transcendence and immanence. For example, Hegel, Schelling, and Whitehead tie God's actual existence so strongly to the world that his transcendent essence is an abstraction, an infinite potential for growth that is finitely actualized. Pannenberg has a quasi-traditional definition of eternal infinite transcendence, but he oddly locates it in the future, which is preeminently real but not yet fully actual. In modern panentheism, God's actual transcendence is at most finite, personal, self-conscious, intentional,

---

9. As Neoplatonists throughout this book have pointed out, there is an infinite difference between the infinite and finite, which implies that there is no proportion at all between them.

and actively integrating aspects of his essence into the world, as asserted by Hartshorne, Peacocke, and Clayton. In sum, panentheism strongly ties God's existence to his immanence in the world. God's transcendence does not include the full actual existence of his essential being but grows with the world. Clearly, the relation and proportion of God's actual transcendence and immanence are vastly different in classical theism and panentheism.

God's transcendent actuality also pertains to the Trinity. In classical Christianity, the Triune God—one God in three persons—is fully actual, whether or not God creates. In other words, the ontological Trinity exists whether or not the economic Trinity does. We humans know God as Father, Son, and Holy Spirit only because of God's active presence in creation, the incarnation, and redemption. But the Trinity would have a full, if infinitesimally slightly different life, even if God had not created our world. But because God did choose to create, the ontological Trinity is the economic Trinity. There is some truth in Rahner's Rule.

As noted in the biblical section above, post-Hegelian trinitarian panentheisms that ontologically correlate God's existence with the world have trouble acknowledging the full actuality of the Trinity apart from creation. In effect, they distinguish the ontological Trinity as God's eternal essence from the economic Trinity as his actual existence, making the full actuality of the ontological Trinity dependent on the economic Trinity's integration of the world into itself. For most modern trinitarian panentheists, God's actual existence is not yet fully three or one.

Transcendence and Immanence

Classical Christian theism affirms that all things are eternally present and subject to God in the sense that he eternally knows everything he is capable of creating. In this way all things are immanent in God as possible beings, but they are not constitutive of his nature or existence. Whether God is actually immanent depends on his decision to create. His creation of the world alters the mode of immanence from possible to actual existence. But every aspect of the world remains completely other than God. Space, time, cosmic energy, and cosmic order are not part or aspects or dimensions of the divine being or power but are creatures or artifacts brought into existence by God—conditions, dimensions, and modes of the actual existence of the universe he has created. God's immanence means that all spaces, times, entities, and events in creation are immediately present to him and he to them as their sustainer. God is omnipresent. Classical theism therefore readily affirms that "in him we live and move and have our being" and that "he is nearer than hands and feet." The classical understanding of God's immanence also includes providential divine *concursus*—God's continuously guiding, sustaining, and empowering creation. In classical theism, God can be *absolutely immanent*—unconditionally omnipresent in creation—precisely because he is *absolutely transcendent*. It is simply false to suggest that classical theism denies or ignores the immanence of God. For example, Aquinas not only insists that "God exists in all things" and that "by a certain similitude to corporeal things, all things exist in God"; he even uses the Platonic analogy of the body being in the soul to illustrate this similitude.[10] His unqualified ontological Creator-creature distinction, however, gives the analogy a much different meaning than it has in World-Soul panentheism.

In panentheism, God is only *relatively* immanent because he is only *relatively* transcendent. Classical panentheism makes God ontologically relative to creation when it posits the generation of the world as intrinsic to his nature. Modern relational panentheism goes further and makes his actual existence relative to creation: ontologically, time, space, and primordial cosmic energy are dimensions or modes of God's being or power, not absolutely distinct creations or artifacts. Although God is vastly greater than creatures, according to Hartshorne, Pannenberg, Moltmann, and Peacocke, we share some ontological structures in common—for example, space-time and cause-effect.[11] Although this shared ontology allows panentheists to claim that they can explain God's interaction with the world more readily than classical theism permits, it also reduces the scope and power of God's immanence, limiting it to the shared ontology. In spite of the immanence of all things in the panentheistic God, his presence, knowledge, and power are relative and limited, not complete, immediate, and unconditioned as in classical theism.

Eternity and Time

Most contemporary scholars assume that time and eternity are antithetical modes of being, so that if God is eternal, he cannot act in time. Thus they regard classical theism's claims that God acts in time as incoherent. Could they be mistaken? Plato, Plotinus, and Boethius view eternity as the complete fullness of the divine life that endures without beginning, sequence, or end. Eternity is the enduring, simultaneous presence of the infinite divine life without any succession. Succession is one of the ways in which things

---

10. Aquinas, *ST* Ia, q. 8, esp. art. 1, ad. 2.

11. Classical theism asserts ontological *analogy*: our being is a finite, fallible analogue of God. Modern panentheism asserts partial ontological *coincidence*: creatures share part of God's ontology.

in finite worlds are ordered, so that when God creates the actual world according to his eternal knowledge and will, the events in that world occur in temporal sequence. Time is the serialization of God's eternal knowledge of a possible world, not the contradiction of eternity.[12] This means that all times are immediately present to God. He upholds and knows all things. He does not learn things by observing them happen, take risks, or revise his plans when free creatures surprise him.

God acts toward creation as a whole by concurrently governing, sustaining, and empowering the existence, natures, relationships, and actions of his creatures within the cosmic order. God engages in particular acts by intending that particular events occur in relation to other entities and events. Some of these events have special revelatory, redemptive, or judgmental significance and consequences. God responds and interacts by way of bringing about events that respond to and interact with creatures in their worldly situations according to his eternal will. To illustrate: I am sick, I pray for healing, I sense God's presence, and I recover. My heightened awareness of God and my recovery are God's actions in response to my prayer. God knows and wills this sequence from all eternity, but when it occurs it really is his immediate presence and action, hearing and answering my prayer. How does this account undermine the experience or the actuality of divine interaction with creatures, as critics allege? It does not. It simply provides an alternative explanation of active divine immanence, one that recognizes God's interaction to be more robust, reliable, and efficacious than modern panentheism or open theism can manage.

God's Holiness

The holiness or "separateness" of God is not merely his infinite ontological superiority to finite creatures but also his utter goodness and moral-spiritual perfection. In classical theism there is nothing in the essence or existence of God that is less than absolute excellence. Although God creates the world foreknowing and permitting its sin and evil, in God himself there is no sin, evil, darkness, or chaos. His absolute immanence means that the sin and evil of the world are immediately present to him, and he deals with them in judgment and grace. Even Jesus Christ, who is God incarnate, is like us in every way according to his human nature, including suffering and death, but is without sin (Heb. 4:15). God himself remains completely holy—untainted and unstained by the world.

---

12. Douglas Felch, "From Here to Eternity: A Biblical, Theological, and Analogical Defense of Divine Eternity in Light of Recent Challenges within Analytic Philosophy" (Ph.D. diss., Calvin Theological Seminary, 2005), documents these claims.

Because panentheism asserts that God includes the world ontologically, it cannot affirm his perfect holiness. It can assert a great Creator-creature distinction, and it can affirm that God never wills or does evil. But it inevitably implies that the sin and evil of the world are in God ontologically, either as an undesired part of the greater divine whole or else as the result of the mutually affective interaction of the God-world relation. God's nature and will might be holy, but his actual being inevitably includes evil. Even more problematic are the panentheisms that view God as the eternal dialectical unity of oppositional potencies. They posit chaotic, dark, demonic, hellish powers as an element in the eternal nature of God. No variety of panentheism can acknowledge the perfect holiness of God as classical theism can.

Does the Classical God Have Feelings?

Admittedly, classical theism does not allow that creatures affect God as humans affect one another. God does not learn, have his feelings aroused, or realize that he must revise his plans by observing us creatures or obtaining our input by means of the cause-effect processes on which we depend. Biblical assertions of God's reactions are anthropopathic. But must classical theists deny that God has feelings, even though many have done so?

The eternal God can have feelings about particular creatures and situations precisely analogous to his knowledge of them. God can be pleased or angry with the comment I make to my wife tomorrow night just as surely as he knows and permits it from all eternity. But God's pleasure and anger are not *passions or emotions caused in him* by hearing my comment, the way humans acquire these feelings. Classical theism denies that God's feelings are the *effects* of creaturely *causes* just as his knowledge is not learned by observing. Instead God's feelings are *affections*—intentional affective attitudes that he eternally chooses to take toward his creatures. One need not abandon classical theism in order to affirm that "God feels our pain." This is one of the great confusions in contemporary theology. In fact, classical theism can provide a more robust, proactive account of God's feelings than relational theology, an account that does not diminish his ability to deal with the causes of our suffering.

Do Humans Have Free Will?

Classical theism can also acknowledge libertarian freedom, defined as an agent's being able to choose from genuine alternative possibilities. If I, with my psychic-biological-cultural-spiritual makeup, in a given situation, have the capacity to do this, or that, or nothing at all, then I have genuine libertarian choice. If I act on that choice for reasons that I choose in the same way, then I act with libertarian freedom. Many classical theists affirm this view of the will.

Classical theism, however, also holds that whatever I freely choose to do is known to God from all eternity because it is part of the world he has ordained to create. And so it is inevitable that I do it. But *it is not causally necessary or determined* in the sense that God's knowledge and will somehow secretly override my ability to have chosen differently than I do.[13] God is the ultimate cause of my action because he created the world in which I choose to perform it. But I am the agent who, with God's concurrence, freely chooses and performs the action.[14]

In this way classical theism, even Reformed classical theism, can affirm both human freedom and the certain eventuation of God's eternal plan.[15] Free-will theists and most modern panentheists define libertarian freedom as incompatible with any inevitability whatsoever, even what is known to God. If they are right, then classical theism, especially Reformed theology, is incompatible with libertarian freedom. But their definition is highly debatable.[16] Classical theism can provide a tenable account of libertarian freedom.

Supernatural Miracles

Classical Christian theism's affirmation of God's supernatural existence enables it to affirm the ongoing possibility of supernatural miracles. Let us distinguish supernatural and natural miracles. Both are special acts of God in creation. Natural miracles occur in conformity to the natural order as we

13. This position is not compatibilism, which does assert that an agent's action can be both free and causally determined, even by its own nature.

14. Alvin Plantinga distinguishes between "weakly" and "strongly" actualizing. God weakly actualizes and I strongly actualize what results from my action. C. S. Lewis and others use the analogy that a playwright knows his play but the actors freely perform it. This analogy works better for God's knowledge of our actions than for our freedom, however, because free creatures do not have God's script to follow.

15. Reformed Christianity does not hold that all human choices are free. Unregenerate persons are not capable of choosing to love God. God regenerates sinful human hearts, who then freely repent, trust, and love God. (This is a compatibilist account of free will in conversion.) But predestination and election in Reformed theology do not entail that *all* human actions are divinely determined the way that saving faith is, even though some Reformed thinkers think so.

16. Molinists and Arminians also think that divine foreknowledge and libertarian freedom are compatible. Luis de Molina (1535–1600) developed the idea of "middle knowledge," God's hypothetical knowledge of the consequences of every possible contingency, including free human choices. Jacob Arminius (1560–1609) taught that God eternally elected to salvation those whom he foreknew would freely accept the gospel. Here he differs with Reformed theology.

know it. The fire on Elijah's altar, for example, might have been a divinely appointed lightning strike. But other miracles, such as the bodily resurrection of Jesus Christ, are supernatural because they are not possible within the natural order and must involve God's exercising power that he normally does not.[17] The possibility of supernatural miracles readily follows from classical theism's affirmation of God's transcendent existence and his omniscient, omnipotent immanence in the world. It is possible for classical theists to accept the current scientific world picture and also to affirm, as does C. S. Lewis in *Miracles*, the permanent possibility that God acts supernaturally in creation. There is nothing antiscientific, theologically repugnant, or philosophically untenable about affirming supernatural miracles.

Classical panentheism posits sufficient transcendence to allow supernatural miracles. Dionysius, Eriugena, Eckhart, and Nicholas of Cusa believed the biblical miracles. Most modern panentheism, however, shares Enlightenment skepticism about supernatural miracles. Heavily influenced by Spinoza and the scientific Neoplatonism of the seventeenth century, it recasts God's immanence in the world as identical to or completely congruent with the order of nature, thereby eliminating the ontological possibility of supernatural miracles. Most Christian panentheists since Schleiermacher have agreed, sometimes even polemicizing against belief in them. There are exceptions, however. Teilhard's theology contains sufficient divine transcendence to affirm at least the supernatural incarnation and resurrection of Jesus Christ. Pannenberg defends the historical resurrection and regards it as an event that has occurred from the transcendent future, not from "above" (*super*) nature. But most contemporary panentheism is wedded so faithfully to current scientific views of nature that it eliminates supernatural miracles, however explained. On this issue it is just another species of modernist theology that challenges the supernaturalism of traditional Christian theology.

The Problem of Evil and God's Power to Save

Classical theism's affirmation of God's supernatural power raises the question why God allows evil and does not perform supernatural acts to alleviate suffering in the world. Dissatisfaction with traditional answers is

---

17. Biblical Christianity affirms that the miracles reported in Scripture actually occurred, not that they are "supernatural." "Supernatural" is a concept typically determined by the current scientific understanding of what is "natural," which can change as science advances. But until science can explain how miracles such as the bodily resurrection of Jesus Christ are possible within nature, those who believe them ought to admit that they are "supernatural" acts of God.

an important part of the reason most panentheists prefer a more limited view of God's power.

The traditional Augustinian view in the Western church (Roman Catholic and Protestant) has insisted that God created the world good and that it became evil through the disobedience of angels and humans. This disobedience, although known and permitted by God from eternity, is freely chosen and not causally determined by the nature or circumstances of creatures. The mystery in this account is why creatures created good would choose to sin, not whether they are free to do so. Thus creatures are responsible for actual sin and evil even though God ordains and creates the world in which they inevitably become actual. God's choice to create this world in spite of all the evil it contains is consistent with (but not necessarily required by) his goodness because his choice to redeem it eventuates in the greater good of his everlasting kingdom. God knows—although we do not—how the apparently countless instances, horrific kinds, and unjust distributions of evil that he permits are consistent with and conducive to the greater good of his kingdom. The atonement and resurrection of Jesus Christ, the final judgment, and the establishment of God's future kingdom provide the ultimate solution to the problem of evil by rendering justice, eliminating evil, and preserving good. This entire account is not an attempt at a rational theodicy but an understanding of the nature and place of sin and evil within the biblical narrative.

Given God's supernatural omnipotence, traditional Christians (not just their critics) may wonder why he does not intervene more frequently or hasten the end. We know from Scripture only that God has chosen to sustain the fallen world until the return of Christ, which will not occur until he is satisfied with the number of redeemed people. But we have no doubt that God has the supernatural power to transform this world into his everlasting kingdom. We are much comforted by God's power because a candid assessment of this world, especially the sin, evil, dysfunction, and suffering in human history, provides no evidential basis for supposing that the current trajectory of cosmic evolution is tracking God's kingdom. Such optimism founders on the facts of world history. It will take a supernatural miracle to bring the kingdom, as classical Christian theism readily affirms. In sum, classical theism's high view of divine power raises the problem of evil about this world but provides certain hope for God's ultimate solution.

Classical panentheism holds that God is omnipotent but evil is inevitable, and modern panentheism limits God's power to deal with it finally and decisively. We consider each in turn.

Neoplatonism differs from Augustinian Christianity in that it views deficiency (nonbeing) and the tension between good and evil (being and nonbeing) as intrinsic to finite reality. Only God in himself is good, either simply good or good as the eternal harmony of contrary forces. If God generates anything other than himself, the multiple modes of finite being include polarities and tensions that inevitably lead to degeneration, destruction, suffering, and deviance in moral-spiritual creatures. Biological death and moral-spiritual alienation are natural and inevitable for humans in this world. Salvation entails the return of finite things to God: destructive potentiality is actualized and marginalized while greater harmony among finite beings is achieved as they all approach the One. This is the vision of Plotinus, and Schleiermacher, Hegel, Schelling, and Teilhard still clearly articulate its Christian version.

Contemporary panentheism weds Neoplatonism to contemporary cosmology and evolutionary biology, and it ends in the same place. Dysfunction and spiritual alienation are ontologically intrinsic to finite existence. In Christian terms, if God creates a world, it is inevitably good but also fallen, and so are humans. But God's incarnation in the creative-fallen dynamics of the world eventually makes the same evolutionary-historical process redemptive.

In addition, virtually all modern panentheism weakens God's power to save creation by insisting that he does not have or does not exercise determination over creatures but only sustains their freedom. The extent of God's power varies in different versions. The tradition of Schelling speaks of God and humans codetermining their destiny, implying that both have active input. Moltmann views God's power as noncoercive love. Process theology limits God's action to "luring" and "persuading" creatures to seek God's kingdom, allowing them complete freedom to do otherwise. Panentheists such as Teilhard and Pannenberg, who still claim that God is finally "irresistible" or "all-determining," are often criticized by their fellows.

Modern panentheists have several reasons for their position. They believe that God's love and goodness require that he not "control" creatures. They attempt to absolve God of responsibility for evil. And some think that God's power in the world is ontologically limited, that he is constitutionally incapable of controlling creatures. Whatever their reasons, they undercut justification for certainty that God can intervene to save the fallen world and establish the kingdom that they hope for.

We have not addressed a number of other fundamental Christian doctrines, such as the nature and purpose of the incarnation and atonement, that are understood differently in panentheism than in classical theism. The issues considered in this section, however, make clear that there are significant differences between the two theologies on many points in the doctrine of God. In my view, properly nuanced classical theism always does a better job than any kind of panentheism in representing the historic Christian faith.

Philosophical Issues

Panentheists not only claim to present the God of the Bible and explain Christian theology more adequately; they also claim philosophical superiority. Negatively, they charge that classical theism is confused and incoherent, for example, when it asserts that the eternal God acts in time or that human actions can be both free and inevitable. Positively, they claim that panentheism presents arguments and explanations that are more philosophically apt and cogent than those of classical theism.

The previous section has already addressed two alleged incoherences, eternity and time, and God's will and human freedom. This section selects three representative philosophical topics on which panentheists claim the high ground: God's freedom, the mind-body relation as a model for the God-world relation, and the panentheistic proof from the true Infinite.

Divine Freedom

God's freedom to create has already been addressed above as a theological topic. It is also philosophical in that it involves general concepts of freedom, determination, and the will. Many panentheists concede that God naturally creates. Others, including most Christians, claim that creation is a free act. Almost all panentheists in both groups, intentionally or unintentionally, assume a compatibilist view of the will, that an act can both be free and entirely determined as long as it is *self*-determined. Philosophically, this concept of freedom seems incoherent to noncompatibilists. Libertarians point out that it does not entail the possibility of genuine choice among alternatives. Determinists argue that it is straightforward determinism and ought not to be camouflaged in the language of freedom. Generic panentheism does not logically require a compatibilist view of divine freedom. But to the almost universal extent that panentheists hold it, they seem philosophically arbitrary, confused, or incoherent.

The Mind-Body Analogy for God and the World

Not all panentheists adopt the mind-body analogy, and some qualify or criticize it. But those who endorse it claim that it provides the most illuminating framework for understanding how God relates to the world, a framework that classical theism cannot offer.

But the mind-body model for God and the world is philosophically inadequate because it is a poor analogy, at least for high personal panentheism. There are two major disanalogies, the human mind-body relation itself and the human relation to the world.

First, there are far more differences than similarities between how humans are embodied and how the supremely personal God of Hartshorne and some Christian panentheists is supposed to relate to the world. We humans are directly conscious of, and can voluntarily interact with or control, very limited parts and processes of our bodies. I may be aware of a pain in my stomach and respond to it. But my awareness is involuntary and passive, not an empowering, "letting it be free to be itself" relationship. If I act to relieve the pain, I get at it indirectly by taking a pill. Is this a model of how God feels and deals with our pain? When I do engage my body, it is usually by controlling, not by enabling it to be itself. I move my finger or attempt to lower my blood pressure by biofeedback. Furthermore, the vast majority of our presence in our bodies is unconscious and involuntary. In fact, many unconscious events and processes in our bodies and brains shape the modes and contents of our consciousness. The very limited, contingent, and fallible mind-body relation of normal humans is, for the most part, unlike the supremely aware and ubiquitously empowering God of Hartshorne and some Christian panentheists. If God really is like the human mind-body relation, then the panentheisms of Schelling, Alexander, Bergson, and Tillich are more accurate. The divine essence is a primordial Ground, and God's actual personality, mind, and voluntary capacities emerge from nature and grow along with the development of humans in the universe. But a billion years ago a tiny organism, not a human, would have been the best model of God. The point is that the mind-body relation is not a very good philosophical model for Christians and other high personal panentheists. And no panentheist of the Schelling-Alexander type can speak literally of God's knowledge and action in the world prior to, or independent of, human knowledge and action in the world.

A second major disanalogy is that humans relate to a world that is external to their minds and bodies whereas the panentheistic God has no external world. He relates only to his body internally and to ideal possibilities. The best analogy for this God is a guru meditating in a sensory-deprivation chamber, focused entirely on his inner physical-spiritual-potential self. But this mode of being is unusual and unnatural. Normal human life is mainly being-in-the-world, as Heidegger puts it. I see a tree, throw a ball, or walk over and greet another person. Unlike the guru, my mind-body self relates to other mind-body selves and things outside me. Normal embodied personhood is not a good analogy for personal panentheism.

A good model should be as similar as it is dissimilar to what it represents. The person/mind–body relation is not a very good philosophical model for personal panentheism in the two ways indicated. In fact, classical theism's view—that God is a purely spiritual, bodiless being who is universally present to creatures other than himself—seems to do a better job.

The Proof from Infinity

Nicholas of Cusa, Hegel, Hartshorne, Pannenberg, Clayton, and others allege a philosophical proof for their theology—the argument from Infinity. Because God is absolutely infinite, nothing can be completely other or outside him. For, if anything were, then God would be limited by it, that is, finite, that is, not-infinite, which is impossible by definition. Therefore all finite reality and relative infinity (mathematical, spatial, temporal, etc.) must be within the absolutely infinite God, which entails panentheism.

Let us concede that the argument from infinity is sound in a formal sense: in some sense, nothing can be "outside" God. This argument does not prove panentheism, however, if only because classical theism also affirms the conclusion but interprets it differently. Panentheists construe infinity in terms of ontological "in-ness." But classical theists explain it just as well in terms of God's voluntary immanence: All relative infinity and finite existence are immanent in the knowledge and power of God as possibilities he can choose to actualize. If he chooses to actualize them, then they are actually immanent to his omnipotent, omniscient, concurrent presence, but they are not in him ontologically. This alternative demonstrates that panentheism is not entailed by the argument from Infinity.

The Biblical Worldview and Redemptive History

Neoplatonism versus Augustinianism

Much modern Christianity has emphasized the redemptive presence of God in the world. For the most part, it rejects "otherworldly" kinds of spirituality that focus mainly on heaven and the afterlife. This criticism aims not only at fundamentalist, mystical, and charismatic Christianity but also at major theologians, such as Barth and Bultmann, who posit a dualism between the everyday world of history and the realm of revelation and salvation.

Panentheism from Neoplatonism to Moltmann emphasizes the immanence of God in the world. It therefore provides an attractive alternative to traditional and contemporary kinds of dualistic or spiritualistic Christianity. Modern Christian panentheists stress the acts of the biblical God in the creation, the incarnation, and the redemption of the world. Salvation history is integral to world history. The redemption of the whole creation is the theme of the Bible, the biblical worldview.

But panentheism is not alone in emphasizing that God's kingdom and the Christian faith engage this world. Many Christians with traditional views of God also affirm God's saving presence in world history and seek God's kingdom in this life as they hope for it in the life to come. I mention just two examples: Roman Catholic neo-Thomism and the neo-Calvinism of Abraham Kuyper, a Reformed minister in the Netherlands.

In the late nineteenth century, Pope Leo XIII called for a return to the vision of Thomas Aquinas to articulate faith and life for the twentieth century. Catholics have involved themselves in the academic, social, political, economic, and cultural lives of the societies in which they live, in ways that are faithful to Catholic teaching and relevant to contemporary practice. The "worldly evangelism" of Pope John Paul II is an exemplary representation of this movement.

About the same time, a similar movement developed in the Netherlands, spearheaded by Abraham Kuyper, who reawakened and updated original Calvinist engagement in the civic, cultural, and intellectual life of previous centuries. Kuyper founded a university, a newspaper, a political party, and eventually became prime minister of the Netherlands. In this movement, as in neo-Thomism, the point has been to participate in the common life of this world critically but helpfully from the standpoint of the Christian faith—not just theology, but a biblical world-and-life view. Immigrants brought Kuyper's ideas to North America, where they have become a major source of the references to "the biblical worldview" or "the Christian world-and-life view" that are now common among North American Christians.[18]

These two movements are not accidental or unrelated. Both are rooted in Augustine's *City of God*, which addressed how Christians should live in

18. Modesty requires that I relegate to a footnote the seminal role of Calvin College, the school of the Christian Reformed Church, in the promulgation of this vision. Christian scholars, such as Henry Stob, Louis Smedes, H. Evan Runner, Alvin Plantinga, Nicholas Wolterstorff, Richard Mouw, and George Marsden, have made important contributions to the promotion of the idea of a Christian worldview among Christian academics and colleges in North America. Well-known advocates of a Christian worldview, such as Francis Schaeffer and Charles Colson, acknowledge Kuyperian neo-Calvinism as a significant source of their perspective.

and contribute to the Roman Empire while remaining faithful to Christ and his church. Pope Leo returned to Aquinas, and Kuyper returned to Calvin. Both Aquinas and Calvin esteemed Augustine above all the church fathers, although they did not interpret him exactly the same way. Augustinian Christianity engages the world as it seeks the kingdom of God. It too identifies the redemption of creation—grace perfecting nature—as the basic theme of Scripture. It remains alive and well to this day.

So panentheistic and Augustinian Christians both preach creation-redemption-consummation as the basic theme of the Bible and work for the coming kingdom of God. In many ways this common emphasis is a good thing, and mutual cooperation on important social, political, and cultural issues is possible.

But there is a crucial difference between the Augustinian and panentheist versions of the biblical worldview: the nature and place of sin and evil. In Augustinian Christianity, sin and evil are an ontological accident, outcomes that are not natural or inevitable in the fundamental structure of the world.[19] They are inevitable by God's permissive decree but not ontologically inevitable. Thus Augustinians state the theme of Scripture, salvation history, this way: creation-fall-redemption-consummation. This signals that the fall is ontologically and temporally distinct from creation. They therefore affirm that redemption culminating in the consummation of the kingdom, like creation, is a gracious undertaking of God that is not a mere outcome of a natural process. Salvation is an amazing expression of supernatural grace.

Panentheism sees redemptive history differently. More Neoplatonic than Augustinian, it typically views the fall as ontologically inevitable. Finite being entails nonbeing and all the tensions their interaction generates. Being in God's image and being fallen are correlative aspects of humans *as created*. Panentheistic appropriations of evolutionary biology confirm this view: the earliest humans inherited mortality and moral-spiritual ambivalence as they evolved beyond their animal ancestors. Immortality and spiritual perfection were never actual or possible for our first parents. But just as creation and fall are correlative aspects of the cosmic process, so are redemption and consummation. Thus panentheists typically view the biblical narrative of salvation history as a single (dialectical) process of creation-alienation-reconciliation-consummation. This history is the result of God's continuous involvement in the world. The very same (dialectical) process by which creation occurs involves the fall, the reconciliation of the tension between creation and fall,

19. Many Augustinians affirm that some violence in natural processes and animal death are part of the good creation, not consequences of the fall. *Human* death is a consequence of the fall.

and the final harmonization of all things in God. For Christian panentheists, the earthly existence of Jesus Christ is either the central cause of the successful outcome of this process, as for Teilhard, Pannenberg, and Moltmann, or a primary symbol or example of the process, as for Tillich and Cobb. Both panentheist construals of redemptive history give different meanings to core doctrines of the person and work of Jesus Christ and the Holy Spirit than Augustinian Christianity does.

In my view, the panentheistic version of redemptive history looks more like Plotinus's emanation and return of all things to the One, read in terms of the biblical narrative, than a natural reading of the Bible from Genesis to Revelation. But this judgment is predictable, given my Augustinian commitment.

Conclusion

I am not a panentheist because I am convinced that classical theism is more adequate for providing a biblically faithful, philosophically sound articulation of Christian theology, salvation history, and the Christian worldview. I endorse Reformed Christian classical theism.

I wish to affirm fellowship with many Christian theologians, however, who profess or imply panentheism or other kinds of relational (i.e., God and creatures causally interact) theology. I acknowledge all Christian theologians who strive to promote historical ecumenical creedal Christianity, who present a strong, ontological (not merely symbolic or functional) view of the Trinity, who base creation in God's loving freedom, who emphasize that God's action in the incarnation, atonement, and bodily resurrection of Jesus Christ is the historical cause of salvation (not a symbol of a more universal process), and who affirm the certainty of God's coming kingdom, a new heaven and earth that includes the actual existence of God's people in fellowship with him.

I close with brief comments on the kinds of theology identified above: modified classical theism, revised classical theism, Christian panentheism, and non-Christian panentheism. In this way I clarify my own position and indicate my appreciation of theologies with which I differ.

Modified Classical Theism

Some classical Christian theists modify traditional theology to allow God's participation in time. For example, one modification, proposed by William Lane Craig, argues that God in himself is eternal but changes temporally since creating the world. Nicholas Wolterstorff's modification goes deeper:

God in himself is not eternal but *everlasting*, possessing a kind of temporality without beginning, end, or the limitations of creaturely time.[20]

Modifications such as these can be fully consistent with the classical Christian and Reformed doctrine of God, including God's aseity, the Trinity, creation, and the incarnation. Revised classical theism need not hold that God is dependent on, affected by, or limited by his involvement in time—that he learns by observation, runs history as a joint venture, or risks surprises. It can posit that God temporally *fore*knows, *fore*ordains, and *con*curs ("runs with") everything in his plan for the world. Thus the modified version can come to the same conclusions about God's sovereignty and providence as traditional classical theism.

A further modification might be that God *responds* to creatures in earthly time but does so with eternal/everlasting foreknowledge and foreordination. He has always known that he would have compassion on me today, and today he actively does so when I seek him. This position affirms God's temporal response but still remains consistent with traditional confessional theology if it does not suggest that God is *causally* affected by his creatures.

I am generally partial to traditional classical theism because it is the historic Christian position and it is still intellectually tenable. But I am open to minimally modified classical theism and recognize that it has the advantage of presenting a case for classical theism that is probably more accessible and cogent to most contemporary thinkers. Its modified concepts and categories may fit better with current philosophy, science, and views of personhood than those of traditional classical theism. In addition, by allowing that God is, to some extent, in time, the modified version can read Scripture's narrative of God's mighty acts in history more straightforwardly and less anthropomorphically than the traditional version requires. Modified classical theism might therefore present more currently plausible accounts of how God acts and responds in time and especially how Jesus Christ is both true and eternal God and also a real human being in time, space, and the natural order. This is an important consideration in comparing traditional and modified classical theism. They stand together, however, against panentheism.

Is Revised Classical Theism Implicit Panentheism?

Some classical theists (theologians who affirm an unqualified God-creature distinction) revise the traditional view so that it no longer conforms to historic confessional theology. They hold not only that God is, to some

20. See their contributions in Gregory Ganssle, ed., *God and Time: Four Views* (Downers Grove, IL: InterVarsity, 2001).

extent, temporal but also that he is causally affected and limited by his involvement in the temporal order. God is relational and interrelational. He relates through space, time, energy, and the natural order. He learns by experiencing what creatures do. His feelings are aroused by observing them suffer. He does not know what free creatures will do in the future, and therefore he cannot plan specifically how he can and must act in the world to accomplish his purposes. God took a calculated risk when he created the world and never ceases to be surprised by what some unpredictable humans do with the freedom he gives them. The best-known current example of this position is open or free-will theism.

In my view, revisions of classical theism that not only locate but also limit God in space, time, and causality conflict with biblical teaching about God's greatness, knowledge, and power, the certainty of his promises, and specific predictive prophecy.[21] In addition, such revisions model God's interaction with the world more as a large disembodied human person relating to much smaller beings than as the infinite Other who has graciously made us finitely analogous to himself in a few ways.

Revised classical theism of this sort tends toward relational panentheism, if not on a slippery slope. Modern panentheism likewise networks God into the spatial-temporal-causal order of the universe and models the God-world nexus in this relational, Creature-creature way. Whether revised classical theism slides into panentheism depends on whether its ontology of God is substantial or merely relational: If one's very being is constituted by one's relations and interactions with others and if this ontology holds for God as well, then the interaction between God and creatures from the beginning of the world into the everlasting future does significantly constitute the very being of God, which amounts to panentheism. This is the case even if God freely chooses to involve himself in creation, as the open theists and Clayton affirm. Then we have voluntary relational panentheism. The only way that relational theologies can avoid panentheism is by adopting a philosophically old-fashioned view of God as the essentially independent Being whose relations outside himself are contingent and do not constitutively affect his infinite existence or intrinsic identity even if he chooses them to be part of his "story." The end of chapter 7 concluded that open theism is not process theology. But there are other kinds of panentheism. Strong versions of open theism are very close to personal-relational Christian

---

21. See Bruce Ware, *God's Lesser Glory: The Diminished God of Open Theism* (Wheaton, IL: Crossway, 2000); Norman Geisler and H. Wayne House, *The Battle for God: Responding to the Challenge of Neotheism* (Grand Rapids: Kregel, 2001); and John Frame, *No Other God: A Response to Open Theism* (Phillipsburg, NJ: P&R, 2001). The tone of some of these rejoinders is sometimes not as helpful as their arguments.

panentheism, if not instances of it. On this topic, there is little difference between Pinnock and Moltmann, both of whom hold relational theologies and relational ontologies.

Christian Panentheism

Christian panentheism is not necessarily an oxymoron. I judge that it is incompatible with Reformed theology. It is not nearly as good as traditional or modified classical theism in being a theology that exposits Scripture. Much modern Christian panentheism is less adequate than open theism, which at least retains a supernatural view of God's existence, power, revelation, and acts in history. Christian panentheism is last on my scorecard. But the combination of Christianity and panentheism is not necessarily incoherent. Many Christian panentheists and implicit panentheists do affirm the theological positions stated at the beginning of this conclusion. They are therefore legitimate expressions of ecumenical Christianity.[22] I hope that they would regard my position the same way, even if they rank it last, behind open theism. Many Christian panentheists, however, have rejected the entire tradition of classical Christian theism vehemently and sometimes harshly.

I take this position not only to make good on my commitment to open dialogue but also to model Christian ecumenicity for readers who share my theological perspective but might dismiss or even anathematize any theology except traditional classical theism.

Non-Christian Panentheism

I do not, however, affirm everything that claims to be Christian panentheism. Christian theology must strongly affirm the ontological and the economic Trinity. Process theology, for instance, is not able to meet this condition. Christian theology must affirm that God's active presence in the incarnation, atonement, resurrection, and reign of Jesus Christ is the central cause of the salvation of the world, not just a symbol of a more general, universal process. On this score, Teilhard, Pannenberg, and Moltmann qualify, for example, but Tillich and Ruether do not. This issue divides historic Christianity from modern Christian pluralism, not just classical theism from modern panentheism.

22. A number of contributors to Philip Clayton and Arthur Peacocke, eds., *In Whom We Live and Move and Have Our Being: Panentheistic Reflections on God's Presence in a Scientific World* (Grand Rapids: Eerdmans, 2003), are Christian panentheists who affirm the great tradition.

Of the several kinds of panentheism identified in this book,[23] some are obviously closer to biblical Christianity than others. First, (trinitarian) personal panentheism is much more fitting than impersonal-Ground-of-being panentheism. Second, relational panentheism can claim some biblical basis, but there is no warrant in Scripture for part-whole panentheism or models of the God-world relation as the soul (or mind) and body. Third, natural-emanation views of creation are not consistent with Scripture. Christians should emphasize God's love and freedom in creation, and genuine voluntarism is more coherent than a compatibilist view of the divine will. Finally, the balance of determinative power ought to be tilted heavily toward God. If creatures do have libertarian freedom and can influence God, as modern panentheism insists, Christian versions must account for the sufficiency of God's power to bring all things to his appointed end. The final causality of God's activity in history must be determinative even if he does not exercise determinative efficient causality. Mere enabling love is not adequate.

Thus concludes this historical introduction to panentheism and my response to it. May all readers find it, on the whole, to be an instructive, fair, and accurate presentation. May those who share my commitment to historic Christian theology see that nuanced classical theism remains its best expression in spite of its current unpopularity. And may those who disagree be able to see at least the spiritual and intellectual integrity of the brief case made for it here.

---

23. To review: God is either personal or the nonpersonal Ground; creatures are "in God" either as parts of God or as ontologically interrelated with God; God creates by choice, by nature, or both; and either creatures are not free to interact causally with God (classical) or they are (modern).

Name Index

347

Subject Index